"A fascinating social history . . . Makes connections between people linked with the CIA and the widespread availability of LSD during the 1960s."—*Publishers Weekly*

"An important study of cultural history . . . The scholarship is exquisite and the methods sensible."—Allen Ginsberg

"Excellent . . . Captivating . . . A generalist's history that should replace all others."—*San Francisco Chronicle*

"A landmark contribution to the sociopolitical history of the U.S. . . . Some of the liveliest, most absorbing, best-documented historical analyses to appear in recent years . . . A seminal contribution to understanding America's most turbulent modern decade."—*Choice*

"As splendidly written as it is fascinating . . . A remarkable history of an unforgettable time."—*The Oakland Tribune*

"This funny and irreverent book brings it all back."
—*The Washington Post*

"Recounts some of the most bizarre incidents in the history of U.S. intelligence."—*The Boston Globe*

"A monumental social history of psychedelia."
—*The Village Voice*

"A blistering exposé of CIA drug experimentation on Americans. It's all there."—John Stockwell

"Highly readable . . . Well researched . . . Filled with entertaining and bizarre episodes."—*The Detroit Free Press*

Acid Dreams

THE COMPLETE SOCIAL HISTORY OF LSD:
THE CIA, THE SIXTIES, AND BEYOND

MARTIN A. LEE AND BRUCE SHLAIN

With an Introduction by Andrei Codrescu

GROVE PRESS
NEW YORK

Published simultaneously in Canada
Printed in the United States of America

Due to limitations of space, permissions and acknowledgments appear on p. v, which constitutes an extension of this copyright page.

Library of Congress Cataloging-in-Publication Data

    Acid dreams : the complete social history of LSD : the CIA, the
sixties, and beyond / Martin A. Lee and Bruce Shlain.
      p.   cm.
    Includes bibliographical references and index.
    ISBN 0-8021-3062-3
    1. LSD (Drug) 2. Drug abuse—United States. 3. United States.
Central Intelligences Agency. 4. Social history—1960–1970.
5. Social history—1970–   I. Shlain, Bruce. II. Title.
HV5822.L9L45   1992
306'.1—dc20   92-1238

Designed by Abe Lerner

Grove Press
841 Broadway
New York, NY 10003

03 04 05 06 07   20 19 18 17 16 15 14 13

ACKNOWLEDGMENTS

Many people helped to make this book possible. Above all, we wish to express our gratitude to Allen Ginsberg and Dr. Oscar Janiger for their counsel and generosity of spirit. And for their enduring friendship: Bret Eynon, oral historian and New Left scholar, and Jeff Cohen, who nurtured the manuscript in countless ways from start to finish.

We'd also like to thank James Grauerholz for encouraging us in the early going; Carl Oglesby, for his ever-articulate insight, and the other members of the Assassination Information Bureau; Peter Berg and Judy Goldhaft, for sharing their perspective on Haight-Ashbury and the Digger experience; Robert Ranftel, Paul Krassner, and Steven Ben Israel, for their comedic genius; Beverly Isis and Liz Iler, for their unwavering support; and Michael Aldridge, the curator of the Fitz Hugh Ludlow Memorial Library, an invaluable resource for sixties and counterculture historians. Very special appreciation to Michael Rossman, William Burroughs, Peter Stafford, Tim Leary, Bill Adler, Ed Sanders, Mark Dowie, Tim Scully, Jonathan Marshall, Bernard Ohanian, Dorianna Fallo, and the late Julian Beck.

In addition, we'd like to thank Charles Allen, Eugene Anthony, Michael Bowen, Ann Charters, Allen Cohen, Ira Cohen, Jim Fouratt, Todd Gitlin, Abbie Hoffman, Michael Horowitz, Ken Kelley, John Marks, Eric Noble, Dr. Humphry Osmond, John Sinclair, David Solomon, Bill Zirinsky, Miles, and Ken Kesey. And a silent nod to those who preferred that their names not be mentioned.

Our heart-felt appreciation to Alana Lee, for coming through time and again. To Goodwin and Silva Lee, Marvin and Hilda Shlain, and Joe and Emily Krinsky, for providing the kind of support that only family can give.

ACKNOWLEDGMENTS

And to Gayle, for her love and faith.

And finally, we'd like to thank Geri Thoma of the Elaine Markson Literary Agency; Joy Johannessen, for her excellent copy editing; Fred Jordan, our editor; Laura Lindgren, Laura Kane, and the staff at Grove Press.

Martin A. Lee

Bruce Shlain

"We do not see things as they are,
we see them as we are."

—OLD TALMUDIC SAYING

CONTENTS

Introduction

Whose Worlds Are These?

BY ANDREI CODRESCU

In June 1967 the Candyman burst through the door of my pad on Avenue C on New York's Lower East Side. He always burst through the door because that was his style. He could barely contain himself. He dropped his mirrored Peruvian bag on the kitchen table and exclaimed: "Just for you! Czech acid!" The Candyman always had some new kind of acid. That month I had already sampled Window Pane and Sunshine. I didn't know if my system could handle another extended flight to the far reaches. But this Czech acid *was* different. For one thing, it revealed to me that the entire molecular and submolecular structure of the universe was in fact composed of tiny sickles and hammers. Billions and billions of tiny sickles and hammers shimmered in the beauteous symmetry of the material world. I always thought of this particular "commie trip" as a rather private experience brought about by my having been born and raised in Communist Romania, where sickles and hammers were ubiquitous and unavoidable.

I did not doubt what I had seen, but I did doubt whether there was such a thing as Czech acid for the simple reason that Czechoslovakia, like Romania, was a monochromatic world. It seemed clear that if acid had existed in Eastern Europe it would have brought about the collapse of communism there, just as it was bringing about the downfall of a certain kind of dour-faced, simple-minded America. And at that time it didn't look like communism was anywhere near collapse. Well, I was wrong. Reading this extraordinary, superbly researched, suspenseful history of LSD, I find, on page 115, that: "In September 1965 Michael Hollingshead returned to his native London armed with hundreds of copies of the updated *Book of the Dead* and five thousand doses of LSD (which he procured from Czech government laboratories in Prague)." And communism did collapse, though not right then, and acid *did* have quite a bit to do with it. Charter 77, the Czech human rights organization, was founded by Václav Havel in defense of the Plastic People of the Universe, a psychedelic band inspired by the Velvet Underground. Havel himself was in New York in 1968, listening to the Velvets and dreaming, no doubt, of a way out of Cold War ideology.

This tiny revelation is but a parenthetical remark in a story full of surprises, many of which are profoundly unsettling. The drug that connected so many of us to the organic mystery of a vastly alive universe turns out to have been, at least in the beginning, a secret CIA project to find a truth serum. It's frightening to think that CIA spooks have used LSD with electroshock and torture to get information out of prisoners. It's even more frightening that they have used it themselves to little positive effect. Or perhaps not. It's ironic and still scary to think that the CIA tried to control the LSD experiment even though hundreds of thousands were turning on in the heyday of the sixties. Neither the ironies nor the chilling implications stop here. The authors have plowed through thousands of pages of declassified intelligence material to reveal a complex tissue of connections between secret government agencies and the academic world on the one hand, and between the utopian hopes of a generation and the machinations of those same agencies on the other. It's a riveting story that makes the most paranoid and outlandish theories of the sixties seem insufficiently paranoid.

At the same time, in a most persuasive and closely argued way, this sharply documented chronicle tells the story of the fantastic characters of acid: Captain Al Hubbard, Aldous Huxley, Timothy Leary, Owsley, Art Kleps, Ken Kesey, and many, many more. One is quickly immersed in the vibrant collective aura of the times, which, in spite of the CIA and army intelligence, managed to change America forever. The undeniably metaphysical window that LSD opened for so many of us may have unwittingly been opened by those whose interests lay in keeping it shut. It may well be that, seeing their mistake, they have been endeavoring to close it ever since. But the fact is that the brilliant glimpse of a living cosmos did pour through for a while, and it resulted in an unprecedented vision of a different world. One could debate forever the question of how much of what the drug did for us was contingent on the peculiar conditions of that time. The opening, however, was real.

INTRODUCTION

The usefulness of *Acid Dreams* goes beyond nostalgia. In researching the effect of LSD on the psychology, sociology, and politics of the sixties, the authors have given a context to the mythos and poetry that now permeate almost every aspect of high and low American culture. For believers in capital *C* Conspiracy this book should prove a rich mine for reflection. For those, like myself, who believe that conspiracy and control are games that vanish once one ceases to believe in them, this book stands as a much-needed corrective. To history buffs, this is fascinating history. Best of all, this is a thriller about the great mystery of how we of a certain generation got to be who we are.

December 4, 1991

Prologue

October 1977.

Thousands of people jammed the auditorium at the University of California in Santa Cruz. Those who were unable to gain admittance stood outside and pressed their faces against the windows, hoping to catch a glimpse of some of the visiting dignitaries. An all-star lineup of poets, scientists, journalists, and media celebrities had convened for the opening of a weekend conference entitled "LSD: A Generation Later." Topping the bill was the man they call the "Father of the Psychedelic Age."

At seventy-one years of age Dr. Albert Hofmann seemed miscast in his role as hero of such a gathering. His white, closely cropped hair and conservative attire contrasted sharply with the motley appearance of his youthful admirers, who could just as easily have turned out for a rock and roll concert or an antinuke rally. But as he strode to the podium to deliver the evening's keynote address, Dr. Hofmann was greeted by a long and thunderous standing ovation.

"You may be disappointed," he warned the audience. "You may have expected a guru, but instead you meet just a chemist." Whereupon Hofmann launched into a serious scientific discussion of the step-by-step process that led to the discovery of LSD-25, the most potent mind drug known to science at the time. Occasionally he flashed a diagram on the screen and expatiated on the molecular subtleties of hallucinogenic drugs. While much of the technical data soared way above the heads of his listeners, they seemed to love every minute of it.

Dr. Hofmann first synthesized LSD (lysergic acid diethylamide) in 1938 while investigating the chemical and pharmacological properties of ergot, a rye fungus rich in medicinal alkaloids, for Sandoz Laboratories in Basel, Switzerland. At the time he was searching for an analeptic compound (a circulatory stimulant), and LSD was the twenty-fifth in a series of ergot derivatives he concocted; hence the designation LSD-25. Preliminary studies on laboratory animals did not prove significant, and scientists at Sandoz quickly lost interest in the drug. For the next five years the vial of LSD gathered dust on the shelf, until the afternoon of April 16, 1943.

"I had a strange feeling," Hofmann told the assembled masses, "that it would be worthwhile to carry out more profound studies with this compound." In the course of preparing a fresh batch of LSD he accidentally absorbed a small dose through his fingertips, and soon he was overcome by "a remarkable but not unpleasant state of intoxication...characterized by an intense stimulation of the imagination and an altered state of awareness of the world." A knowing chorus of laughter emanated from the audience as Hofmann continued to read from his diary notes. "As I lay in a dazed condition with eyes closed there surged up from me a succession of fantastic, rapidly changing imagery of a striking reality and depth, alternating with a vivid, kaleidoscopic play of colors. This condition gradually passed off after about three hours."

Dr. Hofmann was baffled by his first unplanned excursion into the strange world of LSD. He could not comprehend how this substance could have found its way into his body in sufficient quantity to produce such extraordinary symptoms. In the interest of science, he assured his audience, he decided to experiment on himself. Another boisterous round of applause filled the auditorium.

On April 19, three days after his initial psychedelic voyage, Dr. Hofmann swallowed a mere 250 micrograms (a millionth of an ounce), thinking that such a minuscule amount would have negligible results. But he was in for a surprise. As he bicycled home accompanied by his laboratory assistant, he realized the symptoms were much stronger than before. "I had great difficulty in speaking coherently," he recounted. "My field of vision swayed before me, and objects appeared distorted like images in curved mirrors. I had the impression of being unable to move from the spot, although my assistant told me afterwards that we had cycled at a good pace."

When Hofmann arrived home, he consulted a physician, who was ill equipped to deal with what would later be called a "bad trip." Hofmann did not know if he'd taken a fatal dose or if he'd be lost forever in the twisted corridors of inner space. For a while he feared he was losing his mind: "Occasionally I felt as if I were out of my body....I thought I had died. My 'ego' was suspended somewhere in space and I saw my body lying dead on the sofa."

Somehow Hofmann summoned the courage to endure this mind-wrenching ordeal. As the trip wore on, his psychic condition began to improve, and eventually he was able to explore the hallucinogenic terrain with a modicum of composure. He spent the remaining hours absorbed in a synesthetic swoon, bearing witness as each sound triggered a corresponding optical effect, and vice versa, until he fell into a fitful sleep. The next morning he awoke feeling perfectly fine.

And so it was that Dr. Albert Hofmann made his fateful discovery. Right from the start he sensed that LSD could be an important tool for studying how the mind works, and he was pleased when the scientific community began to use the drug for this purpose. But he did not anticipate that his "problem child," as he later referred to LSD, would have such enormous social and cultural impact in the years to come. Nor could he have foreseen that one day he would be revered as a near-mythic figure by a generation of acid enthusiasts.

"Dr. Hofmann," said Stephen Gaskin, leader of the largest counterculture commune in America, "there are thousands of people on the Farm who feel they owe their lives to you." Gaskin was among the guests invited to participate in a panel discussion on the second day of the colloquium. Its purpose was to provide a forum for counterculture veterans to reflect back upon the halcyon days of the psychedelic movement, which had reached a peak a decade earlier during the infamous Summer of Love, and assess what had since come to pass. Poet Allen Ginsberg likened the event to a "class reunion." He decided to do some homework before joining his fellow acid valedictorians, so he took some LSD on the plane flight to the West Coast. While under the influence of the psychedelic, he began to ponder the disclosures that had recently surfaced in the news media concerning the CIA's use of LSD as a mind control weapon. The possibility that an espionage organization might have promoted the widespread use of LSD was disturbing to Ginsberg, who had been an outspoken advocate of psychedelics during the 1960s. He grabbed a pen and started jotting down some high-altitude thoughts. "Am I, Allen Ginsberg, the product of one of the CIA's lamentable, ill-advised, or triumphantly successful experiments in mind control?" Had the CIA, "by conscious plan or inadvertent Pandora's Box, let loose the whole LSD Fad on the U.S. & the World?"

Ginsberg raised the CIA issue during the conference, but few seemed to take the matter seriously. "The LSD movement was started by the CIA," quipped Timothy Leary with a wide grin on his face. "I wouldn't be here now without the foresight of the CIA scientists." The one-time Pied Piper of the flower children was in top form, laughing and joking with reporters, as though he hadn't been chased halfway around the world by US narcotics police and spent the last few years in prison. "It was no accident," Leary mused. "It was all planned and scripted by the Central Intelligence, and I'm all in favor of Central Intelligence."

A jovial mood prevailed throughout much of the panel discussion. Old comrades who had not seen each other for a long time swapped tales of acid glory and reminisced about the wild and unforgettable escapades of yesteryear. "As I look at my colleagues and myself," said Richard Alpert, one of Leary's original cohorts at Harvard University in the early 1960s, "I see we have proceeded just as we wished to, despite all conditions. I feel that what we are doing today is partly demonstrating that we are not psychotic!" Alpert went on to declare that he didn't care if he ever took LSD again but that he appreciated what his hundreds of trips had taught him and hoped there would be a more favorable climate for serious LSD research in the near future.

Alpert's sentiments were echoed by many of the panelists, who called on the government to reconsider its restrictive policies so that scientists and psychologists could resume studying the drug. There were frequent testimonials to the contributions LSD made to science and society. Acid was praised as a boon to psychotherapy, an enhancer of creativity, a religious sacrament, and a liberator of the human spirit. Dr. Ralph Metzner, the third member of the Harvard triumvirate, suggested that the appearance of LSD constituted nothing less than a turning point in human evolution. It was no coincidence, he maintained, that Dr. Hofmann discovered the effects of LSD shortly after the first nuclear chain reaction was achieved by the Manhattan Project. His remarks seemed to imply that LSD was some sort of divine antidote to the nuclear curse and that humanity must pay heed to the psychedelic revelation if it was to alter its self-destructive course and avert a major catastrophe.

Author Richard Ashley elaborated on the theme of acid as a chemical messiah. As far as he was concerned, LSD provided the most effective means of short-circuiting the mental straitjacket that society imposes on its members. A worldwide police state was a virtual certainty, Ashley predicted, unless more people used psychedelics to raise their consciousness and resist the ominous specter of thought control.

Others were somewhat more cautious in speculating upon the role of hallucinogenic drugs in advanced industrial society. "LSD came along before our culture was ready for it," asserted Dr. Stanley Krippner, a leading parapsychologist who once directed the Maimonides Dream Laboratory in New York. "I think we're still not ready for it. We haven't used it for its greatest potential. Psychedelic substances have been used very wisely in primitive cultures for spiritual and healing purposes. Our culture does not have this framework. We don't have the closeness to God, the closeness to nature, the shamanistic outlook. We've lost all that."

By the time the conference drew to a close, over thirty speakers had rendered their verdicts about LSD and the so-called psychedelic revolution. While it was clear that everyone had been deeply affected by the drug experience and the social movement it inspired, there was no overall consensus as to what it all meant. Each person had his or her ideas about why things happened the way they did and what the future might portend. Some felt that LSD arrived on the scene just in the nick of time, others saw it as a premature discovery, and there were a few who thought it might already be too late. If that wasn't enough to thoroughly confuse the audience, John Lilly, the dolphin scientist, urged his listeners to ignore everything they heard from their elders and make their own discoveries. Ginsberg seconded the motion in his concluding remarks. "We must disentangle ourselves from past suppositions," he counseled. "The words 'psychedelic revolution' are part of a past created largely by media images. We need to throw out the past images."

Less than a month before the Santa Cruz convention, LSD was the main topic at another well-attended gathering. The setting on this occasion was an ornate Senate hearing room on Capitol Hill. The television cameras were ready to roll as Ted Kennedy, chairman of the Senate Subcommittee on Health and Scientific Research, strolled toward the lectern flanked by a few of his aides. During the next two days he would attempt to nail down the elusive details of Operation MK-ULTRA, the principal CIA program involving the development of chemical and biological agents during the Cold War.

In his opening statement Kennedy told a large audience that he hoped these hearings would "close the book on this chapter of the

CIA's life." He then proceeded to question a group of former CIA employees about the Agency's testing of LSD and other drugs on unwitting American citizens. These activities were considered so sensitive that only a handful of people within the CIA even knew about them. A previously classified document explained why the program was shrouded in secrecy: "The knowledge that the Agency is engaging in unethical and illicit activities would have serious repercussions in political and diplomatic circles and would be detrimental to the accomplishment of its mission."

Although most of the testimony had been rehearsed earlier when witnesses met with a Kennedy staff member, the senator from Massachusetts still managed to feign a sense of astonishment when David Rhodes, formerly a CIA psychologist, recounted an ill-fated LSD experiment at a CIA safehouse in the San Francisco Bay area. He described how unsuspecting individuals were recruited from local bars and lured to a party where CIA operatives intended to release LSD in the form of an aerosol spray. But as Rhodes explained, the air currents in the room were unsuitable for dosing the partygoers, so one of his cohorts snuck into the bathroom and tried the spray on himself. The audience chuckled at the thought of grown men spritzing themselves with government acid, while news reporters scribbled their renditions of the headline-making tale.

Throughout the hearings the senators listened to one account after another of bumbling and clumsiness on the part of Agency personnel. Phillip Goldman, a CIA chemical warfare specialist, could have been describing a Three Stooges routine when he told of an attempt to test a launching device for a stink bomb. The projectile hit the window ledge, and the spooks held their noses. There were more laughs when he mentioned a drug-coated swizzle stick that dissolved in a cocktail but left a taste so bitter that no one would drink it. And so forth and so on. This kind of buffoonery proved to be an effective public relations ploy for the CIA, deflecting serious scrutiny from drug-related misdeeds. By stressing ineptitude the Agency conveyed an all too human air. After all, why prosecute a bunch of regular Joes for fooling around with chemicals they could never hope to understand?

The star witness on the second day of the hearings was the CIA's chief sorcerer-scientist, Dr. Sidney Gottlieb, who ran the MK-ULTRA program. Gottlieb, a slight man with short gray hair and a clubfoot, agreed to testify only after receiving a grant of immunity from criminal prosecution. His testimony before the Senate sub-committee marked the first public appearance of this shadowy figure since he left the Agency in 1973. Actually his appearance was "semi-public." Because he suffered from a heart condition, Gottlieb was allowed to speak with the senators in a small antechamber while everyone else listened to the proceedings over a public address system.

The purpose of Operation MK-ULTRA and related programs, Gottlieb explained, was "to investigate whether and how it was possible to modify an individual's behavior by covert means." When asked to elaborate on what the CIA learned from this research, Gottlieb was afflicted by a sudden loss of memory, as if he were under the influence of one of his own amnesia drugs. However, he did confirm earlier reports that prostitutes were used in the safehouse experiments to spike the drinks of unlucky customers while CIA operatives observed, photographed, and recorded the action.

When asked to justify this activity, Gottlieb resorted to the familiar Cold War refrain that had been invoked repeatedly throughout the hearings by other witnesses. The original impetus for the CIA's drug programs, he maintained, stemmed from concern about the aggressive use of behavior-altering techniques against the US by its enemies. Gottlieb claimed there was evidence (which he never shared with the senators) that the Soviets and the Red Chinese might have been mucking about with LSD in the early 1950s. This, he explained, had grave implications for our national security.

At the close of the hearings Kennedy summed up the surreptitious LSD tests by declaring, "These activities are part of history, not the current practice of the CIA." And that was as far as it went. The senators seemed eager to get the whole show over with, even though many issues were far from resolved. Later it was revealed that some of the witnesses conferred among themselves, agreeing to limit their testimony to the minimum degree necessary to satisfy the committee. As Dr. Gottlieb admitted, "The bottom line on this whole business has not yet been written."

Shortly after the Senate forum, a Washington attorney gave us a tip about how to gain access to a special reading room that housed documents pertaining to Operation MK-ULTRA and other CIA mind control projects. The documents had recently been declassified as a result of a Freedom of Information request by researcher John Marks. Located on the bottom floor of the Hyatt Regency Hotel in Rosslyn,

Virginia, the reading room was smoke-filled and crowded with journalists working on deadlines, scouring through a heap of papers as fast as their fingers could turn the pages. We were not bound by such constraints, and we decided to examine the files at an unhurried pace.

Reading through the intelligence records was both exciting and frustrating. Each stack of heavily censored reports contained a hodgepodge of data, much of which seemed trivial. There was no rhyme or reason to their arrangement: financial records, inventory lists, in-house gossip, and letters of recommendation were randomly interspersed with minutes of top-secret meetings and other tantalizing morsels.

We dug in for the long haul, intent on examining every scrap of information related to the CIA's behavior modification programs. Our visits to the reading room became a weekly ritual, and soon we expanded our investigation to include army, navy, and air force documents as well. During the next six months we reviewed approximately twenty thousand pages of previously classified memoranda. We began to think of ourselves as archeologists rather than muckrakers, trying to unearth remnants of a lost history buried underneath layers of secrecy.

In the course of our inquiry we uncovered CIA documents describing experiments in sensory deprivation, sleep teaching, ESP, subliminal projection, electronic brain stimulation, and many other methods that might have applications for behavior modification. One project was designed to turn people into programmed assassins who would kill on automatic command. Another document mentioned "hypnotically-induced anxieties" and "induced pain as a form of physical and psychological control." There were repeated references to exotic drugs and biological agents that caused "headache clusters," uncontrollable twitching or drooling, or a lobotomylike stupor. Deadly chemicals were concocted for the sole purpose of inducing a heart attack or cancer without leaving a clue as to the actual source of the disease. CIA specialists also studied the effects of magnetic fields, ultrasonic vibrations, and other forms of radiant energy on the brain. As one CIA doctor put it, "We lived in a never-never land of 'eyes only' memos and unceasing experimentation."

As it turns out, nearly every drug that appeared on the black market during the 1960s—marijuana, cocaine, heroin, PCP, amyl nitrate, mushrooms, DMT, barbiturates, laughing gas, speed, and many others—had previously been scrutinized, tested, and in some cases refined by CIA and army scientists. But of all the techniques explored by the Agency in its multimillion-dollar twenty-five-year quest to conquer the human mind, none received as much attention or was embraced with such enthusiasm as LSD-25. For a time CIA personnel were completely infatuated with the hallucinogen. Those who first tested LSD in the early 1950s were convinced that it would revolutionize the cloak-and-dagger trade.

As we studied the documents more closely, certain shapes and patterns came alive to us. We began to get a sense of the internal dynamics of the CIA's secret LSD program and how it evolved over the years. The story that emerged was far more complex and rich in detail than the disconnected smattering of information that had surfaced in various press reports and government probes. We were able to understand what the spies were looking for when they first got into LSD, what happened during the initial phase of experimentation, how their attitude changed as they tested the drug on themselves and their associates, and how it was ultimately used in covert operations.

The central irony of LSD is that it has been used both as a weapon and a sacrament, a mind control drug and a mind-expanding chemical. Each of these possibilities generated a unique history: a covert history, on the one hand, rooted in CIA and military experimentation with hallucinogens, and a grassroots history of the drug counterculture that exploded into prominence in the 1960s. At key points the two histories converge and overlap, forming an interface between the CIA's secret drug programs and the rise and fall of the psychedelic movement.

The LSD story is inseparable from the cherished hopes and shattered illusions of the sixties generation. In many ways it provides a key for understanding what happened during that turbulent era, when political and cultural revolution erupted with full fury. And yet, as the decade drew to a close, the youth movement suddenly collapsed and bottomed out, leaving a trail of unanswered questions in its wake. Only by examining both sides of the psychedelic saga— the CIA's mind control program and the drug subculture—can we grasp the true nature of LSD-25 and discern what effect this powerful chemical agent had on the social upheavals of the 1960s.

PART ONE

The Roots of Psychedelia

I

In The Beginning
There Was Madness . . .

THE TRUTH SEEKERS

In the spring of 1942 General William "Wild Bill" Donovan, chief of the Office of Strategic Services (OSS), the CIA's wartime predecessor, assembled a half-dozen prestigious American scientists and asked them to undertake a top-secret research program. Their mission, Donovan explained, was to develop a speech-inducing drug for use in intelligence interrogations. He insisted that the need for such a weapon was so acute as to warrant any and every attempt to find it.

The use of drugs by secret agents had long been a part of cloak-and-dagger folklore, but this would be the first concerted attempt on the part of an American espionage organization to modify human behavior through chemical means. "We were not afraid to try things that had never been done before," asserted Donovan, who was known for his freewheeling and unconventional approach to the spy trade. The OSS chief pressed his associates to come up with a substance that could break down the psychological defenses of enemy spies and POWs, thereby causing an uninhibited disclosure of classified information. Such a drug would also be useful for screening OSS personnel in order to identify German sympathizers, double agents, and potential misfits.

Dr. Windfred Overhulser, superintendent of Saint Elizabeth's Hospital in Washington, DC, was appointed chairman of the research committee. Other members included Dr. Edward Strecker, then president of the American Psychiatric Association, and Harry J. Anslinger, head of the Federal Bureau of Narcotics. The committee surveyed and rejected numerous drugs, including alcohol, barbiturates, and caffeine. Peyote and scopolamine were also tested, but the visions produced by these substances interfered with the interrogation process. Eventually marijuana was chosen as the most likely candidate for a speech-inducing agent.

OSS scientists created a highly potent extract of cannabis, and through a process known as esterification a clear and viscous liquid was obtained. The final product had no color, odor, or taste. It would be nearly impossible to detect when administered surreptitiously, which is exactly what the spies intended to do. "There is no reason to believe that any other nation or group is familiar with the preparation of this particular drug," stated a once classified OSS document. Henceforth the OSS referred to the marijuana extract as "TD" —a rather transparent cover for "Truth Drug."

Various ways of administering TD were tried on witting and unwitting subjects. OSS operatives found that the medicated goo could "be injected into any type of food, such as mashed potatoes, butter, salad dressing, or in such things as candy." Another scheme relied on using facial tissues impregnated with the drug. But these methods had their drawbacks. What if someone had a particularly ravenous appetite? Too much TD could knock a subject out and render him useless for interrogation. The OSS eventually determined that the best approach involved the use of a hypodermic syringe to inject a diluted TD solution into a cigarette or cigar. After smoking such an item, the subject would get suitably stoned, at which point a skillful interrogator would move in and try to get him to spill the beans.

The effects of TD were described in an OSS report: "TD appears to relax all inhibitions and to deaden the areas of the brain which govern an individual's discretion and caution. It accentuates the senses and makes manifest any strong characteristics of the individual. Sexual inhibitions are lowered, and the sense of humor is accentuated to the point where any statement or situation can become extremely funny to the subject. On the other hand, a person's unpleasant characteristics may also be heightened. It may be stated that, generally speaking, the reaction will be one of great loquacity and hilarity."*

After testing TD on themselves, their associates, and US military

---

*This was a rather mild and playful assessment of the effects of marijuana compared to the public rantings of Harry Anslinger, the narcotics chief who orchestrated an unrelenting media compaign against "the killer weed."

personnel, OSS agents utilized the drug operationally, although on a limited basis. The results were mixed. In certain instances TD subjects felt a driving necessity "to discuss psychologically charged topics. Whatever the individual is trying to withhold will be forced to the top of his subconscious mind." But there were also those who experienced "toxic reactions"—better known in latter-day lingo as "bummers." One unwitting doper became irritable and threatening and complained of feeling like he was "two different people." The peculiar nature of his symptoms precluded any attempt to question him.

That was how it went, from one extreme to the other. At times TD seemed to stimulate "a rush of talk"; on other occasions people got paranoid and didn't say a word. The lack of consistency proved to be a major stumbling block, and "Donovan's dreamers," as his enthusiastic OSS staffers have been called, reluctantly weaned themselves from their reefer madness. A handwritten comment in the margins of an OSS document summed up their stoned escapades: "The drug defies all but the most expert and searching analysis, and for all practical purposes can be considered beyond analysis."

After the war, the CIA and the military picked up where the OSS had left off in the secret search for a truth serum. The navy took the lead when it initiated Project CHATTER in 1947, the same year the CIA was formed. Described as an "offensive" program, CHATTER was supposed to devise means of obtaining information from people independent of their volition but without physical duress. Toward this end Dr. Charles Savage conducted experiments with mescaline (a semi-synthetic extract of the peyote cactus that produces hallucinations similar to those caused by LSD) at the Naval Medical Research Institute in Bethesda, Maryland. But these studies, which involved animal as well as human subjects, did not yield an effective truth serum, and CHATTER was terminated in 1953.

The navy became interested in mescaline as an interrogation agent when American investigators learned of mind control experiments carried out by Nazi doctors at the Dachau concentration camp during World War II. After administering the hallucinogen to thirty prisoners, the Nazis concluded that it was "impossible to impose one's will on another person as in hypnosis even when the strongest dose of mescaline had been given." But the drug still afforded certain advantages to SS interrogators, who were consistently able to draw "even the most intimate secrets from the [subject] when questions

were cleverly put." Not surprisingly, "sentiments of hatred and re-
venge were exposed in every case."

The mescaline experiments at Dachau were described in a lengthy
report by the US Naval Technical Mission, which swept across Europe in search of every scrap of industrial material and scientific
data that could be garnered from the fallen Reich. This mission set
the stage for the wholesale importation of more than six hundred
top Nazi scientists under the auspices of Project Paperclip, which
the CIA supervised during the early years of the Cold War. Among
those who emigrated to the US in such a fashion was Dr. Hubertus
Strughold, the German scientist whose chief subordinates (Dr. Sigmund Ruff and Dr. Sigmund Rascher) were directly involved in
"aviation medicine" experiments at Dachau, which included the
mescaline studies.* Despite recurring allegations that he sanctioned
medical atrocities during the war, Strughold settled in Texas and
became an important figure in America's space program. After Wern-
her von Braun, he was the top Nazi scientist employed by the American government, and he was subsequently hailed by NASA as the
"father of space medicine."

The CIA, meanwhile, had launched an intensive research effort
geared toward developing "special" interrogation techniques. Two
methods showed promise in the late 1940s. The first involved nar-

---

*Strughold's subordinates injected Dachau inmates with gasoline, crushed them
to death in high-altitude pressure chambers, shot them so that potential blood co-
agulants could be tested on their wounds, forced them to stand naked in subfreezing
temperatures or immersed them in tubs of ice water to see how long it would take
before they died. As Charles R. Allen, Jr., author of *From Hitler to Uncle Sam: How
American Intelligence Used Nazi War Criminals*, stated in an article on Strughold,
"There was a clear pattern to the various experiments with poison, gas, deliberate
infestation of victims with malaria, typhus and other virulencies causing instant or
prolonged anguishing to death. Whether the tests concerned high-altitude, freezing
or the potability of sea water; or the shooting of 'volunteers' with gas bullets—the
patent purpose of the entire body of tests conducted at Dachau was to enhance the
effectiveness of Hitler's criminal warfare against humanity."

After the war an Allied tribunal convened at Nuremberg sentenced a number of
Nazi doctors to death for their role in medical atrocities at Dachau and other concentration camps. The judges at Nuremberg subsequently put forward a code of ethics
for scientific research, which stipulated that full voluntary consent must be obtained
from all research subjects and experiments should yield positive results for the benefit
of society that could not be obtained in any other way.

Although Dr. Strughold escaped prosecution, his name later appeared on a master
list of "Reported Nazi War Criminals Residing in the United States" compiled by
the Immigration and Naturalization Service. He currently lives in San Antonio, Texas.

cohypnosis, in which a CIA psychiatrist attempted to induce a trance state after administering a mild sedative. A second technique involved a combination of two different drugs with contradictory effects. A heavy dose of barbiturates was given to knock the subject out, and then he received an injection of a stimulant, usually some type of amphetamine. As he started to come out of a somnambulant state, he would reach a certain ineffable point prior to becoming fully conscious. Described in CIA documents as "the twilight zone," this groggy condition was considered optimal for interrogation.

CIA doctors attempted to extend the stuporous limbo as long as possible. In order to maintain the delicate balance between consciousness and unconsciousness, an intravenous hookup was inserted in both the subject's arms. One set of works contained a downer, the other an upper (the classic "goofball" effect); with a mere flick of the finger an interrogator could regulate the flow of chemicals. The idea was to produce a "push"—a sudden outpouring of thoughts, emotions, confidences, and whatnot. Along this line various combinations were tested: Seconal and Dexedrine; Pentothal and Desoxyn; and depending on the whim of the spy in charge, some marijuana (the old OSS stand-by, which the CIA referred to as "sugar") might be thrown in for good measure.

The goofball approach was not a precision science. There were no strictly prescribed rules or operating procedures regarding what drugs should be employed in a given situation. The CIA interrogators were left to their own devices, and a certain degree of recklessness was perhaps inevitable. In one case, a group of CIA experts hastily drafted a memo after reviewing a report prepared by one of the Agency's special interrogation teams. The medical consultants pointed out that "the amounts of scopolamine administered were extremely heavy." They also noted that the best results were obtained when two or at most three different chemicals were used in a session. In this case, however, heavy dosages of scopolamine were administered along with thiamine, sodium luminal, atropine sulfate, sodium pentothal and caffeine sulfate. One of the CIA's professional consultants in "H" techniques also questioned why hypnosis was attempted "after a long and continuous use of chemicals, after the subject had vomited, and after apparently a maximum tolerance point had been reached with the chemicals." Everyone who read the interrogation report agreed that hypnosis was useless, if not impossible, under

7

such conditions. Nevertheless, the memo concluded by reaffirming that "no criticism is intended whatsoever" and that "the choice of operating weapons" must be left to the agents in the field.

Despite the potential hazards and tenuousness of the procedure as a whole, special interrogations were strongly endorsed by Agency officials. A CIA document dated November 26, 1951, announced, "We're now convinced that we can maintain a subject in a controlled state for a much longer period of time than we heretofore had believed possible. Furthermore, we feel that by use of certain chemicals or combinations, we can, in a very high percentage of cases, produce relevant information." Although these techniques were still considered experimental, the prevailing opinion among members of the special interrogation teams was that there had been enough experiments "to justify giving the green light to operational use of the techniques." "There will be many a failure," a CIA scientist acknowledged, but he was quick to stress that *every success with this method will be pure gravy.*"*

---

*Obtaining information was only one aspect of the interrogation process. Even when CIA officers were able to loosen a subject's tongue, other problems remained, such as how to insure that he would not remember the events that transpired during his stint in the twilight zone. "If by some means we could create a perfect and thoroughly controlled amnesia," a CIA agent declared, "the matter would be simplified, but amnesia is not certain and cannot be guaranteed."

Certain drugs were known to produce amnesia for a matter of hours or days, but this was not sufficient. The CIA also had access to chemicals capable of causing permanent brain damage, but long-term amnesia drugs that would be completely reversible over a twelve-to-eighteen-month period were not available.

This was quite an inconvenience as far as the national security experts were concerned. The question of what to do with subjects of special interrogation sessions—the "disposal problem"—provoked a heated debate inside the Company. The immediate objective was to find a way of holding them "in maximum custody until either operations have progressed to the point where their knowledge is no longer highly sensitive, or the knowledge they possess in general will be of no use to the enemy."

One possibility suggested in CIA documents was to render a person incoherent through psychological and/or pharmacological attack and then have him placed in a mental institution. An unspecified number of subjects were committed involuntarily to insane asylums, including some who were described in CIA memoranda as mentally sound. (This practice, which began in the early 1950s and continued at least until the mid-1960s, invites obvious comparisons to the incarceration of Russian dissidents in psychiatric hospitals because of their political views.) Another option involved "termination with extreme prejudice" (CIA lingo for assassination), but this was hardly an ideal solution in all situations.

In one CIA document the question of disposal was discussed under the heading "LOBOTOMY and Related Operations." A number of individuals who were fully

In an effort to expand its research program the CIA contacted academics and other outside experts who specialized in areas of mutual interest. Liaison was established with the research sections of police departments and criminology laboratories; medical practitioners, professional hypnotists, and psychiatrists were brought on as paid consultants; and various branches of the military provided assistance. Oftentimes these arrangements involved a cover to conceal the CIA's interest in behavior modification. With the bureaucratic apparatus already in place, the CIA's mind control efforts were integrated into a single project under the code name BLUEBIRD. Due to the extreme sensitivity of the project, the usual channels of authorization were bypassed; instead of going through the Projects Review Committee, the proposal for BLUEBIRD was submitted di-

---

cognizant of the disposal problem suggested that lobotomy "might be the answer or at least a partial solution." They argued that "lobotomy would create a person 'who no longer cared,' who had lost all initiative and drive, whose allegiance to ideal or motivating factors no longer existed, and who would probably have, if not complete amnesia, at least a fuzzy or spotty memory for recent and past events." They also pointed out "that certain lobotomy types of operations were simple, quickly performed and not too dangerous."

Along this line a group of CIA scientists entertained the possibility of using an "icepick" lobotomy to render an individual harmless "from a security point of view." A memo dated February 7, 1952, notes that on numerous occasions after using electroshock to produce anesthesia, an unidentified surgeon in the Washington, DC, area performed an operation that involved destroying brain tissue by piercing the skull just above the eye with a fine surgical icepick. This type of psychosurgery had certain advantages, in that it resulted in "nervous confusional and amnesia effects" without leaving a "tell-tale scar." The CIA also experimented with brain surgery via UHF sound waves and at one point during the early 1950s attempted to create a microwave "amnesia beam" that would destroy memory neurons.

Not all CIA officials, however, favored using lobotomy as a disposal technique. Potential drawbacks were cited: surgical risk was great, brain damage could be extensive, and such an operation, if faulty, could produce a "vegetable." Moreover, if the enemy discovered that the CIA was mutilating people's brains for the sake of national security, this information could be exploited as a propaganda weapon.

Other CIA officials opposed lobotomy because it was blatantly inhumane and violated "all concepts of 'fair-play' and the American way of life and [thus] it could never be *officially* [emphasis added] sanctioned or supported." A CIA document dated March 3, 1952, states that while "the USSR and its satellites are capable of any conceivable atrocity against human beings to attain what they think are their ends, we should not—with our high regard for human life—use these techniques unless by using them we save the lives of our own people and the situation is highly critical to the nation's safety."

In the early 1950s, at least $100,000 was designated for a proposed research project geared toward developing "neuro-surgical techniques for Agency interest." It is not known whether this research was ever carried out.

rectly to CIA director Roscoe Hillenkoetter, who authorized the use of unvouchered funds to finance the hush-hush undertaking. With this seal of approval the CIA's first major drug testing program was officially hatched. BLUEBIRD was to remain a carefully guarded secret, for if word of the program leaked out it would have been a great embarrassment and a detriment to American intelligence. As one CIA document put it, BLUEBIRD material was "not fit for public consumption."

From the outset the CIA's mind control program had an explicit domestic angle. A memo dated July 13, 1951, described the Agency's mind-bending efforts as "broad and comprehensive, involving both domestic and overseas activities, and taking into consideration the programs and objectives of other departments, principally the military services." BLUEBIRD activities were designed to create an "exploitable alteration of personality" in selected individuals; specific targets included "potential agents, defectors, refugees, POWs," and a vague category of "others." A number of units within the CIA participated in this endeavor, including the Inspection and Security Staff (the forerunner of the Office of Security), which assumed overall responsibility for running the program and dispatching the special interrogation teams. Colonel Sheffield Edwards, the chairman of the BLUEBIRD steering committee, consistently pushed for a more reliable speech-inducing substance. By the time BLUEBIRD evolved into Operation ARTICHOKE (the formal change in code names occurred in August 1951), Security officials were still searching for the magic technique—the *deus ex machina*—that would guarantee surefire results.

The whole concept of a truth drug was a bit farfetched to begin with. It presupposed that there was a way to chemically bypass the mind's censor and turn the psyche inside out, unleashing a profusion of buried secrets, and that surely some approximation of "truth" would emerge amidst all the personal debris. In this respect the CIA's quest resembled a skewed version of a familiar mythological theme from which such images as the Philosopher's Stone and the Fountain of Youth derive—that through touching or ingesting something one can acquire wisdom, immortality, or eternal peace. It is more than a bit ironic that the biblical inscription on the marble wall of the main lobby at CIA headquarters in Langley, Virginia, reads, "And ye shall know the Truth and the Truth shall set you free."

The freewheeling atmosphere that prevailed during the CIA's early years encouraged an "anything goes" attitude among researchers associated with the mind control program. This was before the Agency's bureaucratic arteries began to harden, and those who participated in Operation ARTICHOKE were intent on leaving no stone unturned in an effort to deliver the ultimate truth drug. A number of agents were sent on fact-finding missions to all corners of the globe to procure samples of rare herbs and botanicals. The results of one such trip were recorded in a heavily deleted document entitled "Exploration of Potential Plant Resources in the Caribbean Region." Among the numerous items mentioned in this report, a few were particularly intriguing. A plant called a "stupid bush," characterized by the CIA as a psychogenic agent and a pernicious weed, was said to proliferate in Puerto Rico and Saint Thomas. Its effects were shrouded in mystery. An "information bush" was also discovered. This shrub stumped CIA experts, who were at a loss to pin down its properties. The "information bush" was listed as a psychogenic agent followed by a lingering question mark. What type of information—prophetic or mundane—might be evoked by this unusual herb was unclear. Nor was it known whether the "information bush" could be used as an antidote to the "stupid bush" or vice versa.

The CIA studied a veritable pharmacopoeia of drugs with the hope of achieving a breakthrough. At one point during the early 1950s Uncle Sam's secret agents viewed cocaine as a potential truth serum. "Cocaine's general effects have been somewhat neglected," noted an astute researcher. Whereupon tests were conducted that enabled the CIA to determine that the precious powder "will produce elation, talkativeness, etc." when administered by injection. "Larger doses," according to a previously classified document, "may cause fearfulness and alarming hallucinations." The document goes on to report that cocaine "counteracts...the catatonia of catatonic schizophrenics" and concludes with the recommendation that the drug be studied further.

A number of cocaine derivatives were also investigated from an interrogation standpoint. Procaine, a synthetic analogue, was tested on mental patients and the results were intriguing. When injected into the frontal lobes of the brain through trephine holes in the skull, the drug "produced free and spontaneous speech within two days in mute schizophrenics." This procedure was rejected as "too surgical for our use." Nevertheless, according to a CIA pharmacologist, "it is possible that such a drug could be gotten into the general circulation of subject without surgery, hypodermic or feeding." He suggested a method known as iontophoresis, which involves using an electric current to transfer the ions of a chosen medicament into the tissues of the body.

The CIA's infatuation with cocaine was short-lived. It may have titillated the nostrils of more than a few spies and produced some heady speculation, but after the initial inspiration it was back to square one. Perhaps their expectations were too high for any drug to accommodate. Or maybe a new approach to the problem was required.

The search for an effective interrogation technique eventually led to heroin. Not the heroin that ex-Nazi pilots under CIA contract smuggled out of the Golden Triangle in Southeast Asia on CIA proprietary airlines during the late 1940s and early 1950s; nor the heroin that was pumped into America's black and brown ghettos after passing through contraband networks controlled by mobsters who moonlighted as CIA hitmen. The Agency's involvement in worldwide heroin traffic, which has been well documented in *The Politics of Heroin in Southeast Asia* by Alfred McCoy, went far beyond the scope of Operation ARTICHOKE, which was primarily concerned with eliciting information from recalcitrant subjects. However, ARTICHOKE scientists did see possible advantages in heroin as a mind control drug. According to a CIA document dated April 26, 1952, heroin was "frequently used by police and intelligence officers *on a routine basis* [emphasis added]." The cold turkey theory of interrogation: CIA operatives determined that heroin and other habit-forming substances "can be useful in reverse because of the stresses produced when they are withdrawn from those who are addicted to their use."

Enter LSD

It was with the hope of finding the long-sought miracle drug that CIA investigators first began to dabble with LSD-25 in the early 1950s. At the time very little was known about the hallucinogen, even in scientific circles. Dr. Werner Stoll, the son of Sandoz president Arthur Stoll and a colleague of Albert Hofmann's, was the first person to investigate the psychological properties of LSD. The results of his study were presented in the *Swiss Archives of Neurology* in 1947. Stoll reported that LSD produced disturbances in perception, hallucinations, and acceleration in thinking; moreover, the drug was found to blunt the usual suspiciousness of schizophrenic patients. No unfavorable aftereffects were described. Two years later in the same journal Stoll contributed a second report entitled "A New Hallucinatory Agent, Active in Very Small Amounts."

The fact that LSD caused hallucinations should not have been a total surprise to the scientific community. Sandoz first became interested in ergot, the natural source of lysergic acid, because of numerous stories passed down through the ages. The rye fungus had a mysterious and contradictory reputation. In China and parts of the Mideast it was thought to possess medicinal qualities, and certain scholars believe that it may have been used in sacred rites in ancient Greece. In other parts of Europe, however, the same fungus was associated with the horrible malady known as St. Anthony's Fire, which struck periodically like the plague. Medieval chronicles tell of villages and towns where nearly everyone went mad for a few days after ergot-diseased rye was unknowingly milled into flour and baked as bread. Men were afflicted with gangrenous limbs that looked like blackened stumps, and pregnant women miscarried. Even in modern times there have been reports of ergot-related epidemics.*

The CIA inherited this ambiguous legacy when it embraced LSD as a mind control drug. An ARTICHOKE document dated October 21, 1951, indicates that acid was tested initially as part of a pilot study of the effects of various chemicals "on the conscious suppression of experimental or non-threat secrets." In addition to lysergic acid this particular survey covered a wide range of substances, including morphine, ether, Benzedrine, ethyl alcohol, and mescaline. "There is no question," noted the author of this report, "that drugs are already on hand (and new ones are being produced) that can destroy integrity and make indiscreet the most dependable individual." The report concluded by recommending that LSD be critically

---

*In 1951 hundreds of respectable citizens in Pont-Saint-Esprit, a small French village, went completely berserk one evening. Some of the town's leading citizens jumped from windows into the Rhone. Others ran through the streets screaming about being chased by lions, tigers, and "bandits with donkey ears." Many died, and those who survived suffered strange aftereffects for weeks. In his book *The Day of St. Anthony's Fire*, John C. Fuller attributes this bizarre outbreak to rye flour contaminated with ergot.

tested "under threat conditions beyond the scope of civilian experimentation." POWs, federal prisoners, and Security officers were mentioned as possible candidates for these field experiments.

In another study designed to ascertain optimal dosage levels for interrogation sessions, a CIA psychiatrist administered LSD to "at least twelve human subjects *of not too high mentality.*" At the outset the subjects were "told only that a new drug was being tested and promised that nothing serious or dangerous would happen to them.... During the intoxication they realized something was happening, but were never told exactly what." A dosage range of 100 to 150 micrograms was finally selected, and the Agency proceeded to test the drug in mock interrogation trials.

Initial reports seemed promising. In one instance LSD was given to an officer who had been instructed not to reveal "a significant military secret." When questioned, however, "he gave all the details of the secret... and after the effects of the LSD had worn off, the officer had no knowledge of revealing the information (complete amnesia)." Favorable reports kept coming in, and when this phase of experimentation was completed, the CIA's Office of Scientific Intelligence (OSI) prepared a lengthy memorandum entitled "Potential New Agent for Unconventional Warfare." LSD was said to be useful "for eliciting true and accurate statements from subjects under its influence during interrogation." Moreover, the data on hand suggested that LSD might help in reviving memories of past experiences.

It almost seemed too good to be true—a drug that unearthed secrets buried deep in the unconscious mind but also caused amnesia during the effective period. The implications were downright astounding. Soon the entire CIA hierarchy was head over heels as news of what appeared to be a major breakthrough sent shock waves rippling through headquarters. (C. P. Snow once said, "The euphoria of secrecy goes to the head.") For years they had searched, and now they were on the verge of finding the Holy Grail of the cloak-and-dagger trade. As one CIA officer recalled, "We had thought at first that this was the secret that was going to unlock the universe."

But the sense of elation did not last long. As the secret research progressed, the CIA ran into problems. Eventually they came to recognize that LSD was not really a truth serum in the classical sense. Accurate information could not always be obtained from people under the influence of LSD because it induced a "marked anxiety and loss of reality contact." Those who received unwitting doses experienced an intense distortion of time, place, and body image, frequently culminating in full-blown paranoid reactions. The bizarre hallucinations caused by the drug often proved more of a hindrance than an aid to the interrogation process. There was always the risk, for example, that an enemy spy who started to trip out would realize he'd been drugged. This could make him overly suspicious and taciturn to the point of clamming up entirely.

There were other pitfalls that made the situation even more precarious from an interrogation standpoint. While anxiety was the predominant characteristic displayed during LSD sessions, some people experienced delusions of grandeur and omnipotence. An entire operation might backfire if someone had an ecstatic or transcendental experience and became convinced that he could defy his interrogators indefinitely. And then there was the question of amnesia, which was not as cut-and-dried as first supposed. Everyone agreed that a person would probably have a difficult time recalling exactly what happened while he was high on LSD, but that didn't mean his mind would be completely blank. While the drug might distort memory to some degree, it did not destroy it.

When CIA scientists tested a drug for speech-inducing purposes and found that it didn't work, they usually put it aside and tried something else. But such was not the case with LSD. Although early reports proved overoptimistic, the Agency was not about to discard such a powerful and unusual substance simply because it did not live up to its original expectations. They had to shift gears. A reassessment of the strategic implications of LSD was necessary. If, strictly speaking, LSD was not a reliable truth drug, then how else could it be used?

CIA researchers were intrigued by this new chemical, but they didn't quite know what to make of it. LSD was significantly different from anything else they knew about. "The most fascinating thing about it," a CIA psychologist recalled, "was that such minute quantities had such a terrific effect." Mere micrograms could create "serious mental confusion...and render the mind temporarily susceptible to suggestion." Moreover, the drug was colorless, odorless, and tasteless, and therefore easily concealed in food and beverage. But it was hard to predict the response to LSD. On certain occasions acid seemed to cause an uninhibited disclosure of information, but oftentimes the overwhelming anxiety experienced by the subject obstructed the interrogation process. And there were unexplainable mood swings—from total panic to boundless blissout. How could one drug produce such extreme and contradictory reactions? It didn't make sense.

As research continued, the situation became even more perplexing. At one point a group of Security officers did an about-face and suggested that acid might best be employed as an anti-interrogation substance: "Since information obtained from a person in a psychotic state would be unrealistic, bizarre, and extremely difficult to assess, the *self-administration* of LSD-25, which is effective in minute doses, might in special circumstances offer an operative temporary protection against interrogation [emphasis added]."

This proposal was somewhat akin to a suicide pill scenario. Secret agents would be equipped with micro-pellets of LSD to take on dangerous assignments. If they fell into enemy hands and were about to be interrogated, they could pop a tab of acid as a preventive measure and babble gibberish. Obviously this idea was impractical, but it showed just how confused the CIA's top scientists were about LSD. First they thought it was a truth serum, then a lie serum, and for a while they didn't know what to think.

To make matters worse, there was a great deal of concern within the Agency that the Soviets and the Red Chinese might also have designs on LSD as an espionage weapon. A survey conducted by the Office of Scientific Intelligence noted that ergot was a commercial product in numerous Eastern Bloc countries. The enigmatic fungus also flourished in the Soviet Union, but Russian ergot had not yet appeared in foreign markets. Could this mean the Soviets were hoarding their supplies? Since information on the chemical structure of LSD was available in scientific journals as early as 1947, the Russians might have been stockpiling raw ergot in order to convert it into a mind control weapon. "Although no Soviet data are available on LSD-25," the OSI study concluded, "it must be assumed that the scientists of the USSR are thoroughly cognizant of the strategic importance of this powerful new drug and are capable of producing it at any time."

Were the Russians really into acid? "I'm sure they were," asserted John Gittlinger, one of the CIA's leading psychologists during the

Cold War, "but if you ask me to prove it, I've never seen any direct proof of it."* While hard evidence of a Soviet LSD connection was lacking, the CIA wasn't about to take any chances. What would happen, for example, if an American spy was caught and dosed by the Commies? The CIA realized that an adversary intelligence service could employ LSD "to produce anxiety or terror in medically unsophisticated subjects unable to distinguish drug-induced psychosis from actual insanity." The only way to be sure that an operative would not freak out under such circumstances would be to give him a taste of LSD (a mind control vaccine?) before he was sent on a sensitive overseas mission. Such a person would know that the effects of the drug were transitory and would therefore be in a better position to handle the experience. CIA documents actually refer to agents who were familiar with LSD as "enlightened operatives."

Along this line, Security officials proposed that LSD be administered to CIA trainee volunteers. Such a procedure would clearly demonstrate to select individuals the effects of hallucinogenic substances upon themselves and their associates. Furthermore, it would provide an opportunity to screen Agency personnel for "anxiety proneness"; those who couldn't pass the acid test would be excluded from certain critical assignments. This suggestion was well received by the ARTICHOKE steering committee, although the representative from the CIA's Medical Office felt that the test should not be "confined merely to male volunteer trainee personnel, but that it should be broadened to include all components of the Agency." According to a CIA document dated November 19, 1953, the Project Committee "verbally concurred in this recommendation."

During the next few years numerous CIA agents tried LSD. Some used the drug on repeated occasions. How did their firsthand experience with acid affect their personalities? How did it affect their attitude toward their work—particularly those who were directly

---

*Internal CIA memoranda dispute the oft-repeated allegation that the Soviet Union and her satellites, including Red China, were engaged in unorthodox methods of altering human behavior. According to a CIA document dated January 14, 1953, "Apparently their major emphasis is on the development of specially-trained teams for obtaining information *without* the use of narcotics, hypnosis, or special mechanical devices [emphasis added]." A memo issued the next day by the Ad Hoc Medical Study Group admitted that "the present state of knowledge indicates little, if any, threat to National Security through 'special interrogation' techniques or agents."

involved in mind control research? What impact did it have on the program as a whole?*

At the outset of the CIA's behavior control endeavors the main emphasis was on speech-inducing drugs. But when acid entered the scene, the entire program assumed a more aggressive posture. The CIA's turned-on strategists came to believe that mind control techniques could be applied to a wide range of operations above and beyond the strict category of "special interrogation." It was almost as if LSD blew the Agency's collective mind-set—or was it mind-rut? With acid acting as a catalyst, the whole idea of what could be done with a drug, or drugs in general, was suddenly transformed.

---

*At the very least, one suspects that a firsthand encounter with LSD would have made the clandestine mentality more receptive to the possibility of ESP, subliminal perception, and other phenomena associated with altered states. The CIA's interest in parapsychology dates back to the late 1940s. A handwritten memo of the period suggests that "hypnotists and telepathists" be contacted as professional consultants on an exploratory basis, but this proposal was initially rejected. It was not until 1952, after the CIA got heavily involved with LSD, that the Agency began funding ESP research.

While parapsychology has long been ridiculed by the scientific establishment, the CIA seriously entertained the notion that such phenomena might be highly significant for the spy trade. The Agency hypothesized that if a number of people in the US were found to have a high ESP capacity, their talent could be assigned to specific intelligence problems. In 1952 the CIA initiated an extensive program involving "the search for and development of exceptionally gifted individuals who can approximate perfect success in ESP performance." The Office of Security, which ran the ARTI-CHOKE project, was urged to follow "all leads on individuals reported to have true clairvoyant powers" so as to be able to subject their claims to "rigorous scientific investigation."

Along this line the CIA began infiltrating séances and occult gatherings. A memo dated April 9, 1953, refers to a domestic—and therefore illegal—operation that required the "planting of a very specialized observer" at a séance in order to obtain "a broad surveillance of all individuals attending the meetings."

The CIA also sought to develop techniques whereby the ESP powers of a group of psychics could be used "to produce factual information that could not be obtained in any other way." If it were possible "to identify the thought of another person several hundred miles away," a CIA scientist explained, "the adaptation to the practical requirements for obtaining secret information should not give serious difficulty." Moreover, "everything that adds anything to our understanding of what is taking place in ESP is likely to give us advantage in the problem of use and control."

In a rather bizarre twist, during the late 1960s the CIA experimented with mediums in an effort to contact (and debrief?) dead agents. These attempts, according to Victor Marchetti, a former high-ranking CIA official, were part of a larger effort to harness psychic powers for various intelligence-related missions that included utilizing clairvoyants to divine the intentions of the Kremlin leadership. Secret ESP research is still being conducted, although CIA spokesmen refuse to comment on the nature of these experiments.

Soon a perfect compound was envisioned for every conceivable circumstance: there would be smart shots, memory erasers, "antivitamins," knock-out drops, "aphrodisiacs for operational use," drugs that caused "headache clusters" or uncontrollable twitching, drugs that could induce cancer, a stroke or a heart attack without leaving a trace as to the source of the ailment. There were chemicals to make a drunk man sober and a sober man as drunk as a fish. Even a "recruitment pill" was contemplated. What's more, according to a document dated May 5, 1955, the CIA placed a high priority on the development of a drug "which will produce 'pure euphoria' with no subsequent letdown."

This is not to suggest that the CIA had given up on LSD. On the contrary, after grappling with the drug for a number of years, the Agency devised new methods of interrogation based on the "far-out" possibilities of this mind-altering substance. When employed as a third-degree tactic, acid enabled the CIA to approach a hostile subject with a great deal of leverage. CIA operatives realized that intense mental confusion could be produced by deliberately attacking a person along psychological lines. Of all the chemicals that caused mental derangement, none was as powerful as LSD. Acid not only made people extremely anxious, it also broke down the character defenses for handling anxiety. A skillful interrogator could exploit this vulnerability by threatening to keep an unwitting subject in a tripped-out state indefinitely unless he spilled the beans. This tactic often proved successful where others had failed. CIA documents indicate that LSD was employed as an aid to interrogation on an operational basis from the mid-1950s through the early 1960s.

Laboratories of the State

When the CIA first became interested in LSD, only a handful of scientists in the United States were engaged in hallucinogenic drug research. At the time there was little private or public support for this relatively new field of experimental psychiatry, and no one had undertaken a systematic investigation of LSD. The CIA's mind control specialists sensed a golden opportunity in the making. With a sizable treasure chest at their disposal they were in a position to boost the careers of scientists whose skill and expertise would be of maximum benefit to the CIA. Almost overnight a whole new market for grants in LSD research sprang into existence as money started pouring through CIA-linked conduits or "cutouts" such as the Geschickter Fund for Medical Research, the Society for the Study of Human Ecology, and the Josiah Macy, Jr. Foundation.

Among those who benefited from the CIA's largesse was Dr. Max Rinkel, the first person to bring LSD to the United States. In 1949 Rinkel, a research psychiatrist, obtained a supply of LSD from Sandoz Pharmaceuticals in Switzerland and gave the drug to his partner, Dr. Robert Hyde, who took the first acid trip in the Western Hemisphere. Rinkel and Hyde went on to organize an LSD study at the Boston Psychopathic Institute, a pioneering mental health clinic affiliated with Harvard University. They tested the drug on one hundred volunteers and reported the initial findings in May 1950 (nearly three years before the CIA began funding their work) at the annual meeting of the American Psychiatric Association. Rinkel announced that LSD produced "a transitory psychotic disturbance" in normal subjects. This was highly significant, for it raised the possibility that mental disorders could be studied objectively in a controlled experimental setting.

Rinkel's hypothesis was supported and expanded upon during the same forum by Dr. Paul Hoch, a prominent psychiatrist who would also proffer his services to the CIA in the years ahead. Hoch reported that the symptoms produced by LSD, mescaline and related drugs were similar to those of schizophrenia: intensity of color perception, hallucinations, depersonalization, intense anxiety, paranoia, and in some cases catatonic manifestations. As Hoch put it, "LSD and Mescaline disorganize the psychic integration of the individual." He believed that the medical profession was fortunate to have access to these substances, for now it would be possible to reconstruct temporary or "model" psychoses in the laboratory. LSD was considered an exceptional research tool in that the subject could provide a detailed description of his experience while he was under the influence of the drug. It was hoped that careful analysis of these data would shed new light on schizophrenia and other enigmatic mental diseases.

Hoch's landmark thesis—that LSD was a "psychotomimetic" or "madness-mimicking" agent—caused a sensation in scientific circles and led to several important and stimulating theories regarding the biochemical basis of schizophrenia. This in turn sparked an upsurge of interest in brain chemistry and opened new vistas in the field of experimental psychiatry. In light of the extremely high potency of LSD, it seemed completely plausible that infinitesimal traces of a psychoactive substance produced through metabolic dysfunction by the human organism might cause psychotic disturbances. Conversely, attempts to alleviate a "lysergic psychosis" might point the way toward curing schizophrenia and other forms of mental illness.*

As it turned out, the model psychosis concept dovetailed particularly well with the secret schemes of the CIA, which also viewed LSD in terms of its ability to blow minds and make people crazy. Thus it is not surprising that the CIA chose to invest in men like Rinkel and Hoch. Most scientists were flattered by the government's interest in their research, and they were eager to assist the CIA in its attempt to unravel the riddle of LSD. This was, after all, the Cold War, and one did not have to be a blue-ribbon hawk or a hard-liner to work in tandem with American intelligence.

In the early 1950s the CIA approached Dr. Nick Bercel, a psychiatrist who maintained a private practice in Los Angeles. Bercel was one of the first people in the United States to work with LSD, and the CIA asked him to consider a haunting proposition. What would happen if the Russians put LSD in the water supply of a large American city? A skillful saboteur could carry enough acid in his coat pocket to turn an entire metropolis into a loony bin, assuming he found a way to distribute it equally. In light of this frightening prospect, would Bercel render a patriotic service by calculating exactly how much LSD would be required to contaminate the water supply of Los Angeles? Bercel consented, and that evening he dissolved a tiny amount of acid in a glass of tap water, only to discover that the chlorine neutralized the drug. "Don't worry," he told his CIA contact, "it won't work."

The Agency took this as a mandate, and another version of LSD was eventually concocted to overcome this drawback. A CIA document states accordingly, "If the concept of contaminating a city's water supply seems, or in actual fact, is found to be far-fetched (this is by no means certain), there is still the possibility of contaminating, say, the water supply of a bomber base or, more easily still, that of a battleship.... Our current work contains the strong

---

*While the miracle cure never panned out, it is worth noting that Thorazine was found to mollify an LSD reaction and subsequently became a standard drug for controlling patients in mental asylums and prisons.

suggestion that LSD-25 will produce hysteria (unaccountable laughing, anxiety, terror)....It requires little imagination to realize what the consequences might be if a battleship's crew were so affected."

The CIA never got in touch with Bercel again, but they monitored his research reports in various medical journals. When Bercel gave LSD to spiders, they spun perfectly symmetrical webs. Animal studies also showed that cats cringed before untreated mice, and fish that normally swam close to the bottom of a water tank hovered near the top. In another experiment Dr. Louis Joylon ("Jolly") West, chairman of the Department of Psychiatry at the University of Oklahoma, injected an elephant with a massive dose of 300,000 micrograms. Dr. West, a CIA contract employee and an avid believer in the notion that hallucinogens were psychotomimetic agents, was trying to duplicate the periodic "rut" madness that overtakes male elephants for about one week each year. But the animal did not experience a model elephant psychosis; it just keeled over and remained in a motionless stupor. In attempting to revive the elephant, West administered a combination of drugs that ended up killing the poor beast.

Research on human subjects showed that LSD lodged primarily in the liver, spleen, and kidneys. Only a tiny amount (.01%) of the original dose entered the brain, and it only remained there for twenty minutes. This was a most curious finding, as the effect of LSD was not evident until the drug had disappeared entirely from the central nervous system. Some scientists thought LSD might act as a trigger mechanism, releasing or inhibiting a naturally occurring substance in the brain, but no one could figure out exactly why the drug had such a dramatic effect on the mind.

Many other questions were in need of clarification. Could the drug be fatal? What was the maximum dose? Were the effects constant, or were there variations according to different personality types? Could the reaction be accentuated by combining LSD with other chemicals? Was there an antidote? Some of these questions overlapped with legitimate medical concerns, and researchers on CIA stipends published unclassified versions of their work in prestigious scientific periodicals. But these accounts omitted secret data given to the CIA on how LSD affected "operationally pertinent categories" such as disturbance of memory, alteration of sex patterns, eliciting information, increasing suggestibility, and creating emotional dependence.

The CIA was particularly interested in psychiatric reports suggesting that LSD could break down familiar behavior patterns, for this raised the possibility of reprogramming or brainwashing. If LSD temporarily altered a person's view of the world and suspended his belief system, CIA doctors surmised, then perhaps Russian spies could be cajoled into switching loyalties while they were tripping. The brainwashing strategy was relatively simple: find the subject's weakest point (his "squeaky board") and bear down on it. Use any combination or synthesis which might "open the mind to the power of suggestion to a degree never hitherto dreamed possible." LSD would be employed to provoke a reality shift, to break someone down and tame him, to find a locus of anonymity and leave a mark there forever.

To explore the feasibility of this approach, the Agency turned to Dr. Ewen Cameron, a respected psychiatrist who served as president of the Canadian, the American, and the World Psychiatric Associations before his death in 1967. Cameron also directed the Allain Memorial Institute at Montreal's McGill University, where he developed a bizarre and unorthodox method for treating schizophrenia. With financial backing from the CIA he tested his method on fifty-three patients at Allain. The so-called treatment started with "sleep therapy," in which subjects were knocked out for months at a time. The next phase, "depatterning," entailed massive electroshock and frequent doses of LSD designed to wipe out past behavior patterns. Then Cameron tried to recondition the mind through a technique known as "psychic driving." The patients, once again heavily sedated, were confined to "sleep rooms" where tape-recorded messages played over and over from speakers under their pillows. Some heard the same message a quarter of a million times.

Cameron's methods were later discredited, and the CIA grudgingly gave up on the notion of LSD as a brainwashing technique. But that was little consolation to those who served as guinea pigs for the CIA's secret mind control projects. Nine of Cameron's former patients have sued the American government for $1,000,000 each, claiming that they are still suffering from the trauma they went through at Allain. These people never agreed to participate in a scientific experiment—a fact which reflects little credit on the CIA, even if Agency officials feared that the Soviets were spurting ahead in the mind control race. The CIA violated the Nuremberg Code for medical ethics by sponsoring experiments on unwitting subjects. Ironically, Dr. Cameron was a member of the Nuremberg tribunal that heard the case against Nazi war criminals who committed atrocities during World War II.

Like the Nazi doctors at Dachau, the CIA victimized certain groups of people who were unable to resist: prisoners, mental patients, foreigners, the terminally ill, sexual deviants, ethnic minorities. One project took place at the Addiction Research Center of the US Public Health Service Hospital in Lexington, Kentucky. Lexington was ostensibly a place where heroin addicts could go to shake a habit, and although it was officially a penitentiary, all the inmates were referred to as "patients." The patients had their own way of referring to the doctors—"hacks" or "croakers"—who patrolled the premises in military uniforms.

The patients at Lexington had no way of knowing that it was one of fifteen penal and mental institutions utilized by the CIA in its super-secret drug development program. To conceal its role the Agency enlisted the aid of the navy and the National Institutes of Mental Health (NIMH), which served as conduits for channeling money to Dr. Harris Isbell, a gung-ho research scientist who remained on the CIA payroll for over a decade. According to CIA documents the directors of NIMH and the National Institutes of Health were fully cognizant of the Agency's "interest" in Isbell's work and offered "full support and protection."

When the CIA came across a new drug (usually supplied by American pharmaceutical firms) that needed testing, they frequently sent it over to their chief doctor at Lexington, where an ample supply of captive guinea pigs was readily available. Over eight hundred compounds were farmed out to Isbell, including LSD and a variety of hallucinogens. It became an open secret among street junkies that if the supply got tight, you could always commit yourself to Lexington, where heroin and morphine were doled out as payment if you volunteered for Isbell's wacky drug experiments. (Small wonder that Lexington had a return rate of 90%.) Dr. Isbell, a longtime member of the Food and Drug Administration's Advisory Committee on the Abuse of Depressant and Stimulant Drugs, defended the volunteer system on the grounds that there was no precedent at the time for offering inmates cash for their services.

24

CIA documents describe experiments conducted by Isbell in which certain patients—nearly all black inmates—were given LSD for more than seventy-five consecutive days. In order to overcome tolerance to the hallucinogen, Isbell administered "double, triple and quadruple doses." A report dated May 5, 1959, comments on an experiment involving psilocybin (a semi-synthetic version of the magic mushroom). Subjects who ingested the drug became extremely anxious, although sometimes there were periods of intense elation marked by "continuous gales of laughter." A few patients felt that they "had become very large, or had shrunk to the size of children. Their hands or feet did not seem to be their own and sometimes took on the appearance of animal paws.... They reported many fantasies or dreamlike states in which they seemed to be elsewhere. Fantastic experiences, such as trips to the moon or living in gorgeous castles, were occasionally reported."

Isbell concluded, "Despite these striking subjective experiences, the patients remained oriented in time, place and person. In most instances, the patients did not lose their insight but realized that the effects were due to the drug. Two of the nine patients, however, did lose insight and felt that their experiences were caused by the experimenters controlling their minds."

In addition to his role as a research scientist, Dr. Isbell served as a go-between for the CIA in its attempt to obtain drug samples from European pharmaceutical concerns which assumed they were providing "medicine" to a US Public Health official. The CIA in turn acted as a research coordinator, passing information, tips, and leads to Isbell and its other contract employees so that they could keep abreast of each other's progress; when a new discovery was made, the CIA would often ask another researcher to conduct a follow-up study for confirmation. One scientist whose work was coordinated with Isbell's in such a manner was Dr. Carl Pfeiffer, a noted pharmacologist from Princeton who tested LSD on inmates at the federal prison in Atlanta and the Bordentown Reformatory in New Jersey.

Isbell, Pfeiffer, Cameron, West, and Hoch—all were part of a network of doctors and scientists who gathered intelligence for the CIA. Through these scholar-informants the Agency stayed on top of the latest developments within the "aboveground" LSD scene, which expanded rapidly during the Cold War. By the mid-1950s numerous independent investigators had undertaken hallucinogenic drug studies, and the CIA was determined not to let the slightest detail escape its grasp. In a communiqué dated May 26, 1954, the Agency ordered all domestic field offices in the United States to monitor scientists engaged in LSD research. People of interest, the memo explained, "will most probably be found in biochemistry departments of universities, mental hospitals, private psychiatric practice.... We do ask that you remember their importance and report their work when it comes to your attention."

The CIA also expended considerable effort to monitor the latest developments in LSD research on a worldwide scale. Drug specialists funded by the Agency made periodic trips to Europe to confer with scientists and representatives of various pharmaceutical concerns, including, of course, Sandoz Laboratories. Initially the Swiss firm provided LSD to investigators all over the world free of charge, in exchange for full access to their research data. (CIA researchers did not comply with this stipulation.) By 1953 Sandoz had decided to deal directly with the US Food and Drug Administration (FDA), which assumed a supervisory role in distributing LSD to American investigators from then on. It was a superb arrangement as far as the CIA was concerned, for the FDA went out of its way to assist the secret drug program. With the FDA as its junior partner, the CIA not only had ready access to supplies of LSD (which Sandoz marketed for a while under the brand name Delysid) but also was able to keep a close eye on independent researchers in the United States.

The CIA would have been content to let the FDA act as an intermediary in its dealings with Sandoz, but business as usual was suspended when the Agency learned of an offer that could not be refused. Prompted by reports that large quantities of the drug were suddenly available, top-level CIA officials authorized the purchase of ten *kilos* of LSD from Sandoz at an estimated price of $240,000—enough for a staggering one hundred million doses. A document dated November 16, 1953, characterized the pending transaction as a "risky operation," but CIA officials felt it was necessary, if only to preclude any attempt the Communists might make to get their hands on the drug. What the CIA intended to do with such an incredible stash of acid was never made clear.

The CIA later found out that Sandoz had never produced LSD in quantities even remotely resembling ten kilograms. Apparently only ten milligrams were for sale, but a CIA contact in Switzerland mistook a kilogram, 1000 grams, for a milligram (.001 grams), which would explain the huge discrepancy. Nevertheless, Sandoz officials were pleased by the CIA's interest in their product, and the two organizations struck up a cooperative relationship. Arthur Stoll, president of Sandoz, agreed to keep the CIA posted whenever new LSD was produced or a shipment was delivered to a customer. Likewise, any information concerning LSD research behind the Iron Curtain would be passed along confidentially.

But the CIA did not want to depend on a foreign company for supplies of a substance considered vital to American security interests. The Agency asked the Eli Lilly Company in Indianapolis to try to synthesize a batch of all-American acid. By mid-1954 Lilly had succeeded in breaking the secret formula held by Sandoz. *"This is a closely guarded secret,"* a CIA document declared, *"and should not be mentioned generally."* Scientists at Lilly assured the CIA that "in a matter of months LSD would be available in tonnage quantities."

Midnight Climax

In a speech before the National Alumni Conference at Princeton University on April 10, 1953, newly appointed CIA director Allen Dulles lectured his audience on "how sinister the battle for men's minds had become in Soviet hands." The human mind, Dulles warned, was a "malleable tool," and the Red Menace had secretly developed "brain perversion techniques." Some of these methods were "so subtle and so abhorrent to our way of life that we have recoiled from facing up to them." Dulles continued, "The minds of selected individuals who are subjected to such treatment...are deprived of the ability to state their own thoughts. Parrot-like, the individuals so conditioned can merely repeat the thoughts which have been implanted in their minds by suggestion from outside. In effect the brain...becomes a phonograph playing a disc put on its spindle by an outside genius over which it has no control."

Three days after delivering this address Dulles authorized Operation MK-ULTRA, the CIA's major drug and mind control program during the Cold War. MK-ULTRA was the brainchild of Richard Helms, a high-ranking member of the Clandestine Services (otherwise known as the "dirty tricks department") who championed such methods throughout his career as an intelligence officer. As Helms explained to Dulles when he first proposed the MK-ULTRA project, "Aside from the offensive potential, the development of a comprehensive capability in this field...gives us a thorough knowledge of the enemy's theoretical potential, thus enabling us to defend ourselves against a foe who might not be as restrained in the use of these techniques as we are."

The supersecret MK-ULTRA program was run by a relatively small unit within the CIA known as the Technical Services Staff (TSS). Originally established as a supplementary funding mechanism to the ARTICHOKE project, MK-ULTRA quickly grew into a mammoth undertaking that outflanked earlier mind control initiatives. For a while both the TSS and the Office of Security (which directed the ARTICHOKE project) were engaged in parallel LSD tests, and a heated rivalry developed between the two groups. Security officials were miffed because they had gotten into acid first and then this new clique started cutting in on what the ARTICHOKE crowd considered their rightful turf.

The internecine conflict grew to the point where the Office of Security decided to have one of its people spy on the TSS. This set off a flurry of memos between the Security informant and his superiors, who were dismayed when they learned that Dr. Sidney Gottlieb, the chemist who directed the MK-ULTRA program, had approved a plan to give acid to unwitting American citizens. The Office of Security had never attempted such a reckless gesture— although it had its own idiosyncrasies; ARTICHOKE operatives, for example, were attempting to have a hypnotized subject kill someone while in a trance.

Whereas the Office of Security utilized LSD as an interrogation weapon, Dr. Gottlieb had other ideas about what to do with the drug. Because the effects of LSD were temporary (in contrast to the fatal nerve agents), Gottlieb saw important strategic advantages for its use in covert operations. For instance, a surreptitious dose of LSD might disrupt a person's thought process and cause him to act strangely or foolishly in public. A CIA document notes that administering LSD "to high officials would be a relatively simple matter and could have a significant effect at key meetings, speeches, etc." But Gottlieb realized there was a considerable difference between testing LSD in a laboratory and using the drug in clandestine operations. In an effort to bridge the gap, he and his TSS colleagues initiated a series of in-house experiments designed to find out what would happen if LSD was given to someone in a "normal" life setting without advance warning.

28

They approached the problem systematically, taking one step at a time, until they reached a point where outsiders were zapped with no explanation whatsoever. First everyone in Technical Services tried LSD. They tripped alone and in groups. A typical experiment involved two people pairing off in a closed room where they observed each other for hours at a time, took notes, and analyzed their experiences. As Gottlieb later explained, "There was an extensive amount of self-experimentation for the reason that we felt that a first hand knowledge of the subjective effects of these drugs [was] important to those of us who were involved in the program."

When they finally learned the hallucinogenic ropes, so to speak, they agreed among themselves to slip LSD into each other's drinks. The target never knew when his turn would come, but as soon as the drug was ingested a TSS colleague would tell him so he could make the necessary preparations—which usually meant taking the rest of the day off. Initially the leaders of MK-ULTRA restricted the surprise acid tests to TSS members, but when this phase had run its course they started dosing other Agency personnel who had never tripped before. Nearly everyone was fair game, and surprise acid trips became something of an occupational hazard among CIA operatives. Such tests were considered necessary because foreknowledge would prejudice the results of the experiment.

Indeed, things were getting a bit raucous down at headquarters. When Security officials discovered what was going on, they began to have serious doubts about the wisdom of the TSS game plan. Moral reservations were not paramount; it was more a sense that the MK-ULTRA staff had become unhinged by the hallucinogen. The Office of Security felt that the TSS should have exercised better judgment in dealing with such a powerful and dangerous chemical. The straw that broke the camel's back came when a Security informant got wind of a plan by a few TSS jokers to put LSD in the punch served at the annual CIA Christmas office party. A Security memo dated December 15, 1954, noted that acid could "produce serious insanity for periods of 8 to 18 hours and possibly for longer." The writer of this memo concluded indignantly and unequivocally that he did "not recommend testing in the Christmas punch bowls usually present at the Christmas office parties."

The purpose of these early acid tests was not to explore mystical realms or higher states of consciousness. On the contrary, the TSS was trying to figure out how to employ LSD in espionage operations.

Nevertheless, there were times when CIA agents found themselves propelled into a visionary world and they were deeply moved by the experience. One MK-ULTRA veteran wept in front of his colleagues at the end of his first trip. "I didn't want to leave it," he explained. "I felt I would be going back to a place where I wouldn't be able to hold on to this kind of beauty." His colleagues assumed he was having a bad trip and wrote a report stating that the drug had made him psychotic.

Adverse reactions often occurred when people were given LSD on an impromptu basis. On one occasion a CIA operative discovered he'd been dosed during his morning coffee break. "He sort of knew he had it," a fellow-agent recalled, "but he couldn't pull himself together. Somehow, when you know you've taken it, you start the process of maintaining your composure. But this grabbed him before he was aware, and it got away from him." Then he got away from them and fled across Washington stoned out of his mind while they searched frantically for their missing comrade. "He reported afterwards," the TSS man continued, "that every automobile that came by was a terrible monster with fantastic eyes, out to get him personally. Each time a car passed he would huddle down against a parapet, terribly frightened. It was a real horror for him. I mean, it was hours of agony ... like being in a dream that never stops—with someone chasing you."

Incidents such as these reaffirmed to the MK-ULTRA crew just how devastating a weapon LSD could be. But this only made them more enthusiastic about the drug. They kept springing it on people in a manner reminiscent of the ritual hazing of fraternity pledges. "It was just too damned informal," a TSS officer later said. "We didn't know much. We were playing around in ignorance. ... We were just naive about what we were doing."

Such pranks claimed their first victim in November 1953, when a group of CIA and army technicians gathered for a three-day work retreat at a remote hunting lodge in the backwoods of Maryland. On the second day of the meeting Dr. Gottlieb spiked the after-dinner cocktails with LSD. As the drug began to take effect, Gottlieb told everyone that they had ingested a mind-altering chemical. By that time the group had become boisterous with laughter and unable to carry on a coherent conversation.

One man was not amused by the unexpected turn of events. Dr.

Frank Olson, an army scientist who specialized in biological warfare research, had never taken LSD before, and he slid into a deep depression. His mood did not lighten when the conference adjourned. Normally a gregarious family man, Olson returned home quiet and withdrawn. When he went to work after the weekend, he asked his boss to fire him because he had "messed up the experiment" during the retreat. Alarmed by his erratic behavior, Olson's superiors contacted the CIA, which sent him to New York to see Dr. Harold Abramson. A respected physician, Abramson taught at Columbia University and was chief of the allergy clinic at Mount Sinai Hospital. He was also one of the CIA's principal LSD researchers and a part-time consultant to the Army Chemical Corps. While these were impressive credentials, Abramson was not a trained psychiatrist, and it was this kind of counseling his patient desperately needed.

For the next few weeks Olson confided his deepest fears to Abramson. He claimed the CIA was putting something in his coffee to make him stay awake at night. He said people were plotting against him and he heard voices at odd hours commanding him to throw away his wallet—which he did, even though it contained several uncashed checks. Dr. Abramson concluded that Olson was mired in "a psychotic state...with delusions of persecution" that had been "crystallized by the LSD experience." Arrangements were made to move him to Chestnut Lodge, a sanitorium in Rockville, Maryland, staffed by CIA-cleared psychiatrists. (Apparently other CIA personnel who suffered from psychiatric disorders were enrolled in this institution.) On his last evening in New York, Olson checked into a room at the Statler Hilton along with a CIA agent assigned to watch him. And then, in the wee hours of the morning, the troubled scientist plunged headlong through a closed window to his death ten floors below.

The Olson suicide had immediate repercussions within the CIA. An elaborate cover-up erased clues to the actual circumstances leading up to his death. Olson's widow was eventually given a government pension, and the full truth of what happened would not be revealed for another twenty years. Meanwhile CIA director Allen Dulles suspended the in-house testing program for a brief period while an internal investigation was conducted. In the end, Gottlieb and his team received only a mildly worded reprimand for exercising "bad judgment," but no records of the incident were kept in their

31

personnel files which would harm their future careers. The importance of LSD eclipsed all other considerations, and the secret acid tests resumed.

Gottlieb was now ready to undertake the final and most daring phase of the MK-ULTRA program: LSD would be given to unwitting targets in real-life situations. But who would actually do the dirty work? While looking through some old OSS files, Gottlieb discovered that marijuana had been tested on unsuspecting subjects in an effort to develop a truth serum. These experiments had been organized by George Hunter White, a tough, old-fashioned narcotics officer who ran a training school for American spies during World War II. Perhaps White would be interested in testing drugs for the CIA. As a matter of protocol Gottlieb first approached Harry Anslinger, chief of the Federal Narcotics Bureau. Anslinger was favorably disposed and agreed to "lend" one of his top men to the CIA on a part-time basis.

Right from the start White had plenty of leeway in running his operations. He rented an apartment in New York's Greenwich Village, and with funds supplied by the CIA he transformed it into a safehouse complete with two-way mirrors, surveillance equipment, and the like. Posing as an artist and a seaman, White lured people back to his pad and slipped them drugs. A clue as to how his subjects fared can be found in White's personal diary, which contains passing references to surprise LSD experiments: "Gloria gets horrors.... Janet sky high." The frequency of bad reactions prompted White to coin his own code word for the drug: "Stormy," which was how he referred to LSD throughout his fourteen-year stint as a CIA operative.

In 1955 White was transferred to San Francisco, where two more safehouses were established. During this period he initiated Operation Midnight Climax, in which drug-addicted prostitutes were hired to pick up men from local bars and bring them back to a CIA-financed bordello. Unknowing customers were treated to drinks laced with LSD while White sat on a portable toilet behind two-way mirrors, sipping martinis and watching every stoned and kinky moment. As payment for their services the hookers received $100 a night, plus a guarantee from White that he'd intercede on their behalf should they be arrested while plying their trade. In addition to providing data about LSD, Midnight Climax enabled the CIA to learn about the sexual proclivities of those who passed through the safehouses. White's harem of prostitutes became the focal point of an extensive CIA study of how to exploit the art of lovemaking for espionage purposes.

When he wasn't operating a national security whorehouse, White would cruise the streets of San Francisco tracking down drug pushers for the Narcotics Bureau. Sometimes after a tough day on the beat he invited his narc buddies up to one of the safehouses for a little "R & R." Occasionally they unzipped their inhibitions and partied on the premises—much to the chagrin of the neighbors, who began to complain about men with guns in shoulder straps chasing after women in various states of undress. Needless to say, there was always plenty of dope around, and the feds sampled everything from hashish to LSD. "So far as I'm concerned," White later told an associate, "'clear thinking' was non-existent while under the influence of any of these drugs. I did feel at times like I was having a 'mind-expanding experience' but this vanished like a dream immediately after the session."

White had quite a scene going for a while. By day he fought to keep drugs out of circulation, and by night he dispensed them to strangers. Not everyone was cut out for this kind of schizophrenic lifestyle, and White often relied on the bottle to reconcile the two extremes. But there were still moments when his Jekyll-and-Hyde routine got the best of him. One night a friend who had helped install bugging equipment for the CIA stopped by the safehouse only to find the roly-poly narcotics officer slumped in front of a full-length mirror. White had just finished polishing off a half gallon of Gibson's. There he sat, with gun in hand, shooting wax slugs at his own reflection.

The safehouse experiments continued without interruption until 1963, when CIA inspector general John Earman accidentally stumbled across the clandestine testing program during a routine inspection of TSS operations. Only a handful of CIA agents outside Technical Services knew about the testing of LSD on unwitting subjects, and Earman took Richard Helms, the prime instigator of MK-ULTRA, to task for not fully briefing the new CIA director, John J. McCone. Although McCone had been handpicked by President Kennedy to replace Allen Dulles as the dean of American intelligence, Helms apparently had his own ideas about who was running the CIA.

Earman had grave misgivings about MK-ULTRA and he prepared a twenty-four-page report that included a comprehensive overview

33

of the drug and mind control projects. In a cover letter to McCone he noted that the "concepts involved in manipulating human behavior are found by many people within and outside the Agency to be distasteful and unethical." But the harshest criticism was reserved for the safehouse experiments, which, in his words, placed "the rights and interests of U.S. citizens in jeopardy." Earman stated that LSD had been tested on "individuals at all social levels, high and low, native American and foreign." Numerous subjects had become ill, and some required hospitalization for days or weeks at a time. Moreover, the sophomoric procedures employed during the safehouse sessions raised serious questions about the validity of the data provided by White, who was hardly a qualified scientist. As Earman pointed out, the CIA had no way of knowing whether White was fudging the results to suit his own ends.

Earman recommended a freeze on unwitting drug tests until the matter was fully considered at the highest level of the CIA. But Helms, then deputy director for covert operations (the number two position within the Agency), defended the program. In a memo dated November 9, 1964, he warned that the CIA's "positive operational capacity to use drugs is diminishing owing to a lack of realistic testing," and he called for a resumption of the safehouse experiments. While admitting that he had "no answer to the moral issue," Helms argued that such tests were necessary "to keep up with Soviet advances in this field."

This Cold War refrain had a familiar ring. Yet only a few months earlier Helms had sung a different tune when J. Lee Rankin, chief counsel of the Warren Commission investigating the Kennedy assassination, asked him to report on Soviet mind control initiatives. Helms stated his views in a document dated June 26, 1964: "Soviet research in the pharmacological agents producing behavioral effects has consistently lagged five years *behind* Western research [emphasis added]." Furthermore, he confidently asserted that the Russians did not have "any singular, new potent drugs...to force a course of action on an individual."

The bureaucratic wrangling at CIA headquarters didn't seem to bother George Hunter White, who kept on sending vouchers for "unorthodox expenses" to Dr. Sidney Gottlieb. No definitive record exists as to when the unwitting acid tests were terminated, but it appears that White and the CIA parted ways when he retired from the Narcotics Bureau in 1966. Afterwards White reflected upon his service for the Agency in a letter to Gottlieb: "I was a very minor missionary, actually a heretic, but I toiled wholeheartedly in the vineyards because it was fun, fun, fun. Where else could a red-blooded American boy lie, kill, cheat, steal, rape, and pillage with the sanction and blessing of the All-Highest?"

By this time the CIA had developed a "stable of drugs," including LSD, that were used in covert operations. The decision to employ LSD on an operational basis was handled through a special committee that reported directly to Richard Helms, who characterized the drug as "dynamite" and asked to be "advised at all times when it was intended for use." A favorite plan involved slipping "P-1" (the code name for LSD when used operationally) to socialist or left-leaning politicians in foreign countries so that they would babble incoherently and discredit themselves in public.

Fidel Castro was among the Third World leaders targeted for surprise acid attacks. When this method proved unworkable, CIA strategists thought of other ways to embarrass the Cuban premier. One scheme involved dusting Castro's shoes with thalium salts to make his beard fall out. Apparently they thought that Castro would lose his charisma along with his hair. Eventually the Agency shifted its focus from bad trips and close shaves to eliminating Castro altogether. Gottlieb and his TSS cohorts were asked to prepare an array of bizarre gadgets and biochemical poisons for a series of murder conspiracies allying the CIA with anti-Castro mercenaries and the Mob.

Egyptian president Gamal Abdal Nasser also figured high on the CIA's hallucinogenic hit list. While he managed to avoid such a fate, others presumably were less fortunate. CIA documents cited in a documentary by ABC News confirm that Gottlieb carried a stash of acid overseas on a number of occasions during the Cold War with the intention of dosing foreign diplomats and statesmen. But the effects of LSD were difficult to predict when employed in such a haphazard manner, and the CIA used LSD only sparingly in operations of this sort.

The Hallucination Battlefield

While the CIA was interested in LSD primarily as an instrument of clandestine warfare, the United States Army pursued a more grandiose scheme. During the Cold War top-level military brass waxed enthusiastic over the prospect of a new kind of chemical weapon that would revolutionize combat. They imagined aircraft swooping over enemy territory releasing clouds of "madness gas" that would disorient people and dissolve their will to resist. This scenario appealed to those in the Pentagon who felt hamstrung by the possibility of a nuclear shoot-out with the Russkies. They realized that new methods of waging limited warfare would have to be developed, and psychochemical weapons seemed to offer an attractive alternative.

According to Major General William Creasy, chemical incapacitants went hand in glove with the strategic requirements of the Cold War. As chief officer of the Army Chemical Corps, Creasy promoted the psychochemical cause with eccentric and visionary zeal. He maintained that this type of warfare was not only feasible but tactically advantageous in certain situations. Consider, for example, the difficult task of dislodging enemy soldiers from a city inhabited by an otherwise friendly population—an industrial center perhaps, bustling with activity. Assume that the city housed numerous museums and cultural landmarks. Why blow to smithereens the best and worst alike with an old-fashioned artillery barrage? The prospect of obliterating the whole kit and caboodle seemed downright foolish to Creasy if you could get away with less.

Suppose instead you found a way to spike the city's water supply or to release a hallucinogen in aerosol form. For twelve to twenty-four hours all the people in the vicinity would be hopelessly giddy, vertiginous, spaced-out. Those under the spell of madness gas would be incapable of raising a whimper of protest while American troops established themselves on what was once forbidden turf. Victory would be a foregone conclusion, as smooth and effortless as the French army in *The King of Hearts* strolling into a town inhabited solely by asylum inmates.

Yes, wouldn't it be nice to take the teeth out of war and at the same time make its result so final? Just blow their minds, move in, and take over; it was that simple—or so Creasy claimed. As soon as the citizenry recovered from their relatively brief stint in the ozone, everyone would return to a nine-to-five schedule. There'd be no fatalities and, except for a few borderline psychotics pushed over the edge by the drug, no sick or wounded needing medical care. Most important, the local economy would have suffered no significant setback.

36

Psychochemical weapons, Creasy argued, offered the most humane way of conducting the dirty business of warfare. He preached a new military gospel: war without death. An era of bloodless combat was just around the proverbial corner. There was only one problem. The sadly misinformed lay public and their elected officials harbored a knee-jerk aversion to chemical weapons.

In May 1959 Creasy took his case directly to the people by granting interviews to reporters and stumping for psychochemicals on a cross-country lecture tour. "I do not contend that driving people crazy—even for a few hours—is a pleasant prospect," he told *This Week* magazine. "But warfare is never pleasant. And to those who feel that *any* kind of chemical weapon is more horrible than conventional weapons, I put this question: Would you rather be temporarily deranged, blinded, or paralyzed by a chemical agent, or burned alive by a conventional fire bomb?"

Creasy testified a short time later to the House Committee on Science and Astronautics. He explained to the bewildered congressmen how a psychochemical "attacks the sensory, perception, and nerve centers of the body...discombobulating them.... Your hearing might be affected, your sight might be affected, your physical balance might be affected." Moreover, these drugs worked so swiftly that people wouldn't even know they'd been hit.

Representative James Fulton (R-Pa.) was disturbed by Creasy's remarks. He wondered if some foreign power might already be subjecting people in the United States to such agents. "How can we determine it?" Fulton asked. "What is the test to see whether we are already being subjected to them? Are we under it now?...Are we the rabbits and the guinea pigs?...How are we to know?"

Simple, said Creasy. If LSD or a related drug was administered to members of Congress, "we could possibly have you dancing on the desks, or shouting Communist speeches."

Fulton gasped. "Have you ever tried them on Congress?"

"I can assure you of one thing," said Creasy. "The Chemical Corps of the Army has not found it necessary to do it up until now."

Creasy's five-star performance succeeded in winning the hearts, minds, and appropriations of Congress and the Joint Chiefs of Staff. A sizable budget increase was awarded to the Chemical Corps for the express purpose of developing a nonlethal incapacitant that could subdue a foe without inflicting permanent injury. Apparently Creasy neglected to inform the congressmen of the death of Harold Blauer

37

in 1953. Blauer, a tennis professional, was the subject of a drug study conducted by a group of doctors working under army contract at the New York State Psychiatric Institute. He died a few hours after receiving an injection of MDA (methyl di-amphetamine, known in latter-day street parlance as the "love drug") supplied by Edgewood Arsenal, headquarters of the Army Chemical Corps. "We didn't know if it was dog piss or what it was we were giving him," an army researcher later admitted.

The scientist who directly oversaw this research project was Dr. Paul Hoch, an early advocate of the theory that LSD and other hallucinogens were essentially psychosis-producing drugs. In succeeding years Hoch performed a number of bizarre experiments for the army while also serving as a CIA consultant. Intraspinal injections of mescaline and LSD were administered to psychiatric patients, causing an "immediate, massive, and almost shocklike picture with higher doses." Aftereffects ("generalized discomfort," "withdrawal," "oddness," and "unreality feelings") lingered for two to three days following the injections. Hoch, who later became New York State Commissioner for Mental Hygiene, also gave LSD to psychiatric patients and then lobotomized them in order to compare the effects of acid before and after psychosurgery. ("It is possible that a certain amount of brain damage is of therapeutic value," Hoch once stated.) In one experiment a hallucinogen was administered along with a local anesthetic and the subject was told to describe his visual experiences as surgeons removed chunks of his cerebral cortex.

Another scientist who rented his services to the CIA as well as the military was Dr. Robert Heath of Tulane University. Heath and his colleagues administered LSD to people and then subjected them to electronic brain stimulation via electrode implant. One test subject became hysterical, lapsed into a trancelike state, and later claimed that the doctors were trying to manipulate her body. She was "obviously having paranoid ideas," commented an army employee.

In addition to sponsoring research at various universities and civilian hospitals, the army conducted extensive in-house studies with LSD. During the late 1950s a series of tests was initiated at Fort Bragg, North Carolina. Their purpose was to determine how well soldiers would fare in the execution of war games while high on acid. Small military units were given EA-1729, the army's secret code number for LSD, and asked to perform various operational exercises, including command-post maneuvers, squad drills, tank driving, radarscope reading, antiaircraft tracking, meteorological and engineering surveys, and so on. The results showed performance ranging "from total incapacity to marked decrease in proficiency." Unbeknownst to the stoned servicemen, some of these exercises were filmed by the army and were later shown to members of Congress to demonstrate the disruptive influence of psychochemicals.

Concerned that LSD might one day be used covertly against an American military unit, certain officials suggested that every Chemical Corps officer should be familiar with the effects of the drug, if only as a precautionary measure. Accordingly nearly two hundred officers assigned to the Chemical Corps school at Fort McClellan, Alabama, were given acid as a supplement to their regular training program. Some staff members even tried to teach classes while tripping.

Additional tests were carried out at the Aberdeen Proving Ground in Maryland; Fort Benning, Georgia; Fort Leavenworth, Kansas; Dugway Proving Ground, Utah; and in various European and Pacific stations. Soldiers at Edgewood Arsenal were given LSD and confined to sensory deprivation chambers; then they were subjected to hostile questioning by intelligence officers. An army report concludes that an "interrogator of limited experience could compel a subject to compromise himself and to sign documents which could place him in jeopardy." With a stronger dose "a state of fear and anxiety could be induced where the subject could be compelled to trade his cooperation for a guarantee of return to normalcy."

Shortly thereafter the military began using LSD as an interrogation weapon on an operational basis, just as the CIA had been doing for years. An army memo dated September 6, 1961, discussed the interrogation procedure: "Stressing techniques employed included silent treatment before or after EA 1729 administration, sustained conventional interrogation prior to EA 1729 interrogation, deprivation of food, drink, sleep or bodily evacuation, sustained isolation prior to EA 1729 administration, hot-cold switches in approach, duress 'pitches,' verbal degradation and bodily discomfort, or dramatized threats to subject's life or mental health."

Documents pertaining to Operation DERBY HAT indicate that an army Special Purpose Team trained in LSD interrogations initiated a series of field tests in the Far East beginning in August 1962. Seven individuals were questioned; all were foreign nationals who had been implicated in drug smuggling or espionage activities, and in each

39

case the EA-1729 technique produced information that had not been obtained through other means. One subject vomited three times and stated that he "wanted to die" after the Special Purpose Team gave him LSD; his reaction was characterized as "moderate." Another went into shock and remained semiconscious for nearly an hour after receiving triple the dosage normally used in these sessions. When he came to, the Special Purpose Team propped him up in a chair and tried to question him, but the subject kept collapsing and hitting his head on the table, oblivious to the pain. A few hours later he started to talk. "The subject often voiced an anti-communist line," an army report noted, "and begged to be spared the torture he was receiving. In this confused state he even asked to be killed in order to alleviate his suffering."*

By the mid-1960s nearly fifteen hundred military personnel had served as guinea pigs in LSD experiments conducted by the US Army Chemical Corps. Some later claimed they were coerced into "volunteering" for these experiments by their superior officers. A number of GI veterans complained they suffered from severe depression and emotional disturbances after the LSD trials. Ironically, there were also reports that soldiers at Edgewood Arsenal were stealing LSD from the laboratories and using it for recreational purposes. Some of these men had taken their first "trip" (the word originally coined by army scientists to describe an LSD session) when acid was given to unsuspecting GIs at mess parties.

Army policy restricted LSD tests to individual volunteers or small groups of military personnel. That was not enough for the leaders of the Chemical Corps. Major General Creasy bemoaned the fact that large-scale testing of psychochemical weapons in the United States was prohibited. "I was attempting to put on, with a good cover story," he grumbled, "to test to see what would happen in subways, for example, when a cloud was laid down on a city. It was denied on reasons that always seemed a little absurd to me."

---

*Upon completion of their mission in November 1962, the Special Purpose Team was told to remain in Japan and wait for further instructions. Arrangements were made to extend their stay in the Pacific Theater for an additional sixty days so that they could travel to Saigon. According to the army inspector general, a letter hand-delivered to the team "allegedly announced the Secretary of Defense's decision to use LSD on Viet Cong POW's."

As it happened, however, LSD was much more effective by ingestion than by inhalation, and the Chemical Corps was unable to figure out an appropriate means for delivering the drug. This precluded any possibility of using LSD as a large-scale battle weapon. Undaunted, the military surrealists and their industrial counterparts forged ahead in search of a drug and a delivery system that could do the job. During the early 1960s Edgewood Arsenal received an average of four hundred chemical "rejects" every month from the major American pharmaceutical firms. Rejects were drugs found to be commercially useless because of their undesirable side effects. Of course, undesirable side effects were precisely what the army was looking for.

It was from Hoffmann-La Roche in Nutley, New Jersey, that Edgewood Arsenal obtained its first sample of a drug called quinuclidinyl benzilate, or BZ for short. The army learned that BZ inhibits the production of a chemical substance that facilitates the transfer of messages along the nerve endings, thereby disrupting normal perceptual patterns. The effects generally last about three days, although symptoms—headaches, giddiness, disorientation, auditory and visual hallucinations, and maniacal behavior—have been known to persist for as long as six weeks. "During the period of acute effects," noted an army doctor, "the person is completely out of touch with his environment."

Dr. Van Sim, who served as chief of the Clinical Research Division at Edgewood, made it a practice to try all new chemicals himself before testing them on volunteers. Sim said he sampled LSD "on several occasions." Did he enjoy getting high, or were his acid trips simply a patriotic duty? "It's not a matter of compulsiveness or wanting to be the first to try a material," Sim stated. "With my experience I am often able to change the design of future experiments. . . . This allows more comprehensive tests to be conducted later, with maximum effective usefulness of inexperienced volunteers. I'm trying to defeat the compound, and if I can, we don't have to drag out the tests at the expense of a lot of time and money."

With BZ Dr. Sim seems to have met his match. "It zonked me for three days. I kept falling down and the people at the lab assigned someone to follow me around with a mattress. I woke up from it after three days without a bruise." For his efforts Sim received the Decoration for Exceptional Civilian Service and was cited for exposing himself to dangerous drugs "at the risk of grave personal injury."

According to Dr. Solomon Snyder, a leading psychopharmacologist at Johns Hopkins University, which conducted drug research for the Chemical Corps, "The army's testing of LSD was just a sideshow compared to its use of BZ." Clinical studies with EA-2277 (the code number for BZ) were initiated at Edgewood Arsenal in 1959 and continued until 1975. During this period an estimated twenty-eight hundred soldiers were exposed to the superhallucinogen. A number of military personnel have since come forward claiming that they were never the same after their encounter with BZ. Robert Bowen, a former air force enlisted man, felt disoriented for several weeks after his exposure. Bowen said the drug produced a temporary feeling of insanity but that he reacted less severely than other test subjects. One paratrooper lost all muscle control for a time and later seemed totally divorced from reality. "The last time I saw him," said Bowen, "he was taking a shower in his uniform and smoking a cigar."*

After extensive clinical testing at Edgewood Arsenal, the army concluded that BZ was better suited than LSD as a chemical warfare agent for a number of reasons. While acid could knock a person "off his rocker," to use Chemical Corps jargon, BZ would also put him "on the floor" (render him physically immobile). This unique combination—both "off the rocker" and "on the floor"—was exactly what the army sought from an incapacitant. Moreover, BZ was cheaper to produce, more reliable, and packed a stronger punch than LSD. Most important, BZ could be dispersed as an aerosol mist that would float with the wind across city or battlefield. Some advantage was also found in the fact that test subjects lapsed into a state of "semi-quiet delirium" and had no memory of their BZ experience.

This was not to belittle lysergic acid. Although LSD never found a place in the army's arsenal, the drug undoubtedly left its mark on the military mind. Once again LSD seems to have acted primarily as a catalyst. Before acid touched the fancy of army strategists, Creasy's vision of a new kind of warfare was merely a pipe dream. With LSD it suddenly became a real possibility.

*Pentagon spokespeople insist that the potential hazards of such experimentation were "supposed" to be fully explained to all volunteers. But as Dr. Snyder noted, nobody "can tell you for sure BZ won't have a long-lasting effect. With an initial effect of eighty hours compared to eight for LSD you would have to worry more about its long-lasting or recurrent effects."

During the early 1960s the CIA and the military began to phase out their in-house acid tests in favor of more powerful chemicals such as BZ, which became the army's standard incapacitating agent. By this time the superhallucinogen was ready for deployment in a grenade, a 750-pound cluster bomb, and at least one other large-scale bomb. In addition the army tested a number of other advanced BZ munitions, including mortar, artillery, and missile warheads. The superhallucinogen was reportedly employed by American troops as a counterinsurgency weapon in Vietnam, and according to CIA documents there may be contingency plans to use the drug in the event of a major civilian insurrection. As Creasy warned shortly after he retired from the Army Chemical Corps, "We will use these things as we very well see fit, when we think it is in the best interest of the US and their allies."

2

Psychedelic Pioneers

THE ORIGINAL CAPTAIN TRIPS

The stout crew-cut figure riding in the Rolls-Royce was a mystery to those who knew him. A spy by profession, he lived a life of intrigue and adventure befitting his chosen career. Born dirt poor in Kentucky, he served with the OSS during the Second World War and went on to make a fortune as a uranium entrepreneur. His prestigious government and business connections read like a Who's Who of the power elite in North America. His name was Captain Alfred M. Hubbard. His friends called him "Cappy," and he was known as the "Johnny Appleseed of LSD."

The blustery, rum-drinking Hubbard is widely credited with being the first person to emphasize LSD's potential as a visionary or transcendental drug. His faith in the LSD revelation was such that he made it his life's mission to turn on as many men and women as possible. "Most people are walking in their sleep," he said. "Turn them around, start them in the opposite direction and they wouldn't even know the difference." But there was a quick way to remedy that—give them a good dose of LSD and "let them see themselves for what they are."

That Hubbard, of all people, should have emerged as the first genuine LSD apostle is all the more curious in light of his long-standing affiliation with the cloak-and-dagger trade. Indeed, he was no run-of-the-mill spook. As a high-level OSS officer, the Captain directed an extremely sensitive covert operation that involved smuggling weapons and war material to Great Britain prior to the attack on Pearl Harbor. In pitch darkness he sailed ships without lights up the coast to Vancouver, where they were refitted and used as destroyers by the British navy. He also flew planes to the border, took them apart, towed the pieces into Canada, and sent them to England. These activities began with the quiet approval of President Roosevelt

44

nearly a year and a half before the US officially entered the war. To get around the neutrality snag, Hubbard became a Canadian citizen in a mock procedure. While based in Vancouver (where he later settled), he personally handled several million dollars filtered by the OSS through the American consulate to finance a multitude of covert operations in Europe. All this, of course, was highly illegal, and President Truman later issued a special pardon with kudos to the Captain and his men.

Not long after receiving this presidential commendation, Hubbard was introduced to LSD by Dr. Ronald Sandison of Great Britain. During his first acid trip in 1951, he claimed to have witnessed his own conception. "It was the deepest mystical thing I've ever seen," the Captain recounted. "I saw myself as a tiny mite in a big swamp with a spark of intelligence. I saw my mother and father having intercourse. It was all clear."

Hubbard, then forty-nine years old, eagerly sought out others familiar with hallucinogenic drugs. He contacted Dr. Humphry Osmond, a young British psychiatrist who was working with LSD and mescaline at Weyburn Hospital in Saskatchewan, Canada. Like most other researchers in the field, Osmond was primarily interested in psychosis and mental illness. In 1952 he shocked the medical world by drawing attention to the structural similarity between the mescaline and adrenaline molecules, implying that schizophrenia might be a form of self-intoxication caused by the body mistakenly producing its own hallucinogenic compounds. Osmond noted that mescaline enabled a normal person to see the world through the eyes of a schizophrenic, and he suggested that the drug be used as a tool for training doctors, nurses, and other hospital personnel to understand their patients from a more intimate perspective.

Osmond's research attracted widespread attention within scientific circles. The CIA, ever intent on knowing the latest facts as early as possible, quickly sent informants to find out what was happening at Weyburn Hospital. Unbeknownst to Osmond and his cohorts, throughout the next decade they were contacted on repeated occasions by Agency personnel. Indeed, it was impossible for an LSD researcher not to rub shoulders with the espionage establishment, for the CIA was monitoring the entire scene.*

Osmond's reports also caught the eye of Aldous Huxley, the em-

*Osmond left Canada in 1963 and joined a group of researchers at the Princeton Neuropsychiatric Institute. There he worked closely with Dr. Bernard Aaronson,

inent British novelist who for years had been preoccupied with the specter of drug-induced thought control. In 1931 Huxley wrote *Brave New World*, a futuristic vision of a totalitarian society in which the World Controllers chemically coerced the population into loving its servitude. While Huxley grappled with the question of human freedom under pharmacological attack, he also recognized that certain drugs, particularly the hallucinogens, produced radical changes in consciousness that could have a profound and beneficial effect. Upon learning of Osmond's work, he decided to offer himself as a guinea pig.

Huxley seemed like the perfect subject. A learned man steeped in many disciplines, he was also gifted with a writer's eloquence. Even if the drug confounded him, it would not tongue-tie him, for he was a glorious talker. But Osmond was still a bit apprehensive. "I did not relish the possibility, however remote, of being the man who drove Aldous Huxley mad," he explained. His worries proved to be unfounded.

In May 1953, less than a month after the CIA initiated Operation MK-ULTRA, Huxley tried mescaline for the first time at his home in Hollywood Hills, California, under Osmond's supervision. "It was," according to Huxley, "without question the most extraordinary and significant experience this side of the Beatific Vision." Moreover, "it opens up a host of philosophical problems, throws intense light and raises all manner of questions in the field of aesthetics, religion, theory of knowledge."

Huxley described his mescaline adventure in his famous essay *The Doors of Perception* (which took its title from the works of William Blake, the eighteenth-century British poet and visionary artist). With this book Huxley unabashedly declared himself a propagandist for hallucinogenic drugs, and for the first time a large seg-

---

whose studies in hypnosis and altered states of consciousness were funded by the CIA through the Society for the Study of Human Ecology. Osmond and Aaronson later coauthored a popular anthology called *Psychedelics*. Unlike Aaronson, who was unaware of the CIA's interest in his work, Dr. Carl Pfeiffer, another Princeton researcher, had close ties with the CIA. As one of Pfeiffer's associates put it, "Princeton was crawling with agents. They came courting everyone. It was obvious. They would give us whatever we wanted. . . . We realized we were being recruited, but at that time we were flattered that such a prestigious government agency was interested in us." A little too interested, perhaps; a number of scientists soon discovered that their mail was being opened and read by government agents.

ment of the educated public became aware of the existence of these substances. Not surprisingly, the treatise created a storm in literary circles. Some hailed it as a major intellectual statement, others dismissed it as pure quackery. Few critics realized that the book would have such an enormous impact in years to come.

In *The Doors of Perception* Huxley elaborated on Henri Bergson's theory that the brain and the nervous system are not the source of the cognitive process but rather a screening mechanism or "reducing valve" that transmits but a tiny fraction of "the Mind-at-Large," yielding only the kind of information necessary for everyday matters of survival. If this screening mechanism was temporarily suspended, if the doors of perception were suddenly thrust open by a chemical such as mescaline or LSD, then the world would appear in an entirely new light. When he looked at a small vase of flowers, the mescalinized Huxley saw "what Adam had seen on the morning of creation—the miracle, moment by moment, of naked existence...flowers shining with their own inner light and all but quivering under the pressure of the significance with which they were charged....Words like 'grace' and 'transfiguration' came to my mind."

Huxley obviously was not undergoing an "imitation psychosis." On the contrary, he contended that the chemical mind-changers, when administered in the right kind of situation, could lead to a full-blown mystical experience. He went so far as to predict that a religious revival would "come about as the result of biochemical discoveries that will make it possible for large numbers of men and women to achieve a radical self-transcendence and a deeper understanding of the nature of things."

Huxley recognized that the perceptions afforded by hallucinogens bore a striking similarity to experiences achieved without the use of drugs, either spontaneously or through various spiritual exercises. His writings reflected more than a passing interest in nonchemical methods of altering consciousness, such as hypnosis, sensory deprivation, prolonged sleeplessness, fasting—techniques closely scrutinized by the CIA as well, but for vastly different reasons. Whereas the CIA sought to impose an altered state on its victims in order to control them, Huxley's explorations were self-directed and designed to expand consciousness. He was well aware of the potential dangers of behavior modification techniques and constantly warned of their abuse. Thus it is ironic that he unknowingly consorted with a number of scientists who were engaged in mind control research for the CIA and the US military.*

While writing *Heaven and Hell* (the sequel to *The Doors of Perception*) in 1955, Huxley had his second mescaline experience, this time in the company of Captain Al Hubbard. They were joined by philosopher Gerald Heard, a close friend of Huxley's. "Your nice Captain tried a new experiment—group mescalinization," Huxley wrote to Osmond. "Since I was in a group, the experience had a human content, which the earlier, solitary experience, with its Other Worldly quality and its intensification of aesthetic experience, did not possess.... it was a transcendental experience within *this* world and with human references."

Later that same year, with the Captain again acting as a guide, Huxley took his first dose of LSD. Although he consumed only a tiny amount, the experience was highly significant. "What came through the closed door," he stated, "was the realization—not the knowledge, for this wasn't verbal or abstract—but the direct, total awareness, from the inside, so to say, of Love as the primary and fundamental cosmic fact. These words, of course, have a kind of indecency and must necessarily ring false, seem like twaddle. But the fact remains...I was this fact; or perhaps it would be more accurate to say that this fact occupied the place where I had been."

Huxley and his LSD mentor were a most improbable duo. The coarse, uneducated Captain lacked elegance and restraint ("I'm just a born son of a bitch!" he bellowed), while the tall, slender novelist epitomized the genteel qualities of the British intellectual. Yet the two men were evidently quite taken by each other. Huxley spoke admiringly of "the good Captain" whose uranium exploits served "as a passport into the most exalted spheres of government, business, and ecclesiastical polity." In a letter to Osmond he commented, "What Babes in the Wood we literary gents and professional men are! The great World occasionally requires your services, is mildly

*In his letters Huxley mentioned "my friend Dr. J. West," a reference to Jolly West, who conducted LSD studies for the CIA. At one point, while West was engaged in MK-ULTRA research, Huxley suggested that he hypnotize his subjects prior to administering LSD in order to give them "post-hypnotic suggestions aimed at orienting the drug-induced experience in some desired direction." Needless to say, the CIA was intrigued by this idea. Huxley also lectured on parapsychology at Duke University, where J. B. Rhine (with whom Huxley communicated) was engaged in ESP studies for the CIA and the army.

amused by mine; but its full attention and deference are paid to Uranium and Big Business. So what extraordinary luck that this representative of both these Higher Powers should (a) have become so passionately interested in mescalin and (b) be such a very nice man."

Despite their markedly different styles Huxley and Hubbard shared a unique appreciation of the revelatory aspect of hallucinogenic drugs. It was Hubbard who originally suggested that an LSD-induced mystical experience might harbor unexplored therapeutic potential. He administered large doses of acid to gravely ill alcoholics with the hope that the ensuing experience would lead to a drastic and permanent change in the way they viewed themselves and the world. (According to Bill Wilson, the founder of Alcoholics Anonymous, the most important factor in recovery for alcoholics is "a deep and genuine religious experience.") Once the individual's rigidified notion of himself had been shattered, "extensive emotional re-education" was much more likely. At this point the Captain took over. By using religious symbols to trigger psychic responses, he attempted to assist the patient in forming a new and healthier frame of reference that would carry over after the drug wore off. Hubbard found that everyone who went through this process seemed to benefit from it. A number of former alcoholics described their recovery as nothing short of "miraculous." Buoyed by these results, the Captain proceeded to establish LSD treatment centers at three major hospitals in Canada, most notably Hollywood Hospital in Vancouver, where he resided.

Dr. Humphry Osmond was also working with alcoholics in Saskatchewan, but initially he approached the problem from a different vantage point. Osmond noted that some alcoholics decided to give up the bottle only after they "hit bottom" and suffered the withdrawal symptoms of *delirium tremens*. Could a large dose of LSD or mescaline simulate a controlled attack of the DTs? A "model *delirium tremens*," so to speak, would be considerably less dangerous than the real thing, which normally occurs after years of heavy drinking and often results in death. Osmond's hypothesis was still rooted in the psychotomimetic tradition. But then Hubbard came along and turned the young psychiatrist on to the religious meaning of his "madness mimicking" drug. The Captain showed Osmond how to harness LSD's transcendent potential. Nearly a thousand

49

hard-core alcoholics received high-dose LSD treatment at Weyburn Hospital, and the rate of recovery was significantly higher than for other forms of therapy—an astounding 50%.*

Osmond and his coworkers considered LSD the most remarkable drug they had ever come across. They saw no reason to restrict their studies to alcoholics. If LSD changed the way sick people looked at the world, would it not have as powerful an effect on others as well? With this in mind Osmond and Hubbard came up with the idea that LSD could be used to transform the belief systems of world leaders and thereby further the cause of world peace. Although few are willing to disclose the details of these sessions, a close associate of Hubbard's insisted that they "affected the thinking of the political leadership of North America." Those said to have participated in the LSD sessions include a prime minister, assistants to heads of state, UN representatives, and members of the British parliament. "My job," said Hubbard, "was to sit on the couch next to the psychiatrist and put the people through it, which I did."

Hubbard's influence on the above-ground research scene went far beyond the numerous innovations he introduced: high-dose therapy, group sessions, enhancing the drug effect with strobe lights, and ESP experiments while under the influence of LSD. His impressive standing among business and political leaders in the United States and Canada enabled him to command large supplies of the hallucinogen, which he distributed freely to friends and researchers at considerable personal expense. "Cost me a couple of hundred thousand dollars," he boasted. "I had six thousand bottles of it to begin with." When Dr. Ross MacLean, the medical director at Hollywood Hospital in Vancouver, suggested that they form a partnership and set a price for administering LSD, Hubbard would hear nothing of it. For the Captain had "a mission," as he put it, and making money never entered the picture.

Hubbard promoted his cause with indefatigable zeal, crisscrossing North America and Europe, giving LSD to anyone who would stand still. "People heard about it, and they wanted to try it," he explained.

---

*After thirteen years of utilizing this method, Osmond and his colleagues published their findings: "When psychedelic therapy is given to alcholics, about one-third will remain sober after the therapy is completed and another one-third will be benefited....Our conclusion is that, properly used, LSD therapy can turn a large number of alcoholics into sober members of society. Even more important, this can be done very quickly and therefore very economically."

During the 1950s and early 1960s he turned on thousands of people from all walks of life—policemen, statesmen, captains of industry, church figures, scientists. "They all thought it was the most marvelous thing," he stated. "And I never saw a psychosis in any one of these cases."

When certain US medical officials complained that Hubbard was not a licensed physician and therefore should not be permitted to administer drugs, the Captain just laughed and bought a doctor's degree from a diploma mill in Kentucky. "Dr." Hubbard had such remarkable credentials that he received special permission from Rome to administer LSD within the context of the Catholic faith. "He had kind of an incredible way of getting that sort of thing," said a close associate who claimed to have seen the papers from the Vatican.

Hubbard's converts included the Reverend J. E. Brown, a Catholic priest at the Cathedral of the Holy Rosary in Vancouver. After his initiation into the psychedelic mysteries, Reverend Brown recommended the experience to members of his parish. In a letter to the faithful dated December 8, 1957, he wrote, "We humbly ask Our Heavenly Mother the Virgin Mary, help of all who call upon Her to aid us to know and understand the true qualities of these psychedelics, the full capacities of man's noblest faculties and according to God's laws to use them for the benefit of mankind here and in eternity."

Like a molecule at full boil, the Captain moved about at high speeds in all directions. He traveled around the world in his own plane (he was a registered pilot and master of sea vessels), buying up LSD and stashing it, swapping different drugs, and building an underground supply. "I scattered it as I went along," he recalled. With his leather pouch full of "wampum" he rode the circuit, and those on the receiving end were always grateful. "We waited for him like the little old lady on the prairie waiting for a copy of the Sears Roebuck catalogue," said Dr. Oscar Janiger, a Los Angeles psychiatrist.

Dr. Janiger was part of a small circle of scientists and literary figures in the Los Angeles area who began to use psychedelics at social gatherings in the mid-1950s. In addition to Huxley and Gerald Heard, those who participated in these drug-inspired intellectual discussions included philosopher Alan Watts, deep-sea diver Perry Bivens, and researchers Sidney Cohen, Keith Ditman, and Arthur Chandler. This informal group was the first to use LSD socially rather than clinically. Captain Al Hubbard, the wandering shaman who visited southern California on a regular basis, supplied the group with various chemicals.

"Something had to be done and I tried to do it," Hubbard explained. He was, in his own words, "a catalytic agent" who had a "special, chosen role." While this is certainly an accurate appraisal, he was also another kind of agent—an intelligence agent—which raises some intriguing questions about what he was really up to.

After his legendary exploits with the OSS, the Captain continued to serve as an undercover operative for various agencies within the US government. He had many contacts with the FBI, for example, and he claimed to be a close friend of J. Edgar Hoover's. "That old bugger was tough, really tough," Hubbard said with admiration. But when he tried to turn on the FBI chief, Hoover stubbornly declined. However, the Captain did manage to give the drug to "some top intelligence men in Washington, always with good results."

During the early 1950s Hubbard was asked to join the CIA, but he refused. "They lied so much, cheated so much. I don't like 'em," he snarled. "They're lousy deceivers, sons of the devils themselves." The Captain's beef with the Agency stemmed in part from his un-successful attempt to secure back pay owed to him from his OSS days. "They crooked me," he complained bitterly.

Hubbard was unkindly disposed toward the CIA for other reasons as well. Most important, he didn't approve of what the Agency was doing with his beloved LSD. "The CIA work stinks," he said. "They were misusing it. I tried to tell them how to use it, but even when they were killing people, you couldn't tell them a goddamned thing." (Hubbard was certain that Frank Olson was not the only person who died as a result of the CIA's surprise acid tests.)

"I don't know how Al's Washington affairs were done," Dr. Os-mond admitted. "He was one of those naturally brilliant wheeler-dealers." Indeed, Hubbard seemed to have a knack for popping up in the most unpredictable places. He worked for the Treasury De-partment as a young man during the Capone days, busting moon-shiners and gangsters who were smuggling liquor into the US from Canada. Apparently he was able to ingratiate himself with both sides during Prohibition, as he subsequently became deputy chief of se-curity for the Tropicana Hotel in Las Vegas. "Those Mafia men were always interesting to talk to," Hubbard remarked, "but they never smiled."

The Captain also engaged in undercover work for a number of other government agencies, including the Federal Narcotics Bureau and the Food and Drug Administration (at a time when both organizations were assisting the CIA's drug testing programs). During the mid-1960s he was employed by Teledyne, a major defense subcontractor, as "director of human factors research." In this capacity Hubbard served as adviser and consultant to a combined navy and NASA project that involved testing the effects of psychochemical agents on a newly designed "helicopter avionics system." Teledyne worked closely with various government organizations, including the CIA, to apply these techniques to additional areas of military interest.

While Hubbard was not a CIA operative per se, his particular area of expertise—hallucinogenic drugs—brought him into close contact with elements of the espionage community. The CIA must have known what he was up to, since Sandoz and the FDA kept the Agency informed whenever anyone received shipments of LSD. The Captain, of course, was one of their best customers, having purchased large amounts of the drug on different occasions.

In a sense "the mysterious Al" embodies the irony and ambiguity of the LSD story as a whole. As one of his friends put it, "Cappy was sort of a double agent. He worked for the government, but in his own way he was a rebel." Some call him a "witch doctor," others describe him as "an incurable scoundrel." A most unlikely combination of mystic and redneck, Hubbard above all remains an enigma.

"Al Hubbard was a very strange man," confided a fellow drug researcher, "but he probably knew more about LSD than anyone else in the world." And while his tale has many gaps and fuzzy edges, this much can be established beyond a shadow of a doubt: his enthusiasm for LSD never waned. "Anyone who'll try to tell me that this has all been a big hallucination has got to be out of their mind. ...What I've seen with it has been the truth and nothing but the truth."

And as a parting shot he added, "If you don't think it's amazing, all I've got to say is just go ahead and try it."

Healing Acid

By the late 1950s, according to Robert Bernstein, former assistant surgeon general of the American army, "perhaps by coincidence, LSD was almost simultaneously recognized by the army as a military threat and by certain segments of our US population as a means for self-fulfillment." What puzzling characteristics does LSD possess that give rise to such disparate and seemingly contradictory points of view? How could the same drug be hailed as an unparalleled avenue to transcendental or visionary experiences and denounced as an agent of psychotic interludes?

Originally researchers viewed LSD solely in terms of its ability to create an experimental toxic psychosis. The LSD experience was synonymous with LSD psychosis—"good trips" were no exception. This frame of reference, uniformly shared by scientists at the outset of the 1950s, was typified by the comment of a CIA agent involved in the MK-ULTRA program: "Tripping and psychosis are one and the same. Tripping can be an awful schizoid feeling. Also there are hebephrenics—happy schizos. Their experience is similar to a good trip."

Within a few years, however, reports with a different message began to circulate from Canada. After meeting Captain Hubbard, a small circle of researchers based in Saskatchewan broke with the psychotomimetic definition and started exploring new directions. Dr. Osmond noticed a significant discrepancy between the usual description of the drug experience as a close encounter with lunacy and the kinds of experiences reported by his patients when they were given LSD for their alcoholic problems. They often spoke of an LSD session as insightful and rewarding. Many subjects invoked superlatives, calling it an experience of great beauty. As the research at Weyburn Hospital progressed, it became apparent to Osmond and his cohorts that most people who took LSD did not become insane.

The terminology used to describe the LSD experience in the scientific literature did not sit well with Osmond. Words like *hallucination* and *psychosis* were loaded; they implied negative states of mind. The psychiatric jargon reflected a pathological orientation, whereas a truly objective science would not impose value judgments on chemicals that produced unusual or altered states of consciousness. Aldous Huxley also felt that the language of pathology was inadequate. He and Osmond agreed that a new word had to be invented to encompass the full range of effects of these drugs.

The two men had been close friends ever since Huxley's initial mescaline experience, and they carried on a lively correspondence. At first Huxley proposed the word *phanerothyme*, which derived from roots relating to "spirit" or "soul." A letter to Osmond included the following couplet:

> *To make this trivial world sublime,*
> *Take half a Gramme of phanerothyme.*

To which Osmond responded:

> *To fathom hell or soar angelic*
> *Just take a pinch of psychedelic.*

And so it came to pass that the word *psychedelic* was coined. Osmond introduced it to the psychiatric establishment in 1957. Addressing a meeting of the New York Academy of Sciences, he argued that hallucinogenic drugs did "much more" than mimic psychosis, and therefore an appropriate name must "include concepts of enriching the mind and enlarging the vision." He suggested a neutral term to replace *psychotomimetic*, and his choice was certainly vague enough. Literally translated, *psychedelic* means "mind-manifesting," implying that drugs of this category do not produce a predictable sequence of events but bring to the fore whatever is latent within the unconscious. Accordingly Osmond recognized that LSD could be a valuable tool for psychotherapy. This notion represented a marked departure from the military-medical paradigm, which held that every LSD experience was automatically an experimental psychosis.

Dr. Albert Hofmann, the chemist who discovered LSD, thought Osmond's choice appropriate, for it "corresponds better to the effects of these drugs than *hallucinogenic* or *psychotomimetic*." The model psychosis concept was further called into question by published reports demonstrating that in many ways the comparison between naturally occurring and LSD-induced psychosis was facile. During the mid-1950s, researchers John MacDonald and James Galvin pointed out that schizophrenics did not experience the wealth of visual hallucinations common with LSD and mescaline but were prone to auditory aberrations, unlike drug subjects. Oddly enough, true schizophrenics hardly reacted to LSD unless given massive doses.

As the psychotomimetic paradigm began to weaken, the focus shifted toward investigating the therapeutic potential of LSD. Two forms of LSD therapy arose in the 1950s. The "psycholytic" or "mind-loosening" approach utilized low or moderate dosages of LSD as an adjunct to conventional psychoanalysis. Employed in repeated sessions, the drug was said to speed up the process of psychoexploration by reducing the patient's defensiveness and facilitating the recollection of repressed memories and traumatic experiences. Stripped of his censorious attitude, the subject might experience a catharsis in a detached and heightened state of awareness, allowing him to retain his insights after the effects of the chemical subsided. The low-dose technique was practiced primarily in England, where Dr. Ronald Sandison established the first LSD clinic open to the public in 1953. Before long, additional centers specializing in this type of therapy sprang up in Germany, Holland, France, Italy, Czechoslovakia and several Scandinavian countries.

A different approach caught on more quickly in Canada and the United States. Psychedelic therapy, developed by Captain Al Hubbard and popularized by Dr. Humphry Osmond, was geared toward achieving a mystical or conversion experience. The procedure involved high dosages of LSD, precluding any possibility that the patient's ego defenses could withstand psychic dissolution.

According to this therapeutic model, as the drug starts to take effect there is an unfixing of perceptual constants and the subject's habitual reality ties are suspended. It is as though one were suddenly thrust into a Van Gogh canvas; objects ripple and breathe, an onrush of stimuli bombard and penetrate the body. Sensory functions overlap in a manner that might best be described as polymorphously perverse: one can "hear" colors and "see" sounds. The world is felt to be an extension of the flesh. Existence is no longer a riddle to be solved but a mystery to behold.

During the apotheosis of the acid high, the self-concept may be diminished to the point of depersonalization. As poet Octavio Paz describes in *Alternating Current*, "The self disappears, but no other self appears to occupy the empty space it has left. No god but rather the divine. No faith but rather the primordial feeling that sustains all faith, all hope. Peace in the crater of the volcano, the reconciliation of man—what remains of man—with total presence."

This state of consciousness was thought to be conducive to healing deep-rooted psychological wounds. The task of the therapist was to help the patient understand and assimilate the experience in a way that would maximize personal growth. Best results were obtained when the therapist shed his "doctor" status and assumed the role of guide or mentor, intervening only to help the initiate relax and "go with the flow." To succeed, the therapist had to be well acquainted with the psychedelic terrain; this familiarity could only be gained by taking the drug and learning to direct a positive experience. (Osmond's Golden Rule: "You start with yourself.") It was not uncommon for a guide to take a small amount of LSD during the therapy session to increase his rapport with his patient.

Originally tested on alcoholics in Canada with remarkable results, high-dose therapy was subsequently applied to a wide range of diagnostic categories: juvenile delinquency, narcotics addiction, severe character neurosis, and the like. This approach was particularly effective in treating people who were emotionally blocked; they were able to cut through a lot of psychological red tape, so to speak, and get right to the heart of the matter. Oftentimes those who underwent psychedelic therapy reported dramatic personality changes involving not only the relief of neurotic symptoms but a wholesale revamping of value systems, religious and philosophical beliefs, and basic lifestyle. Numerous patients claimed that a few LSD trips proved more fruitful than years of psychoanalysis—at considerably less expense. In some cases spectacular success was achieved with only one dose of the drug.

LSD was the talk of the town in Hollywood and Beverly Hills in the late 1950s as various movie stars were dosed on the psychiatrist's couch. Participants in such sessions included several of the glamor elite, each capable of generating a flash of publicity. Cary Grant first took LSD under the guidance of Dr. Mortimer Hartmann and then with Dr. Oscar Janiger. His therapy was such a success that he became a zealous missionary for LSD. "All my life," Grant stated, "I've been searching for peace of mind. I'd explored yoga and hypnotism and made several attempts at mysticism. Nothing really seemed to give me what I wanted until this treatment." People from all walks of life echoed Grant's plaudits for the drug, and psychiatrists who practiced LSD therapy were inundated with inquiries.

Beatific, oceanic, redemptive—these words have been used to describe the peak of an LSD trip. But there is another side to it. To be cast about as flotsam in the power draughts of the universe can be a hellish as well as a heavenly ordeal. Both possibilities are rooted in the experience of depersonalization or ego loss. The CIA was not interested in the therapeutic applications of LSD. On the contrary, the men of ARTICHOKE and MK-ULTRA defined the drug as an anxiety-producing agent, and they realized it would be relatively easy to "break" a person who was exposed to highly stressful stimuli while high on acid. As one CIA document instructed, "[Whatever] reduces integrative capacity may serve to increase the possibility of an individual being overwhelmed by frustrations and conflicts hitherto managed successfully." The powerful ego-shattering effects of LSD were ideally suited for this purpose. CIA and military interrogators proceeded to utilize the drug as an instrument of psychological torture.

That LSD can be used to heal as well as maim underscores an essential point: non-drug factors play an important role in determining the subject's response. LSD has no standard effects that are purely pharmacological in nature; the enormous range of experiences produced by the chemical stems from differences in (1) the character structure and attitudinal predispositions (or "set") of the subject, and (2) the immediate situation (or "setting"). If LSD is given in a relaxed and supportive environment and the subject is coached beforehand, the experience can be intensely gratifying. As Dr. Janiger put it, "LSD favors the prepared mind."

For the unprepared mind, however, LSD can be a nightmare. When the drug is administered in a sterile laboratory under fluorescent lights by white-coated physicians who attach electrodes and nonchalantly warn the subject that he will go crazy for a while, the odds favor a psychotomimetic reaction, or "bummer."

This became apparent to poet Allen Ginsberg when he took LSD for the first time at the Mental Research Institute in Palo Alto, California, in 1959. Ginsberg was already familiar with psychedelic substances, having experimented with peyote on a number of occasions. As yet, however, there was no underground supply of LSD, and it was virtually impossible for layfolk to procure samples of the drug. Thus he was pleased when Gregory Bateson,* the anthropologist, put him in touch with a team of doctors in Palo Alto. Ginsberg had no way of knowing that one of the researchers associated with the institute, Dr. Charles Savage, had conducted hallucinogenic drug experiments for the US Navy in the early 1950s.

The experiment was conducted in a small room full of medical

*Formerly a member of the Research and Analysis Branch of the OSS, Bateson was the husband and co-worker of anthropologist Margaret Mead. An exceptional intellect, he was turned on to acid by Dr. Harold Abramson, one of the CIA's chief LSD specialists.

equipment and EEG machines, with no outer windows. Ginsberg was advised that he could listen to whatever music he wanted, so he chose Wagner's *Tristan and Isolde* and a recording of Gertrude Stein. "For some reason," he recalled, "I thought you were supposed to lie down like in a hospital on a psychiatrist's couch and let something slowly engulf you, which is what happened. I lay down and something slowly engulfed me." As he started getting high, Ginsberg was put through a series of psychological tests—word association, Rorschach inkblots, arithmetic problems—which struck him as quite absurd at the time. "What difference does it make?" he kept asking the attendants. While they measured his psychological responses, the poet—having read Huxley—was waiting for God to show up inside his brain.

When it came time for the EEG tests, Ginsberg proposed a rather unusual experiment that had been suggested by his friend William S. Burroughs. He wanted to see what would happen if he looked at a stroboscope blinking in synchronization with his alpha rhythms while he was high on acid. The doctors connected the flicker machine to the EEG apparatus so that the alpha waves emanating from his brain set off the strobe effect. "It was like watching my own inner organism," said Ginsberg. "There was no distinction between inner and outer. Suddenly I got this uncanny sense that I was really no different than all of this mechanical machinery around me. I began thinking that if I let this go on, something awful would happen. I would be absorbed into the electrical network grid of the entire nation. Then I began feeling a slight crackling along the hemispheres of my skull. I felt my soul being sucked out through the light into the wall socket and going out."

Ginsberg had had enough. He asked the doctors to turn the flicker machine off, but the "high anxiety" lingered. The clinical atmosphere of the laboratory made it hard for him to relax. As the trip wore on, he got deeper and deeper into a tangle: "I had the impression that I was an insignificant speck on a giant spider web, and that the spider was slowly coming to get me, and that the spider was God or the Devil—I wasn't sure—but I was the victim. I thought I was trapped in a giant web or network of forces beyond my control that were perhaps experimenting with me or were perhaps from another planet or were from some super-government or cosmic military or science-fiction Big Brother."

Ginsberg spent the evening at the home of Dr. Joe Adams, the man who supervised the experiment. He retired to his room and tried to describe his first acid trip. While still high, he composed the poem "Lysergic Acid," which begins with the following incantation:

> It is a multiple million eyed monster
> it is hidden in all its elephants and selves
> it hummeth in the electric typewriter
> it is electricity connected to itself, if it hath wires
> it is a vast Spiderweb
> and I am on the last millionth infinite tentacle of
>   the spiderweb, a worrier
> lost, separated, a worm, a thought, a self. . .
> I allen Ginsberg a separate consciousness
> I who want to be God . . .

It might appear that such ordeals amounted to a ravaging of the soul rather than its redemption. But Ginsberg thought otherwise. He and the other poets and artists associated with the beat generation sampled a veritable pharmacopoeia of different drugs in various dosages and combinations, and publicly extolled their virtues. They too viewed psychedelics as "truth drugs," but unlike the CIA they were not attempting to control someone else's mind. Rather, they used these substances to assert their creative autonomy. Most of all, the beats wanted to speak the truth about their lives. While the CIA prowled around in secret and hoarded information, the beats were open and candid about their chemically illumined voyages. Intoxicated states were the keystone of beat literature, and they chronicled their insights in poetry and prose. Occasionally they tripped together in small groups and later compared notes on how best to approach a psychedelic session. The beats were mapping uncharted zones of the human psyche, an effort Ginsberg likened to "being part of a cosmic conspiracy . . . to resurrect a lost art or a lost knowledge or a lost consciousness."

The beats' drug shamanism was bound up with romantic excess. In the midst of the spiritual blackout of the Cold War they searched for a "final fix" that would afford the vision of all visions. Their affinity for psychedelics reflected as much a desire to escape from a world they found unbearable as to tap the hidden realms of the psyche. Drugs were instrumental in catalyzing their rebellion against the overwhelming conformity of American culture. The beats had nothing but contempt for the strictures of a society anally fixated on success, cleanliness, and material possession. Whatever the mainstream tried to conceal, denigrate, or otherwise purge from experience, the beats flaunted. Their hunger for new sensations led them to seek transcendence through jazz, marijuana, Buddhist meditation, and the frenetic pace of the hip lifestyle.

It was the beats who railed most forcefully against the ghostly reserve of the 1950s. They understood that the problem was largely social in nature, but it was so extreme that the only sensible response was to become antisocial, to retreat into small groups or cabals of like-minded individuals and pursue radical options outside the cultural norm. The beats were pitchmen for another kind of consciousness. They encouraged the youth of America to take their first groping steps toward a psychological freedom from convention that opened the door to all manner of chemical experimentation. The beats bequeathed an inquisitive attitude, a precocious "set" for approaching the drug experience. As cultural expatriates they linked psychedelics to a tiny groundswell of nonconformity that would grow into a mass rebellion during the next decade.

Psychosis or Gnosis?

Therapeutic studies in the 1950s opened up new areas of investigation for a growing number of young psychiatrists. A particularly promising avenue of inquiry involved using LSD as a tool to explore the creative attributes of the mind. Dr. Oscar Janiger (the first person in the US to conduct a clinical investigation of DMT, or dimethyltryptamine, an extremely powerful short-acting psychedelic) noted that many of his patients reported vivid aesthetic perceptions frequently leading to a greater appreciation of the arts. One of his subjects claimed that a single acid trip was equal to "four years in art school" and urged Janiger to give the drug to other artists. This led to an experiment in which one hundred painters drew pictures before, during, and after an LSD experience. Everyone who participated considered their post-LSD creations personally more meaningful. Impressed by these results, Janiger proceeded to administer the psychedelic to various writers, actors, musicians, and filmmakers, including such notables as Anaïs Nin, André Previn, Jack Nicholson, James Coburn, Ivan Tors, and the great stand-up comedian Lord Buckley.*

While some interesting and highly original works of art have been produced during the acid high, the creative effects of LSD cannot be measured solely in terms of immediate artistic output. Even more important is the enlargement of vision, the acute awareness of vaster potentials that persists long after the drug has worn off. Janiger's subjects frequently commented on the affinity between the drug-induced state and "what they felt might be an essential matrix from which the imaginative process derives." Author William Burroughs, who experimented with hallucinogens on his own, agreed with this assessment: "Under the influence of mescaline I have had the experience of seeing a painting for the first time, and I found later that I could see the painting without using the drug. The same insights into music or the exposure to a powerful consciousness-expanding drug often conveys a permanent increase in the range of experience. Mescaline transports the user to unexplored psychic areas, and he can often find the way back without a chemical guide."

The suggestion that LSD might enhance creativity was vigorously disputed by certain studies purporting to measure the impairment of normal mental functioning during the drugged state. The discrepancy between these studies and the personal testimony of the artists themselves underscored the shortcomings of the scientific *modus operandi*, which relied primarily on performance and aptitude tests and the like. In the end such tests yielded a morass of nebulous and contradictory data that shed little light on the psychological action of psychedelic agents. Dr. Osmond spoke for a growing number of researchers when he wrote, "Our preoccupation with behavior, because it is measurable, has led us to assume that what can be measured must be valuable and vice versa.... An emphasis on the measurable and the reductive has resulted in the limitation of interest by psychiatrists to aspects of experience that fit in with this concept." According to Osmond, the most important features of the LSD experience—the overwhelming beauty, the awe

---

*In the mid-1940s Lord Buckley founded a mescaline club called The Church of the Living Swing. A practitioner of yoga who often appeared in public wearing a tuxedo with tennis sneakers, a big white moustache, and a safari hat, Buckley rented a yacht and threw mescaline parties in the San Francisco Bay with live jazz by Ben Webster and Johnny Puleo and the Harmonicats.

and wonder, the existential challenge, the creative and therapeutic insights —would inevitably elude the scientist who viewed them merely as "epiphenomena of 'objective' happenings."

The so-called objectivist approach was inherently flawed not only because it sought to quantify creative experience but also because it ignored the input of the observer, which always influenced the results of an LSD experiment. An acid high was a state of heightened suggestibility and acute sensitivity to environmental cues. The subject's response was therefore largely influenced by the expectations of the person administering the drug. If the scientist viewed the LSD experience as essentially "psychotic," he unwittingly contributed to this type of response, both through implicit suggestion and because he was not equipped to assist the subject in interpreting the altered state of consciousness. Under these circumstances a paranoid response with serious long-range repercussions was not uncommon. Such results, in turn, led to overgeneralization, to the point where the drug was defined as a stress-inducing agent.

The notion that LSD could be used to *treat* psychological problems seemed downright absurd to certain scientists in light of the drug's long-standing identification with the *simulation* of mental illness. Those who operated within the psychotomimetic framework did not recognize that extrapharmacological variables—inadequate preparation, negative expectations, poorly managed sessions—were responsible for the adverse effects mistakenly attributed to the specific action of the drug. (According to the model psychosis scenario, there was really nothing to manage; just dose them and take the reaction.) They were appalled to learn that some psychotherapists were actually taking LSD with their patients. This was strictly taboo to the behaviorist, who refused to experiment on himself on the grounds that it would impair his ability to remain completely objective.

The chasm between the two schools of thought was not due to a communications breakdown or a lack of familiarity with the drug. The different methodologies were rooted in conflicting ideological frameworks. Behaviorism was still anchored in the materialist world view formalized by Newton; the "psychedelic" evidence was congruent with the revolutionary implications of relativity theory and quantum mechanics. The belief in scientific objectivity had been shaken in 1927 when physicist Werner Heisenberg enunciated the "uncertainty principle," which held that in subatomic physics the observer inevitably influenced the movement of the particles being observed. LSD research and many other types of studies suggested that an uncertainty principle of sorts was operative in psychology as well, in that the results were conditioned by the investigator's preconceptions. The "pure" observer was an illusion, and those who thought they could conduct an experiment without "contaminating" the results were deceiving themselves.

Aldous Huxley felt that the "scientific" approach was utterly hopeless. "Those idiots want to be Pavlovians," he said, "[but] Pavlov never saw an animal in its natural state, only under duress. The 'scientific' LSD boys do the same with their subjects. No wonder they report psychotics." The practitioners of psychedelic therapy, on the other hand, were cognizant of the complex interaction between set and setting, and they worked to facilitate insight and personal growth.

Of course, even the best set and setting could not always guarantee an easy, pleasant, or uncomplicated experience. The goal of a therapeutic session was not to have a "good trip" per se but to work through emotional, creative or intellectual blockages and further the process of self-discovery—an ordeal that could be very painful at times. Certain schools of psychiatry—R. D. Laing, for example—recognized that "freaking out" might actually herald a positive breakthrough to a new level of awareness if properly integrated by the patient.* The idea that a turbulent acid trip could have therapeutic consequences reflected an ancient understanding of the human psyche and the principles governing the healing process.

The "perilous passing" through the chaotic realm of the bummer was structured into the drug rituals of primitive societies as part of the sacred "vision-quest." The key figure in the hallucinogenic drama was the shaman, the witch doctor, the medicine man (or woman, as was often the case) who gave song to dreams and provided spiritual access for the entire tribe. A connoisseur of the drug-induced trance state, the shaman derived his or her strength from confronting the

---

*Whereas most psychedelic therapists were prepared to assist their patients should difficulties arise, Dr. Salvador Roquet, a maverick Mexican psychiatrist, consciously sought to induce a bummer as part of his "treatment." Roquet utilized various hallucinogenic drugs, including LSD, psilocybin, mescaline, datura, and ketamine. Known as "a master of bad trips" and "a pusher of death," Roquet subjected people to adverse stimuli while they were drugged; Jewish subjects, for example, were given acid and then forced to listen to a recording of Hitler's speeches.

terror of ego death—the quintessential trial by fire that was seen as a necessary prelude to an ecstatic rebirth, the resurrection of a new personality.

The drug experience informed every aspect of life in traditional cultures. With the aid of hallucinogenic plants the witch doctor cured the sick, communicated with the spirits of the dead, foretold the future, and initiated young people in coming-of-age rites. The use of mind-altering substances within an ethos of combat and aggression was also common in primitive communities. Whatever the specific purpose, the shaman always employed the hallucinogen in a ceremonial context. An elaborate set of rituals governed every step of the process, from gathering the roots and herbs to preparing and administering the brew. The power plants were often poisonous and could be fatal if not prepared properly. Only a ritually clean person who had endured weeks or months of prayer and fasting, often in isolation from the community, was deemed ready to ingest these substances. Because of the shaman's familiarity with states of consciousness induced by hallucinogenic drugs, he or she was considered qualified to pilot others through the experience.

"Primitive man," wrote Huxley in 1931, "explored the pharmacological avenues of escape from the world with astounding thoroughness. Our ancestors left almost no natural stimulant, or hallucinant, or stupefacient, undiscovered." To Huxley, the urge for transcendence and visionary experience was nothing less than a biological imperative. "Always and everywhere," he asserted, "human beings have felt the radical inadequacy of being their insulated selves and not something else, something wider, something in the Wordsworthian phrase, 'far more deeply interfused.' . . . I live, yet not I, but wine or opium or peyotyl or hashish liveth in me. To go beyond the insulated self is such a liberation that, even when self-transcendence is through nausea into frenzy, through cramps into hallucinations and coma, the drug-induced experience has been regarded by primitives and even by the highly civilized as intrinsically divine."

The use of mind-altering drugs as religious sacraments was not restricted to a particular time and place but characterized nearly every society on the planet (with the possible exception of certain Eskimo and Polynesian communities). For the Aztecs there was peyote and ololiuqui, a small lentil-like seed containing lysergic acid; the Aborigines of Australia chewed pituri, a desert shrub; the

65

natives of the Upper Amazon had yagé, the telepathic vine. Those who floated into a sacred space after ingesting these substances often projected ecstatic qualities onto the plants themselves. Certain scholars believe that the fabled Soma of the ancient Vedic religion in northern India was actually the fly agaric mushroom, and there is strong evidence that ergot, from which LSD is derived, was the mysterious *kykeon* used for over two thousand years by the ancient Greeks in the annual Eleusinian Mysteries.*

When Christianity was adopted as the official creed of the Roman Empire in the fourth century, all other religions, including the Mysteries, were banished. Christian propagandists called for the destruction of the pagan drug cults that had spread throughout Europe after the Roman conquest. Like its shamanistic forebears, paganism was rooted in rapture rather than faith or doctrine; its mode of expression was myth and ritual, and those who carried on the forbidden traditions possessed a vast storehouse of knowledge about herbs and special medicaments. The witches of the Middle Ages concocted brews with various hallucinogenic compounds—belladonna, thorn apple, henbane and bufotenine (derived from the sweat gland of the toad *Bufo marinus*)—and when the moon was full they flew off on their imaginary broomsticks to commune with spirits.†

The ruthless suppression of European witchcraft by the Holy Inquisition coincided with attempts to stamp out indigenous drug use

---

*In *The Road to Eleusis* authors Albert Hofmann, Gordon Wasson, and Carl Ruck present convincing evidence that the Eleusinian Mysteries, the oldest religion in the West, centered around a mass tripping ritual. For two millennia pilgrims journeyed from all over the world to take part in the Mysteries and drink of the sacred *kykeon*— a holy brew laced with ergot. The setting for the Mysteries was carefully devised to maximize the transcendental aura. After drinking the spiritual potion, the initiates would listen to ceremonial music and ponder the texts of Demeter, goddess of grain (symbolizing renewal, spring, fecundity, and possibly the ergot fungus, which grows on barley, from which the *kykeon* was made). At the climax of the initiation a beam of sunlight would flood the chamber. This vision was said to be the culminating experience of a lifetime, man's redemption from death. As the poet Pindar wrote, "Happy is he who, having seen these rites, goes below the hollow earth; for he knows the end of life and its god-sent beginning." Plato, Aristotle and Sophocles were among those who participated in this secret ritual.

†While the passing of time and the destruction of documentary evidence by the church has concealed the full scope of the ritual use of hallucinogens in Europe, scattered references suggest that a widespread psychedelic underground existed during the Middle Ages. Walter Map, a twelfth-century ecclesiastic, told of certain heretical sects that offered innocent people a "heavenly food" proclaiming, "Often you will see...angelic visions, in which sustained by their consolation, you can visit whatsoever place you wish without delay or difficulties."

among the colonized natives of the New World. The Spanish outlawed peyote and coca leaves in the Americas, and the British later
tried to banish kava use in Tahiti. Such edicts were part of an imperialist effort to impose a new social order that stigmatized the
psychedelic experience as a form of madness or possession by evil
spirits. It wasn't until the late eighteenth century that industrial
civilization produced its own "devil's advocate," which spoke in a
passionate and lyrical voice. The romantic rebellion signified "a
return of the repressed" as drugs were embraced by the visionary
poets and artists who lived as outcasts in their own society. Laud-
anum, a tincture of opium, catalyzed the literary talents of Cole-
ridge, Poe, Swinburne, De Quincey, and Elizabeth Barrett Browning,
while the best-known French writers, including Baudelaire, de Ner-
val, and Victor Hugo, gathered at Le Club des Haschischins, a pro-
tobohemian enclave in Paris founded by Théophile Gautier in 1844.*

For the visionary poets modern society was the bummer, and they
often viewed the drug experience as a tortured means to a fuller
existence, to a life more innately human. It was with the hope of
alleviating his own tortured mental condition that Antonin Artaud
made an intercontinental trek in the 1930s to participate in the
peyote ritual of the Tarahumara Indians in the Mexican highlands.
Artaud did not undertake such a risky journey as a tourist or an
anthropologist but as someone who wished to be healed, as a spiritual exile seeking to regain "a Truth which the world of Europe is
losing." The desperate Frenchman experienced a monumental bummer—"the cataclysm which was my body ... this dislocated assem-
blage, this piece of damaged geology." Yet somehow, despite the
nightmare visions and the somatic discomfort, he managed to scratch
out a perception of the Infinite. "Once one has experienced a visionary state of mind," Artaud wrote in *The Peyote Dance*, "one
can no longer confuse the lie with truth. One has seen where one
comes from and who one is, and one no longer doubts what one is.
There is no emotion or external influence that can divert one from
this reality."

Like Artaud and the romantic poets, some psychiatrists who used
LSD in a therapeutic context believed that a disruptive experience

---

*Gautier was turned on to hashish by J. J. Moreau de Tours, a French doctor who
attempted to correlate the effects of cannabis with the manifestations of mental
illness. Moreau, the first person to put forward the notion of a drug-induced "model
psychosis," supplied hashish to the literary giants who frequented Gautier's club.

67

could have a curative effect if allowed to proceed to resolution. Many other researchers, however, dismissed transcendental insight as either "happy psychosis" or a lot of nonsense. The knee-jerk reaction on the part of the psychotomimetic stalwarts was indicative of a deeply ingrained prejudice against certain varieties of experience. In advanced industrial societies "paranormal" states of consciousness are readily disparaged as "abnormal" or pathological. Such attitudes, cultural as much as professional, played a crucial role in circum- scribing the horizon of scientific investigation into hallucinogenic agents.

Thomas Kuhn, in *The Structure of Scientific Revolutions*, argues that the scientist's overriding need to make sense of his data compels him to mold it to the prevailing scientific paradigm, which defines "legitimate" problems and methods for a given historical era. There are moments, however, when the orthodox framework cannot bear the weight of irrefutable new evidence. A period of controversy ensues until a new paradigm emerges to encompass and transcend the previous ideology. During this transition period scientists who buck the status quo are often castigated as eccentric, irresponsible, and unscientific. Galileo, for example, was branded a lunatic and a heretic for suggesting that the earth revolved around the sun. In a similar fashion the psychedelic evidence challenged the entrenched world view of the psychiatric establishment, and proponents of LSD therapy were summarily denounced and ridiculed by those who were fixated on the model psychosis concept.

Dr. Humphry Osmond defended his position by emphasizing that the pathological bias, from a historical perspective, was clearly the exception and not the rule. In many cultures that were less sophisticated technologically but more so ecologically, the drug-induced trance state was revered as an enlargement of reality rather than a deviation from it. Osmond pleaded with his fellow researchers not to dismiss something that struck them as unusual or different simply because "it transcends those fashionable ruts of thinking that we dignify by calling logic and reason." He urged psychiatrists to change their outlook in order to realize the full potential of psychedelics.

While many young doctors rallied to his call, there were others, including certain influential scientists working under CIA and military contract, who refused to budge from the psychotomimetic posture. The debate between the two camps came to a head at the first international conference on LSD therapy in 1959. Sponsored by the Josiah Macy, Jr. Foundation (at times a CIA conduit), it was perhaps the most important gathering of LSD researchers to date for it enabled workers in the field to compare notes and analyze their findings as a group. The conference was chaired by Dr. Paul Hoch, a prominent and well-connected scientist who was, in the words of Sanford Unger, "an opinion leader." Hoch was also a longtime CIA consultant and a contract employee of the US Army Chemical Corps. Dr. Harold Abramson, a veteran of the CIA's MK-ULTRA program, served as recording secretary, and a number of other scientists who rented their services to the CIA and the military were featured speakers. Hoch and Abramson did not just stumble into their respective roles at this event. Their status as dominant figures in aboveground LSD research suggests the extent to which covert interests influenced the course of the debate over hallucinogenic substances and their effects.

Despite ample evidence to the contrary Dr. Hoch stubbornly insisted that LSD and mescaline were "essentially anxiety-producing drugs." He asserted that they were "not especially useful" in a therapeutic context because they disorganize the psychic integration of a person. LSD experiments, according to the chairman, could not be compared with "results obtained in patients where tranquilizing drugs were used to reduce, instead of stir up the patient's symptoms."

Dr. Hoch was incredulous when other participants in the Macy conference reported that their patients found the LSD session beneficial and personally rewarding and were usually eager to take the drug again. "In my experience," Hoch announced, "no patient asks for it again." His experience included the following mescaline experiment conducted on a thirty-six-year-old male diagnosed as a "pseudoneurotic schizophrenic."

> He had some visual hallucinations. He saw dragons and tigers coming to eat him and reacted to these hallucinations with marked anxiety. He also had some illusionary distortions of the objects in the room. The emotional changes were apprehension and fear—at times mounting to panic, persecutory misinterpretation of the environment, fear of death, intense irritability, suspiciousness, perplexity, and feelings of depersonalization. He verbalized the feelings of depersonalization as "floating out of space," seemed "between this life and the next," and had the feeling of being born. The paranoid content concerned essentially why the doctors were

69

taking notes and fear that he would be attacked by them. He also expressed an ecstatic grandiose trend of having the feeling that he was God in heaven and then, however, had the feeling of being in hell.... The mental picture was that of a typical schizophrenic psychosis while the drug influence lasted.

As an afterword, Hoch noted, "This patient received transorbital lobotomy and showed temporarily a marked improvement in all his symptoms, losing most of his tension and anxiety. Postoperatively he was again placed under mescaline. Basically the same manifestations were elicited as prior to the operation with the exception that quantitatively the symptoms were not as marked as before."

Dr. Hoch also tried electroshock treatment on patients who had been given mescaline. "It did not influence the clinical symptoms at all," he reported matter-of-factly. "The patients continued to behave in the same way as prior to electroshock treatment." On the basis of these tests Hoch concluded that electroshock "has no influence on mescaline-produced mental states." He might have revised his "objective" assessment if he had taken the drug himself and had one of his assistants apply the volts while he tripped the lights fantastic. But those who secretly funded his research required only that he dish it out to mental patients and prisoners.

"An interesting theory can always outrun a set of facts," declared psychologist Audrey Holliday. She found the whole psychotomimetic approach guilty of using "unscientific and intemperate terms." Yet the semantic inaccuracies were still being bandied about even when most researchers had agreed that LSD did not really mimic endogenous schizophrenia.

Despite widespread acknowledgment that the model psychosis concept had outlived its usefulness, the psychiatric orientation articulated by those of Dr. Hoch's persuasion prevailed in the end. When it came time to lay down their hand, the medical establishment and the media both "mimicked" the line that for years had been secretly promoted by the CIA and the military—that hallucinogenic drugs were extremely dangerous because they drove people insane, and all this talk about creativity and personal growth was just a lot of hocus pocus. This perception of LSD governed the major policy decisions enacted by the FDA and the drug control apparatus in the years ahead.

The molecular structure of d-lysergic diethylamide.

Dr. Albert Hofmann, the grandfather of the acid generation in his laboratory at Sandoz Pharmaceuticals in Basel, Switzerland.
(Sandoz, AG, Basel)

CC5

SCIENTIFIC INTELLIGENCE MEMORANDUM

POTENTIAL NEW AGENT FOR UNCONVENTIONAL WARFARE

Lysergic Acid Diethylamide (LSD)
(N, N-Diethyllysergamide)

CIA/SI 101–54
5 August 1954

CENTRAL INTELLIGENCE AGENCY

OFFICE OF SCIENTIFIC INTELLIGENCE

Cover page of a once-classified CIA memorandum on LSD-25.

Richard Helms, CIA Director from 1967–1973, described LSD as "dynamite." *(AP/Wide World Photos)*

Dr. Sidney Gottlieb, chief of the CIA's Technical Service Staff, who ran the super-secret MK-ULTRA program. *(George Tames/The New York Times)*

George Hunter White, high-ranking narcotics official, shown in December 1952, when he began administering LSD to unwitting American citizens at the behest of the CIA. "It was fun, fun, fun," White said. "Where else could a red-blooded American lie, kill, cheat, and rape, with the sanction of the all-highest?" *(New York Daily News Photo)*

Major General William Creasy, chief officer of the US Army's Chemical Corps in the 1950's, preached a new military gospel of "war without death." During Congressional testimony Creasy called for the testing of hallucinogenic gases on subways in American cities. *(The New York Times)*

Captain Alfred M. Hubbard, the spy who became the first Johnny Appleseed of LSD. "If you don't think it's amazing," said Hubbard, "just go ahead and try it." *(Courtesy of Bill Darling)*

Aldous Huxley, author of *Doors of Perception*, the seminal psychedelic manifesto, and his wife, Laura. *(AP/Wide World Photos)*

Ralph Metzner (left) and Timothy Leary (right) in front of the palatial Millbrook estate. *(New York Daily News Photo)*

William Mellon Hitchcock (right), millionaire owner of Millbrook, taking part in a Tai Chi session with Leary (left) at the mansion. *(Eugene Anthony)*

The Merry Pranksters traveled across the US in a psychedelic bus in the summer of 1964. *(Eugene Anthony)*

Ken Kesey first turned on to LSD through a government-funded drug program at Stanford. *(UPI/ Bettmann Newsphotos)*

Kesey and the Pranksters hosted a series of acid tests on West Coast.

Thousands "freaked freely" at the three-day Trips Festival in Francisco, January 1966. *(Eugene Anthony)*

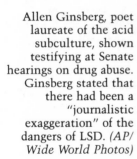

Allen Ginsberg, poet laureate of the acid subculture, shown testifying at Senate hearings on drug abuse. Ginsberg stated that there had been a "journalistic exaggeration" of the dangers of LSD. *(AP/ Wide World Photos)*

Poster announcing the first human be-in.

25,000 gathered in Golden Gate Park for the first human be-in,
January 1967. *(Eugene Anthony)*

Digger street theater in Haight-Ashbury. *(Eugene Anthony)*

Slogan adopted by the flower children.

Anti-war demonstrators at the Pentagon, October 1967. *(Paul Conklin, Time)*

Yippies Abbie Hoffman and Jerry Rubin burning money at the New York Stock Exchange. *(AP/Wide World Photos)*

Undercover police agent posing as a hippie radical. *(AP/Wide World Photos)*

Woodstock rock
festival, August 1969.
*(New York Daily
News Photo)*

Ronald Stark
manufactured 50
million hits of
black market LSD
in the late 1960's
and early 1970's. He
was later exposed as
a CIA informant by
Italian authorities.
(Ansa)

3

Under The Mushroom, Over The Rainbow

MANNA FROM HARVARD

Henry Luce, president of Time-Life, was a busy man during the Cold War. As the preeminent voice of Eisenhower, Dulles, and Pax Americana, he encouraged his correspondents to collaborate with the CIA, and his publishing empire served as a longtime propaganda asset for the Agency. But Luce managed to find the time to experiment with LSD—not for medical reasons, but simply to experience the drug and glean whatever pleasures and insights it might afford. An avid fan of psychedelics, he turned on a half-dozen times in the late 1950s and early 1960s under the supervision of Dr. Sidney Cohen. On one occasion the media magnate claimed he talked to God on the golf course and found that the Old Boy was pretty much on top of things. During another trip the tone-deaf publisher is said to have heard music so enchanting that he walked into a cactus garden and began conducting a phantom orchestra.

Dr. Cohen, attached professionally to UCLA and the Veterans Hospital in Los Angeles, also turned on Henry's wife, Clare Boothe Luce, and a number of other influential Americans. "Oh, sure, we all took acid. It was a creative group—my husband and I and Huxley and [Christopher] Isherwood," recalled Mrs. Luce, who was, by all accounts, the *grande dame* of postwar American politics. (More recently she served as a member of President Reagan's Foreign Intelligence Advisory Board, which oversees covert operations conducted by the CIA.) LSD was fine by Mrs. Luce as long as it remained strictly a drug for the doctors and their friends in the ruling class. But she didn't like the idea that others might also want to partake of the experience. "We wouldn't want everyone doing too much of a good thing," she explained.

By this time, however, psychedelic drugs already had a certain notoriety, largely due to favorable reports in Luce's publishing outlets. In May 1957 *Life* magazine ran a story on the discovery of the "magic mushroom" as part of its Great Adventure series. Written by R. Gordon Wasson, the seventeen-page spread, complete with color photos, was laudatory in every way. Wasson, a vice-president of J. P. Morgan and Company, pursued a lifelong interest in mushrooms as a personal hobby. He and his wife, Valentina, journeyed all over the world, treading a unique path through the back roads of history in an effort to learn about the role of toadstools in primitive societies. Their travels took them to the remote highlands of Mexico, where they met a medicine woman who agreed to serve them teonanacatl, or "God's flesh," as the divine mushrooms were called. As he chewed the bitter fungus, Wasson was determined to resist its effects so as to better observe the ensuing events. But as he explained to the readers of *Life*, his resolve "soon melted before the onslaught of the mushrooms."

> We were never more awake, and the visions came whether our eyes were opened or closed.... They began with art motifs, angular such as might decorate carpets or textiles or wallpaper or the drawing board of an architect. They evolved into palaces with courts, arcades, gardens—resplendent palaces all laid over with semiprecious stones.... Later it was as though the walls of our house had dissolved, and my spirit had flown forth, and I was suspended in mid-air viewing landscapes of mountains, with camel caravans advancing slowly across the slopes, the mountains rising tier above tier to the very heavens.... The thought crossed my mind: could the divine mushrooms be the secret that lay behind the ancient Mysteries? Could the miraculous mobility that I was now enjoying be the explanation for the flying witches that played so important a part in the folklore and fairy tales of northern Europe? These reflections passed through my mind at the very time that I was seeing the visions, for the effect of the mushrooms is to bring about a fission of the spirit, a split in the person, a kind of schizophrenia, with the rational side continuing to reason and to observe the sensations that the other side is enjoying. The mind is attached as by an elastic cord to the vagrant senses.

The visions lasted through the night as Wasson lay on the floor of a tiny hut enraptured by God's flesh. "For the first time," he wrote, "the word ecstasy took on real meaning. For the first time it did not mean someone else's state of mind."

Wasson's account constituted nothing less than a journalistic breakthrough. A mass audience was introduced to the mysterious world of chemical hallucinogens, and soon hundreds of people started flocking to Mexico to find their own *curandero*. At the same time Dr. Albert Hofmann conducted a chemical analysis of the divine mushroom at Sandoz Laboratories. He extracted the active ingredients and synthesized a new compound: psilocybin. Upon learning of Hofmann's achievement, the CIA immediately procured samples from Sandoz and forwarded the material to Dr. Harris Isbell at the Lexington Narcotics Hospital, where it was tested on drug addicts.

Among those whose interest was piqued by Wasson's article in *Life* was a young professor named Timothy Leary. At the time of Wasson's groundbreaking explorations, Leary was pursuing a successful career as a clinical psychologist. Between 1954 and 1959 he was director of clinical research and psychology at the Kaiser Foundation Hospital in Oakland, California. He published extensively in scientific journals and established himself as a rising star in the field of behavioral psychology. He wrote a widely acclaimed psychology textbook and devised a personality test called "The Leary," which was used by the CIA, among other organizations, to test prospective employees.

Leary's work culminated in an appointment as a lecturer at Harvard University, where students and professors had for years served as guinea pigs for CIA- and military-funded LSD experiments. His first semester at Harvard was relatively quiet compared to what lay in store; he taught his classes and collaborated on another psychology textbook. While all seemed well outwardly, Leary was beginning to have second thoughts about the career he had charted for himself in the charmed circle of academe. He was mired in a mid-life crisis stemming from two failed marriages; his first wife had committed suicide. The turning point came in the summer of 1960 while Leary, then thirty-nine years old, was vacationing at a sunny villa in Cuernavaca, Mexico. A friend procured a handful of magic mushrooms from an old Indian woman, and after a bit of prodding Leary washed them down with a few slugs of Carta Blanca. At the time Leary had not even smoked marijuana. Like many who experimented with psychedelics, he found that his first trip had a profound impact on his way of viewing the world. "It was above all and without question the deepest religious experience of my life," he wrote later. "I discovered that beauty, revelation, sensuality, the cellular history of the past, God, the Devil—all lie inside my body, outside my mind." The transcendent implications of that initial journey into inner space convinced him that the normal mind was a "static, repetitive circuit." Leary reevaluated his task as a psychologist; from then on he would dedicate his efforts to exploring substances that hinted at other realities and a new conception of the human psyche.

Leary returned to Harvard and established a psilocybin research project with the approval of Dr. Harry Murray, chairman of the Department of Social Relations. Dr. Murray, who ran the Personality Assessments section of the OSS during World War II, took a keen interest in Leary's work. He volunteered for a psilocybin session, becoming one of the first of many faculty and graduate students to sample the mushroom pill under Leary's guidance. Leary had obtained a supply from Sandoz, which distributed the new drug to researchers free of charge.

Among those most impressed by Leary's research project was Richard Alpert, an assistant professor of education and psychology at Harvard. He and Leary became partners and together set out to investigate the emotional and creative effects of the mushroom pill. At first glance they were an unlikely team, given their contrasting personalities. Alpert, the son of a wealthy New England lawyer, was ten years younger and obsessed with "making it" in the academic world. He seemed to be well on his way, having acquired all the accoutrements of success—the sports car, the cashmere sweaters, the cocktail parties, a faculty post at a prestigious university. The last thing Alpert wanted was to rock the boat and jeopardize his career.

Leary, on the other hand, always had a rebellious streak in him. His mother had dreams of his being a priest, and his father wanted him to become a career military officer. Neither wish came true. Leary passed up an opportunity to attend a Catholic seminary and dropped out of West Point after committing a rules infraction that led to the "silent treatment" (a form of ostracism) by the other cadets for nine months. He later enrolled at Alabama University to study psychology, only to be expelled for getting caught in a girls' dormitory. After a brief stint in the service Leary resumed his psychological studies, earning a doctorate from the University of California at Berkeley. And now he was ready for another tussle with the establishment. In his own words Leary was "handsome, clean-cut, witty, confident, charismatic, and in that inert culture unusually creative."

While drawing up plans for a psilocybin experiment, Leary and Alpert consulted two essays by Aldous Huxley, *The Doors of Per-*

ception and *Heaven and Hell.* By coincidence Huxley was in the area as a visiting lecturer at MIT. The elderly scholar was brought into the project, first as an adviser and then as a participant in a psilocybin experiment. He and Leary took the drug together, and after the session they spoke about what to do with this "philosopher's stone." Huxley felt the best way to bring about vast changes in society was to offer the experience to the talented, the well-born, the intelligent rich, and others in positions of influence.

When Dr. Humphry Osmond passed through Boston, Huxley took him to meet Leary. It was the night of the Kennedy election. "We rode out to his place," Osmond remembered, "and Timothy was wearing his gray-flannel suit and his crew cut. And we had a very interesting discussion with him. That evening after we left, Huxley said, 'What a nice fellow he is!' And then he remarked how wonderful it was to think that this was where it was going to be done —at Harvard. He felt that psychedelics would be good for the Academy. Whereupon I replied, 'I think he's a nice fellow, too. But don't you think he's just a little bit square?' Aldous replied, 'You may well be right. Isn't that, after all, what we want?'"

Leary was a relative latecomer to the psychedelic research scene, but right from the start he and his cohorts made no bones about where they were coming from. "We would avoid the behaviorist approach to others' awareness," Leary asserted. "We were not out to discover new laws, which is to say, to discover the redundant implications of our own premises. We were not to be limited by the pathological point of view. We were not to interpret ecstasy as mania, or calm serenity as catatonia...nor the visionary state as model psychosis."

The first formal experiment conducted by Leary's group was a pioneering venture in criminal psychology. Psilocybin was given to thirty-two inmates at the Massachusetts Correctional Institute in Concord, a maximum security prison, to determine whether the drug would help prisoners change their ways, thereby lowering the recidivism rate. At least one member of Leary's research team took psilocybin with the prisoners while another observer stayed straight for the entire session. The pilot study proved successful in the short term; only 25% of those who took the drug ended up in jail again, as compared to the normal rate of 80%.

Leary's research methodology was quite different from that of the CIA's Dr. Harris Isbell, who administered various hallucinogens, including psilocybin and LSD, to inmates at the Lexington Narcotics Hospital. Some were kept high for six weeks at a stretch. These studies were not designed to rehabilitate criminals; on the contrary, Isbell and the CIA were interested in drugging people to gather more data on the disruptive potential of mind-altering substances. Leary rejected this manipulative approach, believing that research should be conducted *with* subjects rather than *on* them. All of the Concord inmates were briefed beforehand on the effects of the drug, and Leary encouraged his test subjects to provide input and criticism during every phase of the experiment.

Another aspect of Leary's research focused on the relationship between drug-induced and naturally occurring religious experiences. In an unusual experiment he sought to determine whether the transcendent experiences reported during psychedelic sessions were similar to the mystical experiences described in various holy scriptures and reported by saints, prophets, and religious teachers throughout the ages. Although university officials refused to sponsor the experiment, Leary and his assistant, Walter Pahnke, a doctoral candidate at Harvard, proceeded to administer psilocybin to ten theology students and professors in the setting of a Good Friday service, while ten others were given placebos. It was a "double-blind" experiment in that neither Leary nor his subjects knew who was getting the mushroom pill and who was part of the control group. The results of the study were dramatic. Nine out of ten psilocybin recipients reported having an intense religious experience, but only one person from the control group could say the same. In his doctoral dissertation Pahnke concluded that the experiences described by those who had taken the drug were "indistinguishable from, if not identical with" the classical mystical experience.

"The Miracle at Marsh Chapel," as the Good Friday experiment came to be known, generated a highly charged discussion concerning the authenticity of "chemical" or "instant" mysticism. Some religious scholars, such as Walter Houston Clark, professor of the psychology of religion at Andover Newton Theological Seminary, and Huston Smith, professor of philosophy at MIT, supported Leary's contention that with the proper set and setting psychedelics could be used to produce mystical states of consciousness almost at will. These drugs were said to offer not only a means for enhancing spiritual sensitivity; they also opened up the possibility of bringing the religious experience into the laboratory, where it could be scrutinized and perhaps even explained in scientific terms.

This prospect was not greeted with hosannas by orthodox religious teachers, who denigrated the drug experience as a less genuine form of revelation. Psychedelic advocates countered that the apparent ease with which the mystical experience could be triggered by drugs did not negate its spiritual validity. On the contrary, they believed that the high incidence of drug-related religious phenomena, even in cases where an exceptional set and setting were lacking, stemmed from the fact that on a fundamental level the human mind is connected with the Infinite; psychedelics simply made manifest this basic truth. According to Leary, the personal background of the subject did not matter. "You can be a convict or a college professor," he declared. "You'll still have a mystical, transcendental experience that may change your life."

Chemical Crusaders

In addition to a series of formal studies, Leary's group also held psychedelic sessions on their own outside the university. A clinical setting was rejected in favor of the comfortable surroundings of a private apartment where subjects could relax and listen to music by candlelight. Graduate students and selected individuals from the arts were invited to participate in these off-campus experiments, and the vast majority reported positive experiences. "Anyone who wanted to take the voyage was welcome to come along," Leary said.

In December 1960 Allen Ginsberg and Peter Orlovsky arrived at Leary's house in Newton. Although Ginsberg was a veteran of psychedelic trips, he had never tried psilocybin, so when the opportunity presented itself he and Orlovsky jumped at it. The environment provided by Leary was much more congenial than the research institute in Palo Alto where Ginsberg had taken LSD the previous year. After swallowing the mushroom pills, Ginsberg became slightly nauseous, but his initial queasiness subsided as the drug took command of his being. He and Orlovsky were completely overwhelmed. They took off their clothes and padded around the house, a supernatural gleam in their eyes. Ginsberg was inundated by a rush of messianic feelings. "We're going to teach people to stop hating. . . . Start a peace and love movement," he triumphantly proclaimed.

There he stood in Leary's living room, a squinting prophet (he had removed his spectacles) ready to march through the streets stark naked and preach the coming of a new age.

Leary was not particularly enthusiastic about the prospect of one of his test subjects wandering around in public without any clothes in the middle of the winter. He convinced Ginsberg this was not the best tactic. But the beat poet was still full of fire. He wanted to get Kennedy, Khrushchev, and Mao Tse-tung on the phone in a cosmic rap session that would rid them of their petty hangups about warfare. This being impractical, he decided to call Jack Kerouac, author of *On the Road*, the bible of the beat generation. Kerouac was then living with his mother in Northport, Massachusetts. When the operator came on the line, Ginsberg identified himself as God wanting to talk to Kerouac. He repeated his name, spelling it out: G-O-D. When he realized he didn't have Kerouac's number, he shuffled through his address book and tried again. This time he reached Kerouac and insisted that he take the mushroom pills. "I can't leave my mother," Kerouac replied. Ginsberg urged him to bring his mother. Kerouac said he'd take a rain check.

As Ginsberg and Orlovsky were coming down from the six-hour psilocybin high, they put on robes and sat around the kitchen table sipping steamed milk and talking with Leary about the pills. Ginsberg had some forthright ideas about what to do with the synthetic mushroom. As far as he was concerned, psilocybin had vast implications far beyond the world of medicine; psychedelic drugs held the promise of changing mankind and ushering in a new millennium and therefore no one had the right to keep them from the average citizen.

Whereas Huxley had suggested turning on opinion leaders, Ginsberg, the quintessential egalitarian, wanted everyone to have the opportunity to take mind-expanding drugs. His plan was to tell everything, to disseminate as much information as possible. The time was ripe to launch a psychedelic crusade—and what better place to start than Harvard University, the alma mater of president-elect John F. Kennedy? Leary seemed ideally suited to lead such a campaign. A respected academic, he had short hair, wore button-down shirts, and took his role as a scientist quite seriously. How ironic, Ginsberg noted, "that the very technology stereotyping our consciousness and desensitizing our perceptions should throw up its own antidote.... Given such historic Comedy, who should emerge from Harvard University but the one and only Dr. Leary, a respectable human being, a worldly man faced with the task of a Messiah."

Ginsberg's vision of a historic movement that would transform human consciousness struck a responsive chord in Leary. "We were thinking far-out history thoughts at Harvard," the LSD doctor recalled, "believing that it was time (after the shallow and nostalgic fifties) for far-out visions, knowing that America had run out of philosophy, that a new empirical, tangible metaphysics was desperately needed; knowing in our hearts that the old mechanical myths had died at Hiroshima, that the past was over, and that politics could not fill the spiritual vacuum." Leary felt that the limited vision of reality prevailing in modern society was partly attributable to the dominant drugs, alcohol and coffee. Change the drugs, and a change of heart would naturally follow: "Politics, religion, economics, social structure, are based on shared states of consciousness. The cause of social conflict is usually neurological. The cure is biochemical."

The task that lay before them was formidable. Ginsberg pulled out his little black address book and began reeling off the names of people they could turn on: painters, poets, publishers, musicians, and so on. In addition to being one of the most important poets of his time, Ginsberg was a cultural ambassador of sorts. He traveled in various circles, and his contacts were international in scope. He would carry the message to everyone he knew.

Ginsberg was off and running. He returned to New York armed with a stash of psilocybin. At the Five Spot in Greenwich Village he gave the mushroom pills to Theolonius Monk, the great jazz pianist. A few days later Ginsberg dropped by Monk's apartment to check on the results. Monk peered out from behind a crack in the door, smiled, and asked if he had anything stronger. Ginsberg also turned on Dizzy Gillespie, who was evidently quite pleased by the gesture. "Oh yeah," he laughed, "anything that gets you high."

In a sense it was Ginsberg's way of returning a historical favor; the jazz musicians had given marijuana to the beats, and now the beats were turning the jazz cats on to psychedelics. Word of the new drugs spread quickly through the jazz scene, and numerous musicians, including many of the preeminent players in the field, experimented with psychedelics in the early 1960s. John Coltrane, the acknowledged master of the tenor saxophone, took LSD and reported upon returning from his inner voyage that he "perceived the interrelationship of all life forms."

It was through Ginsberg that the existence of Leary's research project came to the attention of the beat network. When Neal Cassady heard about the mushroom pills, he bolted up to Cambridge for a session with the professor. "It's philosophical!" Cassady exclaimed. "This is the Rolls Royce of dope, the ultimate high." Kerouac arranged to sample the mushroom extract without leaving his mother. A "Dear Coach" letter from Kerouac to Leary described his experience tripping at her house on the day President Kennedy was inaugurated.

> Mainly I felt like a floating Khan on a magic carpet with my interesting lieutenants and gods.... We were at the extremist point goofing on clouds watching the movie of existence.... Everybody seemed innocent. . . . It was a definite Satori. Full of psychic clairvoyance (but you must remember that this is not half as good as the peaceful ecstasy of simple Samadhi trance as I described it in *Dharma Bums*).... The faculty of remembering names and what one has learned is heightened so fantastically that we could develop the greatest scholars and scientists in the world with this stuff.

The letter was signed, "Well, okay. Touch football sometime?"

Another writer Ginsberg brought into Leary's circle was the poet Charles Olson, formerly rector of Black Mountain College in North Carolina. A man of overpowering intellect, Olson was fifty years old at the time of his psychedelic initiation. He stood a towering six feet seven inches, had unruly strands of white hair, and spoke in a deep resonant voice. Olson remembered the first time he tried psilocybin: "I was so high on bourbon that I took it as though it was a bunch of peanuts. I kept throwing the peanuts—and the mushroom—into my mouth." He described the experience as "a love feast, a truth pill...it makes you exactly what you are."

Olson had a strong affinity for the mushroom. He thought it a "wretched shame that we don't have it in the common drugstore as a kind of beer, because it's so obviously an attractive and useful, normal food." But he also sensed immediately that psychedelics were a profound threat to the status quo. After the drug wore off, his first words to Leary were, "When they come after you, you can hide at my house." Leary, being an apolitical creature, shrugged off the remark without much thought. Little did he know that the CIA was already keeping an eye on his escapades at Harvard.

Olson admired Leary for his chutzpah, but he also considered the good professor a bit foolhardy in thinking that happiness would descend in one fell swoop if the world was suddenly bemushroomed.

80

"Leary used to argue that this was the decade of the mushroom," Olson commented, "and if we didn't get peace from turning everybody on, the race would be destroyed.... I myself think that was rather thin politics to begin with."

In retrospect Ginsberg admitted, "We were probably too proselytizing." It may have been his messianic enthusiasm that rankled Robert Lowell, the New England poet and Pulitzer Prize winner, who was turned on to psilocybin by Ginsberg. Lowell did not report favorably at the end of the session in his apartment. As Ginsberg was leaving, he tried to reassure Lowell by telling him, "Love conquers all." To which the distinguished poet replied, "Don't be too sure." Writer Arthur Koestler was also critical of the mushroom experience. "This is wonderful, no doubt," he told Leary the day after he tripped. "But it is fake, ersatz. Instant mysticism.... There's no wisdom there. I solved the secret of the universe last night, but this morning I forgot what it was."

But the sternest rebuke to the high-flying optimism of the Harvard group was yet to come. Leary was eager for William Burroughs to take the mushroom pills. Burroughs, author of *Naked Lunch*, was something of a mentor to the beat generation. In the summer of 1961 Leary traveled to Tangiers, where Burroughs was living at the time. He was working on a new novel, *The Soft Machine*, smoking a considerable amount of Moroccan kif, and experimenting with a flicker machine developed by his friend Byron Gysin that caused hallucinations similar to mescaline or LSD. The poets Alan Ansen and Gregory Corso were there for the session along with Leary and Ginsberg. Things got off to a swimming start as they sauntered in the warm moonlight high on psilocybin. But the mood quickly changed once it became apparent that the mushroom was not to Burroughs's liking. "No good, no bueno," he kept shaking his head. He split from the others and waited out the "high" in seclusion.

Burroughs was never into drugs simply for a good time. Despite his psilocybin bummer he agreed to go to Cambridge to participate in further experiments in consciousness alteration. Burroughs looked forward to working with sensory deprivation and submersion tanks, stroboscopes, machines to measure brain waves, and all the technical wonders that a prestigious university could supply. But his hopes were dashed as soon as he arrived at Harvard. All he found was a semipermanent cocktail party with a bunch of starry-eyed intellectuals talking some half-assed jive about brotherly love. Leary

81

kept touting psilocybin as an enlightenment pill, a cure-all for a sick society. To Burroughs, this view was far too simplistic. While agreeing that hallucinogenic drugs could open the doors of perception, he recognized that only the deliberate cultivation of new habits of consciousness could endow such visions with enduring significance. "Remember, anything that can be done chemically can be done in other ways," he insisted. "You don't need drugs to get high, but drugs do serve as a useful shortcut at certain stages of training." Burroughs had already tried drugs as a means of self-realization and was attempting to move on. After a short stint in Cambridge he dropped out of the psychedelic clan for good.

Burroughs was acutely aware of the darker side of American politics, and he had some ominous premonitions about the impending psychedelic revolution. Despite rampant enthusiasm for hallucinogens among his peers, he suspected that sinister forces were also interested in these drugs and that Leary and his sidekicks might be playing right into their hands. Burroughs feared that psychedelics could be used to control rather than liberate the vision-starved masses. He understood that the seeker of enlightenment was especially vulnerable to manipulation from without, and he sounded an urgent warning to this effect in the opening passages of *Nova Express*, published in 1964.

> At the immediate risk of finding myself the most unpopular character of all fiction—and history is fiction—I must say this:
> Bring together state of news—Inquire onward from state to doer—Who monopolized Immortality? Who monopolized Cosmic Consciousness? Who monopolized Love Sex and Dream? Who monopolized Time Life and Fortune? Who took from you what is yours? . . . Listen: Their Garden of Delights is a terminal sewer. . . . Their Immortality Cosmic Consciousness and Love is second-run grade-B shit. . . . Stay out of the Garden of Delights. . . . Throw back their ersatz Immortality. . . . Flush their drug kicks down the drain—*They are poisoning and monopolizing the hallucinogenic drugs—learn to make it without any chemical corn.*

Shortly after Burroughs left Cambridge another figure arrived on the scene who was destined to up the ante considerably. His name was Michael Hollingshead, and he had a profound impact on Leary and his cohorts. An artful Englishman with a keen sense of humor, Hollingshead had once worked for the British Cultural Exchange. While living in New York City, he acquired a full gram of LSD-25 (enough for ten thousand doses), which he divided with his associate

Dr. John Beresford. They mixed the LSD with powdered sugar and distilled water, tasting the divine confection as they spooned it into a mayonnaise jar. Hollingshead had smoked grass and hashish before, but this was another matter entirely. The doors of perception not only swung wide open, they flew off the jambs: "What I had experienced was the equivalent of death's absolution of the body. I had literally stepped forth from the shell of my body into some other strange land of unlikeness which can only be grasped in terms of astonishment and mystery, an ecstatic nirvana."

When he came down from his initial psychedelic voyage, he called Aldous Huxley to ask his advice about what to do with the magic gram of acid. At that point Hollingshead was unsure whether LSD was more confusing than illuminating. The drug had disrupted his sense of self: "The reality on which I had consciously based my personality had dissolved into maya, a hallucinatory facade. Stripped of one kind of reality, and unwilling or unable to benefit from the possibilities of another one, I was acutely aware of my helplessness, my utter transience, my suspension between two worlds, one outside and the other wholly within." Moreover, he was financially destitute and his marriage was falling apart. Huxley was sympathetic. He suggested that Hollingshead go to Harvard and meet Timothy Leary. If there was any single investigator in the United States worth seeing, Huxley assured him, it was Dr. Leary.

Hollingshead took off for Cambridge with his mayonnaise jar. Leary went out of his way to help his visitor. He offered Hollingshead a free room in his attic, loaned him some money, and invited him to join the psilocybin research team. Naturally Leary gave his guest a mushroom session, and though Hollingshead had a good trip, the drug was not as strong as LSD. Hollingshead obliged by offering his host some acid, but Leary was not eager to take it. He was apparently of the opinion that if you had tried one psychedelic you had tried them all.

One night Hollingshead was driving around outside Leary's house with Maynard Ferguson, the trumpet player, and his wife, Flo. They were smoking a joint in the car because illegal drugs were not allowed inside. Hollingshead told them about LSD, and they became very curious. Eventually he fetched his mayonnaise jar, and they all took a hit. Within an hour the drug had started to come on. Flo thought it was fantastic, and Maynard had to agree; it definitely got you there. When Leary noticed that Ferguson's face was glowing like an electric toaster, he decided to join them. He took a heaping spoonful, and soon he was flying.

> It came sudden and irresistible. An endless deep swamp marsh of some other planet teeming and steaming with energy and life, and in the swamp an enormous tree whose branches were foliated out miles high and miles wide. And then this tree, like a cosmic vacuum cleaner, went ssssuuuck, and every cell in my body was swept into the root, twigs, branches, and leaves of this tree. Tumbling and spinning, down the soft fibrous avenues to some central point which was just light. Just light, but not just light. It was the center of Life. A burning, dazzling, throbbing, radiant core, pure pulsing, exulting light. An endless flame that contained everything— sound, touch, cell, seed, sense, soul, sleep, glory, glorifying, God, the hard eye of God. Merged with this pulsing flame it was possible to look out and see and participate in the entire cosmic drama.

Leary was stunned by the power of the drug. In the wake of his first acid trip he wandered about dazed and confused. What to do, he asked himself, now that the mundane routines of life seemed so futile and artificial? Not knowing quite where to turn, he latched onto Hollingshead as his guru. Leary followed him around for days on end, treating the Englishman with awe. He was convinced that this pot-bellied, chain-smoking prankster whose face was pink-veined from alcohol was a messenger from the Good Lord Himself. Richard Alpert and Ralph Metzner, two of Leary's closest associates, were vexed to see him in such a helpless state. They thought he had really blown his mind, and they blamed Hollingshead. But it was only a matter of time before they too sampled the contents of the mayonnaise jar. Hollingshead gave the drug to all the members of the psilocybin project, and from then on LSD was part of their research repertoire.

Those early days at Harvard were charged with a special mystery and excitement. "Turning on" had not yet become identified with a particular lifestyle or set of values, and there were no maps or guideposts to chart the way. To those who embarked upon these shattering inner journeys, anything and everything seemed possible. It was as if all the fetters were suddenly removed. "LSD involved risk," Hollingshead said. "It was anarchistic; it upset our applecarts, torpedoed our cherished illusions, sabotaged our beliefs.... Yet there were some of my circle who, with Rimbaud, could say, 'I dreamed of crusades, senseless voyages of discovery, republics without a history, moral revolution, displacement of races and continents. I believed in all the magics.'"

Not everyone was enchanted by the renegade psychedelic scene at Harvard. A confidential memorandum issued by the CIA's Office of Security, which had utilized LSD for interrogation purposes since the early 1950s, suggested that certain CIA-connected personnel might be involved with Leary's group. This prospect was disconcerting to Security officials, who considered hallucinogenic drugs "extremely dangerous." "Uncontrolled experimentation has in the past resulted in tragic circumstances and for this reason every effort is made to control any involvement with these drugs," a CIA agent reported. The document concluded with a specific directive: "Information concerning the use of this type of drug for experimental or personal reasons should be reported immediately....In addition, any information of Agency personnel involved with...Drs. ALPERT or LEARY, or with any other group engaged in this type of activity should also be reported."

It is known that during this period Leary gave LSD to Mary Pinchot, a painter and a prominent Washington socialite who was married to Cord Meyer, a high-level CIA official. (Meyer oversaw the CIA's infiltration of the US National Student Association and the Congress for Cultural Freedom in Europe, which provided financial support to numerous Cold War liberal intellectuals and writers.) Leary and Pinchot struck up a cordial friendship during her occasional visits to Cambridge in the early 1960s. She asked him to teach her how to guide an LSD session so she could introduce the drug to her circles in Washington. "I have this friend who's a very important man," she confided to Leary. "He's very impressed with what I've told him about my own LSD experience and what other people have told him. He wants to try it himself." Leary was intrigued, but Pinchot wouldn't tell him who she intended to turn on. Nor did she inform her LSD mentor of her marriage to a CIA bigwig.

Leary explained the basic rules about set and setting, emphasizing the importance of a comfortable, sensuous environment for an LSD trip. From time to time Pinchot reported back to him. "I can't give you all the details," she said, "but top people in Washington are turning on. You'd be amazed at the sophistication of some of our leaders. We're getting a little group together . . ." Leary had no way of knowing that Mary Pinchot was one of President Kennedy's girlfriends and that she and JFK smoked pot together in the White House. Pinchot was murdered less than a year after Kennedy was assassinated, and her diary disappeared from her home.

When Leary learned of Pinchot's death, he recalled their conversations about LSD. At various times she had hinted that the CIA was monitoring his activities. Since drug research is of vital importance to American intelligence, Pinchot told him that he'd be allowed to conduct his experiments as long as it didn't get out of hand.

But Leary ignored her advice. In the spring of 1962 he published an article in the *Journal of Atomic Scientists* warning that the Russians might try to subvert the United States by dumping a few pounds of LSD into the water supply of major cities. The only way to prepare for such an attack, Leary maintained, was to dose our own reservoirs first as a civil defense measure so that people would know what to expect. Not surprisingly, this suggestion didn't go over well in the scientific community. A number of CIA- and military-sponsored researchers launched vociferous attacks on Leary and Alpert. Dr. Henry Beecher, an esteemed member of the Harvard Medical School faculty who conducted drug experiments for the CIA, ridiculed Leary's research methodology, stating that it reminded him "of De Quincey's *Confessions of an Opium Eater...* rather than a present-day scientific study of subjective responses to drugs." Dr. Max Rinkel, a veteran of the CIA's MK-ULTRA program, denounced Leary in the *Harvard Alumni Review*, as did Dr. Robert Heath, a longtime CIA and army contract employee. As Heath saw it, the whole notion of consciousness expansion was a meaningless abstraction, and impairing the human nervous system with dangerous chemicals could only result in pathological states that might have long-term negative repercussions.

As word of Leary's acid escapades spread around Harvard, university officials began to get edgy. Tensions reached a boiling point during a faculty meeting in March 1962. Leary's opponents charged that he conducted his drug studies in a nonchalant and irresponsible fashion. Specifically they cited the fact that trained physicians were rarely present; moreover, Leary himself got high with his test subjects. While admitting that he was operating outside the medical framework, Leary stuck to his guns and emphasized that taking LSD with a patient was common practice among many psychiatrists. Besides, since psychedelics were educational as well as medical tools, they should be made available outside the medical profession for investigatory purposes. Just because someone was a physician did not mean he was qualified to administer LSD, Leary argued, especially if he had never tried the drug himself.

Although Leary's volunteers rarely suffered untoward effects, a number of faculty members still had grave misgivings about the psilocybin project. As Dr. Herbert Kelman, recipient of a small grant from the CIA-connected Human Ecology Fund, put it at the meeting, "I question whether this project is being pursued as an intellectual endeavor or whether it is being pursued as a new kind of experience to offer an answer to man's ills."

The following day a sensationalized account of the faculty tussle appeared in the *Harvard Crimson*, the school newspaper. The story was immediately picked up by the Boston press, prompting an investigation by the US Food and Drug Administration, which assisted the CIA's drug testing efforts. A month later Leary was notified that he could not continue his research unless a medical doctor was present when the drugs were administered. LSD, the FDA maintained, was too powerful and unpredictable to be left in the hands of irresponsible individuals, especially when they advocated using it not for scientific or medical purposes but to conjure up so-called religious experiences.

In effect the government had sided with the medical establishment, thereby legitimizing it as the sole authority on these matters. Leary and Alpert were ordered to surrender their supply of psilocybin to the university health service, and a special faculty committee was formed to advise and oversee future experiments. By the end of the year the psilocybin project had been officially terminated. "These drugs apparently cause panic and temporary insanity in many officials who have not taken them," Leary quipped as he grudgingly forked over his stash. The rebellious professor felt that the doctors had a vested interest in keeping psychedelics out of the hands of laymen. He accused the government and the medical establishment of conspiring to suppress valuable methods of research.

Leary's rambunctious style infuriated members of the academic community. Even some of his would-be allies suggested that he tone it down a bit. They feared that his antics might jeopardize other psychedelic researchers. This was also the opinion of Captain Al Hubbard, the incorrigible superspy who visited Leary at Harvard. "I liked Tim when we first met," Hubbard recalled, "but I warned him a dozen times." In no uncertain terms the Captain told Leary to keep his research respectable, to play ball with the system. Hubbard was keenly aware of the potency of Harvard's name and tried to lend a hand by supplying drugs to the young professor. But eventually the two LSD pioneers had a falling-out. "I gave stuff to Leary," said the Captain, "and he turned out to be completely no good....He seemed like a well-intentioned person, but then he went overboard."

The dispute over Leary's research methodology quickly became tangled up with reports that sugar cubes laced with LSD were circulating on the Harvard campus. Unconfirmed stories about wild LSD parties and undergraduates pushing trips on the black market were rife. Leary did little to placate his superiors. "LSD is so powerful," he observed wryly, "that one administered dose can start a thousand rumors." While Leary was never directly accused of dealing drugs, his reputation as a freewheeling and euphoric type led many to assume that he was connected with the underground supply. It was a case of guilt by alleged association, and it proved to be the straw that broke the camel's back.

In May 1963 Richard Alpert was summarily dismissed from his teaching post for violating an agreement not to give LSD to undergraduate students. It was the first time a Harvard faculty member had been fired in the twentieth century. "Some day it will be quite humorous," he told a reporter, "that a professor was fired for supplying a student with 'the most profound educational experience in my life.' That's what he told the Dean it was." A few days later the academic axe fell on Leary as well, after he failed to attend an honors program committee meeting—a rather paltry excuse, but by this time the university higher-ups were glad to get rid of him on any pretext.

Leary was unruffled by the turn of events. LSD, he stated tersely, was "more important than Harvard." He and Alpert fired off a declaration to the *Harvard Review* blasting the university as "the Establishment's apparatus for training consciousness contractors," an "intellectual ministry of defense." The Harvard scandal was hot news. In the coming months most of the major US magazines featured stories on LSD and its foremost proponent. Leary was suddenly "Mr. LSD," and he welcomed the publicity. The extensive media coverage doubtless spurred the growth of the psychedelic underground.

Rebuffed by the academic and medical authorities, Leary decided to take his case directly to the people—in particular, young people.

He was convinced that the revelation and revolution were at hand. The hope for the future rested on a simple equation: the more who turned on, the better. It would be a twentieth-century remake of the Children's Crusade, with legions of stoned youth marching ever onward to the Promised Land. Leary would assume the role of High Priest, urging his brethren to "turn on, tune in, and drop out." With the help of the media his gospel would ring throughout the land. "From this time on," he said, "we saw ourselves as unwitting agents of a social process that was far too powerful for us to control or to more than dimly understand."

The Crackdown

When LSD was first introduced to the United States in 1949, it was well received by the scientific community. Within less than a decade the drug had risen to a position of high standing among psychiatrists. LSD therapy was by no means a fad or a fly-by-night venture. More than one thousand clinical papers were written on the subject, discussing some forty thousand patients. Favorable results were reported when LSD was used to treat severely resistant psychiatric conditions, such as frigidity and other sexual aberrations. A dramatic decrease in autistic symptoms was observed in severely withdrawn children following the administration of LSD. The drug was also found to ease the physical and psychological distress of terminal cancer patients, helping them come to terms with the anguish and mystery of death.* And chronic alcoholics continued to benefit from psychedelic therapy. One enthusiastic researcher went so far as to suggest that with LSD it might be possible to clean out skid row in Los Angeles.

The rate of recovery or significant improvement was often higher with LSD therapy than with traditional methods. Furthermore, its risks were slim compared to the dangers of other commonly used and officially sanctioned procedures such as electroshock, lobotomy, and the so-called anti-psychotic drugs. Dr. Sidney Cohen, the man who turned on Henry and Clare Boothe Luce, attested to the virtues of LSD after conducting an in-depth survey of US and Canadian psychiatrists who had used it as a therapeutic tool. Forty-four doctors

---

*The CIA used terminal cancer patients as guinea pigs for testing knockout drugs and psychochemical weapons under the rubric of Operation MK-ULTRA.

replied to Cohen's questionnaire, providing data on five thousand patients who had taken a total of more than twenty-five thousand doses of either LSD or mescaline. The most frequent complaint voiced by psychedelic therapists was "unmanageability." Only eight instances of "psychotic reaction lasting more than forty-eight hours" were reported in the twenty-five thousand cases surveyed. Not a single case of addiction was indicated, nor any deaths from toxic effects. On the basis of these findings Cohen maintained that "with the proper precautions psychedelics are safe when given to a selected healthy group."

By the early 1960s it appeared that LSD was destined to find a niche on the pharmacologist's shelf. But then the fickle winds of medical policy began to shift. Spokesmen for the American Medical Association (AMA) and the Food and Drug Administration started to denounce the drug, and psychedelic therapy quickly fell into public and professional disrepute. Granted, a certain amount of intransigence arises whenever a new form of treatment threatens to steal the thunder from more conventional methods, but this alone cannot account for the sudden reversal of a promising trend that was ten years in the making.

One reason the medical establishment had such a difficult time coping with the psychedelic evidence was that LSD could not be evaluated like most other drugs. LSD was not a medication in the usual sense; it wasn't guaranteed to relieve a specific symptom such as a cold or headache. In this respect psychedelics were out of kilter with the basic assumptions of Western medicine. The FDA's relationship with this class of chemicals became even more problematic in light of claims that LSD could help the healthy. Most doctors automatically dismissed the notion that drugs might benefit someone who was not obviously ailing.

In 1962 Congress enacted regulations that required the safety and efficacy of a new drug to be proven with respect to the condition for which it was to be marketed commercially. LSD, according to the FDA, did not satisfy these criteria. From then on, authorized distribution of the drug was tightly controlled. Anyone who wanted to work with LSD had to receive special permission from the FDA. The restrictive measures were supposedly designed to weed out "the bad apples," as one report put it, and thereby insure against the misuse of regulated substances. The FDA maintained that it did not want to inhibit legitimate researchers who were "sensitive to their scientific integrity and moral and ethical responsibilities."

By designating LSD an "experimental drug," the FDA had in effect ruled that it could only be used for research purposes and never as part of general psychiatric practice. Consequently it became nearly impossible for psychiatrists to obtain psychedelics legally. Some of the most distinguished and experienced investigators were forced to abandon their work, and the conditions that might have demonstrated LSD's therapeutic potential virtually ceased to exist. "It was a very intense period," Dr. Oscar Janiger recalled. "The drug experience brought together many people of diverse interests. We built up a sizeable amount of data...and then the whole thing just fell in on us. Many who formerly were regarded as groundbreakers making an important contribution suddenly found themselves disenfranchised."

Certain officials suggested that those who practiced psychedelic therapy were themselves to blame for the crackdown on LSD research. In a thinly veiled reference to Leary, Drs. Jonathan Cole and Robert Katz of the National Institutes for Mental Health expressed concern that some investigators "may have been subject to the deleterious and seductive effects of these agents." AMA president Roy Grinkler harped on the same theme, proclaiming, "At one time it was impossible to find an investigator willing to work with LSD-25 who was not himself an 'addict.'"

As far as Grinkler was concerned, the elimination of psychedelic studies was necessary to insure the health and safety of the American public. In a widely circulated editorial that echoed the psychosis-producing view of hallucinogens, the AMA president stated, "Latent psychotics are disintegrating under the influence of even single doses; long-continued LSD experiences are subtly creating a psychopathology. Psychic addiction is being developed." He issued an urgent warning to the psychiatric profession that "greater morbidity, and even mortality, is in store for patients unless controls are developed against the unwise use of LSD-25."

Many LSD researchers were quick to point an accusing finger at Leary for bringing the government's wrath down on everybody. But is it plausible that one wayward individual was single-handedly responsible for provoking a 180-degree shift in official government policy with respect to psychedelic research? Was the FDA simply overreacting to Leary's flamboyant style, or were there other forces at work?

Up until the early 1960s LSD studies had flourished without government restrictions and the CIA had sponsored numerous research projects to enhance its mind control capabilities. In 1962, however, the Technical Services Staff, which ran the MK-ULTRA program, began to orient its behavioral activities exclusively toward operations and away from peripheral long-range studies. This new strategy resulted in the withdrawal of support for many academics and private researchers. Extensive LSD testing was no longer a top priority for the MK-ULTRA crew, which had already learned enough about the drug to understand how it could best be applied in selected covert operations. They had given up on the notion that LSD was "the secret that was going to unlock the universe." While acid was still an important part of the cloak-and-dagger arsenal, by this time the CIA and the army had developed a series of superhallucinogens such as the highly touted BZ, which was thought to hold greater promise as a mind control weapon.

The CIA and the military were not inhibited by the new drug laws enacted during the early 1960s. A special clause in the regulatory policy allowed the FDA to issue "selective exemptions," which meant that favored researchers would not be subject to restrictive measures. With this convenient loophole the FDA never attempted to oversee in-house pharmacological research conducted by the CIA and the military services. Secret arrangements were made whereby these organizations did not even have to file a formal "Claim for Exemption," or IND request. The FDA simply ignored all studies that were classified for reasons of national security, and CIA and military investigators were given free reign to conduct their covert experimentation. Apparently, in the eyes of the FDA, those seeking to develop hallucinogens as weapons were somehow more "sensitive to their scientific integrity and moral and ethical responsibilities" than independent researchers dedicated to exploring the therapeutic potential of LSD.

In 1965 Congress passed the Drug Abuse Control Amendments, which resulted in even tighter restrictions on psychedelic research. The illicit manufacture and sale of LSD was declared a misdemeanor (oddly enough, possession was not yet outlawed). All investigators without IND exemptions were required to turn in their remaining supplies to the FDA, which retained legal jurisdiction over psychedelics. Adverse publicity forced Sandoz to stop marketing LSD entirely in April 1966, and the number of research projects fell to a mere handful.

The decision to curtail LSD experimentation was the subject of a congressional probe into the organization and coordination of federal drug research and regulatory programs. The inquiry in the spring of 1966 was led by Senator Robert Kennedy (D-N.Y.), whose wife, Ethel, reportedly underwent LSD therapy with Dr. Ross MacLean (a close associate of Captain Hubbard's) at Hollywood Hospital in Vancouver. Senator Kennedy asked officials of the FDA and the NIMH to explain why so many LSD projects were suddenly canned. When they evaded the issue, Kennedy became annoyed. "Why if they were worthwhile six months ago, why aren't they worthwhile now?" he demanded repeatedly. The dialogue seesawed back and forth, but no satisfactory answer was forthcoming. "Why didn't you just let them continue?" asked the senator. "We keep going around and around.... If I could get a flat answer about that I would be happy. Is there a misunderstanding about my question?"

Kennedy insinuated that the regulatory agencies were attempting to thwart potentially valuable research. He stressed the importance of a balanced outlook with respect to LSD: "I think we have given too much emphasis and so much attention to the fact that it can be dangerous and that it can hurt an individual who uses it... that perhaps to some extent we have lost sight of the fact that it can be very, very helpful in our society if used properly."

Kennedy's plea fell on deaf ears. The FDA steadfastly refused to alter the course it had chosen. In 1967 a Psychotomimetic Advisory Committee (a joint FDA/NIMH venture) was established to process all research applications. Members of this committee included Dr. Harris Isbell and Dr. Carl Pfeiffer, two longtime CIA contract employees. Shortly thereafter the NIMH terminated its last in-house LSD project involving human subjects. In 1968 the Drug Abuse Control Amendments were modified to make possession of LSD a misdemeanor and sale a felony. Responsibility for enforcing the law was shifted from the FDA to the newly formed Bureau of Narcotics and Dangerous Drugs. Two years later psychedelic drugs were placed in the Schedule I category—a classification reserved for drugs of abuse that have no medical value.

While aboveground research was being phased out, the CIA and the military continued to experiment with an ever more potent variety of hallucinogens.* In effect the policies of the regulatory agencies were themselves "regulated" by the unique requirements of these secret programs. As an official of the Department of Health, Education and Welfare (of which the FDA was part) explained, "We are abdicating our statutory responsibilities in this area out of a desire to be courteous to the Department of Defense...rather than out of legal inability to handle classified materials." The same courtesy was proffered to the CIA. The FDA collaborated with the Agency in other ways as well. FDA personnel with special security clearances served as consultants for chemical warfare projects. Information concerning new developments in the field of psychopharmacology was exchanged through confidential channels. The FDA also provided laboratory facilities and samples of new drugs that might prove useful to the CIA.

In light of the FDA's relationship with the intelligence community, it is highly unlikely that a major policy decision regarding LSD would have been made against the wishes of the CIA. If the Agency had wanted aboveground LSD studies to proliferate, they would have. But this type of research was no longer essential as far as the CIA was concerned. The spymasters viewed LSD as a strategic substance, as well as a threat to national security, by virtue of its psychotomimetic properties, which had been fully explored during the 1950s. Creative or therapeutic considerations were not part of the covert game plan. When push came to shove, the medical establishment implemented a policy based on the psychosis-producing view—that is to say, the CIA's view—of hallucinogens, even though this perspective was vigorously contested by many scientists.

By the early 1960s, when the new regulatory policy was enacted, a large number of people had already heard about LSD. Some were

---

*During this period the Army Chemical Corps and the CIA's Office of Research and Development initiated a project to create new compounds "that could be used offensively." A major portion of the OFTEN/CHICKWIT Program, as the joint effort was called, was geared toward incapacitants. A CIA memo dated March 8, 1971, indicates that a backlog of more than twenty-six thousand drugs had been acquired "for future screening." Information gathered from this screening process was catalogued and data-banked in a "large, closely held" computer system that monitored worldwide developments in pharmacology. Under the auspices of OFTEN/CHICKWIT at least seven hallucinogens similar to BZ were tested; inmates at Holmsburg prison in Pennsylvania were used as test subjects for some of the drugs. Very little is known about these experiments, although CIA documents mention "several laboratory accidents" in which a drug designated EA-3167 produced "prolonged psychotic effects in laboratory personnel."

eager to try the drug, but they no longer had access to psychedelic therapists, who were the original "gatekeepers," so to speak. "The whole thing was just moving geometrically," Dr. Oscar Janiger recalled. "Obviously those people who couldn't get it from us would be seeking to get it elsewhere." A certain momentum had been generated—thanks in no small part to the CIA—and it quickly reached a point where the government could no longer contain it. Black market acid began to turn up on the street to meet the growing demand. This remarkable social phenomenon continued to gather strength despite the repeated admonitions of educators, doctors and politicians. Soon the "laboratory" would stretch across the entire continent as millions of young investigators undertook their own experiments with this consciousness-quaking chemical.

4

Preaching LSD

HIGH SURREALISM

After their expulsion from Harvard, Leary and Alpert were determined to carry out additional studies in the religious use of psychedelic drugs. They set up a grassroots nonprofit group called the International Federation for Internal Freedom (IFIF), whose ranks quickly swelled to three thousand dues-paying members. Local offices sprang up in Boston, New York, and Los Angeles. IFIF believed that everyone should be allowed to use mind-expanding chemicals because the "internal freedom" they provided was a personal and not a governmental matter. They envisioned a society in which large numbers of people would seek higher consciousness, ecstasy, and enlightenment through hallucinogens. "It's only a matter of time," Leary stated confidently, "until the psychedelic experience will be accepted. We see ourselves as modest heros, an educational tool to facilitate the development of new social forms.... We're simply trying to get back to man's sense of nearness to himself and others, the sense of social reality which civilized man has lost. We're in step with the basic needs of the human race, and those who oppose us are *far out*."

In the summer of 1963 IFIF moved its headquarters to a hotel in Zihuatanejo, Mexico, a lush tropical paradise two hundred miles north of Acapulco. There they sponsored an experiment in transcendental living based on the utopian writings and visionary insights of Aldous Huxley. Leary invited Dr. Albert Hofmann to participate in a seminar on drug research at the hotel, emphasizing that broadcast and print journalists from the most important mass media would be present. Hofmann demurred; he was disturbed by Leary's publicity-conscious approach. Huxley declined an offer to join the fledgling movement on similar grounds. He was seriously ill at the time. On November 22, the same day President Kennedy was assassinated, Huxley passed away after receiving his last request: an intravenous injection of LSD-25 given by his wife. As she administered the psychedelic, Laura Huxley saw "this immense expression of complete bliss and love." She whispered, "Light and free you let go, darling, forward and up...you are going toward the light."

During its short but spectacular career the chemical utopia at Zihuatanejo was deluged with over five thousand applicants—far more than IFIF could handle. The group's activities revolved around a tower on the beach in which at least one person at all times maintained a solemn vigil while high on LSD. The ritual changing of the guard took place at sunrise and sunset, and to be chosen for a stretch in the tower was considered a privilege. Beatnik and bohemian types were not allowed to participate in the program, but that did not stop them from pitching tents nearby. Smoking marijuana and lounging in the sun, these scruffy uninvited guests did little to enhance IFIF's reputation; nor did rumors of the all-night orgies that were supposedly commonplace in the hotel. Scarcely six weeks after they had arrived, lurid reports in the Mexican press led to the expulsion of the LSD colonists.

Leary and Alpert returned to the US with their small but energetic band of followers and began to look for an alternative base of operations. During this period they rubbed shoulders with some of the richest jet-setters on the Eastern seaboard, including William Mellon Hitchcock, a tall, handsome stockbroker in his twenties. Hitchcock was the grandson of William Larimer Hitchcock, founder of Gulf Oil, and a nephew of Pittsburgh financier Andrew Mellon, who served as treasury secretary during Prohibition.

Thanks to a sizable inheritance and a family trust fund that provided him with $15,000 *per week* in spending money, Billy Hitchcock was in a position to offer a lot more than moral support to the psychedelic movement. He first turned on to LSD after his sister, Peggy, the director of IFIF's New York branch, introduced him to Leary. They hit it off immediately, and Hitchcock made his family's four-thousand-acre estate in Dutchess County, New York, available to the psychedelic clan for a nominal five-hundred-dollar monthly rent. At the center of the estate sat a turreted sixty-four-room mansion known as Millbrook, surrounded by polo fields, stables, beautiful pine forests, tennis courts, a lake, a large gatehouse, and a picturesque fountain. Two hours from New York City by car, this idyllic spread served as the grand backdrop for the next phase of the chemical crusade.

With a new headquarters at Millbrook, IFIF was disbanded and replaced by another organization, the Castalia Foundation, named after the intellectual colony in Hermann Hesse's *The Glass Bead Game*. Leary, a great fan of Hesse, felt that this particular book illuminated many of the problems he and his cohorts would confront while trying to apply the psychedelic experience to social living. Specifically Leary was concerned about the relationship between the mystic community and the rest of society. He did not want Millbrook to degenerate into a haven for isolated intellectuals. His group would avoid this perennial pitfall by remaining socially relevant. They would undertake the spiritual search in a communal setting and report back to the rest of the world. They would keep records, compile statistics, and publish articles in their own journal, *The Psychedelic Review*. Above all they would become an active, educative, and regenerative force, an example for others to follow.

A core group of approximately thirty men and women gathered at Millbrook, including many acid veterans from the early days at Harvard. They were rejoined by Michael Hollingshead, who had left the group in early 1963 to work in New York City with an organization known as the Agora Scientific Trust. Hollingshead had quite a scene going for a while at his Fifth Avenue apartment. The entire place was laced with LSD—the food, the furnishings, etc.—and anyone who came through the door (even the knobs were spiked) inevitably wound up stoned. He threw some wild parties at which everybody was dosed; those in attendance included people from the United Nations whom he knew from his days at the British Cultural Exchange. But when Hollingshead learned of Hitchcock's generous offer, he knew it was time to pack his bags and head upstate. That's where the action was, and he wanted to be part of it.

The Millbrook residents were a tight-knit group. They shared a common lifestyle geared toward exploring the realities of their own nervous systems in a creative rather than a clinical setting. Their goal was to discover and cultivate the divinity within each person. The permanent members of the household regularly tripped together, rotating as shaman in "follow the leader" sessions involving high doses of LSD-25. The elusive aim of these group sessions was to break through to the other side without losing the love and radiance of the acid high during the crucial reentry period. Various methods were devised to facilitate a permanent spiritual transformation. Since many in the group had backgrounds in behavioral psychology, it came natural to them to keep a scorecard of their changing states of consciousness. On certain days a bell would ring four times an hour starting at 9:00 A.M. The bell was a signal to stop and record what they were doing then, what "game" they were playing. They thought that by paying more attention to shifting motivations and interpersonal dynamics they could learn to transcend their habitual routines. They compared scorecards and rapped endlessly about how LSD was affecting them.

In many ways the scene at Millbrook was like a fairy tale. The mansion itself was beautifully furnished with Persian carpets, crystal chandeliers, and a baronial fireplace, and all the rooms were full of elaborate psychedelic art. There were large aquariums with unusual fish, while other animals—dogs, cats, goats—wandered freely through the house. People stayed up all night tripping and prancing around the estate. (A stash of liquid acid had spilled in Richard Alpert's suitcase, soaking his underwear, when the psychedelic fraternity was traveling back from Zihuatanejo, so anyone could get high merely by sucking on his briefs.) Everyone was always either just coming down from a trip or planning to take one. Some dropped acid for ten days straight, increasing the dosage and mixing in other drugs. Even the children and dogs were said to have taken LSD.

Millbrook was a constant party, but one infused with a sense of purpose and optimism. The residents saw themselves as the vanguard of a psychic revolution that would transform the entire society. Victory seemed inevitable because they thought they had a means of producing guaranteed mystical insight. As Hollingshead described it, "We lived out a myth which had not yet been integrated into our personalities. Millbrook was itself the work of art. . . . Like Kafka's Castle, it gave out messages into the aether in the form of one high resonant sound which vibrated on the ears of the world, as if it were trying to penetrate beyond the barrier separating 'us' from 'them.' We felt satisfied that our goal was Every Man's, a project of Every Man's private ambition. We sought for that unitary state of divine harmony, an existence in which only the sense of wonder remains, and all fear gone."

Billy Hitchcock, the millionaire padrone, never really entered into the close camaraderie of the Millbrook circle. He lived a half-mile from the "big house" in his own private bungalow, a four-bedroom gardener's cottage with a Japanese bath in the basement. There he carried on a social life befitting a scion of one of the country's wealthiest families. Hitchcock never totally broke with his old routines even though he had begun turning on. He still kept in close contact with his friends from New York and with various brokers and investors who visited his bungalow for private parties. Some of these people were introduced to LSD through Hitchcock, but it became a running joke at Millbrook that you should not turn on your lawyer or anyone who had to take care of business for you, lest he drop his briefcase and head for the psychedelic sunset. Hitchcock would usually be on the phone all morning talking with Swiss and Bahamian bankers, setting up business meetings and fast-money deals. By afternoon he had taken care of his monetary affairs and would occasionally join the scene at the mansion.

Why Hitchcock decided to throw his weight behind the psychedelic cause is still something of a mystery. Was he simply a millionaire acid buff, a wayward son of the ruling class who dug Leary's trip? Or did he have something else up his sleeve? "Mr. Billy," as his servants affectionately called him, claimed he got involved with LSD because kicking the establishment in the teeth was exciting. Of course, since Hitchcock was the establishment, some questioned what he was really up to. Michael Hollingshead, for one, never fully trusted him. Most residents, however, thought Hitchcock a charming fellow. As one insider commented, "It hardly registered that he owned the place. He had a happy, open way of talking, perfect manners—a sort of Frank Merriwether type who had somehow fallen into a pool of gold and come up smelling like marijuana."

Hitchcock got along well with Leary and often joined the acid fellowship in group trips. At times he became very emotional and vulnerable on LSD. One night he had to be reassured that he did indeed own the estate. But unlike the others, Mr. Billy tended not to verbalize his feelings. He never developed any metaphysical system about the LSD experience, which was rather peculiar since everyone at Millbrook was into some kind of half- or full-cocked philosophy. Hitchcock's interest in LSD did not appear to be a simple matter of spiritual enrichment. He was not one to wax poetic over the prospect of merging with the Oversoul. When asked at the outset of one group session what question he wanted answered by the acid trip, he replied, "How can I make more money on the stock market?"

Timothy Leary, the eternal optimist, did not seem bothered by

100

such rock-hard considerations. The early days at Millbrook were in many ways a felicitous time for him. He married a beautiful Swedish model named Nina Schlebrugge in an open-air wedding on the grounds of the estate, with everyone decked out in Elizabethan attire. Tripped out on the surrealistic spectacle they had created, the guests passed through the reception line with gifts of cocaine, reefer, and psychedelics. For their honeymoon (it proved to be a short-lived marriage) Leary and his princess made a pilgrimage to India, where they tripped on acid at least once a week and smoked hash the rest of the time. During this meditative hiatus Leary ruminated upon what lay ahead. He now conceived of himself as a "neurologician," having discarded his academic career forever. He was convinced that it would be a psychedelic century. Tim laid out blueprints for man's next five hundred years, surpassing even his own stoned hubris. When he returned to Millbrook a month and a half later, he shared his insights with the group.

Although a legal crackdown was a subject few were willing to contemplate, some of the Millbrook residents had a clear premonition that they only had a few trouble-free years to play with this fantastic new energy. If so, they had to make the most of it. They experimented with drugs in a bold, innovative, sometimes reckless fashion, and the results were often surprising. One night Richard Alpert retired early with a bad cold. Hollingshead and a friend named Arnie Hendin decided to fix him up. When they couldn't rouse him, they gave him a shot of DMT (a short-acting superpsychedelic) in the buttocks. Alpert sat bolt upright, and before the DMT wore off they fed him an additional 800 mikes (micrograms) of LSD in a spoon. Three stereo systems were blasting Coltrane, Stockhausen, and Beethoven simultaneously. A sea of rocky sounds enveloped Alpert as he swirled through a neurological flux. When he came down from his trip, he found that his cold symptoms had completely disappeared.

Richard Alpert had come a long way since the days when he was moving up the academic ladder at Harvard University. "I had a lot of identities that I called Richard Alpert. I played the cello, I flew an airplane, I was charming. I was a Jewish boy making good in Boston." But he gave it all up for a new cause, which he embraced with the zeal of a true believer. His faith was such that he became convinced during an acid trip at Millbrook that he could actually fly. To test this hypothesis in the soundest empirical fashion, he jumped out a second story window. Alpert broke his leg but endured the discomfort amiably; the experiment, he thought, had been a noble one.

Millbrook was Psychedelic Central for the whole East Coast. Like a magnet, it attracted illustrious visitors from all walks of life. The doors were always open, and people were constantly coming and going. Among the musicians who passed through the estate were Maynard Ferguson, Steve Swallow, Charles Lloyd, and the irascible genius of the acoustic bass, Charles Mingus. Other guests included philosopher Alan Watts, psychiatrists Humphry Osmond and R. D. Laing, cartoonist Saul Steinberg, and actress Viva Superstar, a prominent figure in Andy Warhol's avant-garde art circle in New York City.

During the mid-1960s at the Factory, as Warhol's aluminum-foil-walled studio was called, people indulged in every drug they could get their hands on. Occasionally members of Warhol's eyelash set dropped in on the ever-obliging "Dr. Jake" for a quick poke of euphoria. When he came to Millbrook, Dr. Jake added psychedelics to his speedball injections, much to everyone's immediate gratification. As it turned out, Dr. Max "Feelgood" Jacobson served as John F. Kennedy's personal physician during the Camelot presidency. He often administered "vitamin" injections that left JFK flushed and excited, leading some to speculate that the shots included methamphetamine and/or cocaine.

Paul Krassner, editor of a satirical journal, *The Realist*, and a future founding father of the Yippies, also had a session at Millbrook. "My LSD experience began with a solid hour of what my guide [Hollingshead] described as cosmic laughter," Krassner recalled. "The more I laughed, the more I tried to think of depressing things— specifically, the atrocities being committed in Vietnam—and the more wild my laughter became." He laughed so hard that he threw up. Krassner (who later gave acid to fellow comedians Groucho Marx and Lenny Bruce) tried to put his first trip into perspective: "LSD was fun...but if I never take it again, I'll be happy. I enjoy coping with reality. Napalm is burning someone to death in Vietnam this very minute, but I'm alive, and that's what I was really laughing at: the oneness of tragedy and absurdity. The climactic message I got while high was: IT'S VERY FUNNY."

One day a NASA scientist named Steve Groff turned up at Millbrook. Dr. Groff wanted to observe how Leary and his clan ran their sessions. They gave him some acid, and he in turn provided samples of a secret drug known only as JB-118, which the military had developed as an incapacitating agent. Similar to the army's BZ, this potent superhallucinogen simulated a kind of free fall, at the same time triggering bizarre visions. (NASA reportedly gave hallucinogenic drugs to astronauts in training as a way of preparing them for the weightlessness of outer space.) A few of the Millbrook regulars tried the space drug, and Ralph Metzner described the results.

> Objects are seen that are not objectively there, and other objects that are present, are not perceived. For example, one subject saw a man sitting on a chair in the middle of the room and talked with him. When the subject walked close, man and chair disappeared. All of the subjects reported, and were observed, walking into doors or furniture, which they had not seen. Sometimes the basis of the hallucinations was clear, e.g., a coat on a bed would be seen as a small dog. In other instances, no such transformation seemed to underlie the hallucination. For example, one subject saw a friend of his, the size of a three story building, crawling around the garden on his hands and knees, eating the tops of trees.

Things were considerably less dramatic for the common folk and the curious who paid to attend weekend experimental workshops at Millbrook. These bimonthly seminars were tongue-in-cheek affairs for the regular residents, but they were necessary in order to raise money for rent and living expenses. The idea was to offer people an opportunity to explore psychedelic-type realities by means of Buddhist meditation, yoga, encounter groups, and other nonchemical techniques. When the visitors arrived, a rule of silence was imposed so that the general vibe was not brought down by frivolous discussion. And to keep the food bill at a minimum, breakfast was turned into an experience in sensory association. Guests were told to think about how their tastes were color-conditioned, after which they were served a meal of green scrambled eggs, purple oatmeal, and black milk (accomplished through nonpsychedelic vegetable dye). Few ate heartily.

Meanwhile, hundreds of letters asking about LSD poured into Millbrook from those who couldn't make it in person. A ten-point scale was devised for replies, with "one" calling for a dull "Dear Sir" form letter and "ten" meaning a totally way-out response. The replies to Arthur Kleps, a virtual unknown who would soon make his presence felt at Millbrook, were consistently in the eight and nine point range.

In 1960, while still a graduate student in psychology, Kleps sent away to the Delta Chemical Company for five hundred milligrams of mescaline sulfate. After swallowing the bitter powder, he spun through an unforgettable ten-hour journey: "All night I alternated between eyes-open terror and eyes-closed astonishment. With eye-lids shut I saw a succession of elaborate scenes which lasted a few seconds each before being replaced by the next in line. Extra-terrestrial civilizations. Jungles. Organic computer interiors. Ani-mated cartoons. Abstract light shows . . ." For the next four years Kleps kept this experience more or less to himself, "thinking about small things like sex, money, and politics." However, when he dis-covered that there was a group of intellectuals taking psychedelics on the grounds of a country estate, writing papers about trip realities, and having a great time, Kleps decided he was "just being chicken." School psychology went out the window; it was high time to start catching up with the psychedelic pacesetters, and the only way to do that was to join them.

Kleps did not fit into the scene so readily. The first time he took acid at Millbrook he wound up brandishing a gun, and Hollingshead promptly threw him out of the house. Despite this initial faux pas, Kleps was later admitted as a resident of the gatehouse. He was more of an epistemological hard-liner than the others, who in his opinion wanted nothing better than to have unusual experiences and pro-claim them religiously significant. Kleps was straining to develop a metaphysical system that would encompass the far-reaching impli-cations of psychedelics, brooding over such basic questions as "What is mind?" and "What is the external world?" His solipsistic excur-sions were frowned upon as nit-picking, strictly a downer. "You're on a bad trip, Art," said Leary, who scolded the newcomer for drink-ing too much and not grooving with a more cosmic perspective.

In those days a high dose of LSD was viewed as a solution for almost anything, and someone had the bright idea that it might solve the "Kleps problem." One of his comrades—Kleps swore it was Hollingshead—placed a few thousand mikes of pure Sandoz in a snifter of brandy beside his bedstand. Before he even rubbed the sleep out of his eyes, Kleps downed the brandy. A few minutes later he realized he was having trouble brushing his teeth. "I was knocked to the floor as all normal sensation and motor control left my body. The sun, roaring like an avalanche, was headed straight for me, expanding like a bomb and filling my consciousness in less time than it takes to describe it. It *swirled* clockwise, and made two and one half turns before I lost all normal consciousness and passed out, right there on the floor." As he groveled on all fours he got a shot of Thorazine in the rear, but it failed to bring him down. He spent the last hours of the trip sitting in a bed in the lotus position. As Kleps told it, a big book appeared, suspended in space about three feet in front of him, the pages turning automatically, every letter illuminated in gold against sky-blue pages. It was only years later, when he read a description of the two and one half turns that characterize the classic kundalini experience, that he came to an understanding of what he went through the day he'd been "bombed," as the parlance had it. None of the Millbrook priests would acknowledge that a release of kundalini energy was what happened to Kleps; maybe they thought he wasn't spiritually mature or pure enough to have had "the big one."

Kleps, however, thought himself sufficiently advanced on the spiritual path to found his own psychedelic religion, the Neo-American Boohoo Church. Formed in 1966, the Boohoos claimed that their use of LSD was sacramental, similar to the peyote rituals practiced by Indians of the Native American Church, and should therefore be protected under law. Not surprisingly, the Boohoos lost their case in court when the judge ruled that an organization with "Row, Row, Row Your Boat" as its theme song was not serious enough to qualify as a church. "Apparently," Kleps concluded, "those in control of the instrumentalities of coercive power in the United States had no difficulty in recognizing a psychedelic religion as a psychedelic religion when that religion was safely encapsulated in a racial minority group living outside the mainstream of American life."

Kleps, whom Leary described as the "mad monk" and an "ecclesiastical guerrilla," was particularly sensitive to the dangers of elevating institutional forms to the level of eternal verities, and so included elements of foolishness and buffoonery in his church. The church catechism is contained in his *Boohoo Bible,* full of cartoons, true-or-false tests, and a variety of hilarious liturgical observations on such topics as "How to Guide a Session for Maximum Mind Loss" and "The Bombardment and Annihilation of the Planet Saturn." Small monthly dues entitled members to a psychedelic coloring book as well as copies of the religious bulletin *Divine Toad Sweat,* emblazoned with the church motto, "Victory over Horseshit." Leary was a bit miffed: "Art, this is not a psychedelic love

105

message. It's a whiskey trip." But the Chief Boohoo was adamant: "It's my trip, take it or leave it."

Kleps sent diplomalike announcements to five hundred people across America certifying that they were Boohoos. Billy Hitchcock became a Boohoo during the same period in which he was immersed in some questionable financial dealings with Resorts International, a Bahamian-based gambling consortium suspected of having ties to organized crime. Kleps was always on Hitchcock's case, trying to pump him for money or wheedle him out of it or steal it. This didn't seem to bother Hitchcock much. What the hell, he figured, at least Kleps was more interesting than most of the others.

The Psychedelic Manual

Life at Millbrook had a mythic dimension that was nourished by a sense of having embarked upon a journey into unknown waters. Once they had eaten the apple of expanded consciousness, there was no going back. The umbilical cord that tied them to the world of the mundane was irretrievably sundered. Caught between a past that was no longer accessible and a future without precedent, they had only one option: to plunge headlong into the moment, to ride the crest of the wave that was still building, even if they could not see where it would take them. All they had was each other, their audacity and sense of humor, and plenty of LSD. Sooner or later, as everyone realized, the trip would have to come to an end. And what then? They celebrated their own transience by bathing in an atmosphere of hijinks and adventure. The incredible had become commonplace; ecstasy merged with confusion; dream and reality were interchangeable.

Even though they became more familiar with the psychedelic terrain over the years, the profound sense of disorientation that characterized their first trips lingered to some degree among the Millbrook residents. LSD had opened the floodgates of the unconscious, both personal and collective, and all kinds of strange flora and fauna were emerging. They didn't know quite what to make of it; some of it made sense, some of it didn't. Not enough time had elapsed for their insights to take root and mature. They tried to put their fingers on a definite truth, but there was nothing solid to grasp. It was all slippery, ambiguous, dialectical; everything implied its opposite. Old meanings had been annihilated, new ones were yet to be articulated. In searching for a language to describe essentially non-verbal experiences, they kept running up against a built-in credibility gap. As Kleps put it, "For every clarification that one arrives at by discussing these matters with others, there is a corresponding reinforcement of an illusion or misunderstanding. The only reliable way to get there is by closing one's eyes and jumping blindly into nowhere. It is only in such leaps, motivated by whatever passion, perversity, or dedication, that the adhesive grip of duality is escaped and the way made clear for the unconditioned light."

Despite all the changes they had undergone, Leary and his associates were still basically psychologists who felt compelled to figure it all out. But acid had overturned their dogmas and left them dangling precariously in an intellectual limbo that was reinforced by the hermetic environment of the Millbrook estate. As far as they were concerned, nothing less than the entire history of human thought had to be reconsidered in light of the psychedelic experience. Kleps parodied their dilemma in his chronicle of the Millbrook years, describing the arrival of LSD as "The Big Crash" in whose wake the intellectual history of mankind fluctuated madly on the cosmic exchange.

Zen and Buddhist stock rose sharply while Yoga, Brahmanist and Vedantist issues plummeted.... In London, Blake enjoyed a mild rise, Hume skyrocketed, Aldous Huxley weakened, then held, and penny-a-share issues such as Aleister Crowley and Yeats disappeared entirely from view. ... In Paris, former glamor stocks like Sartre and Camus began to look a little green around the gills.... such superficially disparate stocks as Thoreau, Nabokov, Borges, and Norman O. Brown were driven to undreamed of levels.... All the Zen masters spiralled into the blue.... Freud and Jung went through wild gyrations resembling an aerial dogfight, before both sank gradually to earth.... the I Ching went through the roof. The Gita crashed. . . . Shakespeare, unlike almost every other stock being traded, remained absolutely stable.

The sense of psychic displacement was felt most acutely by Timothy Leary. Even though years had passed since his first acid trip, he could still say, "I have never recovered from that shattering ontological confrontation. I have never been able to take myself, my mind, and the social world around me seriously." Now that he was aware of "countless realities," routine existence had been revealed to him as "illusory"; but that did not make it any less problematic. He confided to Kleps that at times he had the uncanny sensation that his head was running down his shoulders, and that he had even considered having himself committed. Whenever Leary took LSD, he relived a "recurring science fiction paranoia. Suddenly I am on camera in an ancient television show. . . . All my life routines a pathetic clown act."

Leary particularly wanted to develop an organized framework for understanding the potentials released by psychedelic drugs. He set out to devise a manual or program that would serve as a guide for acid initiates on their jaunts through higher consciousness. Given that there were no extant myths or models in his own tradition, he looked to the only sources that dealt directly with such matters— the ancient books of the East. In *The Tibetan Book of the Dead*, Leary found a text that was "incredibly specific about the sequence and nature of experiences encountered in the ecstatic state." With a little intellectual tinkering the self-proclaimed priest-scholars Leary, Alpert, and Metzner produced an "updated" interpretation of the ancient scripture. They represented it not as a treatise for the dead but as an instruction manual on how to confront the Clear Light of the Void during the acid peak "with a minimum of fear and confusion."

The *Tibetan Book of the Dead* was first linked to the psychedelic experience by Aldous Huxley in *The Doors of Perception*. Huxley reported that at one point he felt himself on the verge of panic, terrified by the prospect of losing his ego. He compared his dread with that of the Tibetan dead man who could not face the Clear Light, preferring rebirth and "the comforting darkness of selfhood." Huxley said that if you began a trip the wrong way "everything that happened would be proof of the conspiracy against you. It would all be self-validating. You couldn't draw a breath without knowing it was part of the plot." He thought that perhaps he could hold the terror at bay by fixing his attention on what *The Tibetan Book of the Dead* called the Clear Light, but only "if there were somebody there to tell me about the Clear Light. One couldn't do it by oneself. That's the point, I suppose, of the Tibetan ritual—somebody sitting there all the time and telling you what's what."

Leary took Huxley's remarks literally and turned *The Tibetan Book of the Dead* into a psychedelic manual. While Huxley had referred to it in an essay written *after* his psychedelic experience in order to clarify it, Leary promoted the book as a guide before and during the trip. This strategy represented a significant departure from the procedures employed by Dr. Humphry Osmond and other psychedelic therapists of the previous decade who simply sought to help subjects relax and remain open to the experience without defining what was supposed to occur. Leary now presented turning on as a process of initiation into a great brotherhood of free souls christened by the mind-blowing apprehension of the Clear Light during the peak of an acid trip. While the Eastern vibes surrounding the acid sessions at Millbrook may have been benign, Leary's methodology was in some ways analogous to that of the CIA and the military, which also "programmed" trips, although with a very different objective. Eventually Ralph Metzner and Michael Hollingshead were forced to admit that programming a trip was much more difficult than they had originally anticipated. LSD did not easily lend itself to step-by-step goal-oriented instructions, which more often than not created more confusion than they dispelled.

There was a great deal of disagreement among seasoned acid veterans as to the real meaning of the vision of the Clear Light. Hollingshead experienced something akin to it but did not consider it the final nirvana: "Let's face it—LSD is not the key to a new metaphysics of being or a politics of ecstasy. The 'pure light' of an acid session is not this—it may even be the apotheosis of distractions, the ultimate and most dangerous temptation. But it does allow one to live at least for a time in the light of the knowledge that every moment of time is a window into eternity, that the absolute is manifest in every appearance and relationship."

The experience in which eternity takes root in the waking state is brief, yet its significance is profound. It may take months, years, even a lifetime to come to terms with this fleeting moment of vision. Any experience so overwhelming, so incomprehensible to normal waking consciousness, carries with it a tendency to rationalize it as quickly as possible. Art Kleps felt that the peak of a major death-rebirth experience was no time for making formulations; on the contrary, he insisted that one should fight this urge: "If you can't let go and instead grab the first lifesaver or bit of wreckage that floats near your thrashing form, you will come down firmly believing that the lifesaver you grabbed was the meaning of the trip rather than the exit from it. Your new personality will be defined, not in terms of the truth, but in terms of the particular lie you happened to grab at the crucial moment."

It would appear that Leary succumbed to this "LSD temptation" when he developed the notion that a person could tune in to his genetic code while high on acid. "Is it entirely inconceivable," he mused, "that our cortical cells, or the machinery inside the cellular nucleus, 'remembers' back along the unbroken chain of electrical transformations that connects every one of us back to that original thunderbolt in the pre-Cambrian mud?" Leary suggested that by taking LSD he could commune with the "evolutionary program" and actually make contact with the ultimate source of intelligence: DNA. He turned his cellular visions into a kind of psychedelic Darwinism, positing the reading of the individual genetic code as a universal truth: "God does exist and is to me this energy process; the language of God is the DNA code."

Kleps took issue with Leary's conception of a good trip. He insisted that people who never had mystical experiences on acid could learn just as much as those who did. He thought Leary placed too much emphasis on pleasurable visions. "Nine times out of ten, talk about bad trips resolves itself into a naive identification of pleasurable visionary scenes and sensory appreciation of the present (during the trip) with 'goodness.' When such people find themselves in a few Hell-worlds here and there, they think that something is seriously amiss." For Kleps LSD was never supposed to be *easier* than traditional methods of self-realization; it was only "faster and sneakier." According to the Chief Boohoo, you could be devoured by demons during a psychedelic experience and it still might be a good trip if you came out of it feeling that it was worthwhile. Kleps maintained that striving for a preconceived visionary end in the acid high only complicated things and led to bummers.

> It is as if [Leary] deliberately and with malice aforethought polluted the stream at its source and gave half the kids in psychedelic society a bad set to start out with. Almost every acidhead I talked to for years afterwards told me he had, as a novice, used *The Tibetan Book of the Dead* as a "guide"—and every one of them reported unnecessary anxiety, colossal bummers, disillusionment, and eventual frustration and exasperation, for which, in most cases, they blamed themselves, not Tim or the book. They were not "pure" enough, or perhaps the "Lord of Death" did not deign to transform them because they were not worthy of His attentions, etc., etc.

The psychedelic biography of Allen Ginsberg illustrates the futility of the programmed trip, be it self-initiated or imposed from without. Ginsberg found that even self-programming could create formidable psychic tensions often resulting in awful bummers. His desire for a heavenly illumination, which he sought through LSD, was a carry-over from a powerful non-drug experience he had in 1948. Ginsberg was then living in a sublet apartment in Harlem. While reading William Blake's "Ah, Sunflower!" he heard a deep resounding voice. He immediately recognized it as Blake's own voice emerging from the dead. Ginsberg felt his body afloat, suffused with brilliance. Everything he looked at appeared in a new light. He was struck by an overpowering conviction that he had been born to experience this universal spirit.

When Ginsberg began using psychedelic drugs, his Blake vision was his reference point. As he put it, LSD gave access to "what I, as a poet, have called previously aesthetic, poetic, transcendental, or mystical awareness." But he ran into trouble when he attempted to recapture the cosmic heights of his Blakeian episode via drugs. He wanted to write a poem under the influence of LSD that would evoke a sense of divinity, but he found that the act of writing interrupted the multitudinous details inundating his nervous system. The tension between the romantic vision of illumination and the simultaneous urge to communicate it turned his divine quests into bum trips. Ginsberg described his frustration in numerous poems he composed while high on acid and other psychedelics: "The Reply," "Magic Psalm," "Mescaline," and "Lysergic Acid."

Ginsberg had been painting himself into a corner with drugs, thinking that he should take acid to cleanse his soul and trying too hard to attain some sort of satori. He felt a compulsive obligation to use LSD again and again to break down his identity and conquer his obsession with mortality. His growing paranoia with regard to psychedelics came to a climax when he ingested yagé in Peru in 1960. Again he was primed for divine revelation, but instead "the whole fucking cosmos broke loose around me, I think the strongest and worst I've ever had it. . . . I felt faced by Death . . . got nauseous, rushed out and began vomiting, all covered with snakes, like a Snake Seraph, colored serpents in aureole all around my body, I felt like a snake vomiting out the universe—or a Jivaro in head-dress with fangs vomiting up in realization of the murder of the Universe—my death to come—everyone's death to come—all unready—I unready."

Toward the end of 1961 Ginsberg undertook a spiritual pilgrimage to India to come to terms with his unsettling drug visions. On the way he stopped in Israel to talk with Martin Buber, the eminent

Jewish philosopher, who emphasized human relationships and advised him not to get caught up in confrontation with a nonhuman universe. Ginsberg received a similar message in India from Swami Sivananda, who told him, "Your own heart is your guru." These encounters set the stage for a sudden realization that came to him a few months later, during the final days of his long journey. While riding a train in Japan in mid-1963, he had an ecstatic conversion experience, an inexplicable but deeply felt resolution of his trials with psychedelics. The relief was so great that he wept on the train. Inspired by this breakthrough, he pulled out a pencil and wrote a poem called "The Change: Kyoto-Tokyo Express," which signaled a turning point in his spiritual search.

Ginsberg had been seeking divinity through out-of-the-body trips on psychedelics. In trying to superimpose the acid high on his old memory of a cosmic vision, he was not living in the present; he was blocking himself. Now he saw the futility of attempting to conjure visions of a blissful imaginary universe when the secret lay within his own mortal flesh. In this moment of profound insight he understood that truth could only be experienced within the framework of the body; therefore, the overarching mystical imperative was to become one with his own skin. He was not so much renouncing drugs as refusing to be dominated by them or by the obligation to take psychological risks with chemicals to enlarge his consciousness. "I spent about fifteen, twenty years," Ginsberg reflected, "trying to recreate the Blake experience in my head, and so wasted my time. It's just like somebody taking acid and wanting to have a God trip and straining to see God, and instead, naturally, seeing all sorts of diabolical machines coming up around him, seeing hells instead of heavens. So I did finally conclude that the bum trip on acid as well as the bum trip on normal consciousness came from attempting to grasp, desiring a preconceived end, a preconceived universe, rather than entering a universe not conceivable, not even born, not describable."

Secure in his sense of self, his mind calmed, Ginsberg had a different personal set for his subsequent LSD trips, which took on a whole new character for him. He began to enjoy himself while he was high. After all he had been through, Ginsberg finally realized that the experience of peaking on LSD is above all one of an open horizon, a field of presence in the widest sense. Any clutching at the Eternal or the Clear Light or the hidden message of the DNA code necessarily became a fixation, an objectification, and therefore an inauthentic relationship to the infinite openness of psychedelic consciousness. Once Ginsberg was able to direct his attention outside himself, there were no heavy judgments required by acid, just an appreciation of the world that lay before him.

The Hard Sell

Despite criticisms of trip programming, Leary still saw advantages in working with a manual: if a particular spiritual state could be consistently reproduced, there was a good chance the psychedelic movement would really take off. Hence the adoption of the *The Tibetan Book of the Dead* as the first LSD guidebook. Since the movement's only "activism" was the psychedelic session, the first step was to persuade people to take the drug. Leary aimed his message at those whose hearts and minds were still up for grabs: the younger generation. He saw himself as the orchestrator of a mass cultural phenomenon. His goal was to encourage large numbers of American youth to decondition themselves away from the work-duty ethic by means of psychedelic drugs. Leary insisted that the insane rat race was the real "narcotic escape" and that people could find a new kind of harmony by dropping out and "sanitizing" themselves with large helpings of LSD. He advised taking the drug repeatedly in order to transcend the mind's habitual fixations: "Find the wisdom in yourself. Unhook the ambitions and the symbolic drives and the mental connections which keep you addicted and tied to the immediate tribal game."

To those in the inner circle it quickly became apparent that the psychedelic movement "would be sold like beer, not champagne," as Kleps put it. Whether or not the liberation was bogus, the style was strictly Madison Avenue. Leary not only hyped LSD as a shortcut to mystical enlightenment but also fused it with something that had proven mass appeal: sex. In his 1966 *Playboy* interview he discussed psychedelics in the broad social context of "erotic politics" and "hedonic engineering." Acid was portrayed as a "cure" for homosexuality and a means of inhabiting a supremely sensual reality. "In a carefully prepared, loving LSD session," Leary stated, "a woman will inevitably have several hundred orgasms. The three inevitable goals of the LSD session are to discover and make love with God, to discover and make love with yourself, and to discover and make love with a woman.... That is what the LSD experience is all about. Merging, yielding, flowing, union, communion. It's all love-making.... The sexual impact is, of course, the open but private secret about LSD."

Leary had a knack for telling his audiences exactly what they wanted to hear. He could be all things to all people; whatever guise he chose, the gist of the message was essentially the same. "It's all God's flesh," he insisted. "LSD is always a sacrament: whether you are a silly thirteen-year-old popping a sugar cube on your boy-friend's motorcycle, or a theatrical agent giving pot to a girl to get her horny...or even a psychiatrist giving LSD to an unsuspecting patient to do a scientific study."

Leary's public pronouncements were calculated to seduce and frighten. He taunted his critics and prospective followers with bra-zen epigrams: "You have to go out of your mind to use your head." As he saw it, Western culture had reached such a critical impasse that one couldn't afford *not* to experiment with LSD. Regardless of how dangerous such a venture might seem to the uninitiated, the potential benefits were simply too great to pass up: "I would say that at present our society is so insane, that even if the risks were fifty-fifty that if you took LSD you would be permanently insane, I still think that the risk is worth taking, as long as the person knows that that's the risk."

Leary was a kind of carnival barker for the psychedelic movement. He had no compunctions about using the media to promote LSD. "Tim had what we needed," said Kleps. "He had the 'dreams' of the true salesman." Leary was quite candid about his role as a media mogul. "Of course I'm a charlatan," he often joked in public. "Aren't we all?" To Leary the PR was all pretense, a cosmic put-on. That was what he had learned from LSD—all social roles were a game, and he could change personalities like so many different sets of clothing as the occasion warranted. His close friends never took him seriously as a guru or prophet or high priest. As Hollingshead com-mented, "It was easier to see him as an inspired impresario, an Apollinaire or Cocteau."

During the mid-1960s, Millbrook attracted considerable publicity. TV crews filmed regularly at the estate, bringing even more notoriety to Leary, who quickly became one of the most famous and contro-versial figures in America. Leary knew he could get more coverage by making provocative statements, and he played upon the public's infatuation with the sensational. He realized that the press was not an organ for disseminating truth; no matter what one said, it would always be distorted by straight journalists. Thus, even when the media castigated him as everything from an "irresponsible egotist" to a "madman" hooked on acid, he was not in the least flustered. On the contrary, such outbursts seemed to be grist for his mill. Any publicity was a walking stick, as far as Leary was concerned, and if it came down to choosing between no publicity and bad publicity, he would opt for the latter. Leary was confident that the subliminal message—LSD could take you to extraordinary places—would come through between the lines and young people would turn on in greater and greater numbers.

The Millbrook clan not only had their sights set on America; their aspirations were international in scope. In September 1965 Michael Hollingshead returned to his native London armed with hundreds of copies of the updated *Book of the Dead* and five thousand doses of LSD (which he procured from Czech government laboratories in Prague). Hollingshead felt there was very little understanding of LSD in England, but he intended to change that. He proceeded to establish the World Psychedelic Center in the fashionable Kings Road district of London, attracting the likes of Jo Berke (a psychiatrist working with R. D. Laing), the writer and philosopher Alexander Trocchi, multimedia artist Ian Sommerville, filmmaker Roman Polanski, and numerous musicians including Donovan, Peter and Gordon, Eric Clapton, Paul McCartney, and the Rolling Stones.

London was a swinging scene in the mid-1960s, and psychedelics were an intrinsic part of the cultural renaissance that revolved around the rock music explosion. Strangely enough, hardly anyone under twenty-one listened to the radio in England, as the BBC monopolized the airwaves with dance music and symphonies. To compensate for the lack of commercial channels, a group of go-getters organized a network of pirate radio stations that operated offshore beyond the three-mile national limit but within transmitting distance of population centers all along the coast. The entire country was surrounded by small seacraft, and when they started beaming rock music, everyone bought transistors and tuned in. Hollingshead dug the setup. Every week he would emerge from his London apartment wearing his long coat, pink glasses, and wry smile, to be taken by motorboat to a floating pirate station near the Thames. He tripped with the deejays, rapped, played music, and laughed. There was no censorship of any kind. Needless to say, the British authorities were not amused.

During this period Hollingshead smoked pot and hash constantly, dropped acid three times a week in doses often exceeding 500 micrograms, and began using hard drugs. He obtained a doctor's prescription for Methedrine, and after working up to seven injections a day he found himself at the mercy of a nonmiraculous addiction. His gargantuan appetite for drugs turned him into a near zombie. In this condition he was hardly capable of keeping his own house in order, let alone leading a psychedelic revolution in Britain. All hell finally broke loose one night at a party thrown by Hollingshead and his wacked-out colleagues. They decided to offer punch with LSD and without, but someone went ahead and spiked the whole batch. Suddenly there were over a hundred and fifty people at his pad stoned out of their minds, including a lot of unsuspecting folks. Among those who turned on accidentally were a couple of undercover policemen masquerading as hipsters.

When reports of this gala event surfaced in the London press, Hollingshead suspected his number might be up. A few days later the bobbies came to his flat and arrested him for possession of less than an ounce of hash. Hollingshead showed up in court high on LSD and who knows what else, and was sentenced to twenty-one months in Wormwood Scrubs. He managed to smuggle an ample supply of acid into prison, but it was not his custom to turn on other inmates. However, he made an exception in the case of George Blake, the convicted spy who penetrated the highest echelons of British intelligence and passed information to the Russian KGB. Blake was serving the sixth year of a forty-three-year sentence when he met Hollingshead. His interest was aroused as soon as he learned that Hollingshead had hung out with Leary, and they arranged one Sunday afternoon to take LSD behind bars. As the session progressed, Blake became noticeably tense and paranoid. He thought he had been given a truth serum, and he accused Hollingshead of being a secret service agent. The spy finally settled down and spent the last hours of his trip reflecting upon his future and whether he'd be able to stand many more years of incarceration. A few weeks later Blake escaped by scaling the prison wall with a rope ladder. When last heard from, he was living in Moscow and working in the Cairo section of the Soviet Foreign Ministry.

Hollingshead wasn't the only one in legal trouble. Leary had been busted in December 1965 after he and his daughter were caught transporting three ounces of pot across the Mexican border into Laredo, Texas. Leary was fined $30,000 in addition to receiving a maximum sentence of thirty years. While his lawyers appealed the verdict, Leary returned to Millbrook, but the political harassment continued. Relations between the acid commune and the affluent townsfolk of conservative Dutchess County were always a bit strained, to say the least. When the town bigwigs heard that some of the local teenagers were hanging around Millbrook, they pressured the sheriff to put an end to the shenanigans of Leary and company. At the time the Dutchess County prosecutor was none other than G. Gordon Liddy, the future Waterbugger whose arsenal of dirty tricks included LSD and other hallucinogens to neutralize political enemies of the Nixon administration. But these events were still a few years in the offing.

As far as Liddy was concerned, Leary and his pernicious band of dope fiends epitomized the moral infection that was sweeping the land. He was eager to raid the Millbrook estate, where, as he put it, "the panties were dropping as fast as the acid." He and a team of deputies staked out the mansion for months, waiting for the right moment to make an arrest that would stick. Early one morning in April 1966 they decided to act. Crouched behind the bushes with their binoculars, they noticed some kind of film being shown in the house. Splendid, thought Liddy, jockeying for a peek at what he hoped was a pornographic display; the prospect of exposing a citadel of smut as well as a den of dopers was fine by him. He must have been disappointed to find that the film only showed a waterfall.

The deputies made their entry in classic "no-knock" fashion, kicking in the front door and charging up the main stairwell. They were greeted by Leary bouncing down the stairs in nothing but a shirt. A warrant was read aloud, and Leary was finally persuaded to put on a pair of pants. The search continued for five hours; a small amount of marijuana was found, but no other drugs. Leary accused the police of using Gestapo tactics and violating his constitutional rights. When the Supreme Court ruled that suspects must be informed of their legal rights at the time of arrest, the bust was thrown out of court. Leary had escaped on a technicality, but Liddy was still hot on the case. Roadblocks were set up around the estate, and anyone who wanted to visit had to submit to a lengthy, humiliating strip search. The state of siege grew more intense, until the commune was forced to disband in the spring of 1967. The golden age of anarchy at Millbrook had come to an end.

5

The All-American Trip

THE GREAT FREAK FORWARD

Of the notorious acid proselytizers of the 1960s, it was perhaps Ken Kesey who best understood the futility of trying to label the LSD experience. Kesey, like Ginsberg and many others, was first turned on to acid through a federally funded research program. He was a graduate student at Stanford University's creative writing program in 1960 when he heard about some experiments being conducted at the Veterans Hospital in Menlo Park. Volunteers were paid $75 a day for the privilege of serving as guinea pigs in a study of "psychotomimetic drugs."

Kesey, a burly, blue-eyed ex-high school wrestling champion, experienced some wild states of consciousness in the clinic. While stoned on acid, he felt he could see right through the doctors, who had never taken the drug themselves and had no idea what it really did. A few weeks later he showed up at the Veterans Hospital as a night attendant in the psychiatric ward, where there was an array of psychedelics—LSD, mescaline, Ditran, and a mysterious substance known only as IT-290. Soon the drugs were circulating among Kesey's friends in the collegiate bohemia of Perry Lane. Sometimes he would go to work flying on LSD and spend hours leaning on a mop pondering the nature of insanity. "Before I took drugs," said Kesey, "I didn't know why the guys in the psycho ward at the VA Hospital were there. I didn't understand them. After I took LSD, suddenly I saw it. I saw it all. I listened to them and watched them, and I saw that what they were saying and doing was not so crazy after all." Slowly his first novel, *One Flew Over the Cuckoo's Nest*, came to him.

The Perry Lane community went through some rapid changes as more and more people started turning on. A psychedelic party scene developed around the consumption of Kesey's notorious Venison

Chili, a dish laced with liberal helpings of LSD. Among those who dined "electric" were artist Roy Seburn, dancer Chloe Scott, a young musician named Jerry Garcia, and writers Robert Stone (Dog Soldiers, A Flag for Sunrise) and Larry McMurtry (Hud, Terms of Endearment). The tripping collegians quickly developed a taste for exotica in the way of mind-altering chemicals, and they procured hundreds of peyote buttons via mail order from a company in Laredo, Texas.

Folklore has it that large amounts of the Native American sacrament often produce visions indigenous to the drug's ancient traditions and locale. Sure enough, Kesey took peyote and had a vision of a strange, primitive face. It was the face of an Indian, Chief Broom, who became a central character in One Flew Over the Cuckoo's Nest. Writing at times on peyote or LSD, Kesey told the story through the eyes of the schizophrenic Indian. The other main character, McMurphy, was the literary prototype of the new Ken Kesey, a boisterous rebel scheming to blow the mind of the authoritarian Big Nurse. The book received fabulous reviews, and its success gave the psychedelic scene a curious legitimacy; one could have one's cake (LSD) and write the great American novel too.

With his earnings from the book, Kesey bought himself a place in La Honda, fifty miles south of San Francisco. There he finished his second novel, Sometimes a Great Notion. With powerful amplifiers strung up in the trees belting out rock and roll, his country home became a magnet for beatniks, college professors, and a new breed of doper—the acidhead. Along with the original Perry Lane crowd, Ken Babbs, an old friend of Kesey's who had flown helicopters for the marines in Vietnam, started to hang out at La Honda. They all took LSD together on numerous occasions. For them acid was a means of eradicating the unconscious structures that interfered with experiencing the magical dimensions of the here and now, the ever-widening Present. As Kesey put it, "The first drug trips were, for most of us, shell-shattering ordeals that left us blinking kneedeep in the cracked crusts of our pie-in-the-sky personalities. Suddenly people were stripped before one another and behold: we were beautiful. Naked and helpless and sensitive as a snake after skinning, but far more human than that shining knightmare that had stood creaking in previous parade rest. We were alive and life was us."

Out of the happenings at La Honda came Kesey's famous Merry

Pranksters. The Pranksters did not have to trek across continents, as the beats had done earlier, to find a witch doctor or *curandero* who could administer the power plant. With plenty of LSD on hand, they could just as easily have continued to trip in the warm California sun with the outdoor speakers twanging out tunes by Dylan and the Beatles. But travel was still attached to the bohemian lifestyle as a metaphor for spiritual discovery. The Pranksters purchased a 1939 International Harvester school bus and refurbished it with bunks, refrigerators, shelves, and a sink. They put a hole in the roof so people could sit up top and play music, and they wired the entire vehicle so they could broadcast from within and pick up sounds from outside as well. En masse the Pranksters swarmed over the weather-beaten body with paintbrushes, producing the first psychedelic motor transport done in bright, swirling colors. A sign hung on the rear end which read, "Caution: Weird Load." Emblazoned on the front of the bus was the word "FURTHUR" (with two u's), which aptly summed up the Prankster ethos. There were twenty-odd people aboard, and the entire crew was ready for "the great freak forward."

The Pranksters dressed in elaborate costumes, donning capes and masks, painting themselves with Day-Glo, and wearing pieces of the American flag. They took names befitting their new psychedelic identities. Among the women were Mountain Girl, Sensuous X, Gretchen Fetchin the Slime Queen, and Doris Delay. Ken Babbs was Intrepid Traveler. The magnetic Kesey was Swashbuckler. And Mike Hagen, trying to keep his movie camera steady while the bus lurched down the road, was Mal Function. The Pranksters were constantly filming an epic saga that would star everybody. Kesey's slogan— "Get them into your movie before they get you into theirs"—was not just a conviction but a strategy.

As they disembarked from the bus with the loudspeakers blasting rock and roll, the Pranksters were well aware that they looked to straight citizens like inhabitants of another planet. That was exactly what they intended. They were into "tootling the multitudes," doing whatever was necessary to blow minds and keep folks off balance. "The purpose of psychedelics," said Kesey, "is to learn the conditioned responses of people and then to prank them. That's the only way to get people to ask questions, and until they ask questions they're going to remain conditioned robots." During the 1964 presidential campaign the Pranksters drove into Phoenix decked out in

American flag regalia, waving Old Glory and demonstrating with a huge placard that stated, "A Vote for Barry Goldwater is a Vote for Fun."

The driver of the psychedelic bus was Neal Cassady, the aging beat avatar, who had recently been released from San Quentin after serving two years for possession of a single joint of marijuana. Though the years in prison did not totally wither his joyful manner, the experience hardened him. The essence of Cassady's style remained the mad exultation in the moment, but his identification with sheer speed was even more compulsive; he ate amphetamines constantly. With Cassady at the helm the Pranksters retraced the mythic path forged by the beat protagonists some years before. As Ginsberg wrote, "Neal Cassady drove Jack Kerouac to Mexico in a prophetic automobile the same Denver Cassady that one decade later drove Ken Kesey's Kosmos-patterned schoolbus on a Kafka-circus tour over the roads of an awakening nation."

When Cassady joined Kesey's group, his legendary reputation preceded him. Some of the Pranksters were awed by him, others did not fully accept him at first. Ginsberg wondered if the Pranksters truly appreciated his brilliance, or were taking advantage of him in some sense. He was Neal Cassady, the "holy primitive"; the atmosphere on the bus encouraged him to *perform*, to show these younger men and women what real craziness was. His presence lent a certain edge-quality to the general pranking. Indeed, one wonders what extrasensory space he must have inhabited to pull off some of his incredible antics.

On their way to New York the Pranksters passed through the Blue Ridge Mountains. On the steepest downhill road, with Kesey perched atop the bus and everyone stoned on LSD, Cassady decided to career all the way down hill without touching the brakes while the Stars and Stripes streamed in the wind. Nobody told him he shouldn't have taken the risk, because nobody on the bus told anybody not to do anything—especially not for the reason that it was "crazy." Lunacy was not an absolute for the Pranksters; they had moved beyond the world of the Big Nurse and voluntarily embarked upon a trip that was insane by conventional standards. When Cassady took the whole crew with him towards either death or his own version of satori, he was simply going "furthur." This prank was Cassady's way of saying that it was easy to claim, "We're all one," but another thing entirely to act as if everyone's life were his to risk.

Through such gratuitous acts Cassady became a kind of teacher for the group. He was the Zen lunatic whose gestures embodied the bohemian commitment to spontaneity and authenticity. Kesey described Cassady's spiritual path as "the yoga of a man driven to the cliff edge by the grassfire of an entire nation's burning material madness. Rather than be consumed by this he jumped, choosing to sort things out in the fast-flying but smogfree moments of a life with no retreat."

Cassady represented for the Pranksters an ideal of thought and action fusing into a vibrant whole, into pure up-front being. They assumed that whatever was inside a person would come out during the trip (LSD had a way of making this happen); everyone agreed this did not mean that whatever spewed forth would always be beautiful and lovey-dovey. Weird behavior was commonplace on the bus, and awards were given out regularly for "Most Disgusting Trip." The idea really was to go "furthur," to explore the unknown, to feel no limit as to what might be discovered and expressed on acid. It was in this sense that a mission was taking shape among the Pranksters. It had nothing to do with the salvation of the world; it was more a feeling, a "synching" together that created an atmosphere of "creeping religiosity." As a group they searched for a unified consciousness that would outstrip once and for all the pseudo-reality they had left behind.

The Pranksters were in high spirits when they finally hit New York City. Cassady secured an apartment for a powwow between Kesey's group and his old friends Ginsberg and Kerouac. Would the original white hipsters accept these psychedelic neobohemians as kindred spirits? The environment was typical for the Pranksters, with tapes echoing and lights flashing off mirrors. An American flag covered the sofa. Kerouac felt out of place amidst the madness. He and Kesey didn't have much to say to each other. Kerouac walked over to the sofa, carefully folded the flag, and asked the Pranksters if they were Communists. He left early with Cassady and returned to his home in Massachusetts, where he lived with his mother. As Tom Wolfe described the meeting, "It was like hail and farewell. Kerouac was the old star. Kesey was the wild new comet from the West heading christ knew where."

If there was anybody who could dig where the Pranksters were coming from, they figured it had to be Leary's group. After traveling a few thousand miles, they were not going to pass up the chance to visit Millbrook, the only other psychedelic commune they knew of. The Pranksters expected a heartwarming reception, but upon their arrival they were not exactly embraced. Things were friendly but somehow cool. Everyone was waiting for the momentous meeting between Kesey and Leary. However, Leary would not meet with the Pranksters. He was supposedly on a very serious three-day trip upstairs in the mansion and could not be disturbed. Kesey was bewildered by this turn of events, but as the Pranksters grew more familiar with the Millbrook scene, they began to understand why they made everyone so uptight. The Millbrook group was essentially made up of behavioral scientists who kept records of their mental states, wrote papers, and put out a journal. Leary and his people were going the scholarly route, giving lectures and such; they had nothing to gain by associating with a bunch of grinning, filthy bums wearing buckskins and face paint. The distance between the East Coast intellectuals and Kesey's clan was cavernous. As Michael Hollingshead recalled the encounter, "They thought we were square and we thought they were crazy."

The general atmosphere of quietude—the special meditation rooms, the statues of the Buddha, the emphasis on *The Tibetan Book of the Dead*—was unbearably stuffy to the Pranksters, who dubbed the whole thing "the Crypt Trip." In this scene there was no room for electronics, no guitars or videotapes, no American flags, and well, no freakiness. Kesey was not at all interested in structuring the set and setting of an LSD trip so that a spiritual experience would result. Why did acid require picturesque countryside or a fancy apartment with objets d'art to groove on and Bach's Suite in B Minor playing on the stereo? A psychedelic adventure on the bus needed no preconceived spiritual overtones; it could be experienced in the context of a family scene, a musical jam, or a plain old party. The Pranksters thought it was fine just going with the flow, taking acid in the midst of whatever was happening, no matter how disorienting or unusual the situation.

It was, after all, a question of style, East Coast versus West Coast. The Merry Pranksters were born in California, starting out as a party of outlandish proportions that evolved into a stoned encounter group on wheels. Kesey, having first turned on to LSD in a government drug testing program, saw the whole phenomenon of grassroots tripping as "the revolt of the guinea pigs." Now that he had taken LSD out of the laboratory and away from the white smocks, any notion of a medically sanitized or controlled psychedelic experience was abhorrent to him. Programming the LSD trip with Tibetan vibes struck him as a romantic retreat, a turning back, submitting to another culture's ideas rather than getting into the uniqueness of the American trip.

Kesey the psychedelic populist was attempting to broaden the very nature of the tripping experience by incorporating as many different scenes and viewpoints as possible. "When you've got something like we've got," he explained, "you can't just sit on it and possess it, you've got to move off of it and give it to other people. It only works if you bring other people into it." Toward this end the Pranksters staged a series of public initiations, the Electric Kool-Aid Acid Tests of the mid-1960s, which turned on hundreds of people at a single session. The acid tests were weird carnivals with videotapes, flashing strobes, live improvised rock and roll by the Grateful Dead, lots of bizarre costumes, and dancing.

The ultimate example of Kesey's attempt to get everybody into the Prankster movie was when he turned on the hoariest outlaw group of them all, the Hell's Angels. Kesey had met the Angels in the summer of 1965 through Hunter Thompson, the notorious Doctor of Gonzo, who was then writing a book about the motorcycle gang. Whatever the reason (perhaps the bit of redneck in Kesey), he smoked a joint with some of the Angels and they hit it off right away. "We're in the same business," Kesey told them. "You break people's bones, I break people's heads." He invited his new friends to La Honda for a party. The Pranksters laid in unlimited quantities of beer and strung a huge banner across the lawn welcoming the Hell's Angels. The bash would be a reunion of sorts; the old Perry Lane people were there, along with Allen Ginsberg, Richard Alpert, and a lot of San Francisco and Berkeley intellectuals. The Pranksters got ready for the Angels the way they got ready for anything—by dropping acid. The local townsfolk prepared themselves by huddling nervously behind locked doors, while the police turned out to greet the visitors with ten squad cars and live ammunition.

Kesey had really done it this time. A bunch of spaced-out bohemians getting high was one thing, but a violent motorcycle gang was something else again. Even among the Pranksters there was some uncertainty about their guests. The trepidation thermometer must have been sky-high as the Angels roared into La Honda with skulls, crossbones, and swastikas embellishing their denim jackets.

But once the Angels dug into the beer, the tension eased considerably. The Pranksters were probably the first outsiders actually to accept the Angels. To Kesey's group they were fellow outlaws with just as little tolerance for hypocrisy or compromise. An atmosphere of peaceful coexistence was established, and then acid was doled out as a party favor.

Contrary to certain dire expectations of brutal carnage wreaked by drug-twisted criminals, the LSD made the bikers rather docile. They all walked around in a daze, mingling with the radicals, pacifists, and intellectuals. There was Allen Ginsberg, the epitome of much they despised, a gay New York poet chanting Hare Krishna and dancing with his finger cymbals, and the Angels were actually digging him. It was quite a spectacle. The befuddled policemen stayed outside the grounds with their red flashers blinking through the trees. With so many of the Angels bombed out of their minds, the cops deemed it wise to keep their distance.

The party went on for two days—a monument to what the Pranksters had set out to accomplish on the '64 bus trip. They had broken through the worst hang-up intellectuals have—the "real life" hang-up. After this first bash the Angels hung around Kesey's for the next six weeks, attending numerous Prankster parties. Their presence added a certain voltage that was unforgettable for those in attendance. Hunter Thompson wrote that if he could repeat any of his early acid trips, it would be one of the Hell's Angels parties in La Honda. "It was a very electric atmosphere. If the Angels lent a feeling of menace, they also made it more interesting... and far more alive than anything likely to come out of a controlled experiment or a politely brittle gathering of well-educated truth-seekers looking for wisdom in a capsule. Dropping acid with the Angels was an adventure; they were too ignorant to know what to expect, and too wild to care."

Acid and the New Left

Kesey's scene was all the rage in the Bay Area. Among others, it attracted a number of people who were involved with the Free Speech Movement (FSM) that arose on the Berkeley campus of the University of California in the fall of 1964. This was a period of unbridled optimism and enthusiasm among student activists. The Cold War had finally thawed, and many were eager to flex their political muscle for a variety of issues: civil rights, disarmament, university re-form, and so forth. Nothing less than a wholesale transformation of society was thought to be in the offing. The cities would be reno-vated, the institutions remade, the downtrodden uplifted, and justice would ultimately prevail. It was a moment saturated with possibil-ity, and those who joined the protest struggle were confident, in the words of Lautréamont, that "the storms of youth precede brilliant days."

The FSM was a groundbreaking event as students asserted their right to organize politically on campus in the face of attempts by the university administration to ban such activity. At a mass rally in front of Sproul Hall attended by thousands, Mario Savio, a curly-haired twenty-one-year-old FSM spokesperson, delivered a stirring address in which he denounced the university as a factory for pro-cessing students—its raw material—into standardized personnel. "There's a time when the operation of the machine becomes so odious, makes one so sick at heart that you can't take part, you can't even tacitly take part, and you have to put your body upon the gears and the wheels, upon all the apparatus, and you've got to stop it. You've got to indicate to the people who run it, the people who own it, that unless you're free the machine will be prevented from working."

On cue the demonstrators marched into the administrative offices and occupied four floors of Sproul Hall. During the next thirty hours, they established a "liberated" zone with areas designated for polit-ical discussion, entertainment, study hall, kitchen, infirmary, legal aid, alternative classes, and steering committee meetings; the roof was reserved for couples who wanted to sleep together and people who wanted to smoke pot. In effect, they created an embryonic version of the future society, the "beloved community," which they hoped to bring about through social activism.

The young radicals were fashioning the beginnings of a unique political gestalt that encompassed a dual-pronged radical project. They believed that challenging entrenched authority entailed a con-certed attempt to alter the institutions and policy-making apparatus that had been usurped by a self-serving power elite; at the same time, they sought to lead lives that embodied the social changes they desired. For sixties activists, the quest for social justice was in many ways a direct extension of the search for personal authenticity. They were as much concerned with questions of psychic liberation as with economic and political issues. Their demand for a high-energy, freewheeling, erotic culture was a keystone of their anti-authoritarian crusade.

The FSM and other emerging New Left organizations attracted not only those who were steeped in campus politics but also a sizable contingent of social "dropouts" who hung out on the periphery of the academic scene. Although these people rarely attended classes, in a sense they constituted the heart and soul of the new lifestyle emerging in and around various college towns all across America. Hunter Thompson described the nonstudent left in *The Nation* in 1965:

> Social radicals tend to be "arty." Their gigs are poetry and folk music, rather than politics, although many are fervently committed to the civil rights movement. Their political bent is Left, but their real interests are writing, painting, good sex, good sounds, and free marijuana. The realities of politics put them off, although they don't mind lending their talents to a demonstration here and there, or even getting arrested for a good cause. They have quit one system and they don't want to be organized into another; they feel they have more important things to do.

For the new bohemians, radicalism had become a way of life. Moving against the structures of antifreedom involved distinctive modes of dress and speech, how you wore your hair, what you smoked, the kind of music you listened to, and so forth. Getting stoned and floating through the day formed the basis of an almost ritualized existence for these people. Finding the clothes, making the connection, copping the dope and smoking it, and leavening the mixture with one's ongoing experience was in many ways a full-time job in itself.

To the conventional observer this lifestyle appeared shiftless, useless, and parasitic. Invariably the root of this creeping social disease was traced to those evil drugs and that unhealthy lust for kicks they inspired, which was allegedly ruining the lives of so many young people. But drug use was not simply for kicks, an end in itself, even if that was how the straight press and the schoolteachers portrayed it. Indeed, if one insisted on calling it a kick, then it was more like a swift kick in the rump of the establishment.

During the nascent phase of the student movement, taking drugs was a way of saying "No!" to authority, of bucking the status quo. Drug use and radical politics often went hand in hand. If a certain percentage of young people in a given college town were smoking pot or dropping acid, then there was generally a corresponding level of political activism. Not everyone who turned on was also involved in political protest, but there was a significant overlap between the two groups. Many people associated with the FSM, including half the members of the steering committee, were getting high. In this respect Berkeley was not much different from other schools; it was just the leading edge of the political and cultural groundswell that would soon sweep the entire country.

The act of consuming the forbidden fruit was politicized by the mere fact that it was illegal. When you smoked marijuana, you immediately became aware of the glaring contradiction between the way you experienced reality in your own body and the official descriptions by the government and the media. That pot was not the big bugaboo that it had been cracked up to be was irrefutable evidence that the authorities either did not tell the truth or did not know what they were talking about. Its continued illegality was proof that lying and/or stupidity was a cornerstone of government policy. When young people got high, they knew this existentially, from the inside out. They saw through the great hoax, the cover story concerning not only the narcotics laws but the entire system. Smoking dope was thus an important political catalyst, for it enabled many a budding radical to begin questioning the official mythology of the governing class.

It is impossible to understand the politics of LSD without also considering the politics of marijuana, as the two were linked within the drug subculture. The popularity of both substances was inseparable from the outlaw ethos surrounding their use. Dope was an initiation into a cult of secrecy, with blinds drawn, incense burning to hide the smell, and music playing as the joint was ritualistically passed around a circle of friends. Said Michael Rossman, a veteran of the Berkeley Free Speech Movement, "When a young person took his first puff of psychoactive smoke, he also drew in the psychoactive culture as a whole, the entire matrix of law and association surrounding the drug, its induction and transaction. One inhaled a certain way of dressing, talking, acting, certain attitudes. One became a youth criminal against the State."

That dope was fun *and* illegal made the experience all the more exciting. The toking ritual drew people together in a unique way, so that they felt as if they were part of a loose tribe. Who you got high with was as important as what you got high on, for you shared parts of yourself along with the smoke. There was a natural intimacy about toking up with friends that facilitated the revelation of hitherto hidden facets of personality. (The OSS was right to select marijuana as a truth drug, for it does help loosen reserve and stimulate loquaciousness.) As a mild relaxant that also enhanced awareness, pot was frequently smoked in conjunction with some other activity, such as reading, listening to music or making love. The decidedly sensual effects of marijuana often put people on a different timetable. Getting stoned was a reprieve from dead time, school time, television time, punch-the-clock time, and that was what made the drug so attractive.

Once you had smoked marijuana and enjoyed the experience, an interest in other drugs was natural. For many people lighting up was a prelude to tripping out; the set they took off the smoking high disposed them favorably toward LSD. Although acid and grass are both aesthetic enhancers, the strength of LSD put it in a whole other category. Tripping is a very special type of activity, mentally as well as physically. It can include moments of astonishing insight and supermellow serenity ("a peace which passeth all understanding"), but always lurking at the edge of the psychedelic aura is the specter of something deadly serious. Whereas pot is mild enough to be playful, acid is an intense and unremitting dose of bacchanalia. Unlike marijuana intoxication, which can be regulated by the number of puffs, the acid high cannot be controlled once the tab or sugar cube is ingested. The sheer duration of an LSD trip—eight to twelve hours and sometimes longer—requires a much greater commitment than smoking a "jay."

In some sense one is forced to *earn* whatever psychological truths can be gleaned from having the mind stretched to unknown limits by a psychedelic. That was what Kesey and the Merry Pranksters meant when they invited people to try and "pass the Acid Test." The willingness to endure what could be a rather harrowing ordeal was for many young men and women a way of cutting the last umbilical cord to everything the older generation had designated as safe and sanitized. If smoking marijuana turned people into social outlaws, acid led many to see themselves as cosmic fugitives.

The decision to experiment with LSD for the first time was often as important as the experience itself. One had to muster a certain amount of courage to commit a transgression of this sort. It wasn't because dropping acid was against the law (the drug didn't become illegal until late 1966); nevertheless, a leap of faith was required since no one could be sure what lay in store after the deed was done. The only certainty was uncertainty, but that did not dissuade the young from going one on one with the Abyss. Too much was at stake to refuse the gamble. For those who made the leap, the prospect of not taking LSD was even more awesome than the nagging question mark that loomed on the horizon. (Or, as the sixties wall graffiti proclaimed, "Reality is a crutch for those who can't face acid.") Their primary motive was not to escape from the "real" world but to experience by whatever means necessary some sort of existential uplift that might shed light on the quagmire of the self.

Psychedelic initiates were willing to pay some heavy dues as they explored a host of mind-altering chemicals. Before LSD became a staple of the street, the most frequently used "brain food" was the foul-tasting peyote, which induced nausea, cramps, and vomiting. (Michael McClure compared peyote to the smell of "a dead wet dog on a cool morning.") In the late 1950s and early 1960s, peyote buttons could be purchased via mail order from a cactus farm in Texas. Other naturally occurring hallucinogens were also available—morning glory seeds, the Hawaiian baby wood rose, and nutmeg (used by many prison inmates, including Malcolm X before his conversion to Islam). Such drugs frequently resulted in aching joints, weak muscles and a powerful hangover the next day, but that was all part of the "trip." The passion with which young people embraced these substances, despite the attendant somatic discomfort, was indicative of an overriding conviction that psychedelics were a means to liberation, a way of confronting oneself in cosmic dramas, just as Huxley and the beats had described.

If any single theme dominated young people in the 1960s, it was the search for a new way of seeing, a new relation to the world. LSD was a means of exciting consciousness and provoking visions, a kind of hurried magic enabling youthful seekers to recapture the resonance of life that society had denied. Drugs were a passport to an uncharted landscape of risk and sensation, and those who entered the forbidden territory moved quickly into areas where most adults could offer little assistance. The drama enacted in this zone of enchantment was totally alien to the academic curriculum, which failed to provide the necessary tools to deal with the rewards and pitfalls one might encounter on such a journey.

Experimenting with LSD and other hallucinogens often created a feeling of separation or alienation from people who hadn't had the experience. Not surprisingly, those who turned on found it increasingly difficult to identify with anyone of a distinctly older mindset; instead their own peer group became the primary source of information as young people assumed the task of educating themselves. They were committed not so much to a predetermined objective as to a process of self-discovery that was open-ended and ripe with images of tomorrow. Their infatuation with psychedelics was symbolic of an attempt to seize control of the means of mental production in a very personal sense. They would get by—and high—with a little help from their friends, learning what they had to know before or after or in spite of school, so that in the midst of a period of chaos and confusion they might find a way to forge a link with the future.

Carl Oglesby, former president of Students for a Democratic Society (SDS), the leading national New Left organization in the 1960s, reflected on how the psychological underpinnings of taking LSD and rebelling against authority were complementary.

> The acid experience is so concrete. It draws a line right across your life—before and after LSD—in the same way you felt that your step into radical politics drew a sharp division. People talked about that, the change you go through, how fast the change could happen on an individual level and how liberating and glorious it was. Change was seen as survival, as the strategy of health. Nothing could stand for that overall sense of going through profound changes so well as the immediate, powerful and explicit transformation that you went through when you dropped acid. In the same way, bursting through the barricades redefined you as a new person. It's not necessarily that the actual content of the LSD experience contributed to politically radical or revolutionary consciousness—it was just that the experience shared the structural characteristics of political rebellion, and resonated those changes so that the two became independent prongs of an over-arching transcending rebellion that took in the person and the State at the same time.

The first big surge of street acid hit the college scene in 1965, just when the political situation in the United States was heating up. The mid-1960s were pervaded by a sense of daily apocalypse: President Johnson escalated the war in Vietnam, Malcolm X was assassinated, twenty thousand marines conducted a "police action" in the Dominican Republic, and the Watts rebellion caught fire in Los Angeles. During this volatile historical moment the New Left seized the time as well as the attention of the national media, grabbing headlines and making waves. The publicity windfall opened up hitherto undreamed-of possibilities in terms of reaching a large portion of the citizenry but also posed unprecedented challenges for the New Left.

Vietnam was the first television war, and it was the war, more than any other issue, that radicalized people and spurred them to direct action. By the same token the antiwar movement was the first opposition movement to emerge under the full glare of the media spotlight. SDS was catapulted into prominence in April 1965, when it sponsored a rally in Washington, DC, to protest LBJ's decision to initiate the sustained bombing of North Vietnam. Thirty thousand people showed up for this demonstration, far more than had been expected, and the media coverage was extensive. A flood of newly radicalized recruits joined SDS and its influence expanded considerably.

Of course, SDS was only part of the New Left or "the Movement," as insiders called it, and the Movement itself was part of a larger cultural upheaval that occurred during this period. Nearly everything was being questioned and most things tried in an orgy of experiment that shook the nation at its roots. Students everywhere were rejecting mainstream values, turning on to drugs, and marching in the streets. There were teach-ins, sit-ins, mass draft card burnings, guerrilla theater, and other forms of high-spirited protest, as the New Left abandoned a reformist approach and entered a phase of active resistance.

Life seemed to be one grand eruption of creative energy in the mid-1960s, and many thought the crosshatch of cultural and political rebellion was workable and exciting. The hipster and the activist represented two poles of the radical experience. Both shared a contempt for middle-class values, a disdain for authority, and a passion for expression. But there were also significant tensions between the two camps. Each had different ideas about how to achieve personal liberation and remake the world. The first signs of friction became evident not long after the New Left burst into the limelight and large amounts of black market acid hit selected college campuses.

In October 1965 Ken Kesey addressed the Berkeley Vietnam Day rally, an event that was part of the first International Days of Protest, when young radicals in a hundred cities throughout the Western world demonstrated against the war. The Berkeley rally attracted nearly fifteen thousand people who listened to folksingers and a slate of antiwar notables including Allen Ginsberg and Lawrence Ferlinghetti. Kesey showed up with a band of Merry Pranksters in the old psychedelic school bus, which had been painted blood-red for the occasion and covered with swastikas, hammers and sickles, the American eagle, and other nationalist symbols.

Kesey's entourage, which included a number of mean-looking Hell's Angels, grew restless while the antiwar speakers riled up the crowd about the genocide across the ocean. The Chief Prankster was disturbed by the angry overtones of what was supposed to be a peace demonstration. The lack of humor amidst all the self-righteous rhetoric rubbed him the wrong way. When it was his turn to speak, he strolled to the mike in his Day-Glo helmet and windbreaker and proceeded to shock the audience by saying that wars had been fought for ten thousand years and they weren't going to change anything by parading around with signs and slogans. Then he pulled out a harmonica and regaled the crowd with a squalling rendition of "Home on the Range." "Do you want to know how to stop the war?" Kesey screamed. "Just turn your backs on it, fuck it!" And then he walked away.

Kesey represented those elements of the hip scene that emphasized personal liberation without any strategic concern whatsoever; the task of remodeling themselves took precedence over changing institutions or government policy. This posture rankled hard-core politicos who were committed to busting the system that had driven them into limbo. Their opinion of Kesey did not improve the following day when the Hell's Angels began to hassle antiwar activists as they set off toward the US Army installation in Oakland in an attempt to block trains carrying American troops destined for Vietnam.

Bob Dylan was in the Bay Area during the Berkeley Vietnam Day protest, and the march organizers sent Allen Ginsberg to ask him to lead the demonstration. But Dylan was not interested. "There's no left wing and right wing," he said, "just up wing and down wing." He did make a modest proposal, however. He would agree to participate only if it was a festive rally with a sense of irony. If the marchers would carry placards with pictures of lemons or watermelons or words like "orange" or "automobile," then he would join

134

in. Not surprisingly, his whimsical offer was refused.

Dylan's attitude toward antiwar protest disappointed many New Left activists who had once revered him as the folk avatar of the civil rights movement. In his early finger-pointing songs Dylan took on all the sins of the parent culture and spit them back in verse, addressing obvious issues of social justice: antinuke, antiboss, antiexploitation. He sang to hundreds of thousands in August 1963 at a huge rally in Washington, DC, which culminated in Martin Luther King's eloquent "I have a dream" speech. To all appearances it should have been a moment of crowning glory for Dylan, but instead it was a time of crisis for him both as an artist and as a spokesman for social change.

Dylan was caught up in a symbiotic relationship with the inequities of society. His protest songs had made him rich and famous, but where was it all going? The pressures attendant upon his sudden notoriety, as well as his growing doubts about the ability of the Movement to revitalize American life, distanced him from his earlier material. During this period of self-examination Dylan did what he had done when he left his hometown in Minnesota to pursue a career as a folksinger—"strike another match and start anew."

With a small entourage of friends and musicians he holed up in Woodstock, an artist colony in upstate New York, and opened himself to various new influences. Everyone around him was popping pills and experimenting with acid and mushrooms, and Dylan himself entered a period of protracted drug use. At the time he was fond of saying that he was "pro-chemistry": "Being a musician means—depending on how far you go—getting to the depths of where you are at. And most any musician would try anything to get to those depths, because playing music is an immediate thing—as opposed to putting paint on a canvas, which is a calculated thing. Your spirit flies when you are playing music. So, with music, you tend to look deeper and deeper inside yourself to find the music."

It was obvious listening to Dylan's 1965 album, *Bringing It All Back Home*, that he was exploring new directions. The shift in his aesthetic was drastic, as if, like the figure in Cocteau's film *The Blood of a Poet*, he had looked at his own poetic image in the mirror until he convulsively splashed through it. Determined to express the full range of his imagination in song, he plunged into strange, beautiful and chaotic worlds. "Mr. Tambourine Man" is an invo-

135

cation to a mystical journey through "the foggy ruins of time." The lyrics are appropriately vague; the Tambourine Man may be the pusher, the drug, or the experience itself. But the ambience of the work is unmistakably that of early dawn, the hour of the wolf, when all hangs in an eerie balance, as at the end of a long and difficult LSD trip.

On the same album Dylan made his most explicit statement on the outlaw quality of the drug subculture. "Subterranean Homesick Blues" is a paean to the paranoid head-space associated with the use of controlled substances. The opening stanza describes Johnny the bathtub chemist in the basement "mixing up the medicine" while the narc in "the trenchcoat" waits to be paid off. Dylan goes on to offer some homespun advice: keep a low profile, avoid the heat, yet maintain a certain awareness—"Don't try No-Doz"—and above all rely on your intuition—"You don't need a weatherman to know which way the wind blows." (A group of militant SDS radicals would later take their name from this line, calling themselves "the Weathermen.")

In these brilliant and unprecedented works Dylan exorcised the knee-jerk moralism of the topical protest song in favor of his search for a sustaining vision. At first many Dylan fans had a hard time with his new material. For starters one side of *Bringing It All Back Home* featured electric accompaniment, which Dylan had never used before, and this was strictly taboo as far as the folkies were concerned. To confound matters, these elusive and evocative compositions did not seem to have a single message or ultimate meaning. The interpretation of a Dylan song usually said more about the interpreter than about the song or Dylan, which was what the songs were about anyway—facing oneself.

Dylan showcased his new music at the Newport Folk Festival in July 1965. His set completely shattered the expectations of his audience. On the hallowed ground of Newport—where Pete Seeger sang of peace and freedom, where Dylan himself had sung "Blowin' in the Wind" with Peter, Paul and Mary just two years earlier—Bobby D. gave the quintessential protopunk performance. He did three electric numbers with a backup band, but the loud, pulsing electronic rock drowned out a lot of the lyrics, causing some in the crowd to scream and heckle the musicians. This wasn't the Dylan they knew, who had provided a musical backdrop to their most intimate hopes. With some prodding Dylan returned with his acoustic guitar and sang "It's All Over Now, Baby Blue." While this encore somewhat mollified the scandalized audience of folkies, the real message was that the black-and-white politics of the folk era was over.*

The process Dylan inaugurated with *Bringing It All Back Home* characterized his output during the mid-1960s. The songs on *Highway 61 Revisited*, also released in 1965, were testaments to the mystic trials he suffered during his heavy drug period. In his first international chart-buster, "Like a Rolling Stone," Dylan asked the musical question of how it feels to face the Void. This remarkable song combined his most withering vocal sneer with a joyously uplifting melody to capture the combination of fear and exhilaration that accompanied his listeners' first groping steps out of the boredom and security of middle-class suburbia. "How does it *feel*," he moaned, "to be on your own, a complete unknown . . ." Never was an artist more in synch with his time and his cultural moment. He was inside the psyches of millions. Phil Ochs described Dylan during this period as acid incarnate: "He was LSD on stage."

Before Dylan went electric—that is to say, psychedelic—folk was the music of moral conscience, while rock was the Dionysian backbeat glorifying the baser pleasures of sex and speed. But the moment Dylan plugged in his guitar, social critique went Top Forty and rock, with its growing audience, became a vehicle of protest. His songs, along with those of other turned-on folk-rockers who followed in his footsteps—Simon and Garfunkel, The Byrds, Buffalo Springfield, The Lovin' Spoonful—became an instant body of oral tradition appealing to an enormous audience of disaffected youth. The idealism of folk was wedded to the anger and exuberance of rock music, and before long many of the same people who trashed Dylan for selling out and leaving the protest movement in the lurch began to rock out.

Dylan's emergence as a rock and roller was part and parcel of his problematic self-exploration with psychedelic drugs in the mid-1960s. The vastly accelerated personal changes Dylan underwent as he moved from protest to transcendence were archetypical of a rite of passage experienced by thousands of turned-on youth. Dylan knew

---

*In 1965 the Student Nonviolent Coordinating Committee (SNCC), the radical youth wing of the civil rights movement, expelled white activists from its ranks and introduced black power as a counterpoint to integration.

that everyone had to go through the process of individuation on their own, that neither he nor anyone else could lead the masses to that other shore. To those who were attempting to navigate such treacherous waters, his only suggestion was: "Everybody must get stoned."

PART TWO

Acid for the Masses

6

From Hip To Hippie

BEFORE THE DELUGE

The initial breeding ground for the large-scale use of psychedelics was the social and artistic fringe areas associated with the beat phenomenon. For some years prior to the emergence of LSD as a street drug, the number of people whose lives were influenced by psychedelics had been slowly building to a critical mass, until they became visible on both coasts as distinct communities. The most significant expression of the new psychedelic lifestyle was centered in the Haight-Ashbury district of San Francisco. It was in the Haight that the cultural rebellion fueled by LSD happened so vividly and with such intensity that it attracted worldwide attention.

Situated on the periphery of Golden Gate Park, this quiet, multiracial, and somewhat run-down neighborhood first became a haven for nonconformists in the early 1960s, when tourists, gangster elements, thrill seekers, and narcs squeezed the life out of the hip scene in North Beach. A good number of beatnik refugees migrated across town to the Haight, where ramshackle Victorians were available at low rent. The next few years were a gestation period in which Haight-Ashbury continued to evolve as a gathering point for the creatively alienated. Increasing numbers of Berkeley radicals, fed up with academia, joined the artists, musicians, and bearded habitués who were probing eccentricity and other forms of dissent.

By 1965, Haight-Ashbury was a vibrant neobohemian enclave, a community on the cusp of a major transition. A small psychedelic city-state was taking shape, and those who inhabited the open urban space within its invisible borders adhered to a set of laws and rhythms completely different from the nine-to-five routine that governed straight society. More than anything the Haight was a unique state of mind, an arena of exploration and celebration. The new hipsters had cast aside the syndrome of alienation and despair that saddled many of their beatnik forebears. The accent shifted from solitude to communion, from the individual to the interpersonal. The new sensibility was particularly evident in musical preferences. The sound of the in-crowd was no longer folk or jazz but the bouncing rhythms of rock and roll that could incite an audience to boogie in unison almost as a single organism.

Music happenings were a cornerstone of the cultural revival in the Haight, providing a locus around which a new community consciousness coalesced. One of the early energy-movers in the local rock scene was Chet Helms. A couple of years earlier, Helms had forsaken a future as a Baptist minister and hitchhiked from Texas with a young blues singer named Janis Joplin. Together these two rolling stones traveled the asphalt networks of America in search of kindred spirits until they settled in the Haight. Joplin fell in with other musicians, joining what would later become Big Brother and the Holding Company, and Helms formed the Family Dog, an organization dedicated to what was then the rather novel proposition that people should be encouraged to dance at rock concerts.

On October 16, 1965, the Family Dog held its first rock extravaganza at the Longshoreman's Hall, a dome-shaped union headquarters near Fisherman's Wharf. Dubbed "A Tribute to Dr. Strange," the evening featured the city's premier psychedelic rock band, the Jefferson Airplane, and a handful of other local acts. A large crowd turned out for this inaugural event, including quite a few political radicals who participated in the Berkeley Vietnam Day rally earlier the same day. Everyone was decked out in weird costumes. There were even a few Hell's Angels in attendance, and they joined the snake-dance weaving circles and figure eights through the hall.

The Family Dog dance was a huge success, and soon these concerts became a staple of the hip community. Each weekend people converged at auditoriums such as the Avalon Ballroom for all-night festivals that combined the seemingly incongruous elements of spirituality and debauch. Thoroughly stoned on grass and acid and each other, they rediscovered the crushing joy of the dance, pouring it all out in a frenzy that frequently bordered on the religious. When rock music was performed with all its potential fury, a special kind of delirium took hold. Attending such performances amounted to a total assault on the senses: the electric sound washed in visceral waves over the dancers, unleashing intense psychic energies and

142

driving the audience further and further toward public trance. Flashing strobes, light shows, body paint, outrageous getups—it was mass environmental theater, an oblivion of limbs and minds in motion. For a brief moment outside of time these young people lived out the implications of André Breton's surrealist invocation: "Beauty will be CONVULSIVE or will not be at all."

No affair in the Haight better illustrated how far these rock events had strayed from conventional entertainment than the Trips Festival staged by Ken Kesey and the Merry Pranksters in January 1966. "The general tone of things," Kesey advertised, "has moved on from the self-conscious happenings to a more jubilant occasion where the audience participates because it's more fun to do so than not. Audience dancing is an assumed part of all the shows, and the audience is invited to wear ecstatic dress and to bring their own gadgets (A.C. outlets will be provided)." This was a wide-open three-day LSD party with just about every sight and sound imaginable: mime exhibitions, guerrilla theater, a "Congress of Wonders," and live mikes and sound equipment for anyone to play with. Closed-circuit television cameras were set up on the dance floor so people could watch themselves shake and swing. Music blasted at ear-splitting volumes while Day-Glo bodies bounced gleefully on trampolines. At one point Kesey flashed from a projector, "Anyone who knows he is God please go up on stage."

Jerry ("Captain Trips") Garcia, the lead guitarist of the Grateful Dead,* one of the bands that performed at the Trips Festival, tried to put his finger on what made those early events so special:

> What the Kesey thing was depended on who *you* were when you were there. It was open, a tapestry, a mandala—it was whatever you made it. ...When it was moving right, you could dig that there was something that it was getting toward, something like ordered chaos, or some *region* of chaos.... Everybody would be high and flashing and going through insane changes during which everything would be *demolished*, man, and spilled and broken and affected, and after that, another thing would happen, maybe smoothing out the chaos, then another.... Thousands of people, man, all helplessly stoned, all finding themselves in a room of

---

*The first member of the Grateful Dead to turn on to LSD was Robert Hunter, the Dead lyricist, who participated in a government-sponsored drug study at Stanford University during the early 1960s. Hunter later recommended the experience to the other band members.

thousands of people, none of whom any of them were afraid of. It was magic, far-out beautiful magic.

The Trips Festival was a shot of adrenalin for the entire hip scene in the Haight. The head population began to realize its growing strength in numbers. Scores of local bands were forming, their names indicative of their psychedelic orientation: Blue Cheer, Clear Light, Daily Flash, the Loading Zone, Morning Glory, Celestial Hysteria, Ball Point Banana, Flamin' Groovies, the Electric Flag, the Weeds... There was even a band called the CIA (Citizens for Interplanetary Activities). Some of the groups—notably the Jefferson Airplane, Big Brother and the Holding Company, Quicksilver Messenger Service, Country Joe and the Fish, and, of course, the Grateful Dead—established themselves as first-rate performers. Their music was rooted in folk and blues, but the rhythms mutated under the influence of LSD and the raw power of electricity. Acid rock, as the San Francisco sound was called, was unique not only as a genre but also as praxis. The musicians viewed themselves first and foremost as community artists, and they often played outdoors for free as a tribute to their constituency. Even when there was a cover charge, Chet Helms and the Family Dog usually waived it for friends and neighbors. People revered Helms for this, but because of his generosity he frequently lost money and could not always pay the bands.

It was only later, when acid rock went national in the summer of 1967, that the scene began to change. Whether it was the profit motive or just that the euphoric spirit of the early days was becoming harder to sustain, some of the originals felt that things were going sour. An up-and-coming rock promoter named Bill Graham was holding shows at the Fillmore auditorium and handling the biggest acts. Unlike Chet Helms, who ran his dance shows more like a church, Graham was in it strictly for the bucks. Although he refused to turn on, he was tuned in enough to see that light shows and acid rock could have mass appeal. Before long, high-powered record execs were knocking at his door.

While a lot of young people didn't dig Graham's "short-haired" attitude toward business, he did manage to stage an ongoing musical shindig, and he also supported the talented poster artists who would soon make psychedelic art an international style. It was under Graham's patronage that the rock club emerged as a significant cultural institution. (He also booked nonrock acts such as Lenny Bruce, who performed at the Fillmore in 1966 shortly before he died of a heroin overdose.) The rock and roll shows Graham promoted became the new social ritual, above all a music for heads and a powerful reinforcement for the spread of psychedelics.

The acid rock celebration was not confined to the concert hall but poured over into the street, which became the focal point of life in the Haight. The street was center stage, the place where you walked, talked, and dressed any way you wanted. With the pleasant climate you could hang out on the street most of the time, bombarded by a perpetual parade of stimuli—wild costumes, spontaneous theater, assorted antics, wandering minstrels. People were not just striking poses. To patrol the street in full regalia was an act of defiance, an open refusal to buy into the System. But it was also something more. For those who exchanged knowing smiles during their daily rounds, the long hair, beads, and bare feet were not only a symbol of estrangement but a positive leap of consciousness, an affirmation of a radically different set of personal and social priorities.

The Haight was becoming a testing area for fresh shapes of human experience. Dwellers in the acid ghetto frequently clustered into tribal or "intentional" family units. They practiced communal living arrangements in which private property was restricted to a bare minimum. Sexual exclusivity was often rejected in favor of group marriage. The loosening of sexual mores was in part an expression of a growing appetite for a common spirituality. Hangups or restrictions of any sort could only impede the healing process, which entailed nothing less than the reinstatement of ecstasy as the fulcrum of daily life.

Excitement was brewing in the Haight. Although the straight world had scarcely begun to notice what was happening, the psychedelic city-state was having its brief golden age. The energy was unmistakably sky-high; poets and dreamers had the upper hand. One way or another, it all revolved around drugs. The psychedelic experience was the common chord of shared consciousness that unified the entire community. People talked about acid all the time, how it blew apart preconceptions and put you through intense changes. "It seemed like we were in a time machine," said Stephen Gaskin, a self-styled Haight-Ashbury orator. "Nearly anything we did was cool in a sense because it was all learning.... It was all paying attention, and you couldn't build experiments fast enough to catch acid."

Haight-Ashbury was the world's original psychedelic supermarket, the place where acid was first sold on a mass scale. The undisputed king of the illicit LSD trade was Augustus Owsley Stanley III, a dapper individual who could rap for hours on topics ranging from acid rock to Einsteinian physics. Owsley's personal history is something of an enigma—what can you say about someone who ate four steaks a day because he was convinced that vegetables were poison? His father was a government attorney, and his grandfather a US senator from Kentucky. Owsley had been expelled in the ninth grade for bringing intoxicating beverages onto school grounds, after which he was shunted from one prep school to the next. By the age of eighteen he had severed all family ties. He then did a short hitch in the air force, drifted around the West Coast for a few years and hooked up with Melissa Cargill, a young Berkeley chemistry major. Together they began to mass-produce the LSD that would make him a youth culture legend.

Owsley's product first hit the streets in February 1965, during the halcyon days of the early Acid Tests. Though his career as a bootleg chemist led him to adopt a reclusive lifestyle, he did pop up now and again on the psychedelic scene. He visited Millbrook and was on hand to freak freely at some wild parties hosted by Kesey. Owsley was so impressed by the music of the Grateful Dead that he became a patron to the band. During this period he also met Tim Scully, a Berkeley science prodigy whose IQ tipped the scales. He and Scully traveled for a while with the Merry Pranksters. Scully's skills as an electronics wiz came in handy on the psychedelic bus, and he helped design sound equipment for the Dead. But Owsley was more interested in his knowledge of chemicals—which was formidable. Scully became his apprentice, and together they set up an underground laboratory in Point Richmond, California, in the spring of 1966.

Known throughout the Haight as "the unofficial mayor of San Francisco," Owsley cultivated an image as a wizard-alchemist whose intentions with LSD were priestly and magical. Over the years he developed a rather esoteric view of LSD and its potential. He was convinced, for example, that the psychic "vibes" in the laboratory at the precise moment when the raw ingredients of LSD were being mixed had a strong influence on what kind of trips people would have. Owsley was obsessed with making his product as pure as possible—even purer than Sandoz, which described LSD in its scientific reports as a yellowish crystalline substance. As he mastered his illicit craft, Owsley found a way to refine the crystal so that it appeared blue-white under a fluorescent lamp; moreover, if the crystals were shaken, they emitted flashes of light, which meant that LSD in its pure form was piezoluminescent—a property shared by a very small number of compounds.

At first Owsley produced LSD in a powder form that could be doled out in gelatin capsules. He also sold it as a liquid ("Mother's Milk"), tinted light blue so that distributors could keep track of which sugar cubes had been spiked. But it was hard to control the dosage with this method, so Owsley invested in a professional pill press and soon he started dyeing his tablets a different color each time he turned out a new shipment. Although there was no difference between the tablets (each contained a carefully measured 250 micrograms), street folklore ascribed specific qualities to every color: red was said to be exceptionally mellow, green was edgy, and blue was the perfect compromise.

By putting out high-quality merchandise and color-coding his tablets, Owsley was able to stay a few steps ahead of his competitors. Even in the Haight, where he was by far the principal source of LSD, there were other brands available on the black market. But Owsley acid was universally recognized as the most potent, and it was revered by turned-on youth. "Every time we'd make another batch and release it on the street," Scully recalled, "something beautiful would flower, and of course we believed it was all because of what we were doing. We believed that we were the architects of social change, that our mission was to change the world substantially, and what was going on in the Haight was a sort of laboratory experiment, a microscopic sample of what would happen worldwide."

Drug trafficking in the Haight quickly grew to enormous dimensions as people came from all over to cop in large quantities. With his commanding position in the underground market, Owsley kept the retail price of LSD at a steady $2.00 per trip. He and his assistants are said to have manufactured four million hits in the mid-1960s, and he probably gave away as much as he sold. Of course there was money to be made, and Owsley and the others made plenty, but financial considerations were not the sole motivation. The local dealers saw themselves as performing an important community service: "consciousness raising". They distributed acid because they believed in the drug, and while making their deliveries they also functioned as wandering rap specialists, bearers of news, gossip, rumor, and folk wisdom.

It was perhaps inevitable that those who tripped out would often worship LSD and deify its catalytic properties. And who could blame them in the early days, when so many were heady with optimism? The most ardent enthusiasts looked to LSD as something capable, in and of itself, of ushering in the Kingdom of Heaven on earth. The drug was hailed as an elixir of truth, a psychic solvent that could cleanse the heart of greed and envy and break the barriers of separateness. Needless to say, these young romantics had no idea that the CIA's "enlightened" operatives had been dropping acid since the early 1950s without being moved to trade in their blow darts, shellfish toxin, and extreme prejudices for flowers, love beads and peace signs. If the spies had their minds blown by the drug, it was generally in the direction of bizarre James Bond scenarios like putting thalium salts in Castro's shoes to make his beard fall out.

When Ron and Jay Thelin opened the Psychedelic Shop near the corner of Haight and Ashbury in January 1966, they had a clear-cut purpose: spread the word about LSD. The Psychedelic Shop was unique among the numerous storefronts popping up in the Haight to cater to the hip population. At a time when information about LSD was passed primarily by word of mouth, it served as a place to hang out, gossip, and trade drugs. The shelves were stocked with books, smoking paraphernalia, dance posters, paisley fabrics, imported bells—in short, anything an acidhead might be interested in. The Thelin brothers also installed the first community bulletin board. They had a rather benign vision of the country's manifest destiny. Haight Street, Ron Thelin rhapsodized, would soon become "a world-famous dope center. There would be fine tea shops with big jars of fine marijuana, and chemist shops with the finest psychedelic chemicals."

The Thelin brothers were turned on to acid by Allen Cohen, who was then dealing some of Owsley's finest. Cohen ended up working part-time at the Psychedelic Shop and later became editor of the *Oracle*, a psychedelic tabloid backed by the Thelins. The *Oracle* printed articles on eastern mysticism, macrobiotics, yoga, astrology, and whatever else fit into the "new age" scheme of things. The pages were occasionally sprayed with perfume and were often difficult to read because the colored type was slanted to evoke the undulating shapes that characterize LSD hallucinations.

While most people in the Haight were probably in tune with Kesey's cosmic giggle, the *Oracle* group was particularly keen on Timothy Leary's trip. They took their cues from the ex-Harvard professor who spoke in clichés about acid as an evolutionary tool that could guarantee religious epiphanies. *Oracle* philosophy was Leary philosophy; Ron Thelin summed up the newspaper's editorial slant: "To show that LSD provides a profound experience.... To get everyone to turn on, tune in, and drop out."

When the *Oracle* first started publishing, there was already considerable tension between the police and the hip community. Pot busts were becoming more frequent, and the California legislature had recently passed an edict banning the use of LSD. The new law was slated to go into effect on October 6, 1966. The date took on mystical meaning for the *Oracle* group. In the Bible "666" is a symbol of the Beast, the AntiChrist, the precursor of Apocalypse; the law against LSD was interpreted as a demonic act, a violation of a people's God-given right to experience their own divinity. But the *Oracle* group did not want another angry showdown with the authorities. Instead of protesting the new law, they decided to organize a gala event that would expose the falsity of the legal system. "We were not guilty of using illegal substances," Cohen insisted. "We were celebrating transcendental consciousness, the beauty of the universe, the beauty of being."

On the same day that LSD became a controlled substance, the *Oracle* hosted an outdoor gathering called the Love Pageant Rally. It was an expression of the community's steadfast devotion to their chosen sacrament. A few thousand people, far more than expected, assembled peacefully in the Panhandle next to Golden Gate Park. Rock bands played for free, and the master of ceremonies read a manifesto entitled "A Prophecy of a Declaration of Independence": "We hold these truths to be self-evident, that all is equal, that the creation endows us with certain inalienable rights, that among these are: The freedom of the body, the pursuit of joy, and the expansion of consciousness . . ."

At the appropriate moment hundreds of people placed a tab of acid on their outstretched tongues and swallowed in unison. The next year in the Haight would be quite a trip indeed.

Politics of the Bummer

Spring of 1966.

The Senate Subcommittee on Juvenile Delinquency convenes yet another round of hearings in Washington, DC, to deal with the growing "LSD problem." Chairman Thomas Dodd, a conservative Democrat from Connecticut and a noted Communist hunter, speaks out against the use of psychedelic drugs. He dismisses consciousness expansion as an alibi for sheer kicks and proposes strict new laws aimed at "the pseudo-intellectuals who advocate the use of drugs in search for some imaginary freedoms of the mind and in search for higher psychic experiences." Quick and drastic measures are necessary, Dodd asserts, because the LSD scourge is spreading at an alarming rate among America's youth.

A parade of scientists, health officials, and law enforcement experts render their verdict: the unsupervised use of LSD for nonmedical purposes can only lead to tragic results. L-S-D spells instant psychosis and a tendency toward bizarre behavior and capricious fits of violence. What is more, the psychotic interlude can recur at any moment without warning (the "flashback phenomenon"). Other perils are cited: those who take the drug exhibit a disturbing tendency to withdraw from productive activity, and some end up drifting aimlessly through life. To complete the hatchet job, the experts resort to their favorite ploy—the domino theory of drug abuse: the neophyte starts with marijuana and LSD and inevitably winds up hooked on heroin.

The bad rap on acid was sensationalized in the establishment press, which had been focusing on the detrimental effects of LSD since the Harvard scandal. Typical scare headlines from the mid-1960s read: "GIRL 5, EATS LSD AND GOES WILD". . . "A MONSTER IN OUR MIDST—A DRUG CALLED LSD". . . "THRILL DRUG WARPS MIND, KILLS." In March 1966 *Life* magazine ran a cover story entitled "LSD: The Exploding Threat of the Mind Drug That Got Out of Control," which described the psychedelic experience as chemical Russian roulette in which the player gambled with his sanity. Pictures of people on acid cowering in corners, beyond communication, were used to underscore the message that LSD "could be a one-way trip to an asylum, prison, or grave." *Life*, whose publisher, Henry Luce, had once spoken favorably of psychedelics, didn't pull any punches: "A person

...can become permanently deranged through a single terrifying LSD experience. Hospitals report case after case where people arrive in a state of mental disorganization, unable to distinguish their bodies from their surroundings.... it brings out the very worst in some people. LSD is being dropped in girls' drinks. Terrifying parties are being given with a surprise in the punch. The Humane Society is picking up disoriented dogs. . . ."

The smear campaign paid off. In April 1966 Sandoz Pharmaceuticals recalled all the LSD it had distributed to scientists for research purposes, bringing to a halt nearly all government-sponsored experiments in the US (with the exception of the secret research conducted by the CIA and the military). Politicians issued pronunciamentos against the drug, hoping to ride the coattails of the full scale LSD panic that was sweeping the land. One government official went so far as to characterize LSD as "the greatest threat facing the country today... more dangerous than the Vietnam War."

Amidst this atmosphere of near hysteria a few spokesmen for the burgeoning acid subculture were called to testify before the Senate subcommittee. Timothy Leary offered an olive branch to the politicians, suggesting that a moratorium on LSD might be appropriate. (A few months earlier Leary had been convicted of attempting to smuggle marijuana into the US, for which he received the heaviest sentence ever meted out for possession of pot—thirty years in prison and a $30,000 fine. His case was being appealed at the time of the Senate hearings.) Dressed in a suit and tie, with neatly trimmed hair, Leary announced he would urge everyone to stop taking LSD for a year if the lawmakers refrained from banning the drug. Repressive legislation, Leary warned, would usher in an era of prohibition that would be "much more onerous and anguished" than the moonshining days of the 1920s and 1930s. "We do not want amateur or black-market sale or distribution of LSD," said Leary. "You don't know what you are getting."

Leary claimed that he had always been opposed to the indiscriminate of psychedelics. "For six years I have been in the unfortunate position of warning society that this was going to happen. We knew there was going to be an LSD panic. We saw it coming the way a meteorologist can see a hurricane coming. . . . But every attempt has been made to keep it underground. All that energy just cannot be kept underground." To insure good-quality LSD and proper use of the drug, Leary proposed seminars for high school and college students at special psychedelic training centers. These institutions would license responsible adults who wished to utilize LSD "for serious purposes, such as spiritual growth, pursuit of knowledge, or in their own personal development." And what about the lad who chooses military service rather than college? asked Senator Ted Kennedy, a member of the Juvenile Delinquency Subcommittee. "I should think that in the Army of the future," Leary responded, "LSD will be used to expand consciousness so that these men can do their duties more effectively."

Arthur Kleps grew peeved as he watched the politicians react with scorn and derision to Leary's testimony. When it was his turn to speak, he decided to get tough with his interlocutors. "Would you mind telling me if you are really called Chief Boohoo?" asked one southern senator. "I'm afraid so," Kleps replied. Whereupon he launched into one of the most outrageous diatribes ever delivered on Capitol Hill.

"It is difficult for us to imagine what it is like to have been born in 1948," Kleps ranted, "but it is very much like being born into an insane asylum." The Chief Boohoo was particularly irked by FDA commissioner Goddard's contention that LSD-induced mind expansion was "pure bunk" since it could not be measured by objective tests. "If I were to give you an IQ test and during the administration one of the walls of the room opened up giving you a vision of the blazing glories of the central galactic suns, and at the same time your childhood began to unreel before your inner eye like a three-dimensional color movie, you would not do well on the intelligence test."

Kleps spoke with righteous vengeance. "We are not drug addicts, we are not criminals, we are free men, and we will react to persecution the way free men have always reacted." If Leary was imprisoned, Kleps threatened, then all hell would break loose. There'd be a religious civil war. "I'd rather see the prison system become inoperable, and it would be if large amounts of LSD were delivered into the prison and distributed among the inmates....We would have to regard these places as concentration camps where people are being imprisoned because of their religion....I would resort to violence....This is the way this country started...."

When Allen Ginsberg took the stand, he tried to placate the committee by explaining in a calm and dignified tone that many people who took LSD were motivated by a desire for long-lasting beneficial effects rather than the immediate flash. In an effort to communicate the nature of the LSD experience, he invoked his own psychedelic history. He told of writing the second part of *Howl* on peyote and having fearful visions when he ingested yagé in Peru. He said he had stopped taking psychedelics for a few years, until 1965, when he dropped acid in Big Sur on the same day President Johnson was scheduled for a gallbladder operation. It was scarcely a week before the Berkeley Vietnam Day demonstration at which Ginsberg was slated to speak. A great deal of hostility to Johnson policy was percolating in radical circles. Ginsberg thought of the ailing president and the impending protest. Impressed by the majesty of the wooded landscape and the ocean cliffs, the poet realized that more harsh words and negative vibrations would not help the situation. While high on acid, he knelt and prayed for Johnson's health in psychedelic reconciliation with his anger about the administration's Vietnam debacle.

All of this was Ginsberg's way of telling the senators that LSD could have a positive effect on consciousness. For a healthy individual, he asserted, the drug posed a negligible risk—whereupon the bearded bard was quickly rebuffed by Senator Jacob Javits of New York, who reminded him that as a layman he was not qualified to comment on the medical aspects of LSD. But Ginsberg would not recant. He insisted that there had been a journalistic exaggeration of the dangers of LSD, and he warned that laws enacted in a climate of ignorance and hysteria would almost certainly create more problems than they solved.

Certain government officials also expressed reservations about new legislation to ban LSD. "I have a strong feeling," said Dr. Stanley Yolles, former director of NIMH, "that if we make the possession of LSD illegal, it will drive it further underground and make what perhaps is the beginning of a flaunting of authority...a more pathological process and a more strongly accented act of rebellion." Yolles believed that punitive measures would actually spur the growth of the illicit drug market—which was exactly what happened.

Historically in the United States repressive controls have been targeted at drugs identified with the poor, the underprivileged, and racial minorities; often such controls were enacted in times of social crisis (the reefer of the black and brown ghettos was outlawed during the Depression, for example). During the 1960s psychedelic drugs became associated with cultural and political rebellion, but in this case the user population was composed primarily of well-educated white middle-class youth. As a symbol of generational conflict acid provided a convenient scapegoat for the guardians of the status quo, who embraced the anti-LSD crusade as a high-consensus issue in an era otherwise riddled with political schisms. By invoking the specter of hallucinogenic drugs, conservative politicians implicitly attacked the groups that opposed the war in Vietnam. Certainly it was a lot easier to discredit the radical cause if the rest of society could be convinced that those uppity radicals were out of their minds—and the LSD craze was touted as sure proof of that.

"We are now in a position to understand the real reason for the condemnation of hallucinogens and why their use is punished," wrote Octavio Paz in *Alternating Current*. "The authorities do not behave as though they were trying to stamp out a harmful vice, but as though they were attempting to stamp out dissidence. Since this is a form of dissidence that is becoming more widespread, the prohibition takes on the proportion of a campaign against a spiritual contagion, against an *opinion*. What the authorities are displaying is *ideological zeal:* they are punishing a heresy, not a crime."

Indeed, if it were simply a matter of public health, it would be hard to explain all the hubbub about LSD when other commonly used substances are far more injurious: six million Americans are addicted to alcohol; ten million consume enough caffeine to cause health problems; over fifty million smoke cigarettes, which have been linked to lung cancer; and barbiturates (usually in conjunction with alcohol) are responsible for 90% of drug-related deaths each year. Nevertheless, President Johnson mentioned only LSD in his State of the Union address of 1968 (the year LSD possession was reclassified as a felony) when hyping his war against dangerous drugs.

LSD was also singled out as Public Enemy Number One by the mass media, which whipped America into a virtual frenzy over psychedelic drugs. It wasn't enough to convey the false impression that LSD probably caused permanent insanity; all of a sudden the press conjured up the frightening prospect of couples giving birth to some kind of octopus because acid had scrambled their chromosomes. However, when the Army Chemical Corps ran in-house studies to assess the potential hazards of LSD "from a tissue or genetic standpoint," it could not duplicate these findings. "Although human chromosome breaks have been reported by others, we found them much more frequently from caffeine and many other substances," stated

154

Dr. Van Sim, chief of clinical research at Edgewood Arsenal during the 1960s and early 1970s. "We were unable to demonstrate any damage by LSD to any system used." But army officials never uttered a public peep while the so-called facts about LSD and chromosome damage were trumpeted over and over again by the mass media. Nor did the CIA attempt to set the record straight, even though the Agency had access to the same classified reports as Dr. Sim by virtue of a long-standing liaison between the CIA and the research and development staff at Edgewood.

The chromosome hoax had all the earmarks of a media-hyped disinformation campaign against psychedelic drugs. Hardly a day passed in the mid-1960s without yet another story about people freaking out and hurling themselves from windows while high on acid. At the same time, Leary and his cohorts kept churning out magical proclamations about mind expansion, groovy highs, and utopian prospects. ("Can the world live without LSD?" asked the *East Village Other*, an underground newspaper. Their answer, of course, was no.) The combination of dire warnings and ecstatic praise created a highly polarized atmosphere. LSD acquired the emotional and magnetic pull of the taboo, and as a result, more and more people decided to try the drug.

The political controversy surrounding LSD was not an abstract debate that had little bearing on daily use and experimentation. On the contrary, the barrage of contradictory messages conveyed by the straight and alternative press made the situation all the more precarious for the acid initiate. During an acid trip one is in a state of extreme susceptibility to an infinite variety of stimuli, including pressures from the immediate environment as well as more subtle influences stemming from the overall cultural matrix—that invisible field of presence which informs the psychological framework of the subject. Given the highly politicized environment of the 1960s, it is not surprising that taking LSD was accompanied by a considerable degree of anxiety and apprehension. Those who were willing to risk their own sanity to attain ecstasy or expanded consciousness often had unsettling experiences on acid.

How many people actually had bummers on LSD? More than many an acid buff would probably care to admit. In his paper "Social and Political Sources of Drug Effects: The Case of Bad Trips on Psychedelics," Richard Bunce, a research sociologist at the School of Public Health in Berkeley, California, cited statistics based on a survey he conducted in which nearly 50% of those questioned reported having had a bad acid trip during the 1960s. The high percentage was in part a consequence of the widespread anxiety that ensued after LSD was declared illegal in late 1966. These witch-hunting laws created a hostile environment that predisposed people toward more traumatic reactions. As the level of hostility rose, so did the frequency of "marginal psychoses" attributable to LSD. By the mid-1970s, however, the emotionally charged atmosphere had subsided, and the percentage of bad trips dropped accordingly. "We can explain the substantial historical decline in the incidence of bad trips," Bunce concluded, "by reference to variations in the political culture which informs its use."

But what did Bunce mean when he spoke of bad trips? To be sure, there were tragic incidents involving LSD, but only a small percentage of those who experimented with the drug required hospitalization. For most people the hellish vision was only temporary, and because it was temporary it was also in some sense salutary. Difficult experiences were relatively common during LSD trips, but they were often thought to be useful, especially when one worked through their meaning with a therapist or friend. But the potential efficacy of the so-called bummer was never acknowledged by the mass media, which portrayed a bad acid trip as a no-exit situation, rather than an existential challenge. This climate of fear predisposed some people to panic as soon as anxiety set in, thinking that a bout with utter insanity was imminent.

The interpretation of the bummer as pure psychosis—the standard psychotomimetic analysis—was initially promoted by scientists connected with the US Army and the CIA. In addition to influencing the debate over LSD and its effects, the CIA and the military, through their complicity in the dissemination of false information about LSD and chromosome damage, helped create a negative set and setting on a collective scale for those who turned on during the late 1960s and early 1970s.

"That was a mean and dirty trick," said Ken Kesey in reference to the chromosome hoax. Kesey recalled the early days of acid glory before the media created the bad trip: "We didn't have bummers back then." Laura Huxley also lamented the passing of that era of relative innocence, when LSD had not yet become a household word:

How lucky those of us are who approached LSD before it had either the demoniacal or paradisical vibrations it has now—when it had no echoes of gurus and heroes, doctors or delinquents. We went into the experience not knowing what would happen, not expecting that it would be like the experience of someone at last Saturday night's party, or like that of Mary Jones, whose hallucinated, frightened eyes stare at me from the pages of a magazine. LSD—those three now famous letters were free of association with scientific righteousness and beatnik conformity, with earthly paradise and parental loving care—also free from closemindedness, obscurantism and bigotry. The unconscious identification with those ideas, feelings and fears inevitably occurs now, with disastrous consequences.

The First Human Be-In

As the Love Pageant Rally drew to a close and the crowd began to drift away from the Panhandle, the organizers of the stoned festival exulted in their achievement. That same evening members of the *Oracle* group gathered at the home of Michael Bowen to consider their next step. Bowen was a key personality within the *Oracle* clique, and his studio served for a time as the office of the psychedelic tabloid. A painter with beatnik roots, he spent much of his time depicting third eyes and occult symbols amid swirls of bright color. When he wasn't putting the brush to an acid-influenced canvas, he acted as a self-appointed liaison between the *Oracle* staff and various psychedelic and artistic luminaries such as Allen Ginsberg, Timothy Leary, and Lawrence Ferlinghetti.

Some years earlier Bowen had fallen under the singular and charismatic influence of a mysterious guru-type figure named John Starr Cooke. A man of wealth and influential family connections, Cooke was no stranger to high-level CIA personnel. His sister, Alice, to whom he was very close, was married to Roger Kent, a prominent figure in the California state Democratic party; Roger's brother, Sherman Kent, was head of the CIA's National Board of Estimates (an extremely powerful position) and served as CIA director Allen Dulles's right-hand man during the Cold War. John Cooke hobnobbed with Sherman Kent at annual family reunions and is said to have made the acquaintance of a number of CIA operatives while traveling in Europe.

Driven by an avid interest in the occult, Cooke journeyed around the world befriending an assortment of mystics and spiritual teachers. In the early 1950s he became a close confidant of L. Ron Hubbard, the ex-navy officer who founded the Scientology organization. Cooke rose high in the ranks of the newly formed religious cult. (He was

157

the first "clear" in America, meaning he had attained the level of an advanced Scientology initiate.) Before long, however, he grew disillusioned with Hubbard and they parted ways. A few years later, while living in Algiers, Cooke was stricken with polio, which left him crippled and confined to a wheelchair for the rest of his life. Despite his physical disability he was revered by a Sufi sect in northern Africa as a great healer and a saint. Some of his admirers claimed he could activate shakti, or kundalini energy, and induce a blissful spinal seizure merely by touching people on the forehead.

By the early 1960s Cooke had moved back to California, where he immersed himself in an intensive study of the tarot. Word quickly spread through the West Coast occult circuit about an extraordinary psychic who possessed a tarot deck with the handwritten annotations of its previous owner, the infamous Aleister Crowley. Crowds of young people started to flock to Carmel to visit Cooke, and they were not disappointed. With a bald head, goatee, and piercing gray eyes, Cooke looked as though he belonged behind a crystal ball. Shortly after he participated in a series of "channeling" sessions, which resulted in the New Tarot Deck for the Aquarian Age, he had his first taste of LSD-25. Apparently he found the psychedelic to his liking, as he proceeded to drop acid nearly every day for a two-year period. According to one of his disciple-associates, Cooke was also something of a bacchant. At times his penchant for alcohol and acid left him drunk and crazed in his wheelchair.

While the Haight was in its heyday, Cooke was sequestered at a secluded outpost in Cuernavaca, Mexico (his home until he died in 1976), from whence he directed a small but dedicated band of acid evangelists known as the Psychedelic Rangers. Michael Bowen was a member of this group. At Cooke's instruction a half-dozen Rangers were dispatched to various psychedelic hot spots in North America and Europe. Bowen went to Millbrook to try and influence the thinking of Leary's clan and lure some of them back to Mexico where Cooke was leading séances while high on acid. Among those who are said to have visited the crippled psychic were Ralph Metzner, songwriter Leonard Cohen, Andrija Puharich, who conducted parapsychology and drug experiments for the US military in the late 1950s, and Seymour ("The Head") Lazare, a wealthy business associate of William Mellon Hitchcock's.

Following Cooke's "master plan," the Psychedelic Rangers targeted selected individuals for high-dose LSD initiations. They employed 2,000 to 3,000 micrograms (100 to 250 micrograms is usually sufficient for a full-blown acid trip) during a single session in an effort to bring about a rapid and permanent transformation of psychological disposition. Bowen claims he furnished acid to a number of well-known public figures, including comedian Dick Gregory and Jerry Rubin, the future Yippie leader. He also turned on certain journalists (among them a reporter for *Life* magazine) with the hope that they might see the Clear Light, as it were, and present a more favorable picture of LSD in the press.

Cooke and his Psychedelic Rangers believed that by spreading the LSD revelation they were helping to enlighten mankind. They fancied themselves cosmic Good Guys secretly battling the Forces of Darkness in an all-out struggle that would ultimately determine the destiny of the planet. Their world view was distinctly Manichaean: Eros versus Thanatos, the great mythic showdown, with history merely the echo of these titanic opposites locked in eternal conflict. In this respect their perceptions were akin to those of another group of psychedelic devotees who operated in secret while invoking a Manichaean demonology to justify their activities. Nourished by the dual specter of an all-powerful enemy (Communism) and a permanently threatened national security, the CIA assumed the role of America's first line of defense. In its never-ending battle against the Red Menace the cult of intelligence utilized every weapon at its disposal, including covert LSD warfare.

In 1966 Michael Bowen settled in Haight-Ashbury, at the specific request of John Cooke. The two men communicated on a regular basis, keeping each other abreast of new developments within the burgeoning youth culture. When the *Oracle* people convened at Bowen's pad after the Love Pageant Rally, he dutifully called his spiritual adviser to tell him what had transpired. During their conversation, according to Bowen, the plan for an even bigger event was conceived: a "Gathering of the Tribes," a spiritual occasion of otherworldly dimensions that would raise the vibration of the entire planet. The Haight would host the Happening of happenings. It would be the first Human Be-In.

One of the main purposes of the be-in, as formulated by Cooke, Bowen, and the rest of the *Oracle* crew, was to bring together cultural and political rebels who did not always see eye to eye on strategies for liberation. In effect the goal was to psychedelicize the radical left. Toward this end the organizers decided to include at least one

159

representative of the Berkeley activist community among the list of invited speakers. Bowen suggested Jerry Rubin, a leader of the Berkeley Vietnam Day protest, who was still a devoted Marxist although he had recently turned on to acid (evidence, according to Bowen, that the LSD reconditioning process was only partially successful). A permit was secured to hold the demonstration on the Polo Grounds of Golden Gate Park on January 14, 1967. Five different posters were printed to advertise the be-in, including one with a picture of a Plains Indian on horseback holding an electric guitar. The posters appeared in shopwindows, on kiosks, and on coffeehouse bulletin boards. The *Berkeley Barb*, the Bay Area's first underground newspaper, announced the event on the front page with a banner headline.

The publicity campaign was not solely directed at the radical and hip population. The organizers had their sights set on a much wider horizon. They wanted to send a message throughout the world that a new dawn was breaking and the time had come for all good men and women to abandon their exploitative posture toward the earth lest apocalypse spare them the task. Buoyed by an instinctive understanding of McLuhan, the *Oracle* group realized that in an age of instant communication any event could acquire worldwide significance with the proper press coverage. "We knew we had the tiger by the tail," said Allen Cohen. "We knew that anything we did would attract the attention of the mass media."

The be-in was staged as much for the press corps and TV cameras as for the hip community. A few days prior to January 14, the organizers held a meeting with reporters. "For ten years," declared a press release, "a new nation has grown inside the robot flesh of the old. Before your eyes a new free vital soul is reconnecting the living centers of the American body.... Berkeley political activists and the love generation of the Haight-Ashbury will join together...to powwow, celebrate, and prophesy the epoch of liberation, love, peace, compassion, and unity of mankind.... Hang your fear at the door and join the future. If you do not believe, please wipe your eyes and see."

True to expectations, it was an unforgettable afternoon. Over twenty-five thousand men, women, and children assembled around a makeshift stage at the edge of an open meadow. Gary Snyder opened the proceedings by blowing on a white-beaded conch shell. Beside him were other poets from the beatnik era—Michael McClure, Lawrence Ferlinghetti, Lenore Kandel—while a group of Hell's Angels guarded the PA system. (Many Angels had settled in the Haight, where they served as self-appointed protectors of the acid community.) Allen Ginsberg chanted OM and clinked his finger cymbals. Just two months earlier, in a "Public Solitude" address at a church in Boston, Ginsberg had proposed that every American in good health over the age of fourteen "try the chemical LSD at least once . . . that, if necessary, we have a mass emotional nervous breakdown in these States once and for all." But there was no need to reiterate such remarks on this unseasonably warm winter day in San Francisco. The be-in was a healing affair, a feast for the senses, with music, poetry, sunshine, bells, robes, talismans, incense, feathers, and flags. The smell of marijuana lingered over the park slope, and acid flowed like lemonade.

"Welcome," said a calm, clear voice from the platform. "Welcome to the first manifestation of the Brave New World." It was a rather ironic way of introducing the hip superstars who were about to address the crowd. Clad like a holy man in white pajamas, Timothy Leary teased the audience with one-liners such as "The only way out is in." The High Priest of the psychedelic movement spoke of expanded consciousness as the "Fifth Freedom," urging everyone to start their own religion—which was exactly what he and his Millbrook friends had done. Leary's be-in appearance was part of a barnstorming tour to promote his new group, the League for Spiritual Discovery. The League had only two commandments—"Thou shalt not alter the consciousness of thy fellow man" and "Thou shalt not prevent thy fellow man from altering his own consciousness." A tireless proselytizer, Leary had presided over a series of "psychedelic religious celebrations" featuring dramatic re-enactments of the lives of the Buddha, Christ, Mohammed, etc. The purpose of these well-advertised, well-financed productions (one promoter called them the "best thing since vaudeville") was to reproduce the effects of an acid trip without drugs. But Leary's traveling light show was antique by Bay Area standards.

For some people Leary's brief sermon at the be-in marked the highlight of the afternoon. It didn't matter that they had heard it all before; they accepted as gospel every word he'd uttered since he came out of the academic closet and turned into the Pied Piper of the acid generation. But others were not particularly impressed by Tim's laconic manifesto. ("We could even tolerate *him*!" commented

161

one Haight-Ashbury resident in describing the community's live-and-let-live attitude.) The Pope of Dope was trying to symbolize in rather outmoded ways a religious revival that defied traditional categories. After all, why invoke catechisms and commandments when the sheer fact of being alive in that corner of time and space was sufficiently intoxicating?

The be-in was not organized to protest a specific government ordinance or policy. Thousands of people had come together to do nothing in particular, which in itself was quite something. They sat on the grass, shared food and wine, and marveled at how peaceful everyone was. There wasn't even a single uniformed policeman around to spoil the party. At one point a man parachuted down from the sky within view of the gathering. A rumor spread that it was none other than Owsley, the premier acid chemist, descending upon the faithful in waves of billowing white silk. It was just another piece of instant mythos that characterized the day. As Michael McClure put it, "The be-in was a blossom. It was a flower. It was out in the weather. It didn't have all its petals. There were worms in the rose. It was perfect in its imperfections. It was what it was— and there had never been anything like it before."

The be-in was the culmination of everything that had been brewing in the Haight, and people were still buzzing from it weeks later. If LSD already had a reputation as a drug of peace and love, the be-in swelled it to gigantic proportions. Those who basked in the afterglow of this "epochal event," as Ginsberg referred to it, were convinced that acid constituted nothing less than a pharmacological key to world peace—not a peace negotiated through compromise and treaties, but a veritable "Glad State" based on mutual recognition of the supranational Godhead. If only President Johnson turned on to the "right stuff," many an acidhead effused, surely the war in Vietnam would be over in a matter of days! Richard Alpert spoke as a true believer when he claimed that twenty-five thousand freaks represented a political force. "In about seven or eight years," he predicted, "the psychedelic population of the United States will be able to vote anybody into office they wanted to.... Imagine what it would be like to have anybody in high political office with our understanding of the universe. I mean, let's just imagine if Bobby Kennedy had a fully expanded consciousness. Just imagine him in his position, what he would be able to do."

Even if one did not succumb to this kind of puerile thinking, it was hard to remain immune to the messianic fervor associated with the psychedelic upsurge. Juxtaposed with the grim realities of nine-to-five and the nuke, LSD seemed to herald an alternative, a new way of life. During the peak of an acid high one could wink at a turned-on sister or brother, who might also catch a glimpse of a happily-ever-after ending. Or beginning. No need to pin it down. No mix of words or meanings could recapture that overwhelming sense of *promise.* Such sentiments were immortalized in a stitch of drug-inspired prose by Hunter Thompson: "There was a fantastic universal sense that whatever we were doing was *right,* that we were winning.... And that, I think, was the handle—that sense of inevitable victory over the forces of Old and Evil. Not in any mean or military sense; we didn't need that. Our energy would simply *prevail.* There was no point in fighting—on our side or theirs. We had all the momentum; we were riding the crest of a high and beautiful wave."

The grandiosity generated by the be-in was reinforced and exaggerated by the tremendous airplay the event received. Just as the organizers had intended, the be-in attracted not only national but international notice. It marked the beginning of a concentrated media assault on the Haight-Ashbury. Soon it became the most overexposed neighborhood in the country as reporters from all over the world zeroed in on the psychedelic underground. Nearly every major American media outlet, including all the big TV networks, ran features on the hip community, and for a time it seemed that the rest of the country was mesmerized by this baffling lifestyle revolution. *San Francisco Chronicle* columnist Herb Caen bestowed a new title on the cultural rebels, branding the whole lot "hippies." Other descriptions, such as "flower children" and "love generation," reeled off the presses and into the mainstream vocabulary, providing straight society with an assortment of ready-made labels to pin on an otherwise inscrutable phenomenon. Hippies became *the Other,* the very people "our parents warned us against," and this negative definition quickly congealed into a national obsession. The public response was typically ambivalent; the flower children were variously treated as threats to public order or as harmless buffoons. Ronald Reagan, then governor of California, described a hippie as someone who "dresses like Tarzan, has hair like Jane, and smells like Cheetah."

Yet for all the ridicule, there was something deeply disturbing about the youth subculture that begged for an explanation. Why had the sons and daughters of white middle-class America forsaken the affluent lifestyle of their parents? Why did they give up the plush, easy routine of the suburbs to crash in a crowded commune? And why did they blow their minds with dangerous drugs? A panoply of pundits offered interpretations as to what it all meant. To some the hippies were a barometer of a sick society, a warning to industrial civilization of its impending collapse. Others compared them to the early Christians because of their commitment to universal brotherhood and love for all mankind. A journalist from *Time* suggested that "in their independence of material possessions and their emphasis on peacefulness and honesty, hippies lead considerably more virtuous lives than the great majority of their fellow citizens." (This was quite a switch from an earlier assessment by the same publication, which dismissed the longhairs as utopian dreamers in search of a "zero-hour day and freakouts for all.") More than a few commentators projected absurd hopes on the youthful dropouts, claiming that they were "the most significant development of the twentieth century," "the salvation of the Western world," "the incarnation of the gospel," and so forth and so on. Indeed, it was possible for reporters, sociologists, educators, clergymen, or psychologists to find nearly anything they wanted in the Haight. And some of the hippies actually believed what was written about them.

The media coverage in the wake of the be-in obscured the fact that the *Oracle* group failed to accomplish one of its major goals: the unification—if only on a symbolic level—of political radicals and psychedelic dropouts. If anything, the be-in tended to underscore the differences between the two camps. This tension was crystallized when Jerry Rubin addressed the mind-blown throng. His aggressive ranting about the danger of the war in Vietnam, and the greater danger of doing nothing to stop it, seemed out of context at the peaceful gathering, and the audience generally ignored his speech. Except for Ginsberg, no one else mentioned the bloodshed in Southeast Asia.

The apolitical tone of the event was disconcerting to New Left activists, who had once looked upon their hipster brethren as spiritual allies. The radicals disagreed with acid eaters who thought they could elevate the world simply by elevating themselves. This wistful notion was shared by hippies, dropouts, and others in the LSD subculture who believed that massive change would only come about when enough people expanded their consciousness. They rejected the possibility of revamping the social order through political activity, opting instead for a lifestyle that celebrated political disengagement.

Not surprisingly, hard-core politicos were critical of some of the more bizarre manifestations of the acid scene. In an article for *Ramparts* magazine, the leading left-wing monthly of the late 1960s, Warren Hinckle attacked the Haight-Ashbury community for its mindless mystagogy, druggy excess, and latent fascist tendencies. Veteran political organizers, however, were not about to ignore the hippie phenomenon. They saw masses of youth all across the country getting off on this vague peace-and-love kick, and they made efforts to lure them into the political camp. In the spring of 1967 antiwar activists in New York sponsored Flower Power Day; handbills for the event made it look like a be-in, and rock bands were scheduled to entertain the marchers. By this time signs of an emerging counterculture were everywhere: bell-bottoms, work shirts, beads, light shows, pot parties, transistors pulsing with acid rock. People started showing up at political meetings in costume, the style firmly hippiesque, and it became increasingly difficult to discern where protest ended and lifestyle began.

This interaction was certainly evident at the SDS national office in Chicago, where staff members lived and slept together in communal apartments. They shared drug experiences—mostly marijuana, but also LSD—that engendered a sense of closeness and unity. But even as they got stoned during their daily activities, the SDS staffers were always cognizant of the difference between changing their heads and changing the system. "The hip thing," explained former SDS president Carl Oglesby, "was fundamentally a mass introspection, a drug-boosted look-in. The New Left, on the other hand, went out to the world from a set of shared moral perceptions about race, war, and imperialism; it was recreating a private moral judgment as a public political act. Of course, the hippie's every instinct indisposed him to war and made him wholly eager to demonstrate this, provided someone else set the stage. But he was satisfied to act without strategic thought, without any sense of political plan, except that the more people who smoked grass, the better off the country would be."

The leaders of SDS saw grass as a mild pleasure rather than a social panacea. LSD, however, was a bit more problematic. A strong dose of acid could dredge up all sorts of weirdness that had little to do with the world of *Realpolitik;* if anything, all the psychic debris was likely to be more distracting than stimulating when it came to questions of strategy and organization. Bob Dylan's nightmare surrealism, so much admired by student radicals, was heavily influenced by psychedelics, and he withdrew from political protest during the peak of his acid phase to probe the tangled roots of the self. The Dylan saga was proof to some that drugs in general and acid in particular nurtured a privatistic tendency within the youth culture, or perhaps that the ingrained privatism of American life insinuated itself in such a way as to use the chemical high for its own purposes. In either case, certain activists were concerned about the long-range implications of the drug scene.

A few days after the be-in, the *Oracle* hosted a hip summit conference focusing on "the whole problem of whether to drop out or take over," as philosopher Alan Watts put it. Watts was joined by Allen Ginsberg, Gary Snyder, and Timothy Leary, who made no bones about where he stood on the issue. In his opinion the psychedelic and antiwar movements were completely incompatible. "The choice is between being rebellious and being religious," he declared. "Don't vote. Don't politic. Don't petition. You can't do *anything* about America politically." To Leary there was no real difference between capitalism and Communism, between Ronald Reagan and Fidel Castro; both were hung up on competitive power politics. And so were the student activists, whom he denigrated as "young men with menopausal minds." Leary dismissed any action that did not emanate from an expanded consciousness as "robot behavior." "People should not be allowed to talk politics," he stated, "except on all fours."

Watts cautioned against imposing a particular vision on the world, but Leary persisted. As far as he was concerned, the psychedelic subculture was the only game in town. Forget about civil rights and exploitation, forget about the war; dropping out *was* the revolution. "The first thing you have to do is completely detach yourself from anything inside the plastic, robot Establishment." And then what? Leary envisioned the Haight as a launching pad for thousands of young people who would gallantly band together in small tribes and wander the United States and Western Europe, living off the fat of what he contemptuously called the unenlightened "mineral culture" (technological society). He preached his own version of lysergic Leninism—the nation-state would eventually wither away as more and more people turned on. ("Let the *State Disintegrate*" was one of his less successful slogans.) In the meantime the hippies would "stamp out reality," as the famous button read, by loving the establishment to death.

Leary's rap was such an affront to the radical community that at one point when he brought his traveling religious road show to the Bay Area, the editors of the *Berkeley Barb* urged antiwar activists to demonstrate against the acid guru. Even his ostensible allies were put off by his apolitical stance. Gary Snyder felt that dropping out could easily mean copping out unless people cultivated techniques of self-sufficiency as a prerequisite to building a new social order. He did not want to reject those who made tremendous sacrifices for the cause of social justice, although he hoped they could be brought around to what he considered "a more profound vision of themselves and society." That was where LSD might prove useful—to help broaden the very definition of politics and thereby enhance the historical vision of the New Left. Snyder understood that student radicalism and the psychedelic subculture derived from similar roots, and he tried to encourage a creative dialogue between the two.

The flower power ethos was in some sense a caricatured extension of the nonviolent pacifist ideology that dominated the early history of the New Left. During the mid-1960s the psychedelic underground plugged into the spiritual rhetoric of the civil rights movement, which had nothing to do with "expanded consciousness" per se. Although acid in and of itself does not imply a particular moral framework or political outlook, as a nonspecific catalyst of psychic *and social* processes (the two realms are intimately connected) it brings out "the flavors and ingredients of whatever happens to be cooking in the cultural stew," as Michael Rossman put it. That LSD and the subculture it inspired came to be so closely associated with peace and love and tra-la-la was in no small part due to the prevailing left-wing political gestalt of passive resistance.

The rhetoric of nonviolent pacifism constituted only one aspect of the legacy that was adopted by the acid subculture. Members of the Berkeley Free Speech Movement, SDS, and the Student Nonviolent Coordinating Committee (SNCC), the radical youth wing of the civil rights movement, were trying to create alternative structures within which "the loving community" could flourish. This notion—which harked back to the Wobblies' slogan a half-century earlier, "Forming the new society within the shell of the old"—

167

became a moving force in the Haight. By early 1967 a number of thriving alternative institutions already existed in the psychedelic city-state: the *Oracle*, the Community Switchboard, the Hip Job Coop, Happening House (a cooperative teaching venture), Radio Free Hashbury; in coming months the Free Medical Clinic would open its doors. Even the neighborhood merchants formed a business council, HIP (Haight Independent Proprietors). The idea of building a parallel society smack-dab in the belly of the beast held great appeal to many a shell-shocked pacifist who'd grown weary of sit-ins, demonstrations, and police violence. For these people the futility of trying to reform the system was amply confirmed by the landslide election of Ronald Reagan as governor of California. They were ready for a different approach; rather than try to overhaul the social and economic structures of mass commercial society, they would simply try to outflank them.

By dropping out and joining the Haight-Ashbury scene, young people were not necessarily renouncing their commitment to social change. But they felt that the personal and the political could not be split into separate categories. Human liberation was something to be acted out because it was right on, a better way to live, rather than an item petitioned for during protest hour. If, as Charles Olson proposed, "the private is public, and the public is where we behave," then the clearest political statement was how people chose to comport themselves on a daily basis. This premise informed the hip penumbra of the radical left, that widening sphere where culture and politics overlapped in ways both complementary and problematic. The Haight became a crucible of dynamic interchange as left-wing activists cross-fertilized with turned-on poets, drifters, artists, and dropouts who were refashioning themselves into living articulations of the struggle against bureaucracy. A hybrid army of young rebels was on the move: politicos loosened up and grew their hair long, antiwar posters appeared in psychedelic design, and demonstrations incorporated more colorful elements of music, dance, and absurdity.

The hippies, for their part, never completely deserted the peace movement, despite Leary's proddings. At their best they represented an edge where the perspectives and tactics of the New Left were being transformed. Although there were important distinctions that placed the two groups at either end of the spectrum of dissent, the common ground they shared was significant. Both were expressions of the "Great Refusal," and the existential project they embraced was essentially the same: the regeneration of personality. The cultural renaissance fueled by LSD was the force that broke the stranglehold of bourgeois morality and the Protestant work ethic. It provided the passionate underpinning for a lifestyle that existed on the far side of power politics. Above all it insisted upon a revolution that would not only destroy the political bonds that shackle and diminish us but would also, in the words of Antonin Artaud, "turn and face man, face the body of man himself, and decide once and for all to demand that *he change.*"

The Capital Of Forever

STONE FREE

Something's astir on Haight Street. Thousands of hippies are making the scene when a roving band of mysterious characters suddenly appears among the day-trippers, passing out handbills that bear two enigmatic phrases: Street Menu and Carte de Venue ("Your ticket to somewhere"). It's the beginning of a street theater spectacle put on by a gangster performing troupe who call themselves the Diggers. The theme on this occasion is "The Death of Money and the Birth of Free." A bizarre funeral cortege is making its way up LSD Avenue. Leading the procession is a group of women mourners dressed in black singing "Get out my life why don't you babe . . ." to the tune of Chopin's *Funeral March*. They are followed by three hooded figures hoisting a silver dollar sign on a stick and a half-dozen pallbearers carrying a black-diaped coffin. Even stranger are the huge animal masks—at least five feet high—worn by the pallbearers.

There won't be any reruns of this event, no encores or applause—in fact, there aren't even any spectators. Everyone's part of the show. The entire neighborhood becomes the stage as twenty death-walkers at the rear of the funeral march give away flutes, flowers, penny-whistles, and lollipops in preparation for the next "act," so to speak, a cacophonous orchestration mocking the law against being a public nuisance. Public nuisance equals public "new sense," get it? Hundreds of hippies line both sides of the street with instruments in hand, goofing and spoofing, and so it goes, one scene after another for hours at a time.

As twilight approaches, a few hundred rearview car mirrors procured from a junkyard are distributed to the mischievous masses, who are encouraged to climb atop the buildings and reflect the setting sun down onto the street. Meanwhile a chorus of women in silver bell-bottom pants, bolero tops, and tie-dye outfits raises a banner of marbleized paper inscribed with a poem and chants back and forth to some other women perched on the rooftops. Thousands pick up the cue and chant poetry, and soon the police arrive to clear the mob scene—a rather formidable task, considering that the crowd has swelled to unmanageable proportions. The spontaneous interaction between cops and hippies (call it a riot) becomes part of the performance. It's all for free—a free-for-all: anarchist antics scripted to make something wide-open happen. "Street events are rituals of release. Re-claiming of territory (sundown, traffic, public joy) through spirit," proclaimed a Digger manifesto. "No one can control the single circuit-breaking moment that charges games with critical reality. If the glass is cut, if the cushioned distance of the media is removed, the patients may never respond as normals again. They will become life actors...a cast of freed beings."

The Diggers burst upon the scene in the summer of 1966, when a number of actors broke away from the San Francisco Mime Troupe and formed their own loose-knit collective. They felt that the Mime Troupe's political satire was too formal, a predictable rehash of left-wing ideas that failed to appreciate the Haight's unique potential for a new kind of social theater—"a poetry of festivals and crowds, with people pouring into the streets," as Artaud put it. The debate over dropping out versus political engagement was a moot point to the Diggers. Their imaginative pageants were beyond codification, challenging the assumptions of the New Left as well as the psychedelic religious fringe.

The Diggers took their name from a seventeenth-century English farming group that preached and practiced a form of revolutionary communism. Convinced that money and private property were the work of the Devil, the original Diggers claimed squatters' rights for the people and gave free food to the needy. When Lord Protector Cromwell announced the Enclosure Act, which allowed landowners to cordon off public lands for their own use, the Diggers responded by digging the soil (hence their name) and planting a garden in the Commons Area. Their defiance provoked the wrath of Cromwell and his Roundheads, who charged the upstarts with "encouraging the looser and disordered sort of people into greater boldness." The ministers began exhorting their congregations to go out and give the troublemakers hell, and a wave of bloody repression ensued.

Like their British forebears, the San Francisco Diggers believed that the world was run by a cabal of greedy liars and thieves. It was downright foolish to expect the perpetrators to redress the ills they had created, for to deal with a system that was rotten to the core—either by fighting it or joining it—could only lead to further corruption. The Diggers never protested for or against anything, refusing to be seduced by the romantic pretensions of the New Left, whose faith in the efficacy of telling Truth to Power betrayed its own naiveté. That was how the Diggers saw it, and they had no intention of squandering their energy on angry leftist protest that would end up filling a twenty-second slot on the TV news. Peace marches and demonstrations might provide an outlet for private frustrations—a dose of solidarity for temporary relief of alienation—but it seemed doubtful to the Diggers that all the word-slinging and finger-pointing would amount to much in terms of real change.

If you wanted a better world, the Diggers maintained, then it was up to you to make it happen, because no one else—least of all the fraudulent politicians—would hand it over on a silver platter. To take back what was rightfully theirs, people had to assume their own freedom in the here and now: "No frozen moments for tomorrow's fantasy revolution!" The Diggers went about their business as if utopia were already a social fact and everyone were free. They chided other lefties for being stodgy, dull, and fixated on social models (Cuba, China, Vietnam) that had little relevance to the situation in the United States. The goal of revolution, as far as the Diggers were concerned, was not merely to seize the wealth hoarded by a handful of the filthy rich and spread it among the hapless masses. A simple transference of power, a redistribution of things already valued, constituted only a degree of liberation. At best it was a prelude to an overall transformation of values culminating in a revolt against the very concepts of power, property, and hierarchy.

The Diggers sensed a tremendous opportunity in the mid-1960s to experiment with what postindustrial society might look like assuming the human species survived its next cataclysmic moment. Although the precise features of this new social order were never consistently articulated, one could begin by postulating the abolition of the division between labor and leisure, so that the logic of the game once again took precedence in human affairs. It was a game they played for keeps. "Western society has destroyed itself," stated the *Digger Papers*. "The culture is extinct. Politics are as dead as the culture they supported. Ours is the first skirmish of an enormous struggle, infinite in its implications."

Tough, charismatic, and streetwise, the Diggers illuminated the Haight with wild strokes of artistic genius. In acting out their version of an alternative society, they emerged as the avant-garde of American anarchism, a homespun tradition that went back to the previous century and had recently taken a detour through psychedelics. For the Diggers LSD was "hard kicks," a way of extending oneself to the perimeters of existence where something spectacular and awesome might occur. Acid imbued their eyes with a visionary gleam and provided the distance that enabled them to see how they matched up against the grand scheme of life. But the Diggers never copped to the notion that everything would be groovy if everyone turned on. The *Oracle*'s transcendental twaddle struck them as vapid and elitist. They scoffed at those who took drugs to discover the hidden truth and mystery of being.

The Diggers viewed acid in terms of personal fulfillment, but always within a social context. They were more activist-oriented than revelatory; things were real when people did them, and what they did had to relate to the basics: food, clothing, shelter, creativity. As a counterpoint to the vague love ethic of the flower children, they promoted the no-nonsense ethic of "FREE!" When they began serving free meals in the Panhandle in the autumn of 1966, it wasn't a one-shot publicity stunt. This Robin Hood routine actually continued on a daily basis for more than a year. Any hippie—or straight, for that matter—who was hungry merely had to show up at the park at 4:00 P.M., walk through a large orange scaffold (a "Free Frame of Reference"), and chow down. The Diggers also set up a Free Store, which distributed a wide range of "liberated goods" (most of which had been donated by local shopkeepers). There was even a basket with "free money" in it, if anyone was short on cash. The Diggers were dead set against profiteering of any kind, whether it involved dope dealing or HIP merchants hawking psychedelic souvenirs during tourist season. They insisted that any hippie worth his salt had to drop out of America's true national pastime—the money game. "The US standard of living is a bourgeois baby blanket for executives who scream in their sleep. . . . Our fight is with those who would kill us through dumb work, insane wars, dull money morality."

The media portrayed the Digger thing as a goodwill gig, a "hip Salvation Army." Of course they missed the point entirely. Charity was not what motivated the free service initiatives. The Diggers were attempting to lay the groundwork for a collective apparatus,

173

an alternative power base capable of providing the necessary resources so that people wouldn't have to depend on the system or the state to get by. The gist was practical but also theatrical. Inject FREE into any event, and it could turn into theater. FREE was "social acid" that blew apart conditioned responses and called into question prevalent cultural attitudes about class, status, morality, consumerism, etc. Like LSD, FREE could shake people out of the rut of ordinary perception and catalyze some sort of revelation. This was the upshot of Digger activities: to make street theater into an art form, a social opera that would ignite and liberate the human spirit.

To the Diggers FREE also meant not claiming credit for what they did. Anonymity was a cornerstone of their operations, and it greatly enhanced their mystique as a group. Of the dozen men and women who initially formed the Diggers, there was no single leader or spokesperson. Whoever had a good idea became the prime mover of that project; others pitched in if the spirit moved them. People did what they were good at doing, but they also made a point of keeping out of the media spotlight. They were wary of the media not only because it distorted everything but also because it was hierarchical, an intermediary between people and the world. Worst of all, it purported to tell people "the way it is," when everyone should be their own source of news. The Diggers had little tolerance for reporters and made life difficult for them whenever they came around for interviews. On one occasion a journalist from the *Saturday Evening Post* dropped by the Free Store and asked to speak with the manager. He was told that the manager was a shy person who didn't like to answer questions but would make an exception in this instance. The man from the *Post* was then introduced to a *Newsweek* reporter who had been told the same thing. The two press stiffs questioned each other in a corner for twenty minutes before discovering that they'd been duped.

The Diggers' aggressive anarchism ran into conflict with the *Oracle* group, which went out of its way to accommodate the Fourth Estate as part of the publicity campaign for the be-in. Although the Diggers had not been specifically invited to the be-in, they showed up anyway and gave out free food and ten thousand hits of "white lightning" acid Owsley had recently concocted. But that did not mean they approved of the be-in format, which was dominated by media personalities and centered around a stage—the same old hierarchical mode. In contrast to the *Oracle*'s shoot-the-moon scenario

of one huge global turn-on, the Diggers focused on the immediate
nitty-gritty concerns of their own community. They set up crash
pads and a free medical service for the young runaways who started
flocking to the Haight after the be-in; they facilitated group rituals
(often coinciding with solstice and equinox celebrations) as a way
of unifying the spaced-out zone of hip; and they kept up their criticism of the HIP merchants and media sycophants whose "psychedelic logorrhea" prevented them from getting down to brass tacks
and dealing with the serious problems that plagued the acid ghetto.

A lot of changes had taken place as a result of the media blitz.
The local press was having a field day, with reporters from the *Chronicle* and the *Examiner* engaged in a running contest to see who could
come up with the most lurid details about the human zoo on Haight
Street. They took a complex social phenomenon, reduced it to a few
sensationalistic elements, and repeated the same tripe over and over
again. In every edition there were stories dwelling on dope, prom-
iscuity, long hair, filth, and bizarre behavior—themes that reflected
the prurient interests and prejudices of straight journalists locked
into the usual middle-class stereotypes about bohemia. The sensational press coverage was tantamount to a full-scale advertising campaign—albeit of a twisted sort—and the neighborhood became a
magnet for people who were into just what the media reported: sex,
drugs, dirt, weirdness, all the seamiest aspects of the hippie trip. A
different crowd filtered into the acid ghetto, and although it passed
unnoticed at first, the original community began to disintegrate.

The psychedelic style had a certain meaning for the first wave of
self-conscious innovators who were engaged in acting out communal
modes of existence. Mundane objects such as love beads and peace
insignias were tokens of self-imposed exile that communicated a
forbidden identity; they warned the straight world of a threat and
issued an oblique challenge to consumer society. But this meaning
was not readily apparent to the multitudes who turned on for the
first time after the be-in. Before long, teenyboppers and "plastic
hippies" from the suburbs started frequenting the hip hotspots for
some weekend entertainment. Department stores blossomed out in
paisley swirls and psychedelic color schemes, and hippie lingo entered into common usage; suddenly everyone was "rapping" about
"doing their own thing." Long hair, beads, and dope—anyone could
be a hippie by following the latest fashions.

The exceptional attention Haight-Ashbury received—its contin-

ual newsworthiness—undermined the spontaneity of the psychedelic style and created a schism within the acid ghetto. On the one
hand, there were the LSD veterans whose images and definitions of
psychedelia stemmed from a grassroots sensibility that arose organ-
ically during the early- and mid-1960s; on the other hand, there were
the Johnny-come-lately flower power trippers who were keyed into
trendy images of an emerging youth culture. The newcomers began
to mimic a collective reflection of themselves; they learned who
they were (or were supposed to be) and how to act through the media,
which offered a new standard of nonconformity to which they con-
formed. "The media casts nets, creates bags for the identity-hungry
to climb into," a Digger broadside declared. "Your face on TV, your
style immortalized without soul in the captions of the *Chronicle*.
NBC says you exist, ergo I am."

For some the Haight was nothing more than an easy place to pick
up hippie "chicks" or cop a buzz; others knew a fast buck when
they saw one. And then there were those who came just to gawk.
Tourists, carloads of them, bumper to bumper creeping up Haight
Street. The Gray Line bus company announced a "Hippie Hop"—
"a safari through psychedelphia... the only foreign tour within the
continental limits of the United States." Local storefronts suddenly
filled with concession stands pushing "hippieburgers," "lovedogs,"
Day-Glo posters, and an endless assortment of psychedelic gim-
cracks. The street people were turned off by the whole scene and
held up mirrors when tourists peered out of the windows to get a
good look at the weirdos.

The influx of tourists and thrill seekers exacerbated the animosity
between the flower children and the rest of San Francisco, particularly the police and city officials. Businessmen complained that
hippies were clogging the sidewalks in front of their shops and scar-
ing away customers. The cops started busting young people for loi-
tering, panhandling, drug use, and vagrancy. Runaway teenagers who'd
been staying at Digger crash pads were the target of a series of
daylight raids ("sanitation sweeps") led by Ellis D. Sox (the hippies
loved his name), director of the San Francisco Health Department.
By this time the Diggers were mustering their considerable talents
for open confrontations with the authorities who condoned the de-
terioration of their neighborhood. They joined forces with the Communications Company, an underground mimeograph service that
printed and distributed free handbills with on-the-spot news, poetry,

and announcements geared toward prodding the love generation into standing up for its rights. "Stamp out police brutality," suggested a Digger leaflet. "Teach a hippie to fight." With traffic tie-ups becoming a real downer on Haight Street, the Diggers elected to take matters into their own hands. On Easter Sunday 1967 a six-block area was effectively closed to cars as thousands of longhairs rejoiced and danced on the pavement, shouting "LSD, LSD!" and "The streets belong to the people!" By evening the police had arrested a dozen people, including a twelve-year-old boy.

Tempers were already at a boiling point when the *Chronicle* picked up an offhand comment by a Digger and turned it into a front-page banner headline: "HIPPIES WARN CITY — 100,000 WILL INVADE HAIGHT ASHBURY THIS SUMMER." Images of a psychedelic *Grapes of Wrath* sent city officials into a tizzy. The mayor immediately declared "war on the Haight," and shortly thereafter the San Francisco Board of Supervisors passed a resolution stating that hippies were officially unwelcome in their town. A futile gesture, to be sure, as the press kept on predicting that a deluge of acid eaters would descend upon the Golden Gated city as soon as school let out for the summer.

As self-fulfilling prophecies went, this one couldn't be beat. The acid ghetto was headed for a forced consciousness expansion of the rudest sort unless someone figured out a way to stabilize an already overloaded community. The crisis was so grave that various community groups — including the Diggers, the *Oracle* people, the HIP merchants, and the Family Dog — put aside their differences and tried to work out strategies for housing and feeding the media-hyped masses. They proposed that Golden Gate Park be turned into a huge free campground, but the city's political leaders balked at the idea. The Diggers countered by organizing a feed-in on the steps of City Hall. They dished out free spaghetti and meat sauce to government workers and circulated a leaflet that read, "Say if you are hungry, we will feed you, and if you are tired, we will give you a place to rest. This is to affirm responsibility. We merely provide food, shelter and clothing because it should be done."

Some took it as an omen when the Monterey Pop Festival drew nearly fifty thousand people to the Bay Area shortly before the summer solstice, becoming the largest rock and roll event of its time. Flyers at the Human Be-In had first announced the festival, a nonprofit affair with the slogan "Music, love, and flowers." Monterey featured a lineup of psychedelic superstars, including Janis Joplin, the Byrds, the Grateful Dead, and Jimi Hendrix. Joplin pulled out all the stops in a total freak-rock performance that was seen by millions in D. A. Pennebaker's film of the concert. But it was Hendrix who really stole the show when he ended his first American appearance by kneeling in front of his electric guitar and setting it on fire. For the country as a whole, the acid rock era really began with Monterey. Scott McKenzie summed up what it all portended for the Haight when he sang his hit single during the final set: "If you're going to San Francisco, be sure to wear flowers in your hair."

The entire city braced itself in uneasy anticipation as young people started pouring into the Haight. They came in droves, a ragtag army of tattered pilgrims who'd gone AWOL from the Great Society. Propelled by a gut-level emptiness, they rode the crest of Kerouac's bum romance, searching for kicks or comfort or a spiritual calling—anything that might relieve the burden of nonliving that gnawed at their insides. They believed that it would be like the newspapers said, that somewhere at the other end of the rainbow was Haight-Ashbury, the Capital of Forever, where beautiful people cared for each other, where all would be provided and everyone could do their own thing without being hassled.

But the Haight was hardly a paradise during the so-called Summer of Love. The early days of acid glory had receded into memory along with the pioneering spirit that once sustained the hip community. Things were getting rougher on the street, and a lot of kids left when the vibes got too heavy. Those who remained were quick to learn the meaning of Dylan's adage about the rules of the road having been lodged: "It's only people's games that you got to dodge." Young runaways had a hard time finding a way to earn a living or even a place to sleep. Some took to begging for spare change, but the transient rut didn't hold much in the way of good luck. It was enough just to avoid getting caught in the wicked undertow of the drug scene, which claimed more than a few victims in the Haight.

Most of the newcomers were less interested in gleaning philosophic or creative insight than in getting stoned as often as possible. They smoked or swallowed anything said to be a psychedelic, and when the visions grew stale they turned to other drugs, especially amphetamines. That such charms were addictive or potentially lethal mattered little, for the dangers belonged to the future, and the future was a slim prospect at best, too improbable to acknowledge with anything but a shrug. For these people Haight-Ashbury was the last hope. They had nowhere else to go. They were the casualties of the Love Generation. You could see them in the early morning fog, huddled in doorways, hungry, sick and numb from exposure, their eyes flirting with vacancy. They were Doomsday's children, strung out on no tomorrow, and their ghostlike features were eerie proof that a black hole was sucking at the heart of the American dynamo.

The Great Summer Dropout

Nineteen sixty-seven was a year of stark contrasts. America's war against the Vietnamese had swollen into a disaster, provoking disgust and condemnation throughout the world. The black ghettos of Detroit and Newark exploded in the summer heat while Aretha Franklin belted out her anthem for women and oppressed minorities: "All I want is a little *respect...*" Yet it was also a moment of high-flying and heretofore unimagined optimism as the youth movement reached a dazzling apogee. (*Time* magazine gave its Man of the Year award in 1967 to "anyone under twenty-five.") Nowhere was the upbeat sentiment of these turbulent times better expressed than by the Beatles, who embodied in their music and personalities the very principle of change itself.

The Beatles were the foremost lyric spokesmen for an entire generation; millions worshiped their verse as holy writ. Their songs were synchronous with the emotional excitement surrounding Haight-Ashbury. The Beatles were a symbol of the communal group that could accomplish anything, and their unprecedented success fueled the optimism of the times in countless ways. Just before the Great Summer Dropout, the Beatles gave the blossoming psychedelic subculture a stunning musical benediction with their release, in June 1967, of the album *Sgt. Pepper's Lonely Hearts Club Band*. Later that month they supplied an anthem for the advocates of flower power, "All You Need Is Love," in the first live international satellite broadcast, to an estimated audience of seven hundred million people. "I declare," stated Timothy Leary, "that the Beatles are mutants. Prototypes of evolutionary agents sent by God with a mysterious power to create a new species—a young race of laughing free men. ...They are the wisest, holiest, most effective avatars the human race has ever produced."

In their early days the Beatles had popped uppers and downers to

179

keep pace with the rigors of the late-night performing circuit in the bars of Hamburg, Germany. They took whatever was around—French blues, purple hearts, and the "yellow submarines" immortalized in their "children's song" of the same name. It wasn't until 1964, after they broke through to rock stardom, that they tried marijuana. The Fab Four got their first whiff of the wacky weed when John Lennon smoked a joint with Bob Dylan at London's Heathrow Airport. It was a happy high, and from then on the Beatles spent much of their time together stoned.

In early 1965 Lennon and his wife, Cynthia, went to dinner with George Harrison at a friend's. The host slipped a couple of sugar cubes of LSD into their after-dinner coffee, and things got a little barmy when they left. Cynthia remembered it as an ordeal. "John was crying and banging his head against the wall. I tried to make myself sick, and couldn't. I tried to go to sleep, and couldn't. It was like a nightmare that wouldn't stop, whatever you did. None of us got over it for about three days." For John the experience was equally terrifying. "We didn't know what was going on," he recalled. "We were just insane. We were out of our heads."

Despite his jarring initiation into psychedelia, within a year John Lennon would be dropping acid as casually as he had once smoked a cigarette. But Lennon was hardly in the vanguard of psychedelic use, which had gained a certain currency among British rock bands in the mid-1960s. A number of pop stars, including Donovan Leitch, Keith Richards, and the Yardbirds, had been introduced to LSD via Michael Hollingshead and his short-lived World Psychedelic Center in London. Soon the turned-on message was being broadcast throughout the English-speaking world, and acid became an international phenomenon. The Rolling Stones announced that "Something Happened to Me Yesterday"; Eric Burdon and the Animals crooned a love song to "A Girl Named Sandoz." Across the ocean in America the Count Five were having a "Psychotic Reaction," the Electric Prunes had "Too Much to Dream Last Night," the Amboy Dukes took a "Journey to the Center of My Mind," and the Byrds flew "Eight Miles High."*

LSD influenced much of mid-1960s rock, but it was the Beatles

---

*LSD-25 made its debut in the pop world on the flip side of a 1962 single by the Gamblers.

who most lavishly and accurately captured the psychic landscape of the altered state. Their first acid-tinged songs appeared on *Revolver* (1966). "She Said She Said" was inspired by a conversation in California with Peter Fonda during Lennon's second LSD trip. Fonda talked about taking acid and experiencing "what it's like to be dead." The album also featured Lennon's "Dr. Robert," a song about a New York physician who dispensed "vitamin shots" to the rich and famous. On the final track, "Tomorow Never Knows," Lennon exhorted his listeners to turn off their minds, relax, and float downstream. Originally titled "The Void," this song was inspired by Leary's *Tibetan Book of the Dead* manual, which Lennon was then reading while high on acid. On it he used the first of many "backward" tapes while tripping in his studio late one night. He even considered having a thousand monks chant in the background. Although this proved unrealistic, it pointed up Lennon's growing obsession with musical special effects, which would reach an apotheosis on *Sgt. Pepper*.

By the time *Sgt. Pepper* was recorded, all of the Beatles were getting high on acid. Paul McCartney, the last Beatle to take LSD, made candid admissions to the press about his use of psychedelics, causing an uproar. "It opened my eyes," he told *Life* magazine. "It made me a better, more honest, more tolerant member of society." If the leaders of the world's nations were to take LSD even once, McCartney insisted, they would be ready to "banish war, poverty and famine."

Teen America got its first look at the psychedelicized Beatles on Dick Clark's *American Bandstand*, in a film clip accompanying the release of "Strawberry Fields Forever." Their hair was longer, they had grown moustaches, and they were dressed in scruffy, slightly outlandish clothes. Lennon especially looked like a different person, with his wire-frame glasses, Fu Manchu, and distant gaze. That was how he appeared on the cover of *Sgt. Pepper*, where on close inspection, according to Lennon, "you can see that two of us are flying, and two aren't." John and George had taken LSD for the photo session.

Sgt. Pepper is a concept album structured as a musical "trip." The Beatles play the part of Sgt. Pepper's Lonely Hearts Club Band, an old-time musical group, that takes its listeners on a sentimental journey through the history of music from ballads and folksongs to dancehall tunes, circus music, and rock and roll. The album includes at least four cuts with overt drug references, and the entire LP utilizes sound effects in novel ways to evoke unique mental images and create an overall psychedelic aesthetic.

It is difficult to overstate this record's importance in galvanizing the acid subculture. For the love generation, *Sgt. Pepper* was nothing less than a revelation, a message from on high. Thousands of people can still recall exactly where and when they first heard the magical chords of "Lucy in the Sky with Diamonds" wafting in the summer breeze. This was the cut on which Lennon celebrated the synesthetic peak of an acid trip. The hallucinatory visions of "tangerine trees," "marmalade skies," "newspaper taxis," and "looking glass ties" mesmerized the multitudes of Beatle fans who listened to *Sgt. Pepper* on pot and acid until the grooves were worn out. Lennon said that the title of the song, rather than standing for LSD, was inspired by his son's drawings, but his disclaimer had little effect on the general interpretation of the lyrics.

The Blue Meanies immediately denounced the album. The ultra-right-wing John Birch Society charged that *Sgt. Pepper* exhibited "an understanding of the principles of brainwashing" and suggested that the Beatles were part of an "international communist conspiracy." Spiro Agnew, then governor of Maryland, led a crusade to ban "With a Little Help from My Friends" because it mentioned getting high. And the BBC actually did ban "A Day in the Life," with Lennon singing "I'd love to turn you on."

In September 1967 the Beatles went on an adventurous trip modeled after the Merry Pranksters' odyssey. Loading a large school bus with freaks and friends, they headed for the British countryside. Like the Pranksters, they also made a movie—an ad-lib, spontaneous dream film entitled *Magical Mystery Tour* (with an album of the same name). During this period there was an abundance of LSD in the Beatles family thanks to Owsley, who supplied several pint-sized vials of electric liquid along with a cache of little pink pills. Lennon was at the height of his acid phase. He used to "trip all the time," as he put it, while living in a country mansion stocked with an extravagant array of tape recorders, video equipment, musical instruments, and whatnot. Since money was no object, he was able to fulfill any LSD-inspired whim at any time of day or night.

By his own estimate Lennon took over one thousand acid trips. His protracted self-investigation with LSD only exacerbated his personal difficulties, as he wrestled with Beatledom and his mounting differences with Paul over the direction the group should take, or even if they should continue as a group. Unbeknownst to millions of their fans, the Beatles, even at the height of their popularity, were well along the winding road to breakup. That acid was becoming problematic for Lennon was evident on some of his psychedelic songs, such as "I Am the Walrus," with its repeated, blankly sung admission "I'm crying."

Eventually the mind-boggled Beatle couldn't stand it anymore. He got so freaked out that he had to stop using the drug, and it took him a while to get his feet back on the ground. "I got a message on acid that you should destroy your ego," he later explained, "and I did, you know. I was reading that stupid book of Leary's [the psychedelic manual based on the *Tibetan Book of the Dead*] and all that shit. We were going through a whole game that everyone went through, and I destroyed myself....I destroyed my ego and I didn't believe I could do anything."

Lennon's obsession with losing his ego typified a certain segment of the acid subculture in the mid- and late 1960s. Those who got heavily into tripping often subscribed to a mythology of ego death that Leary was fond of preaching. The LSD doctor spoke of a chemical doorway through which one could leave the "fake prop-television-set America" and enter the equivalent of the Garden of Eden, a realm of unprogrammed beginnings where there was no distinction between matter and spirit, no individual personality to bear the brunt of life's flickering sadness. To be gratefully dead, from the standpoint of acid folklore, was not merely a symbolic proposition; the zap of superconsciousness that hit whenever a tab of LSD kicked the slats out of the ego might in certain instances be felt as an actual death and rebirth of the body (as the psychiatric studies of Dr. Stanislav Grof seemed to indicate). Acid could send people spinning on a 360-degree tour through their own senses and rekindle childhood's lost "tense of presence," as a Digger broadside stated.

But this experience was fraught with pitfalls, among them a tendency to become attached to the pristine vision, to want to hang on to it for as long as possible. Such an urge presumably could only be satisfied by taking the "utopiate" again and again. But after countless trips and sideshows of the mind one arrived at an impasse: "All right, my mind's been blown....What's next?" Little could be gained from prolonged use of the drug, except perhaps the realization that it was necessary to "graduate acid," as Ken Kesey said. Oftentimes this meant adopting new methods to approximate or recreate the psychedelic experience without a chemical catalyst—via yoga, meditation, organic foods, martial arts, or any of the so-called natural highs. That was what the Beatles concluded when they jumped off the Magical Mystery Tour for a fling with the Maharishi and Transcendental Meditation. "Acid is not the answer," said George Harrison. "It's enabled people to see a bit more, but when you really get hip, you don't need it." Ditto for McCartney: "It was an experience we went through. . . . We're finding new ways of getting there."

For many who turned on during the 1960s there was a sense that LSD had changed all the rules, that the scales had been lifted from their eyes and they'd never be the same. The drug was thought to provide a shortcut to a higher reality, a special way of knowing. But an acid trip's "eight-hour dose of wild surmise," as Charles Perry put it, can have unexpected consequences. People may find themselves straddling the margins of human awareness where all semblance of epistemological decorum vanishes and form and emptiness play tricks on each other. Things are no longer anchored in simple location but rather vibrate in a womb of poetic correspondences. From this vantage point it is tempting to conclude that all worlds are imaginary constructions and that behind the apparent multiplicity of discernible objects there exists a single infinite reality which is consciousness itself. Thus interpreted, consciousness becomes a means mistaken for an end—and without an end or focus it becomes an inversion, giving rise to a specious sort of logic. If the "real war" is strictly an internal affair and each person is responsible for creating the conditions of his own suffering by projecting his skewed egotistical version of reality onto the material plane, does it not follow that the desire to redress social ills is yet another delusion? In this "ultimate" scheme of things all sense of moral obligation and political commitment is rendered absurd by definition.

Herein lay another pitfall of the tripping experience. Even after they stopped taking LSD, many people could still hear the siren song, a vague and muffled invitation to a "higher" calling. Those who responded to that etheric melody were plunged willy-nilly into an abstract vortex of soul-searching, escaping, and "discovering thyself." Some were intensely sincere, and their quest very often was lonely and confusing. The difficulties they faced stemmed in part from the fact that advanced industrial society does not recognize

184

ego loss or peak experience as a particularly worthy objective. Thus it is not surprising that large numbers of turned-on youth looked to non-Occidental traditions—Oriental mysticism, European magic and occultism, and primitive shamanism (especially American Indian lore)—in an attempt to conjure up a coherent framework for understanding their private visions.

Quite a few acidheads and acid graduates subscribed to the Eastern belief that reality is an illusion. They were quick to mouth the phrases of enlightenment—karma, maya, nirvana—but in their adaptation these concepts were coarsened and sentimentalized. The hunger for regenerative spirituality was often deflected into a pseudo-Oriental fatalism: "Why fret over the plight of the world when it's all part of the Divine Dance?" This slipshod philosophy was partially due to the effects of heavy acid tripping—"the haze that blurs the corner of the inner screen," as David Mairowitz said, "a magic that insinuates itself 'cosmically,' establishing spectrum upon confusing spectrum in the broadening of personal horizons. It could cloud up your telescope on the known world and bring on a delirium of vague 'universal' thinking." Or it might just reinforce what poet John Ashbery described as "the pious attitudes of those spiritual bigots whose faces are turned toward eternity and who therefore can see nothing."

The laissez-faire intellectualism that flourished in the acid subculture was particularly evident in the San Francisco *Oracle*, which by now boasted a nationwide circulation of a hundred thousand. The lingo of pop mysticism was sprinkled throughout the pages of the psychedelic tabloid. Sandwiched between various tidbits on ESP, tarot, witchcraft, numerology and the latest drug gossip were announcements of impending UFO landings. Yet in a sense the *Oracle* was merely echoing a trend that had begun to assert itself in American society as a whole. The appetite for spiritual transcendence, the desire to go beyond "the sweating self," in Huxley's words, is an indefatigable urge that assumes many guises—offbeat religious sects, parapsychology, the occult, and so forth. While such phenomena are not necessarily futile diversions, there is an inherent danger in "wanting the ultimate in one leap," as Nietzsche put it, whether by pill or perfect spiritual master. This desperate yearning makes individuals highly vulnerable to manipulation by totalitarian personalities. It was, after all, Charles Manson who wrote a song called "The Ego Is a Too Much Thing."

Manson, an ex-convict and would-be rock musician, had his own scene going in the Haight during the Summer of Love, before he and his family of acid eaters moved to southern California and made headlines as a grisly murder cult in 1969. Claiming to have experienced the crucifixion of Christ during an acid trip, he declared himself the almighty God of Fuck. Then he fed the drug to his harem of females as part of their daily regimen, had intercourse with them while they were high, and cast a corrupting spell over them. To demonstrate their faith they carried out his bloodthirsty schemes.

Manson was only one among numerous mind vamps, power trippers, hustlers, and ripoff artists who hovered over what Mairowitz described as "the ego-death of easy-prey LSD takers" in the Haight. There was a certain type of character who got off on attacking people while they were high and trespassing on their brains. "The whole catalogue of craziness . . . was exposed by acid," commented Stephen Gaskin. There were LSD freaks "who were into ego dominance. . . . That was their hobby and that was what they worked toward." Call it acid fascism or plain old psychological warfare, the hippie community had degenerated to the point where it merely offered a different setting for the same destructive drives omnipresent in straight society. "Rape is as common as bullshit on Haight Street," a Communications Company leaflet declared. "Pretty little sixteen-year-old middle-class chick comes to the Haight to see what it's all about & gets picked up by a seventeen-year-old street dealer who spends all day shooting her full of speed again & again, then feeds her 3000 mikes [twelve times the normal dose] & raffles off her temporarily unemployed body for the biggest Haight Street gang bang since the night before last."

Violent crime increased dramatically as the acid ghetto became a repository for hoods, bikers, derelicts, con men, burnouts, and walking crazies. The shift in sensibility was reflected in the kinds of drugs that were prevalent on the street. First there was a mysterious grass shortage, and then an amphetamine epidemic swept through the Haight. By midsummer 1967 speed rivaled pot and acid as the most widely used substance in the area. The speed syndrome ravaged people mentally and physically. Widespread malnutrition resulted from appetite suppression, and infectious diseases like hepatitis and VD (from unsterilized needles and "free love") were rampant. The Haight-Ashbury Free Clinic was established in response to the mounting health crisis. Among its other functions the clinic offered a special "trip room" where people could ease off the bummers and freakouts that were becoming ever more commonplace in the Haight.

The increase in bad trips was largely due to the fact that inexperienced youngsters were taking psychedelics in a hostile and congested environment. To make matters worse, a number of new mind-twisting chemicals suddenly appeared on the street, including a superpotent hallucinogen known as STP, which could launch an intense three-day trip. "Acid is like being let out of a cage," one user said. "STP is like being shot out of a gun."

STP (2,5 dimethox-4-methylphene-thylamine—the initials stood for "Serenity, Tranquility, Peace") was developed in 1964 by an experimental chemist working for the Dow Chemical Company, which provided samples of the drug to Edgewood Arsenal, headquarters of the US Army Chemical Corps. Scientists at Edgewood tested STP (which was similar in effect to BZ) to see if it could be used as an incapacitating agent, while the CIA utilized the drug in its behavior modification studies. In early 1967, for some inexplicable reason, the formula for STP was released to the scientific community at large. By this time ergotamine tartrate, an essential raw ingredient of LSD, was in short supply, so Owsley, the premier acid chemist, decided to try his hand at STP. Shortly thereafter the drug was circulating in the hippie districts of San Francisco and New York.

STP made its debut in the Haight when five thousand tabs were given away during a solstice celebration marking the onset of the Summer of Love. Few had heard of the drug, but that didn't matter to the crowd of eager pill poppers. They gobbled the gift as if it were an after-dinner mint, and a lot of people were still tripping three days later. The emergency wards at various San Francisco hospitals were filled with freaked-out hippies who feared they'd never come down. The straight doctors assumed they were zonked on LSD and administered Thorazine—the usual treatment—to cool them out. But Thorazine potentiates or increases the effect of STP. It was bummersville in the Haight until people figured out what was going on and word went out to think twice before ingesting the superhallucinogen.

STP was just one of the bizarre drugs that were pumped into the willing arteries of the acid ghetto. According to doctors who worked at the Haight-Ashbury Free Clinic, there was a rash of adverse reactions when a compound purporting to be THC (a synthetic version of marijuana) inundated the Haight. The drug was actually phencyclidine, or PCP—otherwise known as "angel dust"—which had originally been marketed as an animal tranquilizer by Parke-Davis. But the army had other ideas when it tested PCP on American GIs at Edgewood Arsenal in the late 1950s. At the same time the CIA employed Dr. Ewen Cameron to administer PCP to psychiatric patients at the Allain Memorial Institute in Montreal under the rubric of Operation MK-ULTRA. The Agency later stockpiled PCP for use as a "nonlethal incapacitant," although high dosages, according to the CIA's own reports, could "lead to convulsions and death."

Yes, a lot of weird drugs were floating around Haight-Ashbury. The neighborhood was clotted with youngsters whose minds had been jerked around ruthlessly by chemicals touted for their euphoric properties. Much of the LSD turning up on the street was fortified with some sort of additive, usually speed or strychnine,* or in some cases insecticide. But where did this contaminated acid come from? Originally the main source of LSD in the Haight was Owsley, but the scene got totally out of hand with all the media fanfare after the be-in, and renegade chemists started moving in on the drug trade. The Mafia exploited the situation by setting up its own production and distribution networks. In June 1967 James Finlator, chief of the FDA's Bureau of Drug Abuse and Control, announced that "hard core Cosa Nostra-type criminal figures" were behind "an extremely well-organized traffic in hallucinogenic drugs." Consequently the quality of black market LSD began to deteriorate. Signs posted in the Haight expressed the consensus among hippies: "Syndicate acid stinks."

And what was the CIA up to while its perennial partner of convenience, organized crime, was dumping bad acid on the black market? According to a former CIA contract employee, Agency personnel helped underground chemists set up LSD laboratories in the Bay Area during the Summer of Love to "monitor" events in the acid ghetto. But why, if this assertion is true, would the CIA be interested in keeping tabs on the hippie population? Law enforcement is not a plausible explanation, for there were already enough narcs operating in the Haight. Then what was the motive? A CIA agent who claims to have infiltrated the covert LSD network provided a clue

---

*Strychnine, a poison that is lethal in sufficient quantities, was listed in an inventory of biochemical agents stockpiled by the CIA. Other drugs in the CIA's medicine chest included tachrin (a vomit-inducing agent), 2,4 pyrolo ("causes temporary amnesia"), M-246 ("produces paralysis"), neurokinin ("produces severe pain"), digitoxin (for inducing a heart attack), and seven BZ homologues.

when he referred to Haight-Ashbury as a "human guinea pig farm."

And what better place to establish a surveillance operation than the Haight-Ashbury district of San Francisco? A dozen years earlier in the same city, George Hunter White and his CIA colleagues had set up a safehouse and begun testing hallucinogenic drugs on unwitting citizens. White's activities were phased out in the mid-1960s, just when the grassroots acid scene exploded in the Bay Area. Suddenly there was a neighborhood packed full of young people who were ready and willing to gobble experimental chemicals—chemicals that had already been tested in the lab but seldom under actual field conditions.

In addition to the spooks who inserted themselves among the drug dealers, there were scientists with CIA backgrounds who stationed themselves in the acid ghetto for "monitoring" purposes. Dr. Louis Joylon ("Jolly") West,* an old-time LSD investigator for the Agency,

*West was head of the Department of Psychiatry at the University of Oklahoma during the 1950s and early 1960s, when he conducted research into LSD, hypnosis and "the psychobiology of dissociated states" for the CIA. (It was West who administered a massive dose of LSD to an elephant as part of an ill-fated drug experiment.) In 1964 he was called upon to examine Jack Ruby, who had murdered Lee Harvey Oswald, the alleged assassin of President Kennedy. After visiting Ruby in his jail cell, West concluded that he had sunk into a "paranoid state manifested by delusions, visual and auditory hallucinations and suicidal impulses." Ruby was not faking these symptoms, West asserted, since he had vigorously rejected the doctor's repeated suggestions that he was mentally ill. "The true malingerer usually grasps eagerly at such an explanation," said West. Since Ruby would not admit he was crazy, West concluded he was nuts. Catch-22.

Ruby's "delusions" included the belief that an ultra-right-wing conspiracy was behind the death of the president. On the basis of Dr. West's diagnosis, Ruby became a candidate for treatment of mental disorders. Another doctor soon put him on "happy pills," although these drugs did not seem to cheer Ruby up. Two years later he died of cancer while still in prison.

West, meanwhile, moved to Los Angeles, where he served as director of UCLA's Neuropsychiatric Institute, a position he still holds. In the early 1970s he became embroiled in a heated controversy over plans for a Center for the Study and Reduction of Violence. Originally proposed by Governor Ronald Reagan, the violence center would have exceeded even Jack Ruby's worst paranoid nightmares had it not been scuttled by the California State legislature after information about it was leaked to the press.

West, who helped formulate plans for the center, described the program as an attempt "to predict the probability of occurrences" of violent behavior among specific population groups. "The major known correlates of violence," according to West, "are sex (male), age (youthful), ethnicity (black), and urbanicity."

The violence center was to have been housed in a former military base located in a remote area of California. The medical facility at Vacaville prison, the site of a major CIA drug testing program during the late 1960s and early 1970s, was listed rented a pad in the heart of Haight-Ashbury with the intention of studying the hippies in their native habitat. The hippie trip must have held a strange fascination for Jolly West and other CIA scientists who had devoted their talents to exploring the covert potential of mind-altering chemicals during the Cold War. Numerous spies had tried LSD long before flower power became the vogue. They had administered the drug to test subjects and watched unperturbed as the toughest of specimens were reduced to quivering jelly, their confidence and poise demolished under the impact of the hallucinogen. No doubt about it—LSD was a devastating weapon. Richard Helms, CIA director during the late 1960s and early 1970s, had once described the drug as "dynamite"—a word often used by hippie connoisseurs when praising a high-quality psychedelic.

Indeed, it must have been quite a mind-bender for the elite corps of CIA acidheads who ran the secret behavior mod programs when young people started fooling around with the same drug they had once thought would revolutionize the cloak-and-dagger trade. At first they may have passed it off as some sort of twisted fad comparable to goldfish swallowing or cramming a telephone booth, a kind of hula-hooping of the inner self. But soon the number of drug-indulgent youth reached epidemic proportions. The whole thing seemed downright absurd. Why would anyone willingly flirt with psychosis?

Needless to say, the spooks never anticipated that LSD would leave the laboratory this way, but now that the cat was out of the bag they had to ask themselves whether an incredible blunder had been committed somewhere along the line. There was no denying that the CIA was partly responsible for letting loose upon the land an awesome energy whose consequences were still difficult to fathom. As men of science and espionage they were obliged to consider every permutation of havoc that acid might wreak upon a generation of restless juveniles. If LSD makes a person insane—and surely that was what the tests had shown—then would a collective mass not

among the facilities that would have been used to develop treatment models and implement pilot and demonstration programs for the violence center.

Treatments discussed by West included chemical castration, psychosurgery, and the testing of experimental drugs on involuntarily incarcerated individuals. Furthermore, the activities of the Center were to have been coordinated with a California law enforcement program that maintained computer files on "pre-delinquent" children so that they could be treated *before* they made a negative mark on society.

suffer a similar crippling departure from the psychic status quo? A forbidding prospect, these acid casualties, yet seemingly imminent if the present trend continued.

One way or another, something very strange was going on behind the scenes. Rumors of conspiracy circulated among the street people. "The CIA is poisoning the acid these days to make everyone go on bad trips," complained one LSD user. But bad drugs were not the main factor in the decline of the Haight; they merely accelerated a process that began when tons of verbiage started pouring from the press. "The Haight-Ashbury was our town," said Nancy Getz, a close friend of Janis Joplin's. "It was sunshine and flowers and love. And the media got hold of it and ate us and fed us back to ourselves."

With each passing week things got a little heavier, a little freakier, in the Haight. The clincher came when a couple of independent drug dealers were murdered a few days apart; one had his arm cut off, the other was butchered and thrown off a cliff. The hippies were quick to blame the Mob, but nobody knew what had actually happened. Double-crossing, snitching, beatings, burns, and disappearances were endemic to the dope industry, and a number of people had private scores to settle. There was also a lot of friction between white street kids and blacks in the neighboring Fillmore district. For a while it seemed like everyone was packing heat—a blade or a heavy-caliber weapon—as Haight-Ashbury degenerated into a survival-of-the-fittest trip.

A lot of acid veterans couldn't handle the paranoia and split to the countryside, where they hoped to pursue a relatively hassle-free existence on one of the many communes that were springing up in California and the Southwest. These rural enclaves provided a temporary haven for those who needed to mellow out after having their minds blown in a million different directions. Others returned to their former homes or traveled to cities where hippie communities were just starting to take root. The mass exodus from the Haight signaled the end of the Summer of Love. The Diggers marked the changing seasons by staging a symbolic funeral in which "the death of the hippie, devoted son of the mass media" was proclaimed. A coffin filled with hippie ornaments—love beads, bandannas, underground newspapers, etc.—was carried through the neighborhood and laid to rest. The ceremony took place on October 6, 1967—exactly one year after the Love Pageant Rally, when LSD became illegal in California. "We're trying to sabotage the word 'hippie,'" explained

191

Ron Thelin, former proprietor of the Psychedelic Shop and *Oracle* backer who had recently joined ranks with the Diggers. "It's not our word. It has nothing to do with us. We'd like to substitute the words 'Free American' in its place."

By this time the windows of the Psychedelic Shop were boarded up and the Free Clinic had closed its doors for an indefinite period. Haight Street was turned into a one-way avenue and homeowners and merchants vacated the district in increasing numbers. Property values plummeted, and a wave of crime, drug addiction, and police repression turned Haight Street into Desolation Row. The reign of terror lasted for well over a year as cops patrolled the area in riot gear, roughing up longhairs and busting young people indiscriminately. (A neighborhood councilperson condemned Mayor Joseph Alioto for adopting a "domestic Vietnam policy" in the Haight. Alioto's retort: "We're not going to listen to any crybabies complaining about police brutality.") There wasn't any reason to venture into this combat zone except to score some dope, and that probably meant heroin or downers, which had been plentiful since the autumn of 1967. Most street scavengers, the leftovers from the Summer of Love, were into shooting junk or sniffing glue or drinking rotgut alcohol—whatever could deliver them to the land of the endlessly numb.

The Diggers, for their part, attempted to carry on the struggle despite the decline of the Haight. An amazing inborn cleverness kept them going through one crisis after another. They practiced street savvy like a martial art, figuring that the best way to deal with the established powers was to outfox them. Their actions were so provocative and unexpected that the authorities often didn't know how to react. On one occasion a Digger was hauled into FBI headquarters for questioning. As the interrogation was about to commence, he placed a tape recorder on the table and turned it on. The G-man was so flustered he cut the interview short.

In early 1968 the Diggers changed their name to the Free City Collective and issued a manifesto calling for a citywide coalition of "free families" to pool their resources and form survival networks that could sustain a long-term revolutionary effort. They forged alliances with street gangs from the Latin and Chinese ghettos in San Francisco and also worked with the American Indian Movement and the Black Panther party. In response to the intense police harassment that was crippling their community, Free City advocates staged a

192

protracted open-air salon on the steps of City Hall. Every day for three months, they gathered to read poetry, give out copies of the *Free City News*, and carry on outrageously. One of their last events before calling it quits on the summer solstice of 1968 was a Free City Convention (a parody of the upcoming Democratic Convention in Chicago), complete with banners and fanfare and a theme: "A Vote for Me Is a Vote for You."

Beyond the Free City the Diggers were among the first to raise the issue of ecological balance as a political concern. A handful of the original San Francisco activists would resurface in later years as the Planet Drum Foundation, a grassroots organization devoted to articulating biospheric values appropriate to postindustrial society. From city to planet, bioregions instead of nation-states: a politics of living-in-place, reinhabiting where you are. The drum beat could be heard even when the Haight was at its heyday. Listen to a Digger rap it down:

LSD hand-holding is not the end.... We're going to view what we're doing as the best we could come up with. It's only the best, scratch it. Scratch sixty-seven. Summer in San Francisco has been the first Be-Together for Escapees and Refugees.... Our part now coming up is to communicate in direct spinal language.... To push as hard as we can...to move past the Civil War in the United States to our planetary concerns, the forms and modes of which we are now developing.... The species on the planet has to get past the non-living of the last century, that most barren sterile time. The time when men died for wages, when lives were counted against profit-sharing coupons...when coupons and clip-outs became days and nights, when sunup was time to go to work and sundown was exhausted relief or an alcoholic night out.... We're trying to move our minds as sensuous instruments...to move the school of fish we swim in...to move onto the next place that we've got to go because if we don't move from where we are now, the barracuda are going to hit us. And they do. Everytime the tide turns, the barracuda turns. Everybody turns when the tide turns.

8

Peaking In Babylon

A GATHERING STORM

There is the story of the Zen master who tells his student, "Don't think of a carrot." Naturally a carrot is the first image that pops into the student's mind. So, too, the establishment media constantly decried LSD and warned in shrill tones of an epidemic of drug abuse sweeping the nation. The net effect of the immense publicity, even though much of it was negative, was to arouse intense interest and curiosity, leading to ever-widening patterns of use. For in an era of generational disaffection the quickest way to spur adolescent action is to say, "Don't do it!"

The evolution of the psychedelic scene was intimately bound up with the media coverage it attracted. Prior to the big publicity barrage, those who lived in the Haight, New York's East Village, and other hip redoubts did not necessarily think of themselves as belonging to an overarching "counterculture." The quantum leap from community to counterculture was precipitated by the first major media event, the San Francisco be-in of January 1967. The organizers of the be-in consciously sought to use the media to send a message throughout the country. On its own terms the event was an astounding achievement: the psychedelic butterfly fluttered through the TV cameras directly into the hearts and minds of America's restless youth. But the ramifications of this sudden exposure were ambiguous, double-edged. As a result of the be-in, Haight-Ashbury became a national symbol. Shortly thereafter the original fabric of the hip community began to unravel as young people responding to the "hippie temptation" (examined in a CBS documentary of that title) inundated the Haight. In fact it was the media doing the tempting, and the acid ghetto was trampled to death during the Summer of Love, leaving a social sewer in its place.

194

A similar pattern was repeated in the East Village, where a combination of runaways, tourism, and Mafia heroin destroyed a creative scene that had been many years in the making. The psychedelic pioneers in New York were an informal group of beats, students, and pacifists who frequented an arcane bookstore on East Ninth Street run by Eric Loeb; it sold peyote buttons that were on display in the storefront window in the late 1950s. Street acid was available by 1963, and as more people turned on, the gathering places became more explicit: Ed Sanders' Peace Eye Bookstore, the Electric Circus performance space on Saint Mark's Place, Fillmore East on Second Avenue, Tompkins Square and Washington Square Park. There was also an array of coffeeshops, including the Psychedelicatessen, and other conspicuous hangouts offering copies of *Inner Space*, a psychedelic newsletter published by Lynn House. The topography of New York City made the situation all the more intense, and there was plenty of street action leading up to the be-in at the Sheep Meadow in Central Park on Easter Sunday 1967. The New York be-in, organized by Abbie Hoffman, Jim Fouratt, and others, was inspired by its San Francisco prototype. Thousands of glassy-eyed youths smoked pot and gobbled acid while suspicious cops and TV cameramen surrounded the site. The psychedelic community quickly degenerated after this event, and a series of brutal drug murders in the fall of 1967 marked the end of an exotic social experiment.

The decimation of the East Village and the Haight might have been the final chapter of a unique phase in cultural history if not for the profound impact these communities had on American society as a whole. Like a cueball scattering the opening shot, the media laserbeam broke open the energy cluster that had coalesced in these hip enclaves and spread the psychedelic seed throughout the country. Soon there were love-ins and be-ins in nearly every major city in the US as hippie colonies sprang up across the land. Wherever LSD appeared on the scene, it announced itself in obvious ways: long hair, way-out clothing, funny glasses, and overall freakiness. (Frank Zappa, leader of the Los Angeles-based rock group, the Mothers of Invention, defined "freaking out" as "a process whereby an individual casts off outmoded and restricting standards of thinking, dress, and social etiquette in order to express CREATIVELY his relationship to his immediate environment and the social structure as a whole.") People who turned on were entertained and enlightened by distinc-

195

tive modes of art, film, dance, poetry, and, perhaps most important, music. The new electric sound, at once lyrical and dissonant, had broad appeal without losing any of its rebellious bite. For the first time in history young intellectuals and the young masses were not only grooving to the same beat but getting high on the same drugs.

"No corporate leader can afford to ignore the changing social, political and intellectual standard summed up in the phrase 'the generation gap,'" lectured David Rockefeller, chairman of Chase Manhattan Bank, to a group of executives at the University of Chicago's annual management conference in early 1968. By this time Madison Avenue had appropriated hip lingo to sell consumer goods, and snatches of popular songs could be heard in various advertising jingles. Opel promised to "light your fire," while a new brand of laundry detergent was touted as "out of sight." (The hippies, meanwhile, adapted the motto of the megacorporation: "Better living through chemistry.") The mystique of the Haight was ripped off by the bell-bottom salesmen and the promoters of *Hair*, a box-office triumph that took Broadway by storm in the fall of 1967. "LSD, LBJ, FBI, CIA," sang the cast of this widely acclaimed "tribal love-rock musical" which featured nudity, draft card burning, and an AM chartbuster hailing the day when peace would rule the planet and love would steer the stars. America may not have approved of its flower children, but commercially it ate them up.

The styles associated with psychedelic drugs achieved widespread cultural diffusion throughout North America and the Western world thanks to the ubiquitous reach of the mass media. Even those who did not actually sample LSD were apt to wear their hair longer and partake, however indirectly, of the psychedelic groundswell. But LSD had a much deeper effect on those who actually experimented with the drug. The media fanfare surrounding Haight-Ashbury and the Summer of Love catalyzed the sudden explosion of the acid scene. Four million North Americans are said to have tried acid in the late 1960s, and the average user, according to an extensive survey by Dr. Sidney Cohen, Richard Alpert, and Lawrence Schiller, was taking a dose every three or four months. Seventy percent of the turned-on set were of high school or college age, and many of them were involved in radical politics at one time or another.

The burgeoning acid scene raised more than a few eyebrows within the intelligence community, and a number of CIA-connected think tanks, including the Rand Corporation,* analyzed the broader questions relating to the social and political impact of LSD. Based in Santa Monica, California, the Rand Corporation played a crucial role in designing strategies for counter-revolution and pacification that were implemented in Vietnam. In the mid-1960s the think tank approach was expanded to include domestic issues; along this line Rand personnel examined the short- and long-term effect of LSD on personality change. A Rand report by William McGlothlin refers to "changes in dogmatism" and political affiliation: "If some of the subjects are drawn from extreme right or leftwing organizations, it may be possible to obtain additional behavioral measure in terms of the number resigning or becoming inactive."

While Rand Corporation specialists pondered whether LSD might be an antidote to political activism, the Hudson Institute, another think tank with strong ties to the intelligence community, kept tabs on shifting trends within the grassroots psychedelic movement. Founded by Herman Kahn,† one of America's leading nuclear strategists, the Hudson Institute specialized in classified research on national security issues. Kahn experimented with LSD on repeated occasions during the 1960s, and he visited Millbrook and other psychedelic strongholds on the East Coast. From time to time the rotund futurist (Kahn weighed over three hundred pounds) would stroll along Saint Mark's Place in the East Village, observing the flower children and musing on the implications of the acid subculture. At one point he predicted that by the year 2000 there would be an alternative "dropped-out" country within the United States. But Kahn was not overly sympathetic to the psychedelic movement. "He was primarily interested in social control," stated a Hudson Institute consultant who once lectured there on the subject of LSD.

The psychedelic subculture and its relationship to the New Left and the political upheavals of the 1960s was the subject of an investigation by Willis Harmon, who currently heads the Futures De-

---

*James Schlesinger, former CIA director and Secretary of Defense, is a senior strategic analyst at Rand. Henry Rowen, former Rand president, previously served as head of the CIA's National Intelligence Command.

†A well-known futurist, Kahn coauthored a book called *The Year 2000* with Anthony Wiener, a professor at MIT's Center for International Studies. Wiener had previously received a $12,000 grant from the Human Ecology Fund, which served as a cutout for funding numerous CIA behavior control studies under Operation MK-ULTRA.

partment at the Stanford Research Institute (SRI). Located in Palo Alto, California, this prestigious think tank received a number of grants from the US Army to conduct classified research into chemical incapacitants. Harmon made no bones about where he stood with respect to political radicals and the New Left. When Michael Rossman, a veteran of the Berkeley Free Speech Movement, visited SRI headquarters in the early 1970s, Harmon told him, "There's a war going on between your side and mine. And my side is not going to lose."

Harmon was turned on to LSD in the late 1950s by Captain Al Hubbard, the legendary superspy, who took a special interest in his new convert. Shortly thereafter Harmon became vice-president of the International Federation for Advanced Studies (IFAS), an organization devoted to exploring the therapeutic and problem solving potential of LSD. IFAS was the brainchild of Hubbard, who undoubtedly leaned on his political connections in Washington to insure that Harmon and his colleagues would be allowed to continue their drug investigations even after the first big purge of aboveground LSD research by the FDA in the early 1960s. During this period IFAS charged $500 for a single session of high-dose psychedelic therapy—an arrangement that led some critics to accuse IFAS of bilking the public.

Adverse publicity forced IFAS to disband in 1965, whereupon Harmon, who considered himself a disciple of the Captain, became director of the Educational Policy Research Center at SRI. In October 1968 he invited Hubbard, then living in semiretirement in British Columbia, to join SRI as a part-time "special investigative agent." As Harmon stated in a letter to his acid mentor, "Our investigations of some of the current social movements affecting education indicate that the drug usage prevalent among student members of the New Left is not entirely undesigned. Some of it appears to be present as a deliberate weapon aimed at political change. We are concerned with assessing the significance of this as it impacts on matters of long-range educational policy. In this connection it would be advantageous to have you considered in the capacity of a special investigative agent who might have access to relevant data which is not ordinarily available."

Hubbard accepted the offer of a $100 per day consultant's fee, and from then on he was officially employed as a security officer for SRI. "His services to us," explained Harmon, "consisted in gathering various sorts of data regarding student unrest, drug abuse, drug use at schools and universities, causes and nature of radical activities, and similar matters, some of a classified nature."

Hubbard was the ideal person for such a task. He boasted a great deal of experience both in the law enforcement field and in the use of psychedelic drugs. As a special agent for the FDA in the early 1960s, he led the first raids on underground acid labs, and a number of rebel chemists were arrested because of his detective work. The Captain was particularly irked when he learned that LSD in adulterated form was circulating on the black market. To Hubbard this represented degradation of the lowest order. The most precious spiritual substance on earth was being contaminated by a bunch of lousy bathtub chemists out to make a quick buck. The Captain was dead set against illicit drug use. "Impure drugs are very dangerous," he explained, "and the Law takes a dim view of it." He kept a sample of street acid for "comparative purposes" each time he busted an underground LSD factory during the 1960s; most of these outfits, Hubbard maintained, were run by the Mafia.

Even though Hubbard took a lot of acid and was a maverick among his peers, he remained a staunch law-and-order man throughout his life. The crew-cut Captain was the quintessential turned-on patriot, a seasoned spy veteran who admired the likes of J. Edgar Hoover. Above all Hubbard didn't like weirdos—especially long-haired radical weirdos who abused his beloved LSD. Thus he was eager to apply his espionage talents to a secret study of the student movement and the acid subculture. After conferring with Harmon, the Captain donned a khaki uniform, a gold-plated badge, a belt strung with bullets, and a pistol in a shoulder holster. That was the uniform he wore throughout his tenure as an SRI consultant, which lasted until the late 1970s.

Ironically, while Harmon and Hubbard were probing the relationship between drugs and radical politics, a number of New Left activists grappled with a similar question. Political and cultural radicals from both sides of the Atlantic discussed the drug issue at a conference on "the dialectics of liberation," which took place in London during the summer of 1967. Some were wary of mixing acid and politics. "Don't give LSD to Che Guevara, he might stop fighting," said Dr. David Cooper, a British psychiatrist who feared that drugs might undermine political commitment (the same thesis put forward by the Rand Corporation). But others, such as Allen Ginsberg, saw great advantages in a "politics of ecstasy." The pro-LSD faction insisted that acid was a radicalizing factor and that psychedelics would continue to galvanize the youth rebellion.

Obviously there was a great deal of confusion about LSD and its influence on the New Left. But an assessment of the overall impact of LSD cannot be couched solely in terms of whether acid "politicized" or "depoliticized" those who turned on, for the drug is capable of producing a wide range of reactions. A common mistake with respect to LSD was to attribute the personal effects of an acid trip to something inherent in the drug itself; as a result of this subtle transference, acid acquired the qualities of a particular mind-set or milieu, depending on who was experimenting with it. The love-and-peace vibrations thought to be intrinsic to the psychedelic high were largely an amplified reflection of the unique spirit that animated the mid-1960s, just as the CIA's obsession with LSD-induced anxiety and terror mirrored the Cold War paranoia of the espionage establishment.

Strictly speaking, acid is neither a transcendental sacrament, as Leary claimed, nor an anxiety-producing agent, as initially defined by CIA and army scientists. Rather, it is a nonspecific amplifier of psychic and social processes. LSD "makes you more of what you are," Aldous Huxley concluded. "It gives each person what he or she needs." At the same time acid catalyzes whatever forces are already active in a given social milieu and brings forth those that are latent.

Everyone who belongs to a particular culture shares, in the words of Peter Marin, "a condition, a kind of internal landscape,' the psychic shape that a particular time and place assumes within a man as the extent and limit of his perceptions, dreams, and pleasure and pain." This internal landscape was jolted by a series of earthquakes in the 1960s and early 1970s, and psychedelic drugs intensified and accelerated each phase of the youth rebellion as it developed over the years. The crucial turning point occurred in 1967, when the grass-roots acid scene was floodlit by the mass media and young people started turning on in greater numbers than ever before. This period marked the beginning of a new phase of political and countercultural transition. The media would be deeply implicated in everything that happened thereafter.

In effect, the media catalyzed the widespread use of LSD, itself a catalyst, and the pace of events suddenly flew into high gear. The

200

fuse had been lit in 1965, and now it was as if the second stage of that acid-fueled rocket had blasted into hyperspace. The fallout from the psychedelic explosion was enormous, reaching even those who shuddered at the prospect of turning on. Every sector of the New Left was affected by it, if only by contamination or the rush to denounce it. Soon the acid crazies would run amok, trashing what remained of the old political style and further upsetting the equilibrium of a movement that was already wobbling in the glare of publicity. But if LSD knocked things off-balance, it also gave the New Left "its first-ever dose of real fun," as Mairowitz put it, and a lot of young people wanted a piece of the action.

Magical Politics

The peace movement had reached a crossroads in the spring of 1967, after people took to the streets in unprecedented numbers all across the country to protest the war in Vietnam. Despite this tremendous outpouring of public sentiment President Johnson continued to escalate the war effort. American troop strength swelled to nearly a half-million, and young men were returning in body bags at a rate of five hundred a month. All of this was deeply disturbing to David Dellinger, director of the National Mobilization to End the War in Vietnam (otherwise known as the Mobe). Dellinger, an avowed pacifist, was strongly committed to nonviolence, but he questioned whether petitioning the government solely through legal means was an adequate response to the Vietnam debacle. His dilemma was compounded by the fact that the antiwar coalition had grown to encompass a broad range of groups from moderate to radical, each pursuing its own strategy and objectives. The only thing they all agreed on was to meet at the next big event: an antiwar demonstration in Washington, DC, on October 21, 1967, sponsored by Dellinger and the Mobe.

Dellinger feared that anything less than a huge turnout would be depicted in the press as a sign that the peace movement was losing steam. Big demonstrations were essential for media coverage, and the Mobe needed publicity to keep up the momentum. But the prospect of yet another well-mannered, nonviolent event that the government would simply shrug off did not appeal to radical elements. At one point SDS threatened to boycott the protest rally on the grounds that it would "delude" people into thinking they were having an effect on public policy. The Mobe eventually opted for a multitactical approach that included a call for defiant mass resistance at the Pentagon after the main rally at the Lincoln Memorial. To attract as many young people as possible Dellinger invited Jerry Rubin, the noted Berkeley activist, to New York to help organize the Pentagon action.

Rubin had impressive credentials among radicals and youth groups. He was one of the prime movers of the Vietnam Day protest in Berkeley two years earlier, and he led marchers in an attempt to block troop trains. After spending a month in jail for his political work, he was subpoenaed by the House Un-American Activities Committee (HUAC) in Washington. Instead of pleading the Fifth Amendment as most people did when called by HUAC, Rubin entered the hearing room dressed in an American Revolutionary War uniform. "I wear this uniform to symbolize the fact that America was born in revolution, but today America does violence to her own past by denying the right of others to revolution," he told a group of reporters. It was a political ploy designed to make a mockery of the HUAC proceedings; the congressmen were caught off guard, and Rubin's stunt became page-one news throughout the country. The publicity helped him garner 22% of the vote when he ran for mayor of Berkeley the following year on a platform opposing the war and supporting black power and the legalization of marijuana.

As soon as Rubin arrived in New York, he teamed up with Abbie Hoffman, an East Village hippie who'd been a civil rights organizer before he turned on to acid in 1965 courtesy of his roommate, an army psychologist who supplied the LSD. Hoffman got into drugs and grew his curly hair long, but he remained an activist at heart. He was involved in staging the New York be-in during the spring of 1967—an event modeled after the first Human Be-In in San Francisco, which had featured Rubin as a speaker.

Hoffman's politics got a lot saucier after he met a group of San Francisco Diggers in June 1967 at a "Back to the Drawing Boards" conference sponsored by SDS. At this gathering, which took place in Denton, Michigan, a Digger spokesman took off his clothes and challenged everyone else to do likewise. When no one budged, he started tossing tables and chairs around while berating the New Lefties in a burst of "do your own thing" rhetoric for being stodgy and unimaginative in their discussions of strategy. For many of the SDS members it was like watching the sulfurous fumes of hell. But not for Hoffman; he just sat there transfixed, absorbing everything he heard and saw. When he returned to New York he began calling himself "Abbie Digger" and opened a Free Store in the Bowery. Hoffman later published *Steal This Book*, a widely read underground treatise that incorporated much of what he had gleaned from the Diggers.

While Hoffman admired the acid anarchists from San Francisco, he did not share their disdain for using the media as a political tool. "A modern revolutionary headed for the television station, not for the factory," he declared. His eagerness to exploit the TV cameras struck a responsive chord in his newfound friend Jerry Rubin, who was also strongly influenced by the acid scene in San Francisco. ("If everyone did it," Rubin said of LSD, "it would be like heaven on earth.") They got stoned together and shared ideas about building a grand alliance between the bohemian and New Left tendencies. Such a combination, they believed, would provide an inexhaustible source of energy for the Movement. They agreed that the psychedelic sub-culture could be a significant political force, but if more young people were to be drawn into the protest struggle they would have to be engaged theatrically, via long hair, costume, and clever gamesmanship. With this in mind they set their sights on the upcoming march on the Pentagon.

Rubin had picked up a bit of occult folklore from Michael Bowen, the Psychedelic Ranger from Haight-Ashbury who had organized the San Francisco be-in and turned Rubin on to LSD earlier that year. A five-sided figure, Bowen explained, is a symbol of power, and when the figure is pointed north like the Pentagon building in Washington, it represents the forces of evil. This being the case, Bowen introduced the notion of encircling the Pentagon—not to capture it or shut it down, as some militants had urged, but to wound it symbolically. The idea of a mass antiwar ritual appealed to Rubin and Hoffman. At a press conference preceding the demonstration, they announced their intention to exorcise the Pentagon's evil spirits by levitating the building three hundred feet in the air until it started to vibrate and turn orange, whereupon the war in Vietnam would immediately cease. Hoffman also threatened to release a mysterious gas called "LACE," allegedly concocted by Owsley, which "makes you want to take off your clothes, kiss people and make love."

Seventy-five thousand protesters assembled at the Lincoln Memorial, including a sizable number of hippie types dressed in colorful costumes. The motley army of witches, warlocks, sorcerers, and long-haired bards who had come to celebrate the mystic revolution lent a carnival atmosphere to the demonstration. After a rousing prelude of speeches and songs, a large contingent crossed the Arlington Memorial Bridge into Virginia and raced toward the Pentagon, waving banners and shouting antiwar epithets. Some were high on acid when they stormed the grim ziggurat. They surrounded the entire building, dancing and hissing in unison, while soldiers stood guard at all five walls. Posters and slogans memorializing Che Guevara, the Latin revolutionary who had been killed in Bolivia a few weeks earlier, appeared on abutments, and a Viet Cong flag, blue and red with a gold star, fluttered in the breeze. And then the promised exorcism began.

"Out, demons, out!" boomed the voice of Ed Sanders, leader of a burlesque folk-rock ensemble called the Fugs, which provided musical edification for the antiwar constituency. On a flatbed truck in front of the high church of the military-industrial complex, the Fugs worked their "gene-shredding influence" on the crowd. Thousands shrieked their approval—"Out, out, out!"—and the stage was set for an ecstatic confrontation.

The demonstration had become a form of ritual theater, a preview of what politics would be like in the post-Haight-Ashbury era. As Norman Mailer wrote in *The Armies of the Night*, a best selling account of the march on the Pentagon, "Now, here, after several years of the blandest reports from the religious explorers of LSD, vague Tibetan lama goody-goodness auras of religiosity being the only publicly announced or even rumored fruit from all trips back from the buried Atlantis of LSD, now suddenly an entire generation of acid-heads seemed to have said goodbye to easy visions of heaven, no, now the witches were here, and rites of exorcism, and black terrors of the night.... The hippies had gone from Tibet to Christ to the Middle Ages, now they were Revolutionary Alchemists."

Despite their incantations and spells the protesters could not transmute the lead weight of the Pentagon into a golden vision in the sky. But it hardly mattered, for they were celebrating a new kind of activism, a style so authentically unique that it verged on the bizarre. "What possibly they shared," said Mailer, "was the unspoken happy confidence that politics had again become mysterious, had begun to partake of Mystery.... The new generation believed in technology more than any before it, but the generation also believed in LSD, in witches, in tribal knowledge, in orgy, and revolution. It had no respect whatsoever for the unassailable logic of the next step: belief was reserved for the revelatory mystery of the happening where you did not know what was going to happen next; that was what was good about it."

What happened next was not something anyone had expected— in fact, it might never have happened had it not been for the FBI, which attempted to disrupt the antiwar gathering upon learning of a plot to sky-bomb the Pentagon with ten thousand flowers. Peggy Hitchcock (the sister of William Mellon Hitchcock, owner of the Millbrook estate) gave Michael Bowen and friends money to purchase two hundred pounds of daisies for the occasion, but the plan never got off the ground because of a dirty trick by the FBI. J. Edgar Hoover's men answered an ad for a pilot in the *East Village Other* but never showed up at the airport. Bowen was stuck with more flowers than he knew what to do with, so he turned around and drove back to the demonstration. Distributed among the crowd, the flowers were subsequently photographed by the world press protruding from the muzzles of rifles held by the soldiers guarding the Pentagon.

It was one of the spectacular images of the 1960s: the troops with their bayonets sprouting daisies, frozen in a tense face-off with the antiwar activists. By sundown most of the press had left. The police moved in with tear gas and arrested people—over eight hundred in all—and many were brutally beaten. But these tactics did not dampen the spirits of the demonstrators. They were elated by what had transpired. Some felt that it was a watershed event, comparable in magnitude to the Boston Tea Party. "It made me see that we could build a movement by knocking off American symbols," said Rubin. "We had symbolically destroyed the Pentagon, the symbol of the war machine, by throwing blood on it, by pissing on it, dancing on it...painting 'Che lives' on it. It was a total cultural attack on the Pentagon. The media had communicated this all over the country and lots of people identified with us, the besiegers."

After the march Rubin decided to remain in New York with his girlfriend, Nancy Kurshan. They spent the next few months with Hoffman and his wife, Anita, cooking up new stunts so audacious and compelling that the press would have to cover them. "An event doesn't exist until the media announces it," Rubin asserted. "Once the media announces it, it is an event whether or not it exists." He and Hoffman believed that television was little more than an elaborate mirror game the authorities used to pacify the public. In their stoned reveries they dreamed of switching the mirrors around in order to reflect a different set of images that would shock the viewers, blow their minds, and make them confront the idea that there was a crazy alternative to the straight way of life.

Hoffman and Rubin possessed an uncanny knack for showmanship, a sixth sense for what would capture the imagination of young people. But they needed some kind of focal point, a central theme that would enhance the impact of their efforts. On New Year's Day 1968 they dropped acid together so they "could look at the problem *logically*," as Rubin put it, and they hit upon a recipe for social change. Mix one part hippie and one part activist, marinade in Marx (Groucho, not Karl) and McLuhan, season radically with psychedelics, and what do you come up with? Paul Krassner, editor of the *Realist*, a satirical underground magazine, said it first: "Yippie!"— the battle cry of the Youth International Party. It was a name to conjure with, a rallying point for stoned politicos and militant hippies who had merged the "I protest" of the New Left with the "I am" of the counterculture. "We figured we could create a new myth of the dope-taking, freedom-loving, politically committed activist," Rubin explained. "Some day, we dreamed, the myth will grow and grow until there were millions of yippies.... Soon there will be yippies and a Youth International Party throughout the Western world."

The Yippies didn't go along with the notion that being a serious activist meant you couldn't have a good time. Convinced that boredom was a revolutionary sin, they were determined to make outrage contagious on a mass scale. "No need to build a stage," said Hoffman, "it was all around us. Props would be simple and obvious. We would hurl ourselves across the canvas of American society like streaks of splattered paint. Highly visual images would become news, and rumor mongers would rush to spread the excited word."

The Yippies were political pranksters, and their lunatic style of attack played upon the media's insatiable appetite for anything new or eccentric. They knew the press would give them free publicity as long as they flaunted the holy goof: burning money on Wall Street; appearing naked in church; dumping soot and smoke bombs in the lobby of Con Edison's headquarters; mailing Valentine's cards to persons unknown, each containing a joint. Their bombastic antics were framed as political commercials ("advertisements for the revolution") that would mobilize oppositional consciousness and compel people by dramatic example to change their lives. "Our lifestyle—acid, long hair, rock music, sex—is the revolution," Rubin declared.

To the Yippies the masses of American youth were potential revolutionaries who merely had to be "turned on" by media buttons—and by LSD. They believed that acid was a subversive instrument, and they urged everyone to take the drug in order to break the mind-forged manacles that bound people to a repressive society. This presumably would lead to an understanding of why a revolution was necessary, thereby accelerating the dawn of a twentieth-century utopia. "Once one has experienced LSD," said Hoffman, "one realizes that action is the only reality." But what kind of action did the Yippies propose? Drugs made them more willing to gamble on their intuitions. "Mostly it's a catch-as-catch-can affair," Hoffman admitted. "You just get stoned, get the ideas in your head and then do 'em."

TV and LSD: both magical and instantaneous, both ways of leapfrogging the long and arduous task of grassroots political organizing. The Yippies had no predefined strategy other than *épater les bourgeois* (tweaking the nose of the middle class) via media freaking. They rejected the idea of a program as too confining. Ideology was dismissed as "a brain disease." If they had any doctrine at all, it was that people should do "whatever the fuck they want." Rubin described his Yippie vision in the closing passages of *Do It!*

> At community meetings all over the land, Bob Dylan will replace the National Anthem.
> There will be no more jails, courts, or police.
> The White House will become a crash pad for anybody without a place to stay in Washington.
> The world will become one big commune with free food and housing, everything shared.
> All watches and clocks will be destroyed....
> The Pentagon will be replaced by an LSD experimental farm. . . .

The Yippies were not an organization in the formal sense. They had no membership list, no direct relationship with a grassroots, face-to-face constituency, and it was not clear whether their views represented a majority opinion in hip communities; nevertheless, these TV-promoted gadflys became the most celebrated spokesmen for the youth movement. In this respect the Yippies had much in common with Timothy Leary, whose status as leader of the psychedelic movement was certified by the media rather than by those who actually took LSD. Leary also lacked an organizational base but was adept at manipulating the press, which was one of the reasons the Yippies sought him out. "We had many analytical discussions about the tactical necessity of using the media," Leary recalled. But he was not particularly enthusiastic when the Yippies asked him to endorse their cause. Despite the halfhearted response Hoffman acknowledged his debt to the High Priest of LSD: "I studied his technique of karmic salesmanship."

The Yippies were the first group on the left to define themselves solely through the media projections of their flamboyant leaders. On their own terms they were quite successful. They articulated a spirit of revolt that was alive in young people throughout the country and helped foster an antiestablishment consciousness among some who might not have been reached in any other way. But the Yippie approach was not without pitfalls. As former SDS president Todd Gitlin explained, "When movements become too 'mediated,' it becomes hard to tell the difference between a movement and a fad, a movement and a trend, or just a press conference. The results are pernicious for movements. The line between leadership and celebrity becomes very thin. It's easy for leaders to cross over and become wholly unaccountable to a movement base."

Rubin and Hoffman were the two most famous radical celebrities of the 1960s. Their lust for the spotlight, doubtless the product of personal as well as political motives, drove them to new peaks of self-promotion. But the Yippies paid a high price for a ticket on the publicity loop. As four-star attractions in an ongoing radical soap opera, they inadvertently trivialized the very issues they sought to dramatize. The result was a parody of left-wing politics that may have undermined serious efforts to reform America. "I didn't know if I was headed to Hollywood or to jail," Rubin later confessed. "I purposefully manipulated the media, but on a deeper level I see that it was mutual manipulation. To interest the media I needed to express my politics frivolously....If I had given a sober lecture on the history of Vietnam, the media cameras would have turned off."

So the Yippies kept pranking and the cameras kept cranking. The most outlandish, abrasive, and extravagant gestures were the surest to be broadcast, and the media, always hungry for novelty, gave leading roles to those who, in Gitlin's words, "seemed like Central Casting's gift to revolutionary imagery." By no means, however, did

208

the Yippies have a monopoly on movement histrionics in the late 1960s. Indeed, their zany youth cult capers were timid in comparison to the militant theatrics of the Black Panther party.

Founded in 1966 by Huey Newton and Bobby Seale, the Panthers first gained attention the following year when they strolled into the California state capitol building in Sacramento twenty strong, with their leather jackets, black berets on blossoming afros, and loaded Magnum rifles and shotguns, to protest a bill forbidding such weapons in Oakland, where the Panthers were based. The ensuing publicity gave them a big boost, and they began to organize chapters in urban ghettos across the country. Initially their focus was on police brutality and self-defense, but soon the Panthers developed a black socialist ideology and a forthright party program that reflected the influence of Malcolm X, who in the final years of his life had rejected antiwhite bigotry. To promote the party in the community, the Panthers launched a variety of "survival programs," such as free medical clinics, pest control projects, and free breakfast for poor children (black, brown, and white) on a daily basis—an idea that had been suggested by the San Francisco Diggers. Meanwhile they continued to cultivate the symbolism of violence. Their overinflated language, menacing leather attire, and radical cool provoked a great deal of attention in the mainstream press, and thousands of young blacks joined their ranks.

The Panthers rejected the goal of assimilation into a system they saw as repressive and inhumane—a sentiment shared by many white radicals. The black nationalist culture, with its dashikis, tiger-tooth necklaces, and afro haircuts, often espoused values similar to those of the white counterculture: spontaneity, simplicity, respect for individuality and ethnic identity, cooperation rather than competition, and so forth. A number of black activists were also into drugs—mostly marijuana and cocaine—for rest and relaxation. Some of the Panthers, for example, liked to get stoned and listen to Bob Dylan's *Highway 61 Revisited* on headphones. They were particularly impressed by "The Ballad of a Thin Man," which taunted "Mr. Jones," the archetypical honkie who knows something's happening but doesn't know what it is. "These brothers would get halfway high, loaded on something," Bobby Seale recounted, "and they would sit down and play this record over and over and over, especially after they began to hear Huey P. Newton interpret that record. They'd be trying to relate to an understanding about what was going on, 'cause old Bobby [Dylan] did society a big favor when he made that particular sound."

While the black power movement had a strong cultural component, it never embraced LSD, which made only minor inroads into black society during the 1960s. Reality was already too heavy a trip in the ghetto, and many black militants were unkindly disposed toward the black soul singers and rock stars who expressed a preference for hippie drugs in their music: Sly and the Family Stone ("I Want to Take You Higher"), Jimi Hendrix ("Are You Experienced?"), the Chambers Brothers ("Time Has Come Today"), the Temptations ("Cloud Nine" and "Psychedelic Shack"). Certain black radicals, such as A. X. Nicholas, went so far as to denounce these songs as "counterrevolutionary" and urge that they be boycotted by the black community.

Thus it took on added significance when Eldridge Cleaver, minister of information of the Black Panther party, offered to make an alliance with those notoriously wacked-out acidheads the Yippies. "Eldridge wanted a coalition between the Panthers and psychedelic street activists," Rubin explained. So they got together, smoked a lot of grass, and composed a "joint" manifesto called the Panther-Yippie Pipe Dream. "Into the streets!" Cleaver proclaimed. "Let us join together with all those souls in Babylon who are straining for the birth of a new day. A revolutionary generation is on the scene. There are men and women, human beings, in Babylon today. Disenchanted, alienated white youth, the hippies, the yippies and all the unnamed dropouts from the white man's burden, are our allies in this cause." The Black Panther party newspaper later featured an article entitled, "The Hippies Are Not Our Enemies."

The prospect of a genuine coalition between white radicals and black militants sent chills up the spine of the political establishment in the United States, which greatly feared, in the words of former air force secretary Townsend Hoopes, "the fateful merging of antiwar and racial dissension." But the Panther-Yippie alliance was more symbolic than anything else, and only nearsighted observers could have thought otherwise. The Yippies were essentially freelance activists whose shadow organization lacked a community base; hence there was nothing for the Panthers to ally with other than an image, a set of fleeting gestures. But the Yippies and Panthers did share certain important attributes. Both knew how to use the media in creative ways to get their message across, and both were excited about the prospects for an explosive year in 1968.

Gotta Revolution

Few people realized just how intense things would get in 1968, and no one was prepared for the bewildering series of events that unfolded. With each passing month the political temperature rose a few more notches. First there was the Tet offensive launched by the Viet Cong in February, which belied President Johnson's optimistic predictions of an impending US victory. Twenty thousand Americans had already been killed in action, a hundred and ten thousand were wounded, and still there was no sign that the war would be over in the near future. A "dump Johnson" movement mounted by doves within the Democratic party gathered unexpected momentum when Senator Eugene McCarthy decided to challenge LBJ for the presidential nomination. McCarthy scored an impressive showing in the early primaries, and on March 31, 1968, Johnson announced he would not seek reelection.

The demise of LBJ was a great victory for the New Left, but the euphoria passed quickly. Four days after Johnson's abdication Dr. Martin Luther King was assassinated in Memphis. The death of the nation's most gifted civil rights leader sparked the worst domestic strife since the Civil War. There were riots in a hundred and twenty-five cities nationwide, including Washington, DC. Forty-six people died, more than twenty thousand were arrested, and fifty-five thousand federal troops and National Guardsmen were deployed to handle the emergency. In the wake of the ghetto uprisings a nervous Congress passed the so-called Rap Brown amendment, making it a federal crime to cross state lines with the intent to start a riot. This law would be used in subsequent years to prosecute antiwar activists.

Violent confrontations became a normal occurrence in 1968 not only in the ghettos and barrios of America, but also on college campuses throughout the country. The first pitched battle between students and police took place at Columbia University in New York City, the media capital of the world, when the local SDS chapter led a series of actions beginning in late April and lasting for several weeks. Hundreds were injured during the protest, which sent shock

211

waves reverberating through all of academia. "This is a ferocious but effective way to be a student—to be educated," said former SDS president Carl Oglesby. "The policeman's riot club functions like a magic wand under whose hard caress the banal soul grows vivid and the nameless recover their authenticity—a bestower, this wand, of the lost charisma of the modern self: I bleed, therefore I am."

Hundreds of campuses in the US enacted similar confrontations in the coming months. But academic insurrections were by no means exclusively an American phenomenon. During the late 1960s student radicals took to the streets in nearly every country in Western Europe, as well as in Japan, South Africa, Canada, Turkey, Latin America, and a number of Eastern bloc nations. The most dramatic upheaval occurred in Paris in May 1968, when left-wing activists at the Sorbonne succeeded in triggering a nationwide strike that threatened to topple the Gaullist government.

During the peak of the Sorbonne uprising a group of artists and cultural workers got together to discuss how they could best show their support for those who were engaged in running battles with the police. Among those present at the meeting was Julian Beck of the Living Theater, an experimental performing troupe that traveled extensively in Europe. Controversy always surrounded the Living Theater, for they were among the boldest and most innovative experimenters of the 1960s. Their performances included rituals of love, affirmation, nonviolence, and communality drawn from various mystical and contemporary sources: Artaud, the kabbalah, the continuous use of drugs. The thirty members of the Living Theater frequently tripped together and often performed while high on LSD. "We were willing to experiment with anything that would set the mind free," Beck explained. "We were practicing anarchists, and we were talking about freedom in whatever zones it could be acquired. If drug trips were a way of unbinding the mind, we were eager to experiment."

The Living Theater was already heavily into drugs when the police chased them out of New York City in the early 1960s after many of them had been arrested during pacifist demonstrations. They fled to Europe on a wing and a prayer, hoping to avoid the legal hassles that plagued them in the States. Wherever they traveled on the Continent, the Living Theater interacted with the thriving acid subculture that took root in the mid-1960s. In each city they mingled with turned-on artists, poets, dropouts, and other nonconformists

212

who shared their anarchist vision and provided them with cannabis and acid. The Living Theater, in turn, helped to spread the psychedelic creed as they moved from one locale to another.

Amsterdam was the touchstone, the magic city where every drug was readily available. It was also the home of the Provos (short for Provocateurs), a large anarchist tribe whose political art happenings anticipated the style and essence of the San Francisco Diggers. The Provos took Amsterdam by storm in 1965 when they plastered peace insignias across the city streets along with their own logo, an upside down apple, which represented the modern Johnny Appleseed implanting the seeds of a liberating culture. They unrolled reams of newsprint like carpets through the streets of Amsterdam to protest the "daily newspapers which brainwash our people." They also staged proecology rallies and elected several of their pot-smoking members to the city administration.

Provo groups sprang up in Milan, Stockholm, Copenhagen, Brussels, and Antwerp (a transit point for shiploads of Congolese grass) as the drug scene spread rapidly throughout Europe. London emerged as a major psychedelic center in the summer of 1965. Acid was also plentiful in Munich and Berlin, where hippies were called *Gammler.* Rome had its *capellones* who liked to get *stonati* by ingesting *hallucinazione.* LSD trickled into Paris, Zurich, Madrid, and the Greek Isles, and a Czech expatriate reports that young people in Prague were turning on to acid in the months prior to the Russian invasion in August, 1968. As Beck put it,

> LSD carried with it a certain messianic vision, a certain understanding of the meaning of freedom, of the meaning of the as yet unattainable but nevertheless to be obtained erotic fantasy, political fantasy, social fantasy—a sense of oneness, a sense of goodness, a marvelous return to the Garden of Eden morality.... That's why we thought if you could put it into the water system, everybody would wake up and we would be able to realize the changes we were dreaming in terms of societal structures. People wouldn't be able to tolerate things as they were any longer. They'd realize that something is wrong out there, something is wrong inside me, something is too beautiful, too indescribable, too irresistible to put off any longer.

During their travels the Living Theater befriended many leaders of the student movement in Europe, who were also concerned about new selfhood, new human beings, new possibilities. But the hardcore politicos were not overly enthusiastic about psychedelic drugs.

"We pushed reefers on them all the time," Beck recalled. "They were getting high, but not enough." Most left-wing activists in France, Germany, and Italy saw drugs as a pleasant diversion at best; they never thought the most effective way to organize people was to turn them on. As a general rule there was far less overlap between the drug scene and the New Left in Europe than in the United States. This became apparent to the Living Theater when they returned to North America in the summer of 1968, after four and a half years of self-imposed exile.

Much had changed on the cultural and political front in the US during this period. The peace movement, having grown by leaps and bounds, was now a mass movement. Polls showed a majority of Americans disapproved of the administration's Vietnam policy. As opposition to the war became more respectable and mainstream, the New Left as a whole edged toward a more radical posture. The V sign for peace gave way to the clenched fist, denoting a change not so much to violence as to militance. An increasing number of activists came to view the war not as an error in judgment or an aberration of American foreign policy but as the latest in a series of imperialist interventions in many countries. The emphasis on vigorous street tactics and a sweeping anti-imperialist analysis set the young radicals apart from the reform-minded liberals and moderates who after years of bloodshed in Southeast Asia finally decided to give peace a chance.

Buoyed by the surging popularity of the antiwar cause and the heightened tempo of the black rebellion, many people began to take for granted a context of political extremity. Predictions of the coming revolution were rampant, and much of the New Left assumed it was on the threshold of a political transformation that was actually way beyond its means. Indeed, it was hard for radicals not to get carried away as the decade rocked to a bloody climax in 1968. They had forced LBJ into early retirement, and now the whole lousy system seemed to be teetering on the brink. A few shouts, a few kicks, a good hard shove in the right place, and surely Babylon would fall.

This was the unspoken assumption behind the Yippies' decision to stage a massive demonstration at the 1968 Democratic National Convention in Chicago during the last week of August. At the heart of the Yippie scenario was a "Festival of Life" that would offer an enticing alternative to the "death politics" inside the convention

214

hall. Plans for the festival included a variety of counterconvention activities: a nude grope-in for peace and prosperity, a joint-rolling contest, the election of Miss Yippie. All the top rock and roll acts would perform, the hippest poets would recite the best poems. And what demonstration would be complete without a bell-festooned contingent of holy men leading the protesters in life-affirming incantations? There'd be free food for everyone and workshops on drugs, communes, guerrilla theater, first aid, and draft dodging.

It was an ambitious scheme for a group of dope-smoking misfits who had no political organization to speak of. But the Yippies knew they had the media at their beck and call, and they hoped hype would make up for what they lacked on a grassroots level. They tantalized reporters with visions of a Chicago inundated by a million stoned freaks who would force the Democrats to conduct their business under armed guard. The Yippies, meanwhile, would nominate their own presidential candidate—a pig named Pigasus, whom they vowed to eat after he won the election. This, the Yippies maintained, would reverse the normal procedure in which the pig is elected "and proceeds to eat the people."

Of course, the Yippies realized that nowhere near a million people would turn up for the demonstration, but exaggeration was the crux of their organizing strategy. They inflated the figures to attract more publicity, hoping to create a snowball effect and draw a large crowd. "We competed for attention like media junkies after a fix," Rubin admitted. "Television [kept] us escalating our tactics." Whereas a sit-in or a picket line might have made headlines a few years ago, now it took bloody heads and tear gas to get coverage on the evening news. In the months preceding the convention the Yippies flatly predicted violence and spiced up their rhetoric to keep their audience enthralled. "We will burn Chicago to the ground!" "We will fuck on the beaches!" "We demand the Politics of Ecstasy!" "Acid for all!" "Abandon the Creeping Meatball!" And always: "Yippie! Chicago—August 25-30."

A handful of Yippie stalwarts worked long hours at an ad hoc office in New York, printing tens of thousands of posters, leaflets, and buttons as part of the PR campaign for the Festival of Life. Getting stoned was standard operating procedure among office staffers, and their fanciful literature carried their dope-induced hallucinations. They kept in touch with young people throughout the country by issuing sporadic press releases that were picked up by the Liberation News Service and disseminated to three hundred underground newspapers.

The Yippies were preparing monkey-warfare hijinks and other street theater actions, but their plans did not call for organized violence or rioting on the part of demonstrators. Nevertheless, they made no secret of the fact that they relished the possibility of a showdown with the "pigs." By forcing a confrontation the Yippies hoped to reveal the "true nature of the beast," as the saying went, and make the fence-sitters take sides. This, they believed, would automatically benefit the radical cause. "It's not the Republicans and Democrats," Rubin asserted, "it's what America is doing and what it stands for and against. And when that becomes clear in every living room in this country, wow—our side's gonna win."

Victory for the Yippies was nothing less than "total revolution"— or something like that. Just what they actually meant by "revolution for the hell of it" or how such a thing would come to pass was never very clear, but it hardly seemed to matter. They were confident that their moment of shining glory had arrived. "We want the world and we want it now!" sang Jim Morrison of the Doors (who took their name from Huxley's *The Doors of Perception*) in what became the anthem of the young rebels who dismissed any notion of temperate or deliberate change. Those who combined youthful anger with untrammeled experimentation had little patience for the politics of the long haul. Things had developed so quickly and so far beyond expectations that the only honorable course was to take every idea to the limit, to indulge every form of excess. Surely all this energy would lead to something amazing, something chaotic, a crisis so massive that it would sweep aside the gray-haired masters of war and bring the government to its knees. For a generation "born to be wild," anything less seemed like a cowardly evasion of destiny.

And it wasn't just the Yippies who entertained this fantasy. Caught up in their own inflated rhetoric, almost everyone associated with the New Left began to lose track of what was politically feasible. Radicals blithely spoke of revolution as if it were just around the corner, a historical certainty as imminent as tomorrow's sunrise. And why not? The flamboyant images of revolt were everywhere— in the daily papers, in the underground press, on the TV news. In a society thoroughly bombarded by media images, who could tell what was real? Stoned or otherwise, the baby boom rebels were tangled in a net of reflected events, a hall of mirrors; they related to a distorted picture of reality that filtered through the cracked looking glass of the mass media. By focusing on highly charged incidents and giving the greatest airplay to the wildest and most aggressive gestures, the commercial media reinforced and accentuated the social chaos. Add to this confusion the sudden explosion of the acid scene in the wake of the Summer of Love, and one begins to get a sense of the hallucinatory nature of this period.

The revolutionary fervor of the late 1960s was amplified by the widespread use of LSD and other hallucinogens. These drugs tended to blur the distinction between the imaginary and the real, so that daily life for frequent users became infused with the exaggeration of a mythic dream. Many political activists who got high regularly behaved as though they were living in the midst of a revolutionary situation.

"The effect of LSD was really heavy," acknowledged John Sinclair, former head of the White Panther party in Ann Arbor, Michigan. "Acid blew all sense of proportion, all sense of a frame, to smithereens. I mean it just blew the frame right out of the picture.... It gave you a sense of infinite possibility. You could do anything if you just *did it*—totally! You could walk right into the sky." Sinclair now considers this attitude foolhardy. "All your big decisions were made on LSD. And while that might be an exciting way to operate, it's not the most intelligent way. To think that your personal consciousness can overcome historical forces is a mistake."

Sinclair first turned on to psychedelics in the early 1960s, after reading Ginsberg and the beats. Known among his peers as a poet and jazz aficionado, he got involved with the Detroit Artists Workshop and started turning on more frequently with his creative clique. After the Detroit riots in 1967 Sinclair began to study the literature of the black power movement. "Anything to the right of Malcolm X just wasn't happening," he asserted. At the time there was a lot of acid floating around. "In my case it was the idealistic poetry stuff coupled with the black militant stuff and the turned-on black jazz artists," Sinclair recalled, "and all those things came together in my little psyche, 500 mikes a week, and POW! After one particularly stunning LSD experience, I got to the point where I felt that writing and poetry and all that was cool, but it was really important to develop some sort of instrumentation to make it relevant on a larger scale."

Sinclair credits LSD with facilitating the transition from the secretive, cabalistic mentality of the beats to the collective orientation of the 1960s. "When the beatniks started taking acid, it brought us out of the basement, the dark place, the underworld, the fringes of society.... all of a sudden one was filled with a messianic feeling of love, of brotherhood.... LSD gave us the idea it could be different. It was tremendously inspiring. We thought this would alter everything. We were going to take over the world. This was the general belief. It was the LSD.... Acid was amping everything up, driving everything into greater and greater frenzy."

In retrospect Sinclair wonders whether the CIA was behind the acid craze. "They're the ones who had it," he says. But the notion that LSD might have been part of a government plot was the furthest thing from Sinclair's mind when he moved to Ann Arbor with a coterie of radicals in early 1968 and formed the White Panther party. One of their main objectives was to spread the revolutionary message to high schools throughout the Midwest with the help of a politically dedicated rock and roll band, the MC5, which Sinclair managed. "School sucks," declared the White Panther manifesto. "The white honkie culture that has been handed down to us on a plastic platter is meaningless to us! We don't want it! Fuck God in the ass. Fuck your woman until she can't stand up. Fuck everybody you can get your hands on. Our program of rock and roll, dope and fucking in the streets is a program of total freedom for everyone. And we are committed to carrying out our program. We breathe revolution. We are LSD-driven total maniacs in the universe."

When Sinclair heard about the Yippies' plan for Chicago, he thought it was fantastic. "I could never see what was more important than cultural activity, what people did each day to reflect the way they thought and felt about things," he said. "To me that was really political." For a while the White Panthers even considered becoming the Michigan chapter of the Youth International Party. They were, after all, natural allies; like the Yippies, Sinclair was high on the revolutionary potential of drugs and the druggy potential of revolution. The Festival of Life was particularly appealing to the White Panthers, who liked the idea of merging rock music with politics. It was also an opportunity for the MC5 to perform before a national audience. Thus, on grounds of politics and promotion, the Panthers wholeheartedly endorsed the Yippie festival.

With the Democratic Convention only weeks away, the Yippies persisted in needling Mayor Daley as much as possible. They circulated a list of demands including the legalization of marijuana and LSD, the abolition of money, the disarming of the Chicago police, and—not to be overlooked—a statement in favor of general copulation: "We believe that people should fuck all the time, anytime, whomever they wish." When the Yippies slyly let it be known that they intended to put LSD in the water supply (a scenario cooked up by the CIA fifteen years earlier), Daley ordered a round-the-clock guard at the local reservoirs. Hoffman and Rubin countered by threatening to dispatch Yippie girls dressed up as whores, "but young, you know, and nice," who would pick up convention delegates and slip acid into their drinks (another scenario reminiscent of CIA escapades during the Cold War). Moreover, thousands of protesters would run naked through the streets while "Yippie studs" seduced the delegates' wives and daughters.

Apparently these fictive threats touched a raw nerve somewhere and were taken quite seriously by Daley's men. The Yippies were humiliating the old fogies by reminding them of their fading sexuality as well as heaping scorn on their patriotic ideals. Rubin again: "We were dirty, smelly, grimy, foul, loud, dope-crazed, hell-bent and leather-jacketed....We were a public display of filth and shabbiness, living in-the-flesh rejects of middle-class standards. We pissed and shit and fucked in public....We were constantly stoned or tripping on every drug known to man....Dig it! *The future of humanity was in our hands!*"

There was no "fucking in the streets" as the Yippies had promised. But even the thought of such erotic impudence was enough to jack up the angry riot squads and the secret service goons who had assembled in Chicago. Mayor Daley prepared for the acidheads and the foul-mouthed subversives by turning the city into an armed camp. He ordered twelve thousand police to work overtime, and hundreds of undercover agents were deployed on "special assignments." There were also six thousand National Guardsmen ready for action, and an equal number of regular army troops complete with bazookas, barbed-wire jeeps, and tanks. Then he issued a discreet warning: come to Chicago at your own risk.

Daley's intimidation tactics succeeded. In the end only about ten thousand protesters showed up, far fewer than the Yippies had expected. The much-heralded Festival of Life commenced on Sunday, August 25, the day before the convention. The protesters met at Lincoln Park, where acid was passed around in the form of spiked honey. A free rock concert had been announced, but all the musicians stayed away except for Phil Ochs and the MC5. Then the police moved in and started arresting people. Tempers flared on both sides, and the Festival of Life soon became a Festival of Blood.

The street fighting continued for the next five days while the Democrats deliberated inside the convention hall. The confrontation reached a dramatic crescendo during the middle of the week. Thousands of demonstrators massed along Michigan Avenue in front of the Conrad Hilton, where Vice-President Hubert Humphrey, the Democratic nominee, was staying along with many of the convention delegates. It was late at night, but that portion of the street was floodlit for the sake of television. The crowd took up the rousing chant, "The whole world is watching! The whole world is watching."

The National Guard in full battle dress moved into position with M-1 rifles, gas masks, and machine guns mounted on military vehicles. Tear gas was thrown and a gruesome melee ensued. The police attacked with indiscriminate fury, clubbing and macing young and old, male and female, protesters and innocent bystanders. News reporters and photographers were beaten along with the rest, while the powerful lamp of an army helicopter shone down through billowing clouds of orange smoke. Dozens of patrol cars flashed blue siren lights, and the silhouettes of mangled bodies were barely visible in the stroboscopic mist.

"For me, that week in Chicago was far worse than the worst acid trip I'd even heard rumors about," said Hunter Thompson. "It permanently altered my brain chemistry, and my first new idea—when I finally calmed down—was an absolute conviction there was no possibility for any personal truce...in a nation that could hatch and be proud of a malignant monster like Chicago. Suddenly it seemed imperative to get a grip on those who had somehow slipped into power and caused the thing to happen."

Young people throughout the country shared Thompson's sense of urgency, as they watched the unmuzzled savagery of the police on television. (The Walker Commission later attributed the mayhem to a "police riot.") Over a thousand demonstrators had been injured, and one youth died during that tumultuous week. But even more significant than the number of casualties was the profound impact these events had on the New Left as a whole. The Battle of Chicago drew a line across the political landscape, marking the symbolic end of the resistance period and the turn toward revolution. It proved once and for all that the pernicious system was beyond any hope of reform; it would have to be completely dismantled. In the wake of Chicago, many activists concluded that peaceful means of protest, no matter how noble or well-executed, were not enough to eradicate the evils of America; social institutions grounded in violence would resort to violence if any serious challenge to the status quo was mounted.

The Yippies came away from Chicago strengthened in their resolve to fight the establishment by any means necessary. They felt they had won a great victory, and in some ways they were right. The ruthlessness of those in power had been laid bare for all to see in what was perhaps the most memorable media event of sixties protest culture. But the Yippies overlooked a very basic fact: getting TV coverage did not necessarily mean getting their message across. While the street brawl may have shocked some viewers into sympathy for the demonstrators, every poll indicated that a vast majority of the public applauded the brutality of the Chicago police.

To the average citizen the Yippies epitomized the calamitous upsurge of wayward youth gone anti-American and wild. Their obnoxious behavior offended millions who would no longer look upon student protest with indifference, much less with favor. But it wasn't just the Yippies who were putting people on edge. Not since the Civil War had life in America been so disorienting and confusing, so terribly violent, as it was during the late 1960s. Everything seemed to be spinning out of control. The assassinations of Robert Kennedy and Martin Luther King, the ghetto riots, the campus strikes, the soaring crime rate, the spread of drugs, the black power movement— all these factors raised genuine fears that American society was coming apart. And then along came Richard Nixon, the law-and-order candidate, who promised to put the Commie-hippie-freaks in their place. Nixon won the '68 election in the streets of Chicago when the madness of an entire decade spilled into the living rooms of a nation of bewildered onlookers.

"Chicago, I think, was the place where all America was radicalized," wrote Tom Wicker of the *New York Times*. "The miracle of television made it visible to all—pierced, at last, the isolation of one America from the other, exposed to each the power it faced. Everything since Chicago has had a new intensity—that of polarization, of confrontation, of antagonism and fear."

9

Season Of The Witch

ARMED LOVE

It was a typical sixties scene: a group of scruffy, long-haired students stood in a circle passing joints and hash pipes. The setting could have been Berkeley, Ann Arbor or any other hip campus. But these students were actually FBI agents, and the school they attended was known as "Hoover University." Located at Quantico Marine Base in Virginia, this elite academy specialized in training G-men to penetrate left-wing organizations. To cultivate the proper counterculture image, they were told not to wash or bathe for several days before infiltrating a group of radicals. Refresher courses were also held for FBI agents who had successfully immersed themselves in the drug culture of their respective locales. For months they had smoked pot and dropped acid with unsuspecting radicals, and now the turned-on spies had a chance to swap stories with their undercover comrades. Former FBI agent Cril Payne likened the annual seminar to a class reunion. Between lectures on the New Left, drug abuse, and FBI procedure, the G-men would sneak away to the wooded grounds to get stoned while American taxpayers footed the bill.

In the late 1960s the Yippies were infiltrated by an FBI agent named George Demmerle. Known in New York radical circles as "Prince Crazy," Demmerle wore weird costumes, smoked a lot of pot, and instigated some of the most outrageous street theater actions. He also was a member of the YIP steering committee, and he served as Abbie Hoffman's bodyguard during the Chicago convention. At one point Demmerle tried to interest the Yippies in a plan to blow up the Brooklyn Bridge, but fortunately wiser heads prevailed. They never suspected he was a spook; after all, marijuana was a "revolutionary" drug, and no pig could maintain his cover while under the honest influence of the herb (the old truth drug

223

scenario). So the Yippies believed until they learned the extent of the government's penetration of the New Left.

According to Army intelligence documents later obtained by CBS news, nearly one out of six demonstrators at the Chicago convention was an undercover operative. The retinue of spies included Bob Pierson, a Chicago cop disguised as a biker, who latched onto Jerry Rubin during the convention and became his bodyguard. Enthralled by the romantic notion of an alliance between motorcycle gang members and middle-class radicals, the Yippies were easily conned by Pierson's tough-talking rhetoric. He was always in the thick of the street action, throwing stones at police, pulling down American flags, leading crowds in militant chants, and urging protesters to start fires and tie up traffic. Pierson's testimony at the trial of the Chicago Seven was instrumental in putting Rubin behind bars for sixty-six days, before his sentence and those of the other defendants were overturned by an appeals court.

The use of informants and provocateurs was part of a massive *sub rosa* campaign to subvert the forces of dissent in the late 1960s and early 1970s. Joining the FBI in this effort was an alphabet soup of federal agencies: the Internal Revenue Service (IRS), the Bureau of Narcotics and Dangerous Drugs (BNDD), the National Security Agency (NSA), the Federal Communications Commission (FCC), the Law Enforcement Assistance Administration (LEAA), the Department of Health, Education and Welfare (HEW), the intelligence divisions of all the military services, and numerous local police forces. Over a quarter of a million Americans were under "active surveillance" during this period, and dossiers were kept on the lawful political activities and personal lives of millions more. Those affiliated with black militant, antiwar, and New Left* groups were prime targets of dirty tricks and other underhanded tactics designed to stir up factionalism and "neutralize" political activists.

During the Nixon presidency the CIA stepped up its domestic operations even though such activity was outlawed by the Agency's charter. In 1969 the CIA prepared a report entitled "Restless Youth," which concluded that the New Left and black nationalist movements were essentially homegrown phenomena and that foreign ties to American dissidents were insubstantial. That was not what Pres-

---

*The FBI never arrived at a precise definition of the New Left. "It's more or less an attitude, I would think," an FBI official told a senate committee in 1975.

ident Nixon wanted to hear. The "Communist conspiracy" had become an *idée fixe* in the White House, and Nixon pressed CIA director Richard Helms to expand the parameters of Operation CHAOS (an appropriate acronym) and other domestic probes. In addition to monitoring a wide range of liberal and left-wing organizations, the CIA provided training, technical assistance, exotic equipment, and intelligence data to local police departments. The Agency also employed harassment tactics such as sprinkling "itching powder" (concocted by the Technical Services Staff, the unit that oversaw the LSD experiments in the 1950s) on public toilets near leftist meetings, which drove people wild for about three days after they sat down.

The FBI, meanwhile, escalated its secret war against all forms of political and cultural dissent in America. The assault on freedom of expression included a systematic attempt to cripple the underground press, which FBI chief J. Edgar Hoover found loathsome because of its "depraved nature and moral looseness." There was also a concerted campaign to make political arrests by charging radicals with possession of small amounts of marijuana. "Since the use of marijuana and other narcotics is widespread among members of the New Left, you should be on the alert to opportunities to have them arrested on drug charges," Hoover stated in a top-secret FBI memo. "Any information concerning the fact that individuals have marijuana or are engaging in a narcotics party should be immediately furnished to local authorities and they should be encouraged to take action."

Nixon made the issue of drug abuse a cornerstone of his law-and-order campaign during the 1968 election, and when he took office he pushed through a series of no-knock laws allowing police to break into homes of suspected drug users, unannounced and armed to the hilt, to search for a tiny tab of LSD or a pipeful of pot. While no-knock and other draconian legal ploys were allegedly designed to crack down on the abuse of controlled substances, the targets of the antidrug campaign were often involved in radical politics. Examples are legion: in 1969 John Sinclair, leader of the White Panther party in Michigan, was sentenced to nine and a half years in prison for giving two marijuana joints to an undercover officer; Lee Otis Johnson, a black militant and antiwar organizer at Texas Southern University, was given a thirty-year jail term after sharing a joint with a narc; Mark Rudd, an SDS militant who played a prominent role in the uprising at Columbia University, was fingered for drugs by an

225

informant; and police in Buffalo, New York, planted dope in a bookstore run by Martin Sostre, a black anarchist who served six years in prison before Amnesty International successfully interceded on his behalf.

Drug laws were also used to persecute Timothy Leary and other counterculture leaders. An example of this type of harassment came to light in federal court when Jack Martin, a musician who'd been busted on a dope rap, testified that he was asked to turn informant and assist the Federal Narcotics Bureau in framing Allen Ginsberg on a marijuana charge. The FBI and the CIA kept tabs on Ginsberg's activities in the late 1960s and early 1970s, while the narcs maintained a file that included a photograph of the well-known poet "in an indecent pose." The picture was placed in a special vault at BNDD headquarters and marked for "possible future use."

A number of big-name rock musicians were also targeted for surveillance by the FBI. Hoover's men shadowed John Lennon after he and Yoko Ono got involved in radical politics in the US (Lennon's "Give Peace a Chance" became the anthem of the antiwar movement). In addition the FBI kept tabs on Jimi Hendrix, Janis Joplin, Jim Morrison, the Fugs, and other rock stars, many of whom were prosecuted on drug charges. The harassment of rock musicians was part of a crusade against the emerging counterculture and the alternative lifestyles associated with radical politics in the late 1960s. Some rock groups took explicitly political stands, and their music received wide airplay despite halfhearted attempts at government censorship. As a result large numbers of young people were exposed to the rhetoric of radical politics. While rock music certainly did not politicize its entire audience, it reinforced a pervasive anti-authoritarianism and provided an audacious soundtrack to the hopes and anger of the younger generation. High energy rock songs were clarion calls to revolt: the Rolling Stones' "Street Fighting Man," Steppenwolf's "Born to Be Wild," the Doors' "Break on through to the other side," Jefferson Airplane's "We are all outlaws . . ." "All of these and many more items of popular culture thrived in *and reproduced* an apocalyptic, polarized political mood," noted former SDS president Todd Gitlin. "*In ensemble* they shaped a symbolic environment that was conducive to revolutionism out of context, to the inflation of rhetoric and militancy out of proportion to the possible."

After the Chicago convention an increasing number of radicals began to talk about the need for violence to raise the domestic political costs of the war in Vietnam. The revelations of My Lai, the tiger cages, the napalm, the cancer-causing defoliants, the carpet bombings, the delayed-action antipersonnel weapons, the images of daily carnage on television—all this and much more dislocated the sensibilities of young and old alike until it was difficult for some to see anything virtuous in "Amerika" (or "AmeriKKKa"), as it came to be spelled by left-wing militants. The imperial center had to be defeated at all costs for the sake of those who were dying in Southeast Asia.

As every legitimate gesture of dissent was rebuffed by another round of US atrocities, antiwar activists were forced to reconsider their tactics. The overwhelming horror of Vietnam made all political choices seem urgent and simple. Radicals were under tremendous pressure to translate their jargon into action, to demonstrate their revolutionary commitment by pushing militancy to the extreme. Although they did not realize it at the time, the ultramilitants were playing right into the hands of the Nixon administration, which seized upon incidents of violence by protesters to justify the imposition of repressive measures against the antiwar movement as a whole. During this period the New Left became open turf for undercover operatives who spouted revolutionary rhetoric in order to incite others to violence. But covert manipulation was not solely to blame for what happened in the late 1960s. The provocateurs' success depended on a climate of tolerance for their wild suggestions and antics.

Some radical groups didn't need any provocation. The "Up Against the Wall, Motherfucker" collective made their antisocial debut during the New York City garbage strike in early 1968 when they set fire to heaps of rubbish and threw bricks and bottles at firemen who came to douse the blaze. Formed as the Lower East Side chapter of SDS, this band of acid-fueled fanatics supported the student strike at Columbia by occupying a building and sabotaging the school's electrical system. After the strike was over, however, they berated their fellow communards for not slugging it out with the cops. The Motherfuckers proceeded to terrorize other radical organizations, causing havoc at meetings and protest rallies. At one point, they crashed a conference of socialist scholars and denounced the participants as "armchair book-quoting jive-ass honky leftists.... who are the VD of the revolution."

In pursuit of "total revolution" the Motherfuckers divided into small affinity groups and introduced "motion tactics" or "trashing" to SDS. The idea was to get loaded on drugs and run wild through the streets, breaking store windows, spilling trash cans, and smashing windshields in an improvised war dance. It was sheer bravado, a blow for a blow's sake, but there was something almost mystical about it. The political efficacy of trashing was less important than how it felt, the sense of psychic liberation, the existential buzz that came from "doing it in the road." They just wanted to let loose and do whatever they could to put some hurt on the oppressor.

The Motherfuckers saw their role as "a permanent fermenting agent, encouraging action without claiming to lead." In a poster disseminated on the Lower East Side they denounced Timothy Leary and his apolitical followers for "limiting the revolution" with their lightweight metaphysical theories and gooey religious rhetoric. Shortly before they dispersed in 1969 the Motherfuckers issued a manifesto called "Acid Armed Consciousness," which spoke in grandiose terms of picking up the gun and correcting the cosmic imbalance: "We are the freaks of an unknown space/time. . . . We are the eye of the Revolution. . . . Only when we simultaneously see our magic drugs as an ecstatic revolutionary implement, and feel our bodies as the cellular macrocosm and galactic microcosm will our spiral/life energy destroy everything dead as it races over the planet. . . . Blown minds of screaming-singing-beaded-stoned-armed-feathered Future-People are only the sparks of a revolutionary explosion and evolutionary planetary regeneration. Neon Nirvanas finally overload their circuits . . . as we snake dance thru our world trailed by a smokescreen of reefer."

The Motherfuckers might be dismissed as a lunatic fringe had they not prefigured the paramilitary fad that engulfed the New Left as the decade drew to a close. The classic photo from this period appeared on the front page of the *Berkeley Tribe*, an offshoot of the *Berkeley Barb*; it showed a hip couple posing earnestly in front of a wooded commune, the long-haired man with a rifle in hand, and his woman in a granny dress holding a baby on her back. This was the mood of the late 1960s. A lot of self-styled outlaws and freaky-looking people were studying karate and learning how to handle shotguns. Former pacifists were now talking about bloodshed as a necessary evil in political struggle. The underground press published instructions on bomb making, and Yippie tactics of humor and guerrilla theater were supplanted by real guerrilla attacks. *The Anarchist Cookbook* included a recipe for concocting Molotov cocktails as well as LSD. "Acid armed consciousness"—a far cry from flower power, but that was what the Movement had come to since the Summer of Love.

There was no containing the violence any longer. Across the country militants blew up power lines, burned down ROTC headquarters, trashed draft board offices, and traded potshots with police. All told, major demonstrations occurred at nearly three hundred colleges and universities during the spring of 1969, involving a third of the nation's students. A plethora of radical groups sprang up: the Young Lords (a Puerto Rican organization), the Brown Berets (Chicanos), the GI resistance movement, the Gay Liberation Front, the American Indian Movement, the League of Revolutionary Black Workers in the car factories of Detroit. High school students were becoming more militant, and women's liberationists were going after *Playboy* magazine, Wall Street, the Miss America Pageant, and other bastions of sexism. Whether all these groups could cooperate in a comradely way was another matter entirely, but the sum total of their efforts produced a thunderous cacophony that almost sounded like a revolution.

Ironically, just when the New Left was experiencing an unprecedented wave of support, its leading organization, SDS, which claimed almost a hundred thousand members and a million supporters, was being torn asunder by internal contradictions. Chapter meetings throughout the country degenerated into ideological squabbles as the Progressive Labor party (PL), a disciplined Old Left cadre, made a power play and tried to take over SDS. The PL people were cultural conservatives; they wore their hair short, dressed straight, mouthed Marxist dogma, and dismissed lifestyle as a peripheral concern that diverted attention from the true working-class struggle. On repeated occasions PL castigated SDS regulars for being "escapist" and "objectively counterrevolutionary" when they spoke in favor of turning on. (Quite a few SDS members would have agreed with Arthur Kleps when he said, "Marxism is the opiate of the unstoned classes.") PL also criticized propaganda tactics like guerrilla theater and rock bands at rallies as "creeping carnivalism," and they even claimed that Timothy Leary was a CIA agent who pushed acid on the Movement as part of an imperialist plot.

The drug issue wasn't the only axis of division within SDS. Action

229

freaks taunted the "wimps" who emphasized day-to-day grassroots organizing; hippie elements were angry at hard-core militants; and women started to leave the organization in droves, criticizing the New Left for its ingrained male chauvinism. Through it all the ubiquitous FBI and CIA stoked the fires of internal dissension at every given opportunity. A CIA document of April 1969 forecast the fatal rupture that occurred two months later: "The SDS prize continues to be fair game for takeover by any organized communist group on the American scene with the power, prestige, and cunning to do so.... It can be predicted that such efforts will continue until someone succeeds. Then SDS will split and their influence on the American campus can be expected to diminish."

The death knell was sounded at the SDS national conference in Chicago in June 1969, when an ultramilitant faction put forward a position paper called "You Don't Need a Weatherman to Know Which Way the Wind Blows." The title came from a line in Bob Dylan's "Subterranean Homesick Blues," a song full of homespun advice to disaffected youth, with the usual Dylanesque overtones of anti-authoritarianism and rebellion that appealed to many SDS members. The Weathermen, as this group immediately came to be known, announced their intention to form urban guerrilla cadres and carry on the revolution with sporadic gestures of violence. Then they walked out en masse after declaring that they had "expelled" PL from SDS. When the dust settled, there were two groups stridently claiming to be the "real" SDS, neither of which inspired much enthusiasm among students. Just as the CIA had predicted, the split marked the end of SDS as an effective organization, and the collapse of the New Left as a whole soon followed.

The Weathermen's decision to go underground was formulated during a period when many of their key leaders, including chief spokesperson Bernardine Dohrn, were tripping out on LSD. Dohrn, whose fiery personality and good looks raised eyebrows among her male comrades, showed her solidarity with the youth culture when she organized a be-in for Chicago in the spring of 1967. Her enthusiasm for acid was shared by Jeff Jones, a former Motherfucker who joined the Weather contingent when SDS bit the dust.

Some Weather leaders were initially reluctant to experiment with psychedelic drugs. Mark Rudd, who had been chairman of the Action Faction at the Columbia University chapter of SDS, declined numerous offers to turn on with the Crazies (a militant offshoot of the

Yippies) on the grounds that it would interfere with his politics. The Crazies chided Rudd and his cohorts for being straitlaced and ignorant of the youth culture, but Rudd's crowd was not to be persuaded. Finally the Crazies took matters into their own hands and put acid in the wine at a Weather party without telling the hosts. Soon the place exploded into a frenzy of song and dance; afterwards the local leadership agreed that LSD was inherently revolutionary, and they ordered every Weatherperson in New York to take the drug and get "experienced."

Meanwhile the White Panthers were turning on future Weather recruits in Ann Arbor, Michigan. Billy Ayers was a prominent figure in the Jesse James Gang, Ann Arbor's version of the Action Faction, before joining the Weathermen, and he too had reservations about LSD until Ken Kelley, a White Panther who edited an underground newspaper called the *Ann Arbor Argus*, turned him on. "I remember when it hit the Weathermen," said Kelley. "That's when they just got *out there*."

While the Weathermen are an extreme case, the degree to which acid accentuated their militant tendencies underscores an essential truth about the drug: LSD does not make people more or less political; rather, it reinforces and magnifies what's already in their heads. Most of the Weatherpeople (at the outset there were three hundred full-fledged members) came from middle- and upper-middle-class families and their encounter with LSD dredged up a lot of guilt about "white skin privilege." They felt that all white youth, including themselves, were guilty of crimes against Third World people. This guilt, according to Weather logic, could only be purged in sacrificial blood: white blood must flow to prove to blacks, Vietnamese, and other victims of American imperialism that white revolutionaries were serious. Accordingly the Weatherpeople organized themselves into a network of secret cells, each with ten or twelve members, and prepared to undertake armed attacks against the state.

"We have one task," Billy Ayers stated, "and that's to make ourselves into tools of the revolution." Toward this end the Weather collectives embarked upon a rigorous process of internal purification. They sought to overcome their bourgeois cultural conditioning by living in places that were filthy and foul. Sometimes they went without food to save money for more important items, such as guns. They rejected romantic love as a capitalist hangup and abandoned

231

monogamous sexual relations in favor of orgies and freewheeling partner swapping. ("People who fuck together, fight together" was the going slogan.) Their days were filled with weapons training and karate practice; at night they held endless criticism and self-criticism sessions, often with the aid of LSD, in an effort to exorcise their natural passivity and bring themselves closer to that apocalyptic edge where political violence intersects with personal transformation and privileged youth become street fighters. The amount of acid a person could take during these sessions without freaking out was a measure of personal toughness. (For all the talk about the ego-dissolving properties of LSD, the male ego flourished among the Weathermen.)

The communal ingestion of LSD also served as a rudimentary security check. In a manner recalling the CIA's use of LSD as a truth drug, the Weatherpeople attempted to weed out suspected informants by putting them through a group acid test. On one occasion a Weather collective in Cincinnati thought they had identified an agent provocateur when Larry Grathwohl, an ex-Green Beret who had fought in Vietnam, announced during an acid trip, "You're right, I *am* a pig." After mulling over his confession, the Weather cadre concluded he was merely expressing his guilt for having served in the army, and he was accepted into their ranks. They were particularly attracted to Grathwohl's military skills. He supplied guns and drugs and taught them how to make bombs. A few months later Grathwohl fingered two New York Weatherwomen for the FBI.*

When a group of people trip together frequently, it's easy for them to get caught up in a mutually reinforcing world view and lose sight of the degree to which they've drifted off-center, far from the day-to-day perceptions of most individuals. This was particularly true of the Weatherpeople, who lived a very isolated existence. The collective was their whole world. All their waking hours were geared toward making the revolution. They were totally consumed by it— eating less, sleeping less, getting charged up until they were oblivious to the outside world. They used to sing a song to the tune of the Beatle's "Yellow Submarine": "We all live in a weather machine,

---

*Another FBI informant named Horace J. Packer infiltrated SDS and the Weathermen at the University of Washington. Packer later testified that he supplied campus radicals with drugs, weapons and materials for making Molotov cocktails. He also admitted that while posing as a leftwing activist he used acid, speed, mescaline and cocaine.

a weather machine..." And that's how it was; they were like a machine, an integral unit composed of interchangeable parts. "We got carried away," an ex-Weatherwoman admitted. "We were out on a limb with each other.... We thought about picking up the gun all the time. We really thought there was going to be a revolution."

The Weathermen's fantasies about the coming revolution were nourished by the hermetic quality of their own experience and the hectic atmosphere of the late 1960s. Things were moving so fast during this period, people were going through so many changes, the antiwar cause had picked up such incredible momentum, but hardly anyone paused to absorb what was happening. It was easy to lose a sense of balance as the pace of history accelerated. Committed activists felt as though they had lived through several lifetimes in a few months, which inevitably led to widespread exhaustion. "Inside the movement," Todd Gitlin recalled, "one had the sense of being hurled through a time tunnel, of hurtling from event to event without the time to learn from experience."

This dizzying sense of onrushing time was reinforced by the use of psychedelic drugs. An LSD trip encapsulates an enormous amount of experience in a relatively short period; insights that might normally take years to acquire can burst forth in an awesome flurry during an eight-hour acid high. "It was like a cheap form of shrinkdom," Ken Kelley stated. "A week became a decade in terms of your consciousness.... Every single aspect of your life was affected by it. ...It was like if Jesus Christ came for the Second Coming and said, 'Follow me.' That's what LSD was like. No one could believe it. All you knew was that you'd find out more of what was going on in the cosmic scheme of things if you took LSD."

As a catalyst of psychic and social processes, LSD amplified a chaotic cultural milieu which in the late 1960s was completely saturated by the inflated images of the mass media. Both these perceptual technologies—LSD and the media—combined to accelerate the temporal flux and fuel the wishful thinking of the young activists who jumped from rebellion to revolution without knowing what they were really getting into. Television was particularly insidious, reducing history to a series of discontinuous freeze-frames or, as Gitlin put it, "a sequence of tenuously linked exclamation points"—Columbia! Sorbonne! Chicago! In this mythic "event time," each tumultuous confrontation was a peak moment, like an LSD trip, packed full of vivid experience not always easy to assimilate or put into proper context in the short term. "Tripping ratified and gathered into a single day's experience what, in fact, life had become," an SDS veteran explained. "Life was very trippy from about 1968 on in the worst and best sense, and the conflict was, do you go with it or do you escape it?"

Those who lived inside the high-velocity Weather machine chose to go with it no matter what the cost. After months of intensive preparation they plunged into the next mythic showdown, the Days of Rage demonstration in Chicago in October 1969. It was the second anniversary of the death of Che Guevara, and the Weatherpeople were determined to "bring the war back home" by making revolutionary violence a reality inside the Mother Country. Armed with pipes, clubs, poles, motorcycle helmets, gas masks, goggles and flak jackets, six hundred hard-core militants went on a rampage, whipping themselves into a frenzy with Battle of Algiers war whoops. They marched through the streets carrying Viet Cong flags and trashing everything in sight. Hundreds of demonstrators were beaten, a dozen were shot, and half of the Weatherbrigade was arrested within a few hours.

For the Weatherpeople, the violent outburst in Chicago was a way of "upping the cost of imperialism." They had little patience for those who were still hung up on building a broad-based movement. "Organizing is just another way of going slow," said Mark Rudd. He and his cohorts wanted to get on with the business of destruction; everything else was dismissed as liberal dillydallying. Drunk on confrontation and intoxicated by an overblown sense of their capacity to "make history," the Weathermen believed they could overthrow the American system by sheer willpower. Theirs was an acid dream of revolution, and the course they had chosen, more by instinct than by rational planning, sent them hurtling down a one-way road to political oblivion.

The Acid Brotherhood

"Bringing the war back home"—the deeper resonance of the Weather motto returned to haunt the New Left. As millions of Americans took to the streets to protest the Vietnam debacle, the Defense Department was drawn ever more deeply into the problem of containing domestic violence. Military strategists recommended an array of bizarre weapons to quell civil unrest, including the psychochemical incapacitating agent BZ, which had been utilized on a limited basis as a counterinsurgency device in Vietnam.

In March 1966 French journalist Pierre Darcourt described in *L'Express* an action known as Operation White Wing, in which grenades containing BZ were deployed against a Viet Cong battalion of five hundred troops by the First Cavalry Airmobile; only one hundred guerrillas were said to have escaped. According to Dutch author Wil Vervey the superhallucinogen was used on at least five other occasions in Vietnam between 1968 and 1970. In all probability, however, the Vietnam experience showed the drug to be only marginally effective as a counterinsurgency agent, given its tendency to elicit maniacal behavior and the difficulties of controlling the amount of BZ absorbed in a combat situation. As one senior Defense Department official admitted, all the incapacitants "have dosage ranges into lethality. They can clobber people." Despite these drawbacks the army stockpiled no less than fifty tons of BZ, or enough to turn everyone in the world into a stark raving lunatic.

Documents prepared at the army's "limited war laboratory" at Aberdeen Proving Ground in Maryland, one of three major military installations where BZ is stored, indicate that the government seriously considered using the superhallucinogen as a domestic riot control technique. One scheme involved the use of tiny remote-controlled model airplanes nicknamed "mechanical bees." The bees, mounted with hypodermic syringes, would be aimed at selected protesters during a demonstration to render them senseless. Another plan called for spraying BZ gas to incapacitate an unruly mob. A CIA memo dated September 4, 1970, reaffirmed the importance of BZ-type weapons: "Trends in modern police action and warfare indicate the desire to incapacitate reversibly and demoralize, rather than kill, the enemy.... With the advent of highly potent natural products, psychotropic and immobilizing drugs, a new era of law enforcement... is being ushered in."

While American soldiers were waging psychochemical warfare with BZ gas to subdue the Viet Cong, other GIs were dropping acid and tripping out on the battlefield—an ironic development in light of the fact that a few years earlier the army had tested LSD on American servicemen to see if the drug would impair their ability to carry out military maneuvers. Now the soldiers were taking LSD voluntarily in order to incapacitate themselves. "I was stoned every day of my life in Vietnam," a GI acid veteran admitted, "stoned to the gourd. It was the only way to deal with all the horror and the insanity, and that's what everyone did. Everyone was stoned on something."

An authentic drug subculture thrived among American troops in Vietnam. Soldiers often wore beads and peace symbols on their uniforms and grooved to the same rock music that was popular in the States. Words such as "bomb" and "knockout" were coined by soldiers to describe the drug experience and were soon adopted by heads back home. Vietnamese reefer was especially potent, and its widespread use both in the barracks and in the field was a unifying factor among dissident GIs. Pot smoking was so prevalent (80% of American servicemen got stoned) that the military brass never even tried to crack down on it. There was also plenty of heroin available, and soldiers often smoked or injected it (15% of those who saw action in Vietnam returned home as heroin addicts). But nothing compared with getting high on LSD for the first time in a combat situation. "*Apocalypse Now*—that's how it really was," said a former employee of the supersecret Army Security Agency. "After a while, Vietnam *was* an acid trip. Vietnam was psychedelic, even when you weren't tripping."

One type of acid was particularly popular among American ground forces in Vietnam. It was called "orange sunshine," and much of it was smuggled in from southern California during the late 1960s and early 1970s. Far from the rice paddies of Southeast Asia a group known as the Brotherhood of Eternal Love was waging its own holy war of sorts in their tireless efforts to turn the world on to LSD. During their heyday the Brotherhood ran the world's largest illicit LSD ring. Ironically their base of operations was Orange County, home turf of Richard Nixon, Disneyland, and the John Birch Society.

The saga of the Brotherhood of Eternal Love is a bizarre melange of evangelical, starry-eyed hippie dealers, mystic alchemists, and fast-money bankers. Federal investigators described them as a "hippie Mafia" of approximately seven hundred fifty people that allegedly grossed $200,000,000. But the Brotherhood's secret network of smugglers lived by a code different from that associated with organized crime. They were fired with idealism, committed to changing the world by disseminating large quantities of psychedelics. At least that's how it was at the beginning....

It all started back in 1966 when a motorcycle gang from Anaheim, California, led by a stocky, intense man known as Farmer John Griggs,

236

held up a Hollywood producer at gunpoint and robbed him of his stash of Sandoz LSD. A week later the bikers dropped the acid on a hill overlooking Palm Springs in Joshua Tree National Park. They must have seen the Burning Bush, for they threw away their guns and ran around the desert at midnight screaming, "This is it!" The next morning Griggs and company roared back to Anaheim, determined to begin a new life. They experimented with psychedelics on a weekly basis and dabbled in mysticism. Griggs was the proselytizer, the moving spirit of the group. In the summer of 1966 he traveled to Millbrook to meet with Leary, who was quite taken by the ex-hoodlum. "Although unschooled and unlettered he was an impressive person," Leary said of Griggs. "He had this charisma... that sparkle in his eye."

Griggs looked to Leary for guidance, revering the older man as a guru. At the time, the High Priest of LSD was urging everyone to start their own church. This seemed like an excellent idea to Griggs. The Brotherhood of Eternal Love, consisting of approximately thirty original members, was formally established as a tax-exempt entity in October 1966, ten days after LSD was made illegal in the state of California. The articles of incorporation announced the group's objective: "to bring to the world a greater awareness of God through the teachings of Jesus Christ, Buddha, Ramakrishna, Babaji, Paramahansa Yogananda, Mahatma Gandhi, and all true prophets and apostles of God, and to spread the love and wisdom of these great teachers to all men.... We believe this church to be the earthly instrument of God's will. We believe in the sacred right of each individual to commune with God in spirit and in truth as it is empirically revealed to him."

The Brothers settled in Laguna Beach, a small seaside resort thirty miles south of Los Angeles. It was the pure scene, an electric beach community tucked against a semicircle of sandstone hills rising twelve hundred feet above the Pacific. The majestic landscape attracted an artist colony, and the sun and waves brought surfers. John Griggs supplied a lot of LSD for a growing Freaktown where hippies danced barefoot across beaches and mountains murmuring, "Thank you, God." In this exquisite setting the Brothers employed acid as a communal sacrament, hoping eventually to obtain legal permission to expand their consciousness through chemicals in much the same way that the Indians of the Native American Church used peyote. To support their spiritual habit, they opened a storefont in

237

Laguna Beach called Mystic Arts World, which sold health food, books, smoking paraphernalia and other accoutrements of the psychedelic counterculture. The headshop became a meeting place for hippies and freaks of every persuasion, and soon more people wanted to join the fledgling church.

While Mystic Arts provided a steady income, it wasn't enough for the ambitious plans of the Brotherhood. They needed more money to purchase land for their growing membership, so they started dealing drugs—mostly marijuana at first, which they snuck across the border in hundred-pound lots after paying off police officials in Mexico. Within the next few years the Brotherhood of Eternal Love developed into a sophisticated smuggling and distribution network that stretched around the globe. Huge quantities of hashish were brought in from Afghanistan by Brothers equipped with false ID and crew-cut wigs. They eluded the authorities by zigzagging across oceans and continents in transport outfitted with hollow compartments filled with contraband—unloading at one port, sometimes traveling a short distance overland, then reloading at the next port and substituting yet another phony registration for the vehicle. They also sold LSD obtained from Owsley's lieutenants in Haight-Ashbury.

The dealing operation was already in high gear when Timothy Leary decided to pull up roots and head for the West Coast, the Mecca of hippiedom. By the spring of 1967 the Millbrook scene was collapsing. Three rival religious sects (the League for Spiritual Discovery, the Neo-American Boohoo Church, and a Hindu-oriented ashram) had taken up residence at the acid commune, and the entire place was under round-the-clock surveillance by the police. California beckoned, and Billy Hitchcock, the Millbrook patron, decided to move to the Bay Area. He gave Leary a parting check for $14,000 and sent him on his way after evicting everyone else from the estate.

Leary and his new wife, a young ex-model named Rosemary, had a standing invitation from John Griggs to visit Laguna Beach. He was greeted by the Brotherhood like a private heaven-sent prophet, and he acted the part, preaching to the group about love, peace, and enlightenment. Leary enjoyed the adulation as well as the town's mellow atmosphere. He and Rosemary rented a house near the ocean and spent much of their time dropping acid, lolling in the surf, and talking with the hippies on the beach. Leary was very conscious of his role as elder statesman of the town's burgeoning head colony. He tried to stay on good terms with everyone and never missed a chance to flash his trademark grin when he saw a policeman.

But there was one person Leary could not win over. Neal Purcell, a rookie cop, came to Laguna Beach in the fall of 1968. A squat, dark-complected man with a pencil-thin moustache, Purcell harbored a deep animosity toward long-haired skinny-dippers and young women without bras. He considered marijuana and LSD part and parcel of a generational corruption that was destroying the country's moral fiber, and it irked him to see Leary roam freely through town spreading his evil creed while America was going down the tubes.

Purcell had previously been assigned to entice and entrap homosexuals at a nearby beach, but he had bigger things on his mind as he patrolled the quiet residential section of Laguna. He was determined to put the screws to Timothy Leary. Shortly after Christmas 1968 Purcell spotted a station wagon blocking a narrow road. He later claimed that he did not realize it was Leary's until he approached and saw Tim roll down the window, releasing a thick cloud of marijuana smoke. Rosemary sat next to her husband in the front seat while Leary's son, Jack, frolicked in the back, making faces at the officer. Purcell searched the car and came up with two weather-beaten roaches and a few skimpy flakes of pot. "Big deal," said Leary when his nemesis produced the evidence.

Leary was charged with possession of marijuana and released on bail. It was his second drug bust; he was already facing a thirty-year sentence for the snafu in Laredo, Texas, in 1965. Despite his precarious legal status Leary announced his intention to run for governor of California in 1969 against Ronald Reagan. The High Priest had suddenly become political! Midway through his upbeat campaign he got a call from John Lennon and Yoko Ono, who were then conducting their "Bed-ins for Peace" in luxury hotels around the world. They wanted Leary to help them cut their antiwar song "Give Peace a Chance." Leary joined them at their bedside in Montreal while photographers flashed cameras for the international press. Lennon asked Leary what he could do to help his electoral efforts, and the candidate suggested that Lennon write a song. The Beatle began to improvise around Leary's campaign slogan, "Come together, join the party," and soon the song "Come Together" (on the *Abbey Road* album) was playing on California radio stations.

All the notoriety surrounding Leary's movements and pronouncements was something of a mixed blessing for the Brotherhood. They were happy to provide living expenses for the acid guru and finance his frequent travels up to Berkeley, where he rented another house, but Leary attracted a lot of attention—which was exactly what a secret dope-smuggling outfit didn't need. Griggs and several of his cohorts decided to establish a second base of operations at a secluded ranch near Idylwild, California. They bought a three-hundred-acre plot at the arid base of the Santa Ana Mountains to provide a safe haven for their extralegal activities. The Brotherhood occupied a run-down farmhouse surrounded by a circle of seven teepees and grew their own vegetables, which their wives and girlfriends dutifully cooked. A wooden watchtower camouflaged by eucalyptus trees enabled the dealers to spot any unwanted intruders moving up the winding dirt road to their hideaway. They stayed high all the time, smoking as much as thirty joints per day per person and dropping acid whenever the spirit moved them.

The setup was ideal, and everything went smoothly. The Brotherhood even started to deal a new product—hash oil, a gooey resin thirty times more potent than the bricks they were importing from Afghanistan at a rate of a thousand kilos a month. The Brothers were making a lot of money, but that wasn't their sole motivation. They believed they were carrying out a special mission. "It was the Dead End Kids who took acid and fell in love with beauty," stated Michael Hollingshead, who visited the Brotherhood commune in Idylwild. "They were totally committed. They had tremendous determination. They were all very tough; once they were moving dope, they were manic...they did this nonstop thing."

There was just one hitch in the otherwise flawless operation: they lacked a sufficient quantity of LSD for wholesale marketing. Ever since Owsley's arrest in late 1967, a steady supply of high-quality street acid had been hard to come by. The king of the acid underground had been caught red-handed by federal agents at his tabbing factory in Orinda, California, with a large stash of LSD and STP that would have netted $10,000,000 on the black market. He was eventually sentenced to three years in prison and fined $3,000 for tax evasion.

While Owsley slugged it out in the courts, his former assistant, Tim Scully, vowed to carry on the chemical crusade. Flushed with the potential of consciousness expansion, Scully believed that LSD was the solution to man's inhumanity to man and all other problems caused by shortsightedness. His goal was to make as much acid as possible before the inevitable legal crackdown. But Owsley had kept him on a short string financially, and Scully lacked the necessary resources to set up an underground laboratory. His search for monetary support led him to Billy Hitchcock, who was then living in Sausalito, a scenic tourist town just north of San Francisco.

Hitchcock and Scully first became acquainted when the young chemist passed through the psychedelic menagerie at Millbrook in the spring of 1967. They hit it off immediately, and Hitchcock was pleased when Scully called on him again in Sausalito a few months later. They agreed to form a business partnership. Hitchcock would lend him money for supplies and equipment, and Scully would synthesize LSD and other psychedelics. At first Scully proposed that they give the acid away free of charge, but his financial mentor would hear nothing of it. People wouldn't appreciate what they didn't have to pay for, Hitchcock argued, and after all, he was the boss.

Hitchcock also bankrolled another chemist named Nick Sand, who began his illicit career by making DMT, a short-acting superpsychedelic, in his bathtub in Brooklyn. Sand got into the writings of Gurdjieff (a Russian mystic who had been a spy for the czar) and later wound up at Millbrook, where he served as alchemist to Arthur Kleps's Neo-American Boohoo Church. When the Millbrook scene unraveled, Sand followed Hitchcock out to the Bay Area and started making STP in an underground lab in San Francisco. He would have preferred to make acid, but he was hard-pressed, as was Scully, to find ergotamine tartrate (which they referred to as "ET"), one of the key ingredients of LSD-25. Hitchcock saw a way past the bottleneck. He contacted a European source with legitimate access, and Sand and Scully were off and running. The demand for street acid had skyrocketed ever since the Summer of Love, and these young men intended to fill the void created by Owsley's sudden demise.

Sand and Scully met at Hitchcock's house in Sausalito and agreed to work together at the instigation of their host. They were admittedly an odd couple—Scully, the brilliant, sensitive soul with messianic visions, and Sand, the hard-nosed street tough eager for economic gain, who cultivated contacts among all manner of fringe types, including the Hell's Angels. Scully didn't want to have anything to do with the bikers, who had distributed STP for Sand, and a rift quickly developed between the two chemists.

Scully had already manufactured a sizable allotment of LSD when the police discovered his underground drug lab in Denver in June 1968. They seized and tagged all his equipment, which was returned to the young chemist after his lawyers got him off the hook. Shortly after the Denver bust a delegation of Brothers led by John Griggs first made contact with Sand and Scully. The powwow, which had been suggested by Leary, took place at Hitchcock's villa in Sausalito, with the ever-obliging Mr. Billy in attendance. The Brothers were looking for a good connection, and they couldn't have asked for a more righteous brew. A few weeks later Sand traveled south to Idyl-wild to finalize the arrangement.

With the Brotherhood ready to serve as their distribution arm, Sand and Scully embarked upon a full-fledged manufacturing spree. Hitchcock bought some property in Windsor, a small town sixty miles north of San Francisco. He helped Scully move to the premises, hauling large metal drums and wooden crates full of glass beakers, Bunsen burners, flasks, rubber tubing, chromatography columns, vacuum evaporators, and bundles of semiprecious compounds—all the equipment necessary for a sophisticated drug lab. In January, 1969, Sand and Scully went to work, each on a modest $12,000 yearly retainer from Hitchcock. Scully was absolutely meticulous, keeping hour-by-hour logs whenever he made a new batch of acid so there'd be no chance of mistakes. His LSD was said to be purer than Sandoz. Sand, on the other hand, liked to take liberties. He cut his product with a pinch of this or that (usually Methedrine), and sometimes went on binges, working for thirty consecutive days with little sleep or rest. During these marathon sessions Sand inevitably got stoned to the gills from breathing dust particles of LSD and absorbing it through his fingers.

By the time the Windsor lab shut down in June 1969, Sand and Scully had turned out no less than ten million hits of the soon-to-be-famous orange sunshine. The chemists protected themselves by keeping the drug off the streets until they liquidated the entire laboratory. They also experimented with new formulas, concocting a grab bag of psychedelics, some of them scarcely known to the scientific community, let alone narcotics officials. Hitchcock concurrently hired a prestigious New York law firm—Rabinowitz, Boudin and Standard—to research the legal status of obscure hallucinogenic drugs.

At a rock concert in Anaheim, the Brothers' hometown, it suddenly began to rain orange pills. A man in black leather trousers wearing a T-shirt that read "Orange Sunshine Express" was scattering LSD into the air, his long hair flowing behind him. The psychedelic sower was a member of the Brotherhood, and he was handing out as many as a hundred thousand doses in a single day. Leary, meanwhile, began to act as an unofficial publicist for the new product. During his frequent public lectures he made a point of endorsing orange sunshine above all other brands. He even wrote an article for the *East Village Other*, "Deal for Real—the Dealer as Robin Hood," in which he sang the praises of the Brotherhood. The High Priest suggested that as a moral exercise all psychedelic users ought to do a little dealing "to pay tribute to this most honorable profession, brotherhoods or groups of men."

Indeed, if a dealer wanted to impress his clientele, he'd often rap about the Brotherhood, but it wasn't always the Brotherhood of Eternal Love. There were many names: the Brotherhood of Light, or White Light, or whatnot. At one point nearly every hippie in Laguna Beach claimed to be a Brother, and who could dispute them? It was nearly impossible to separate the truth about this elusive organization from the romantic embellishments of stoned-out dopers. The tiny orange pills quickly acquired near-mythic status. "There have got to be cosmic influences connected with Sunshine," an acid buff effused. "There is a fantastic karma to this LSD. If you get on a dealing trip and do not abuse it—trying to make outlandish profits— you realize you have a lot of power on your hands with a tremendous responsibility for a lot of heads. You realize that you are not just selling drugs, but are selling to people a great and important part of their existence."

The magic caught on. In the late 1960s and early 1970s orange sunshine turned up in all fifty states and numerous foreign countries, including such far-flung outposts as Goa Beach in India, the mountains of Nepal, Indonesia, Australia, Japan, South Vietnam, Costa Rica, Israel, and the ancient Muslim shrine of Mecca. Sunshine was truly acid for the Global Village, and its worldwide popularity added to the growing mystique of the Brotherhood, who were already part of the underground mythology of California. If you smoked pot or dropped acid in the late 1960s or early 1970s, you probably heard legendary tales of this secretive group of dopers who were dedicated to making sure that primo stash was available at reasonable prices. "They were very good dealers on a spiritual trip," said a woman who lived on the Brotherhood commune in Idylwild. "They had a great reputation because they had the best dope."

But the image of the Brotherhood as saintly dealers did not tally with the seamier side of the fast-money crowd that gravitated around Billy Hitchcock, the sugar daddy of the LSD counterculture. Hitchcock, ostensibly acting as a broker for a small investment firm called Delafield and Delafield, managed his business affairs by phone from Sausalito. His specialty was setting up tax shelters for various business associates, and he knew exactly what to do with the proceeds from the Brotherhood's missionary work. The dirty cash would be laundered through Bahamian slush funds in the same way professional criminals hid their gains.

Hitchcock served as banker for the Brotherhood of Eternal Love, although later he insisted he was nothing more than a financial adviser. In truth he had a lot to say about how things were done. According to Scully, he was involved in numerous planning sessions at his house in Sausalito. (Sometimes after these meetings they all got stoned and played Monopoly; Mr. Billy always won.) But Hitchcock never expected to make big money from LSD. He was in it more for the adventure. He enjoyed his status as the behind-the-scenes facilitator who brought people together and made connections. Most of all he liked to party, and he wanted to see more folks turn on to acid.

In the spring of 1968 Hitchcock and acid chemist Nick Sand journeyed to the Bahamas, where they stayed at the spacious mansion of Sam Clapp, chairman of the local Fiduciary Trust Company. Clapp was a college chum of Hitchcock's and they had been doing business together for years. They arranged for Sand to open an account under a false name at Clapp's bank. Hitchcock and Sand also looked into the feasibility of setting up an offshore LSD laboratory on one of Bahama's secluded cays—which led some to wonder whether Mr. Billy was "on a Dr. No Trip."

Fiduciary's hermetic banking provisions also appealed to the likes of Bernie Cornfeld and Seymour ("The Head") Lazare, directors of the Swiss-based Investors Overseas Services (IOS), a fast-money laundry for organized crime, corrupt Third World dictators, wealthy expatriates, and freelance swindlers. Cornfeld and Lazare were both acid veterans.* Like everyone else, these hippie arbitrage experts

---

*At one point Cornfeld imagined a critical cash shortage at IOS when there really was none. This set the stage for one of the largest frauds in the history of money. In 1971 an estimated $224,000,000 was siphoned from IOS into the coffers of Robert Vesco, a heroin trafficker and financial contributor to Richard Nixon's 1972 presidential campaign. William Spector, a former OSS operative, claimed that Vesco's

needed a broker, and they found the boyish Mellon heir irresistible. Hitchcock took full advantage of his unlimited borrowing privileges at Fiduciary. At Clapp's urging he poured over $5,000,000 into unregistered "letter stocks" (the kind that aren't traded publicly but tend to show dramatic gains on paper) associated with the Mary Carter Paint Company, later known as Resorts International. It was the single largest chunk of money raised by Resorts, an organization suspected of having ties to organized crime.* Resorts International proceeded to build a casino on an exclusive piece of Bahamian real estate called Paradise Island. A star-studded cast was on hand for the grand opening of the gambling spa, complete with tennis courts, swimming pools, albino beaches, and the clear blue waters of the Caribbean. It was New Year's Eve 1968 and the guest of honor at this gala event was none other than Richard Nixon, who was about to launch a successful bid for the White House. James Crosby, president of Resorts International, contributed $100,000 to Nixon's campaign. Crosby and Bebe Rebozo, Nixon's best friend, mingled with a bevy of movie stars, jet setters, gangsters, and GOP faithful. Billy Hitchcock was also there, idling among the heavies with drink in hand.

In addition to his dealings with Resorts International, Hitchcock maintained a private account at Castle Bank and Trust, a funny-money repository in the Bahamas that catered to mobsters, entertainers, drug dealers, and Republican party fatcats—the same crowd that boozed it up whenever Resorts threw a party on Paradise Isle. A certain Richard M. Nixon was among three hundred prominent Americans who used Castle to deposit their cash. The bank's clientele included actor Tony Curtis, the rock group Creedence Clearwater Revival, *Playboy* publisher Hugh Hefner, Bob Guccione's *Penthouse*, Chiang Kai-shek's daughter and her husband, and billionaire eccentric Howard Hughes.

---

tangled web of corporations served as fronts for various CIA activities and provided cover for CIA agents.

*Eddie Cellini, the brother of a longtime associate of Meyer Lansky, served as the casino manager for Resorts International. Louis Chesler, another Lansky crony, and Wallace Groves, who allegedly had CIA connections, were both partners in a gambling venture with Mary Carter/Resorts. In 1970 Resorts International formed a private intelligence corporation called Intertel, which was staffed largely by ex-CIA, NSA, BNDD, Interpol, and Justice Department officials. Intertel rented its services to a wide range of corporate clients, including ITT, McDonald's, and Howard Hughes's Summa Corporation.

Castle Bank was no ordinary financial institution. Originally set up by the CIA as a funding conduit for a wide range of covert operations in the Caribbean, this sophisticated "money wash" was part of a vast worldwide financial network managed by American intelligence. Specifically the Agency used Castle Bank to facilitate the hidden transfer of huge sums to finance subversion, paramilitary operations, an occasional coup d'état, bribery, and payments to foreign informants. Castle played a key role in funding the CIA's secret war against Cuba—a campaign that drew upon the "patriotic" services of Mob hit teams assembled at the behest of the Agency to assassinate Fidel Castro. The Syndicate, seeking to return to the days when Havana was the brothel of the Caribbean, had a score to settle with the Cuban president. They also had much to gain from a cozy relationship with the CIA, whose clandestine financial network provided a perfect shield for criminal activities. In effect Castle Bank was an intelligence front that covered for the Mob.*

Billy Hitchcock wasn't the only figure in the Mellon clan who rubbed shoulders with the espionage community. A number of Mellons served in the OSS, notably David Bruce, the OSS station chief in London (whose father-in-law, Andrew Mellon, was treasury secretary during the Depression). After the war certain influential members of the Mellon family maintained close ties with the CIA. Mellon family foundations have been used repeatedly as conduits for Agency funds. Furthermore, Richard Helms was a frequent weekend guest of the Mellon patriarchs in Pittsburgh during his tenure as CIA director (1966-1973).

But Billy Hitchcock was clearly the black sheep of the illustrious Mellon flock, and his high-powered family connections showed little

---

*Castle Bank was founded and controlled by Paul Helliwell, a Miami lawyer with long-standing ties to American intelligence. Helliwell's career as a spook dates back to World War II, when he served as chief of special intelligence in China with the OSS. He stayed in the Far East when the CIA was formed and bossed a bevy of spies, including E. Howard Hunt of Watergate fame. In the early 1950s Helliwell organized Sea Supply, a CIA proprietary company that furnished weapons and other material to anti-Communist guerrillas in the hills of Burma, Laos, and Thailand. Based in the Golden Triangle, this mercenary army cultivated fields of opium poppies, and the CIA was drawn immediately into the drug connection. Helliwell also served as paymaster for the ill-fated Bay of Pigs operation in 1961. A few years later he set up Castle Bank, serving in a dual capacity as CIA banker and legal counsel for the Cuban Mafia, which prospered by selling Southeast Asian heroin in the US. Helliwell's law firm also represented Louis Chesler and Wallace Groves, both partners in Resorts International.

246

sympathy when his luck began to falter. The first sign of trouble came when American authorities began to display an unhealthy interest in the financial affairs of Sam Clapp, the manager of Fiduciary Trust, which was headquartered on Jail Street, of all places. That was where Clapp feared he'd end up—in jail—unless he liquidated his bank. Hitchcock, who had been called to testify before the Securities and Exchange Commission regarding Fiduciary Trust, quickly shifted his assets—which included the Brotherhood's drug profits—into a series of new accounts (no names, just numbers) in Switzerland. A total of $67,000,000 illegally sloshed through Paravacini Bank in Berne.

Then something went amiss. Charles Rumsey, Hitchcock's bagman, ran afoul of Customs as he reentered the US in the summer of 1969 with $100,000 in cash. Rumsey choked and fingered his boss, revealing that the money came from various Paravacini accounts in Switzerland. Customs officials alerted the IRS, which already had a thick file on Billy Hitchcock. Freddie Paravacini, owner of the bank, produced a letter stating that the money was a loan, but his credibility was suspect among federal agents. He and Hitchcock had garnered millions from fraudulent stock manipulations. The scam buckled later that year when they gambled on some chancy issues. Both men took a bath, and Paravacini was eventually forced to sell his bank. Most of the LSD booty was squandered in the process—much to the chagrin of Nick Sand and the Brothers. A large chunk of Owsley's money, which Hitchcock had been managing, was also lost due to stock market chicanery.

Hitchcock's personal life was not faring any better. His wife, Aurora, had grown weary of LSD and other shenanigans. She filed for divorce in 1969, claiming in an affidavit that her husband hid profits from illicit drug deals in a Swiss bank. Hitchcock, heeding the advice of his lawyers and accountants, got out his checkbook and forked over $500,000 to the IRS for back taxes and potential fines, but it was too late to head off a full-scale investigation. With the feds breathing down his neck, Mr. Billy decided it was time to withdraw from the acid business. He moved back to the now tranquil Millbrook estate to gear up for a protracted legal battle with the government.

At the same time there were also problems at the Brotherhood commune in Idylwild. In July 1969 Charlene Almeida, a teenage friend of Leary's daughter, drowned in a pond at the ranch. An autopsy revealed traces of LSD in her blood, provoking a raid by the Riverside County sheriff. Leary was charged with contributing to the delinquency of a minor, and five Brothers were sent to jail on pot charges. But the greatest setback occurred in early August when Farmer John Griggs took an overdose of PCP. Griggs refused medical assistance as he lay dying in a teepee at Idylwild. "It's just between me and God," he muttered softly before passing away.

In the aftermath of Griggs's death there was a shakeup in the Brotherhood hierarchy. A different breed took over, and their approach to dealing was more competitive and cutthroat than before. Robert ("Fat Bobby") Andrist became the kingpin of the hashish operation. His counterparts in the LSD trade were Michael Boyd Randall and Nick Sand, who controlled a network that included over thirty regional distributors. They unloaded orange sunshine in parcels of eighty to two hundred fifty thousand, and the supply was quickly dwindling. Sand wanted to commence another manufacturing run, but he was stymied by a lack of raw materials. Hitchcock's source in Europe had dried up, leaving the Brothers in the lurch.

It was at this point that a mysterious figure named Ronald Hadley Stark appeared on the scene. The first time anyone heard of Stark was when one of his emissaries turned up in New York to see Hitchcock. The man claimed to represent a large French LSD operation. He was seeking to unload his product through covert channels. Hitchcock, who was then trying to distance himself from the drug trade, directed his visitor to the Brotherhood ranch. A few weeks later Stark and his assistant traveled to Idylwild.

The Brothers were hesitant initially, but after some verbal sparring Stark proved his sincerity by showing them a kilo of pure LSD. This was a rather impressive credential, to say the least. None of the Brothers had ever seen that much acid in one place before. Stark informed them that he had discovered a new quick process of making high-quality LSD. He laid out his plan to turn on the world—not just the West, but the Soviet Union and the Communist countries as well. Stark had business contacts with the Japanese Mafia, and they could smuggle drugs into the Chinese mainland. He also knew a high-placed Tibetan close to the Dalai Lama. Why not offer him enough LSD to dose all the Chinese troops occupying Tibet? The CIA was then training Tibetan exiles for guerrilla actions in their former homeland, and the hallucinogen could come in handy. The Brothers dug his rap. "We were definitely very gullible in believing the stuff he told us," Scully said.

Stark's talent as a raconteur was enhanced by an insatiable appetite for intrigue and deception. He was adept at dropping names, dates, and places that would change depending upon the situation. At various times he passed himself off as a medical doctor, a gourmet cook, a professional chemist, a collector of fine art. Every story he told was slightly different, and no one knew for certain who he really was. His net worth in 1967 was a paltry $3,000, but a year later he was a millionaire. Stark claimed a relationship to the Whitneys, one of America's richest clans, and attributed his sudden wealth to the deft handling of a family trust fund.

Stark maintained an expensive apartment in Greenwich Village and liked to dine at the best restaurants in immaculate three-piece suits. Yet whenever he visited the Brotherhood ranch, he put on a smelly jellaba or a rumpled shirt and grease-stained tie. Five foot eight, with a bulging waistline, high forehead, and thick, brooding moustache, he could easily come off as a *shlub*, but his motley appearance belied a ruthless and cunning intelligence. Although only in his early thirties, Stark spoke ten languages fluently, including French, German, Italian, Arabic, and Chinese. He was, in short, a genius con artist who could talk circles around just about anybody.

Stark presented himself to the Brothers as the premier fixer, the man who could get anything done. He came across as someone who really knew his way around the world of international finance, claiming to sit on numerous boards of numerous corporations— some legitimate, others illegitimate—that he alone controlled. He promised to use his connections to help the Brothers. Stark warned them that buying real estate openly, as they had done, was much too risky—but his lawyers could remedy the situation by hiding ownership in a maze of shell companies. Before long he assumed Hitchcock's role as banker and money manager for the Brothers' dirty cash.

But Stark got much more involved than Hitchcock, overseeing the production end of the LSD operation in addition to the finances. As *éminence grise* of the psychedelic movement, he had a lot going in his favor, principally a reliable source of raw materials from Czechoslovakia and an excellent manufacturing facility in Paris, which had already produced large quantities of LSD in crystalline form. The acid was dyed orange so as to continue the sunshine legacy, and the Brothers tabbed and distributed it.

Meanwhile the redoubtable Stark dashed to and fro, attending to various business scams in at least a dozen countries. Like a chameleon, he moved swiftly from underground drug factories and hippie communes to posh hotels and private clubs for the rich and famous. He maneuvered on four continents, leaving a trail of ambiguities at every turn. A master of innuendo and disinformation, he preferred to keep his range of contacts ignorant of each other's activities. Oftentimes he concealed the fact that he was an American. His European associates were not privy to his affairs in Africa, and those in Asia knew little about his work in the States. The Brothers, for example, had no idea that he was running a separate cocaine ring in the Bay Area.

Stark compartmentalized the different spheres of his life, managing everything on a "need to know" basis. His *modus operandi* was not unlike that of an intelligence operative. He often claimed to know exactly how things worked in the espionage community. He said he knew lots of spies, and to some of his friends he even boasted of working for the CIA. It was a tip from the Agency, he explained, that prompted him to shut down his French operation in 1971. A few months later he opened another sophisticated production center in Brussels, which masqueraded for two years as a reputable firm engaged in biomedical research. During this period Stark communicated on a regular basis with officials at the American embassy in London. He even elicited their assistance while setting up his Belgian drug lab. By the time it was all over, Stark had made twenty kilos of LSD—enough for fifty million doses! It was by far the largest amount of acid ever to emanate from a single underground source, and most of it was sold in the United States.

Some of the Brothers began to have qualms about the way Stark operated. Scully, for one, decided to retire from the acid business not long after Stark entered the picture in the summer of 1969. There was something unnerving about this newcomer. His slick manner seemed worlds apart from the traditions of the psychedelic movement, and Scully distrusted him. A man with bisexual proclivities, Stark used drugs and sex to manipulate people. Occasionally he made overtures to one of the Brothers. This didn't bother Scully as much as the overall feeling that Stark was an unsavory character. His intuition proved correct, as Stark ended up with nearly all the money and property in his name after the feds broke up the Brotherhood network in the early 1970s.

"He must have pegged us as real softies," said Scully, who attributed much of his own naiveté to an infatuation with LSD. "My friends and I thought that taking acid would necessarily make people very gentle, very honest, very open, and much more concerned about each other and the planet," he explained. "But, in fact, that was just a projection of our own trip. It had nothing to do with reality, and we were able to ignore what was actually happening for a number of years. . . . Many people had different reasons for what they were doing, and they were all coming from wildly different places. Because of the feeling you get when you're stoned on acid—that you're one with others—you think that the people you're with understand you and agree with you, even though that may not be the case at all. I'm sure that led a lot of people astray."

In retrospect Scully realized that the love-and-peace mythology associated with LSD made the scene especially attractive to hustlers and con men who claimed to have lofty motives. This in part explains how a complete stranger like Stark was able to insinuate himself with such ease into the core of the Brotherhood and assume a commanding position within the organization. His fateful appearance at the Idylwild ranch coincided with the unpleasant changes that began in the summer of 1969, when Griggs died and Hitchcock pulled away from the group. Ironically, things started to sour just when the acid generation was celebrating its greatest public triumph on a rain-soaked weekend in upstate New York.

Bad Moon Rising

It was awesome to behold: a wide, sloping pasture paved with humanity, countless bodies nestled together in a swirl of dazzling colors. Close to a half million people had descended upon Max Yasgur's farm in August 1969 to attend the Woodstock music and arts fair. The three-day "Aquarian Exposition" was the greatest be-in of all, and a good many acid heavies came out of the woodwork to join the celebration. A full busload of Merry Pranksters, wildly attired in their Day-Glo costumes and American flags, drove all the way from Springfield, Oregon, where Kesey was sitting out three years' probation for marijuana possession on his brother's farm. The Yippies were also there, along with a rabble of Crazies, Motherfuckers, White Panthers, and Weathermen, who came to politicize the stoned masses. The activists set up booths and a printing press in a choice spot known as "Movement City," situated next to a psychedelic forest where headshops and dealers advertised their wares: "Acid, speed, mushrooms, mesc . . ." As soon as they arrived, the Motherfuckers struck a blow against hip capitalism by tearing down a portion of the wire fence that surrounded the natural amphitheater, and Woodstock became a free festival by default.

But losing money was not the primary concern of the promoters at this point, for they had an enormous problem on their hands. By the second day food was running out, the wells weren't pumping, and trucks couldn't get in to service the overflowing portable toilets. After the first downpour the field turned into an oozing crater of mud, with collapsed tents, bottles, tin cans, and garbage galore giving off a horrible stench. Medical supplies were brought in by army helicopters, conjuring up images of a Vietnam delta under siege, and the press carried a very plausible report that the entire festival site was about to be declared a disaster area.

But there was no disaster—no riots and no violence despite the abominable conditions. What kept the peace was no great secret. Nearly everybody was buzzed on something, and the unarmed policemen, clothed in bright red T-shirts with the words "love" and "peace" emblazoned across the chest, wisely followed a laissez-faire policy and let the dopers do their thing. Orange sunshine was plentiful, and lumps of hash appeared like manna from heaven. Some badly manufactured LSD also circulated among the crowd, and the makeshift hospital staffed by the Hog Farm, a New Mexico-based commune, was crammed with hundreds of freaked-out trippers. For the most part, however, the drugs had a calming effect, and a spirit of goodwill prevailed throughout the weekend. Woodstock "was less a festival than a religious convocation," wrote Myra Friedman in her biography of Janis Joplin. "Its ceremonies were the assertions of lifestyle, and the lifestyle included a celebration of the mystical relationship between drugs and rock.... What ruled was the rock world's *Realpolitik*: you are only as good as the number of joints you smoke, only as blessed as you are high. It was as if Woodstock was the ultimate declaration of dope, not as an incidental euphoriant, but as some kind of necessary virtue."

If rock-dope had become a new American religion, then the musicians were akin to prophets. Thirty-one of the finest musical acts, including a number of San Francisco acid rock bands, performed that weekend. But the real stars of Woodstock were those who sat in the mud and listened to the assembled talent. Never had a hippie gathering been so successful, so impressive by any standard. Here, it seemed, was irrefutable proof of the moral superiority of the new order. The sheer power of the cultural mood was overwhelming. "One, Two, Many Woodstocks," *Rolling Stone* exulted in an article that told of plans to repeat the triumph. Not every segment of the youth culture, however, was wild about what went down at Yasgur's farm. "Fuck hippie capitalism," the Weather Underground declared. "Events like the Woodstock gentleness freakout...indicate that as long as militancy isn't a threat, pig and ruling class approval is forthcoming." The Yippies agreed with their Weather brethren. "The revolution is more than digging rock or turning on," said Abbie Hoffman. "The revolution is about coming together in a struggle for change. It's about the destruction of a system based on bosses and competition and the building of a system based on people and co-operation."

Hoffman was high on acid when he ran on stage at Woodstock to deliver his political rap about the plight of John Sinclair, Pig Nation, and the whole shtick. Just as he started to talk, the microphone went dead, and Peter Townshend, leader of the Who, bonked Hoffman over the head with his electric guitar. So much for the grand alliance of cultural and political rebels that the Yippies were trying to forge under their banner. The two factions were at odds once again, reflecting the old split within the youth movement that became impossible to reconcile as the decade drew to a close.

The once fruitful dialogue between head culture and activist politics had degenerated into acrimonious word-slinging. Jann Wenner, publisher of *Rolling Stone*, the one national magazine that came out of the Haight-Ashbury subculture, dismissed the New Left as "a completely frustrating and pointless exercise of campus politics in a grown-up world." Wenner believed that rock and roll, in and of itself, would bring about the millennium. But the mystical aggrandizement of rock as "the magic that can set you free" concealed the fact that it was just another form of entertainment for most people. While Woodstock showed the vast size of the rock audience, it also symbolized the rapid growth of the music industry, which by 1969 had become a billion-dollar enterprise. Rock and roll was a victim of its own success, and the new music, despite its frequent anti-authoritarian overtones, was easily coopted by the corporate establishment. At one point Columbia Records actually ran an advertising campaign based on the moneymaking slogan, "The Man can't bust our music."

Economic factors had little to do with the original impetus of acid rock—a vital, seething outburst that blew apart the established world of record company rules. The bizarre, twisting rhythms of the early psychedelic bands were too long and formless for AM radio airplay, so there was little national exposure for this type of music. It wasn't until after the major record companies swooped down upon the Haight and used their formidable financial clout to sign, record, and promote the most successful acid rock performers that the San Francisco sound was reduced to formula. Earsplitting volume and light shows became standard fare at concerts. "It's like television, loud, large television," Jerry Garcia of the Grateful Dead said of acid rock after it became institutionalized. "It was a sensitive trip, and it's been lost.... [It] hasn't blown a new mind in years."

The capacity to absorb its critics is among the chief characteristics of American capitalism, and one of the keys to its enduring hegemony. Although they begin by posing a symbolic challenge to the status quo, rebellious styles invariably wind up creating new conventions and new options for industry. Even long hair—the outstanding symbol of revolt in the 1960s (at least for men)—proved to be a commercial bonanza for hairdressers: $20 a clip and everyone could look like their favorite rock star! By the turn of the decade the counterculture had millions of visible adherents. Rock and roll, drugs, and hip fashion were incorporated into the social mainstream like so many eggs being folded into batter.

The Yippies and their allies in the youth movement tried to resist this trend by promoting the myth of a unified counterculture. "We are a people...a nation," said John Sinclair. This unique psycho-geographical entity had its own media, its own music and dance, its own youth ghettos and communes; moreover, its citizens were involved in a struggle for national liberation against the "fascist pigs" of the Mother Country. Abbie Hoffman called the budding youth colony "Woodstock Nation," and in his book of the same title he blasted the movie *Woodstock* for extolling hip capitalism while steering clear of politics. He and his cohorts felt it was high time for the hippies to grow thorns and defend themselves and their lifestyle, which had come under increasing attack. There was even talk of forming the Woodstock People's party, which would serve as the militant vanguard of the psychedelic liberation front.

Such a notion was yet another example of the megalomania of the younger generation, which blithely "mistook its demographic pro-proliferation for real political power," as Stanley Aronowitz put it. (*We Are Everywhere* was the title of Jerry Rubin's second book, which he dedicated to the Weather Underground.) In their stoned hubris the Yippies, the White Panthers, and the Weatherpeople misread the depth of the cultural revolution and its impact on the political situation in America. Their delusions about the omnipotence of the Movement derived in part from their experience with psychedelic drugs. They believed that LSD contained an intrinsic revolutionary message; such a notion, however, was essentially an amplified reflection of their own political inclinations. ("Woodstock was political because everyone was tripping," said Karl Crazy, a member of the YIP steering committee.) Like so many others, the turned-on activists succumbed to the perennial "LSD temptation" and assumed everyone else would have similar insights while buzzed on acid. "I didn't have a sense of how unique I was," John Sinclair later recalled. "I projected so much for so many years that it blinded me from seeing it. . . . LSD did that, you know what I mean—'Everyone is one, and da-da-da.' . . . I just thought that this is how I got to where I was, and I figured everyone was in the same place. . . . I was so deep into it, I didn't see what was going on."

When Sinclair first turned on in the early 1960s, there was a prevailing sense among hip pioneers that acid should be used for initiation, in the way that Huxley implied when he spoke of opening the doors of perception and widening the area of consciousness. Sure, getting high could be loads of fun, but it was rarely a matter of just kicks, a pure recreational buzz; the era demanded more than that. "Drugs had a lot to do with placing people in a historical context— of placing people in a radical position," wrote George Cavaletto for the Liberation News Service. "Using drugs was the revolutionary first step a lot of people took."

By the late 1960s, however, so many people were getting high that the identification of drug use with the sharper forms of cultural and political deviance weakened considerably. Instead of being weapons in a generational war, marijuana and LSD often served as pleasure props, accoutrements of the good life that included water beds, tape decks, golden roach clips, and a host of leisure items. High school kids were popping tabs of acid every weekend as if they were gumdrops. And much of the LSD *was* like candy—full of additives and impurities. The physical contamination of street acid symbolized what was happening throughout the culture. "The pill was no longer a sacrament," said Michael Rossman, "but a commercial token, stripped of its essential husk of love, ritual and supportive searching community."

Many people who tried LSD for the first time during this period indulged their appetite for altered states in a confused, unfocused, and self-destructive manner. This was certainly the case when a horde of young people flocked to the Altamont Speedway in Livermore, California, in December 1969 for a free rock concert featuring the Rolling Stones. With the crowd came the dealers, selling every type of drug, including large quantities of LSD. Mick Jagger floated over the stoned throng in a helicopter with the High Priest himself, Timothy Leary, who was then awaiting trial for his marijuana bust in Laguna Beach the previous year. Even with the long arm of the law preparing a stranglehold for him, Leary still flashed that giant lighthouse of a smile wherever he went. His effusive demeanor gave no hint of a man destined for prison as he and Jagger landed at Altamont. They emerged together, with Leary grinning and waving the peace sign.

Security for the festival was entrusted to the Hell's Angels, who busied themselves guzzling their allotment of beer and eating acid by the handful. Fights broke out near the stage while the Angels faced down a crowd of a quarter to half a million. To make matters worse, there was some contaminated LSD circulating among the audience, but the scene was so violent that people were freaking out regardless of what type of acid they took. The paramedics and physicians from the Haight-Ashbury and Berkeley free clinics treated so many bummers that they ran out of Thorazine in half an hour. Thousands of others suffered cut feet, broken bones, head wounds, and worse as the Angels went on a rampage.

Into this maelstrom walked the Rolling Stones. Leary sat at the side of the stage brooding over a vast sea of bad trippers as they launched into their set. The violence reached its inevitable climax while the Stones did "Sympathy for the Devil," their song about everyone being implicated in life's evils, the sinner and the saint as two sides of the same coin. An eighteen-year-old black named Meredith Hunter was knifed and stomped to death by a gang of Hell's Angels. He was one of four people who died at Altamont. But Jagger couldn't see anything more than swirling shapes and shadows, and the Stones continued to play, at times with amazing beauty and urgency, even as fights erupted in front of them.

Things went from bad to worse as the decade drew to a close. The week of the Altamont fiasco Charles Manson and his "hippie" followers were arrested and charged with the murder of Sharon Tate and four of her friends. The glamorous young film actress, wife of director Roman Polanski, was eight months pregnant with her first child. She was stabbed forty-nine times with a butcher knife in July 1969, and the walls of her mansion in Bel Air, California, were smeared with slogans written in the blood of the victims. Sensational tales of black magic, hypnotism, and intimidation by spell-casting were played up in the national media, which fastened on the Manson case as if the entire youth culture were on trial.

The newspapers made much of the fact that Manson had once been a familiar figure in Haight-Ashbury and that he and his family used acid and chattered about revolution. The lawyers for the defense tried to blame the slayings on the deleterious effects of hallucinogenic drugs—an argument that had about as much credence as the notion that LSD was responsible for generating the good vibes at Woodstock. If the Tate killings showed anything, it was that acid has no implicit moral direction. The Manson affair was a vivid refutation of the sixties myth that anyone who took LSD would automatically become holy or reverential or politically conscious or anything else except stoned.

The canonization of Manson by certain segments of the counterculture was a measure of how desperate and bitter people had become in the final days of the 1960s. Jerry Rubin confessed that he fell in love with Manson's "cherub face and sparkling eyes" when the accused murderer appeared on television. *Tuesday's Child*, an underground paper in Los Angeles, named him Man of the Year and ran his picture with the word "hippie" as the caption. The Weathermen went a step further by lauding Manson as a heroic, acid-ripped street fighter who offed some "rich honky pigs." "Dig it!" exclaimed Bernardine Dohrn. "First they killed those pigs, then they ate dinner in the same room with them, then they even shoved a fork into a victim's stomach! Wild!" The Weatherpeople proclaimed 1970 "the Year of the Fork" in Manson's honor.

Dohrn's remarks, which she later came to regret, were made at the drug-crazed Wargasm conference, otherwise known as the National War Council. Held in Flint, Michigan, over the Christmas holidays in 1969, this meeting was the Weathermen's last public fling before dropping out of sight, a farewell to the shattered remains of SDS and the old Movement, and a final appeal for comrades to join their underground crusade. There was general agreement that armed struggle was necessary to smash the "imperialist motherfucker," and much of the discussion focused on possible terrorist actions. Someone proposed attacking the Strategic Air Command base outside of Dayton, Ohio, to knock out an H-bomb. "It's time to get down," the Weather Bureau declared. "Any kind of action that fucks up the pig's war and helps the people win is a good kind of action."

At the close of the four-day conference the Weatherpeople dropped acid and danced all night long while Sly Stone sang "Thank you for letting me be myself" over and over again on the phonograph. A terpsichorean frenzy filled the room as everyone burst into Indian war whoops and spirited chants: "Women Power!" "Struggling Power!" "Red Army Power!" "Sirhan Sirhan Power!" "Charlie Manson Power!" Some had dressed in hippie garb, with headbands, beads, and capes, while others wore leather jackets and chains for the wargasm climax. "It was like a collective puberty rite," one participant recalled. There was heavy laughing and heavy fucking until the wee hours of the morning, and then they all dispersed. Before long approximately one hundred of the Weather cadre were living clandestinely with the avowed objective of making war on the state.

IO

What A Field Day For The Heat

Timothy Leary was brimming with confidence as he strolled into an Orange County courtroom in February 1970. He predicted he would be acquitted of all charges stemming from his drug bust in Laguna Beach the previous winter. The trial lasted ten days. On the morning the case went to the jury, newspaper headlines in Orange County read, "DRUG CRAZED HIPPIES SLAY MOTHER AND CHILDREN." An army medical officer named McDonald reported that a gang of longhairs descended upon his home and murdered his family, leaving the words "Acid is Groovy, Kill the Pigs" scrawled in blood on the wall. Several years later McDonald himself was convicted of the crime. Initially, however, it seemed like a replay of the Manson affair, and LSD got a lot of negative publicity once again.

It was a bad omen for Timothy Leary. The jury returned a guilty verdict, and Judge Byron K. McMillan sent him to jail immediately without appeal bond. Leary spent five weeks in solitary confinement awaiting sentence. During the interim a US district court in Houston gave him ten years for the Laredo bust in 1965. And then Judge McMillan, calling Leary a "nuisance to society," added another ten to run consecutively with the federal penalty, which meant that Leary, at forty-nine years of age, faced a virtual life sentence.

Leary's friends were outraged. It wasn't just drugs, they charged, but Leary's role as cynosure of the youth movement that incurred the wrath of two vindictive judges. In the activist spirit of the day legal defense committees sprang up on several campuses. Stoned-out hippies shook their heads in sympathy for Leary's plight while Movement politicos decried yet another example of the establishment's assault against the values of the younger generation. But the

LSD doctor wasn't about to rock the boat. He gave no press conferences and refrained from making public declarations that might in any way be construed as inflammatory. At one point Leary was asked to take a commonly used prison personality test that he had helped to develop many years earlier while serving as a research psychologist at the Kaiser Foundation in Oakland. His answers were purposely calculated to make him appear normal, docile, and conforming.

After a few months Leary was transferred to a minimum security prison in San Luis Obispo. He passed the time writing, doing yoga, working out in the yard, and generally keeping a low profile while his lawyers prepared to appeal his case before the Supreme Court. On one occasion Leary tried to prevent an altercation between a guard and an inmate; for this he was chastised in his cell by an SDS militant who claimed that confrontations between "the people" and "the pigs" were inevitable and that by stopping them Leary was only delaying the revolution. The High Priest (who stayed high thanks to a stash of LSD smuggled into prison) contended that a revolution in consciousness had already occurred. He was disturbed that acidheads were now "using violent tactics which were light-years removed from the accelerating and rapidly evolving realities of our space and time."

But the acid militants had a long way to go before they posed a real threat to the governing class. This became apparent when a dynamite blast destroyed a Greenwich Village townhouse in March 1970, killing three Weatherpeople who misconnected a wire while constructing an antipersonnel bomb. It was an ominous curtain raiser for a group of tripped-out urban guerrillas. Shortly thereafter the Weather Underground initiated a wave of dramatic bombings against corporate headquarters, government buildings, and military installations. They always chose symbolic targets that would attract a lot of attention, and nearly every incident was accompanied by an advance warning and an explanation so as to minimize the loss of life and raise the public consciousness. These attacks set the tone for similar actions by small bands of quasi-Weathermen operating in different parts of the country—the New Year's Gang, the Proud Eagle Tribe, the Quartermoon Tribe, the Armed-Love Conspiracy. After a series of explosions on the West Coast a secret guerrilla unit issued a communiqué that stated, "As the beast falls, a new culture of life arises: our families and gardens, our music and acid and weed, their Bank of America burning to the ground."

The Senate Subcommittee on Investigations cited 4,330 bombings in the US from January 1969 to April 1970—an average of more than nine a day. These attacks managed to annoy and embarrass the American government, but violence ultimately was not a winning strategy. Such incidents tarnished the image of the antiwar movement and alienated many mainstream Americans who might otherwise have supported the radical opposition. That was exactly what the Nixon White House wanted; hence the extensive use of provocateurs, who provided weapons and drugs to revolutionary cliques in an effort to discredit the New Left as a whole.

The invasion of Cambodia in the spring of 1970 and the subsequent killing of four students by the National Guard at Kent State sparked another round of demonstrations throughout the US. Over five hundred colleges canceled classes and some shut down for the rest of the semester while four million people vented their rage and frustration by spilling into the streets. But the mass uproar quickly dissipated, for there was no organization to coordinate and sustain the protests. SDS had disintegrated and nothing emerged to replace it. Most activists found themselves suspended in a dizzy political space: between the dogmatic Marxist crazies and the militant acid crazies there was nowhere "left" to turn.

Time and time again the young radicals had put their bodies on the line, but the war kept grinding on. For all their efforts, it seemed like they were getting nowhere. (No one knew that President Nixon secretly kept American B-52s on full nuclear alert in the summer of 1969, but decided not to drop the big one on Hanoi because of what Kissinger described as "the hammer of antiwar pressure.") After years of frenetic struggle, Movement veterans were exhausted and demoralized. "Somewhere in the nightmare of failure and despair that gripped America in the late 1960s," recalls Hunter Thompson, "the emphasis on beating the system by challenging it, by fighting it, gave way to a sort of numb conviction that it made more sense in the long run to flee, or to simply hide, than to fight the bastards on anything even vaguely resembling their own terms."

In their wistful swan song, "Hey Jude," the Beatles offered a musical palliative to a generation of sixties burnouts: "Take a sad song and make it better." The breakup of the Beatles symbolized culturally what Kent State symbolized politically—the end of an era. What followed, according to rock critic Albert Goldman, was "the new depression." Instead of rebellious lyrics there were brooding melodies for those who needed a bridge over troubled waters. A number of rock festivals during the summer of 1970 sought to rekindle the Woodstock feeling, but they were little more than occasions for aimless milling and random violence, with most people turning on simply to turn off.

The shift in orientation was reflected in the new drug lingo: "getting wasted" (a term used by GIs in Vietnam to mean death) became a dominant idiom for chemical experimentation. Nineteen seventy turned into "the year of the middle-class junkie" as large quantities of heroin appeared for the first time in youth culture enclaves. Movement leaders were careful to distinguish between "death drugs" (smack, downers, speed, alcohol) and "people drugs" (marijuana, LSD), but the number of victims from accidental overdose kept increasing. Rock stars were falling like dominos: Hendrix, Joplin, Morrison. . . . Some suspected that the heroin scourge was part of a government plot to pacify the masses of young people. The conspiracy was allegedly set in motion in the fall of 1969, when Nixon initiated Operation Intercept to cut off the supply of marijuana from Mexico. A temporary grass shortage resulted, and then came the influx of heroin—the ultimate pharmacological copout. Subsequent revelations, however, topped any conspiracy theory: the CIA was in cahoots with organized crime; Agency personnel based in Southeast Asia were involved in the heroin trade;* for eight years the drug was smuggled inside returning corpses of American servicemen who had died in Vietnam; and corrupt police pushed junk in New York, Detroit, and other major urban ghettos.

When the social fabric starts to unravel, as it did in the late 1960s, the fabric of the psyche also unravels. People needed to put their lives back together and regain their sanity after the turmoil of those years. For some this meant going off to live in a commune or a farm in the country where they could wage a revolution of purely private expectations. Others took solace in Jesus Freakery or any number of Eastern swamis who promised blissful panaceas for acid casualties on the rebound.

---

*New York Times foreign affairs columnist C. L. Sulzberger was indignant when Allen Ginsberg accused the CIA of trafficking in heroin. But Sulzberger later acknowledged his mistake in a letter to Ginsberg dated April 11, 1978. "I fear I owe you an apology," he told Ginsberg. "I have been reading a succession of pieces about CIA involvement in the dope trade in Southeast Asia and I remember when you first suggested I look into this I thought you were full of beans. Indeed you were right."

Of all the New Age dream-spinners, none made as big a splash as Richard Alpert, whose spiritual odyssey had begun at Harvard when he met Timothy Leary and sampled the magic mushroom. The two professors set out to publicize the virtues of psychedelic drugs, hoping to alter the consciousness of America. But playing second fiddle to Leary was never quite enough for Alpert. Eventually they went their separate ways—Leary to jail, and Alpert to India on a religious quest. A series of cosmic connections brought him to the Himalayas, where he found a guru with the right stuff. What made Alpert so sure? He gave the old man a few thousand mikes of LSD, and it hardly fazed him—which could only mean one thing: he was high *all the time*! Alpert changed his name to Baba Ram Dass and returned home to spread the word.

Ram Dass wrote an autobiographical treatise, *Be Here Now*, which described his conversion to meditation. (Actually it was only a partial conversion; he still took an occasional LSD trip when he yearned for a jolt of expanded consciousness.) The book became a cult best-seller, winning effusive praise from Jerry Rubin and other counter-culture mavens. Ram Dass never intended to build a church or a new religion; his metaphysical meanderings were eclectic, and the gist of his message seemed to be, "Work on yourself." Nothing new, of course, but soothing for an audience of weary radicals who needed some spiritual first aid after years of thankless struggle on the political front.

Ram Dass talked a lot about changing the reality of private consciousness, but he didn't have much to say about changing social reality. "Better to be good than to do good," he pontificated. "Trust your intuitive heart-mind, and see where the wind takes you." It was nifty advice—assuming you were willing to believe that someone or something was tending the proverbial Light at the end of the tunnel. Apparently it was what a lot of people wanted to hear; Ram Dass became a hot ticket on the lecture circuit as the new High Priest. Oftentimes he began with a self-effacing comment: "You may remember me as Mr. LSD, Jr." For years he had lived in Leary's shadow, but now Ram Dass had a chance to do his own thing while Mr. LSD, Sr., languished in prison. He showed little sympathy for his former tripping partner. "If he's there, that's where he should be," Ram Dass asserted. "Tim's in jail because that's his karma. Trust and obey your karma, grow with it."

Such enlightened sophistry did not sit well with Leary. He had

263

spent seven long months behind bars, and there was little prospect of an early release. Karma or no karma, he wanted out. If legal methods didn't work, then he would opt for an immediate solution: escape. An intricate plan was developed with Leary's wife, Rosemary, ferrying messages back and forth among the principals. She was in touch with a radical attorney who arranged for a getaway car to pick Leary up on the highway near the prison. Members of the Brotherhood put up $25,000 to fund the operation, and a group of trained professionals was hired to spirit him out of the country.

On September 12, 1970, Leary slipped across the prison yard while most of the inmates were eating dinner. To scale the wall he had to climb a tree without being noticed. That was relatively easy. He removed his sneakers and padded barefoot along the roof, his silhouette exposed against an overcast sky. Extending from the other side of the roof was a thin steel wire—his path to freedom. Quickly he donned a pair of handball gloves and grabbed the cable, kicking his legs up like a monkey. He could see the car lights on the highway as he pulled himself hand over hand, bouncing and wrenching with each heave, until exhaustion set in. Leary's body ached and perspired as he dangled precariously halfway across the highwire, unsure if he had the strength to continue. After pausing to catch his breath, he mustered every ounce of inner reserve and made it to a utility pole on the other side of the fence. Leary slid down the splintery wood, scrambled toward the road, and waited anxiously at a predesignated spot.

A few minutes later a pickup truck signaled and pulled over. A woman called out the password, "Nino." Leary answered "Kelly" and jumped into the car, overjoyed to be in the company of two young strangers who had come to rescue him. As the vehicle sped away, they handed Leary ID papers for a "Mr. William McNellis." The acid fugitive changed into another set of clothes. His old gear was dumped at a gas station to mislead the police while he switched cars and traveled north to San Francisco. Only then did Leary learn that he'd been rescued by members of the Weather Underground.

Leary was taken to a safehouse in the Bay Area where he met with Bernardine Dohrn, Jeff Jones, and other Weather leaders. In a communiqué mailed to newspapers across the country, the Weather Underground claimed credit for the jailbreak. It was a tremendous propaganda coup for the acid militants. They described Leary as a political prisoner who was "captured for the work he did in helping all of us begin the task of creating a new culture on the barren wasteland that has been imposed on us by Democrats, Republicans, Capitalists and creeps." LSD and marijuana, the Weather cadre asserted, would help make a better world in the future, but for the time being, "we are at war.... we know that peace is only possible in the destruction of U.S. imperialism. We are outlaws. We are free."

Leary was grateful to the Weathermen and enjoyed their company. They got stoned together and planned their next move. Leary needed an effective disguise. He shaved the top of his head, grew a moustache, and dyed his hair. But more than just his physical appearance changed during the time he spent with the Weatherpeople. Leary now thought of himself as a psychedelic revolutionary. He expressed his new political perspective in a manifesto called "Shoot to Live." Disavowing his earlier pacifism, he called for sabotage and other acts of resistance. "To shoot a genocidal robot policeman in defense of life is a sacred act," Leary proclaimed. "World War III is now being waged by short-haired robots whose deliberate aim is to destroy the complex web of free wild life by the imposition of mechanical order. ...Blow the mechanical mind with Holy Acid...dose them...dose them." He urged everyone to "stay high and wage the revolutionary war." In a postscript he warned, "I am armed and should be considered dangerous to anyone who threatens my life and freedom."

Many friends were shocked and dismayed by the turn Leary's mind had taken. Ken Kesey, who was then living on a farm in Oregon, voiced his concern in a letter to Leary. It was an eloquent plea, written on Yom Kippur, the Day of Atonement, after Kesey dropped some orange sunshine.

Dear Good Doctor Timothy:

Congratulations! The only positive memories I have from all my legal experiences was getting away. A good escape almost makes up for the fucking bust.

But listen to me, please, with a stillness. Listen to me as you would to any felon and fugitive and mainly, friend. With stillness, old timer, and patience, because I must say this carefully and with respect for your ears and not the media....I've been doing a media fast, vowing this last summer solstice to try for six months to neither heed nor feed a beast which I am convinced is nourished by the blood and anguish of confrontations which the beast itself promotes. So all magazines, newspapers, TV or radio have been refreshingly absent the last few months. Lots of farming and community and trying to hear the earth and the people without the message filtered through Madison Avenue's dollar. The true news always penetrates anyway.

"Did you hear? Leary flew the coop!"

"Far fucking out!"

Speculations were rampant and joyous. "I hope he gets his ass to India or someplace. Old Leary deserves some good R and R because, shit, man, how long's it been? Ten, twelve years now and right in there all the time taking on all comers and never a whimper and you can *tell*, man, working where it counts inside and out *all* the time . . ."

Then that letter came out. "You read that letter of Leary's in the *Free Press*? Saying it's sacred to shoot cops and that he's armed and dangerous? That doesn't sound like something he'd put out. It sounds like some of them militants trying to jack a buncha people up . . ."

I read the letter. Halfway through I was sure it was you talking. And it grieved me because I perceived that you hadn't escaped after all.

Don't misunderstand me, doctor; I wish in no way to cool your fervor. We all know what is at stake. Unless the material virus that has been burrowing for decades into the spirit of the country is somehow branded and checked, unless our I/It lustings are outgrown and our rapings of the earth and each other stopped, in short unless we become the gentle and enlightened people we all know ourselves capable of becoming, we shall surely lose not only our life and land but, like Esau, our birthright. And worst of all, the birthrights of our children.

In this battle, Timothy, we need every mind and every soul, but oh my doctor we don't need one more nut with a gun. I know what jail makes you feel but don't let them get your head in their cowboys-and-Indians script. If they can plant a deep enough rage in you they make of you an ally. Rage is mainly a media brew anyway, concocted of frustrations and self-pity over a smokey fire of righteousness, for the purpose of making headline ink. What we need, doctor, is inspiration, enlightenment, *creation*, not more headlines. Put down that gun, clear that understandable ire from your Irish heart and pray for the vision wherein lies our only true hope. If it still comes up guns then God be with you in your part of the battle, but if it doesn't come up guns then I beg you to print a reconsideration. I do not mean to scold someone so much my senior in so many ways; I just don't want to lose you. What I really mean is stay cool and alive and high and out of cages.

And keep in mind what somebody, some Harvard holy man I think it was, used to tell us years ago: "The revolution is over and we have won." The poor country still may not survive and even if it does survive and comes again to its feet, there's still years of work and suffering and atonement before we can expect it to walk straight and healthy once more, but the Truth is already in the records: the revolution is over and we have won.

With all my respect and prayers,

Ken Kesey

Leary was in no position to heed Kesey's words. He was in motion, transported from one underground site to another by the Weathermen, preparing to leave the country on a fake passport. His brazen plan was to walk right through Customs disguised as a bland-looking, middle-aged businessman. Leary tested his disguise for the first time with a trip to the movies accompanied by some of the Weatherpeople. They went to *Woodstock*, a film Leary had wanted to see while he stewed in prison. No one recognized the LSD doctor with horn-rimmed glasses and a shiny bald pate.

A few days later the new Leary passed through a metal detector and boarded a TWA flight to Paris. Rosemary joined him on the same plane; she also had a disguise and phony ID. At first they thought of going into seclusion in Europe, but that was no life for a perennial media star like Leary. The Weathermen suggested a quick trip to Algeria, where Eldridge Cleaver and the Black Panthers had set up a government-in-exile. Perhaps Cleaver could help him obtain political asylum in Algiers. It was a romantic script that intrigued Leary—a new society of American exiles in a Third World country, working to unify the revolution.

A Bitter Pill

Tim and Rosemary arrived in Algiers with great expectations. "Panthers are the hope of the world," he wrote to Allen Ginsberg. "How perfect that we were received here and protected by young Blacks. Algeria is perfect. Great political satori! Socialism works here.... Eldridge is a genial genius. Brilliant! Turned on too!" The Panthers were also enthusiastic. At a "solidarity" press conference, they announced that "Dr. Leary is part of our movement," having previously been active "among the sons and daughters of those imperialist bandit pigs."

The alliance between Cleaver and Leary was hot news, and Algiers was suddenly crawling with media. But the much-publicized meeting of the minds quickly degenerated into a battle of egos. Leary didn't like Cleaver's heavy-handed security measures. All visitors were frisked—even Leary's friends—and drugs were banned from Panther headquarters except on rare occasions when Cleaver said it was okay to get high. In his discussions with Cleaver, Leary emphasized that "you've got to free yourself internally before you attempt to free yourself behaviorally." The Panthers, however, were not receptive to Leary's "spiritual" politics. Nor were they keen on his idea of inviting draft resisters, antiwar activists, hippies, rock stars, Weatherpeople, and other dissident groups to broadcast a "Radio Free America" program throughout Europe. Cleaver had no intention of providing a forum for a multitude of voices on the left. He was quick to brand nearly everyone else "revisionist," heaping ridicule on Stokely Carmichael, Martin Luther King, James Baldwin, LeRoi Jones, and white radicals such as Abbie Hoffman and Jerry Rubin. Soon would come the split with Panther leader Huey Newton, fomented in part by FBI subterfuge.

The FBI was also responsible for stirring up tensions between Leary and his hosts. An undercover operative who had infiltrated the New York chapter of the Black Panther party sent a poison pen letter to Cleaver urging him to discipline Leary for his cavalier, individualistic behavior. Tim and Rosemary were busted at gunpoint at Panther headquarters while black CIA agents who had penetrated Cleaver's entourage monitored the situation. A CIA document dated February 12, 1971, reported that "Panther activities have recently taken some interesting turns. Eldridge Cleaver and his Algiers contingent have apparently become disenchanted with the antics of Tim Leary.... Electing to call their action protective custody, Cleaver and company, on their own authority, have put Tim and Rosemary under house arrest due most probably to Leary's continued use of hallucinogenic drugs."

Leary had smuggled twenty thousand hits of LSD into Algiers and was planning to turn on all of Africa. This scheme didn't impress Cleaver, who was fed up with Leary's stoned gasconades. "Something's wrong with Leary's brain," the Panther chief declared in a communiqué to the underground press. "We want people to gather their wits, sober up and get down to the serious business of destroying the Babylonian empire." As far as Cleaver was concerned, the psychedelic counterculture would henceforth be considered quasi-political, if not downright dangerous. When he spoke of LSD, he invoked the specter of drug-induced totalitarianism. "To all those of you who look to Dr. Leary for inspiration and leadership," Cleaver concluded, "we want to say to you that your god is dead because his mind has been blown by acid."

Leary, for his part, felt he had come up against a new kind of chauvinism—revolutionary chauvinism—and he wanted out. But not so fast. He could leave—at a price. Once again the Brotherhood of Eternal Love came to the rescue, chipping in $25,000 to facilitate Leary's release. As they scrambled to get out of Algiers in early 1971, Tim and Rosemary were aware of the gravity of their predicament. They had no legitimate travel papers and additional advance money for Leary's book on his prison escape (*Diaries of a Hope Fiend*) was not forthcoming. Whoever could help them at this point became an instant ally. A British woman employed as a stringer for *Newsweek* introduced the Learys to a well-educated Algerian bureaucrat named Ali, who made no bones about his association with the CIA. Ali promised to arrange exit visas for them. Rosemary wondered if they could trust such a man. "He's liberal CIA," Tim assured her, "and that's the best mafia you can deal with in the twentieth century."

The fugitive couple fled to Switzerland, hoping to obtain political asylum. Leary spent the first six weeks in jail while Swiss officials reviewed his case. Life behind bars was relatively pleasant thanks to a mysterious benefactor named Michel-Gustave Hauchard, who provided Leary with fine wine and assorted delicacies during his incarceration. Described by Leary as a tall, silver-haired gunrunner, Hauchard had strong enough lines into the Swiss council to secure Leary's release from prison. He also had the funds to bankroll Leary in the high style to which he had become accustomed. Leary nicknamed him "Goldfinger" and accepted an invitation to stay in Lausanne at his luxury penthouse with an exquisite view of the lake. In return Tim merely had to sign away half the money from his forthcoming book to Hauchard.

While in Switzerland, Leary was treated to gourmet lunches, dinners at expensive restaurants, and weekend parties with wealthy foreigners. Old friends such as Billy Hitchcock dropped by to visit. Leary also contacted Dr. Albert Hofmann, the Sandoz chemist who had discovered LSD nearly thirty years earlier. They met for the first time at a cafe in Lausanne. Hofmann told Leary about his informal "wisdom school" centered around psychedelic sessions with leading European intellectuals, including Ernst Jünger, the German novelist and mystic. Leary asked Hofmann about the dangers of LSD, and the elderly scientist insisted there was no evidence of brain damage caused by the drug. The only dangers, he maintained, were psychological and could be avoided by supportive conditions. In the final analysis Dr. Hofmann affirmed the importance of LSD as an "aid to meditation aimed at the mystical experience of a deeper, comprehensive reality."

Leary's legal status remained ambiguous during his eighteen-month sojourn in Switzerland. He was without a valid passport, but he had money, which is tantamount to a passport for a man on the run. When Bantam Books came through with his $250,000 advance (half of which went to Hauchard), Leary bought a spiffy yellow Porsche and a state-of-the-art stereo system. He traveled from one Swiss canton to the next, each allowing him to stay for just so long. His insecure and terminally jangled lifestyle was wearing on Rosemary's nerves. For seven years they had been together through high times and the all too frequent cycle of arrests, trials, convictions, jail, escape, and flight. While Tim was convalescing in a hospital after a minor operation, Rosemary had a love affair with an old friend. Leary was high on acid when he found out what had happened, and he told his wife to pack her bags and leave. It was a final break; he would almost never mention her name again.

With Rosemary gone, Leary was no longer moored to any kind of personal stability. He was floating in his own version of a Fellini film, accompanied by a half-desperate circus of wired, burned-out dopers, self-styled revolutionaries, informers, journalists, and star-fuckers. Besides the mysterious Hauchard, various smugglers and power peddlers offered him deals that only further confused the issue of who his friends really were. Weary of a life in constant flux, perhaps a little bored at age 50, Leary was ready for a change of scene. Soon a woman would enter his life who could have walked off a page of a Thomas Pynchon novel.

It's not clear why Joanna Harcourt-Smith was so intent on tracking Leary down. Born in Saint Moritz, she was a young globe-trotting adventuress who'd been married twice before she met Leary. Her father was a British aristocrat and her step-father one of the wealthiest men in Europe; she was also the niece of Simon Harcourt-Smith, a London publisher.

In the fall of 1972, Joanna met Michel Hauchard for drinks in New York. Hauchard, her ex-lover, bragged that he "owned" Timothy Leary, openly waving the check from his book advance. Joanna boarded the next plane to Geneva, and arranged to meet Leary at a nearby café. Tim was immediately attracted by her wit and sexy smile. As they drove back to Leary's pad, Joanna reached into her pocket, pulled out two hits of windowpane acid, swallowed one, and said of the other, "Whoever eats this will follow me." Leary gobbled the psychedelic, precipitating an all-night session of lovemaking,

270

speaking in French, and overall grokking. The next morning, Tim told his housemates that he had found his perfect love.

Joanna filled a void in Leary's life created by the chaotic events and uncertainties of two years on the lam. She and Tim became almost a single entity. They tripped together, took long baths in a big tub, living only for the moment. But there were still problems with the Swiss authorities. Leary had been denied asylum three times, and he was tired of pleading his case from one canton to the next. Hauchard told him that it wouldn't be safe to stay in Switzerland much longer.

With some prodding from Joanna they decided to drive off in his yellow Porsche for a "honeymoon," even though they were not officially married. In Austria, they were joined by Dennis Martino, whom Leary had met a few years earlier in Laguna Beach through the Brotherhood of Eternal Love. (Martino's twin brother, David, was married to Leary's daughter, Susan.) Martino had participated in numerous drug smuggling operations for the Brotherhood until he was busted for selling marijuana. After serving six months in prison, he jumped probation and fled to Europe.

By this time a federal task force composed of thirteen agencies—including the FBI, CIA, BNDD, IRS, Customs, and the State Department—was gearing up for a major crackdown on the Brotherhood. Operation BEL, as the Brotherhood sting was called, scored its first major victory in August 1972, when narcotics agents arrested forty people in three different states. The predawn raids were ordered on the basis of twenty-nine secret indictments handed down by an Orange County grand jury. They marked the culmination of a yearlong investigation that netted a million and a half LSD tablets, two and a half tons of hashish, thirty gallons of hash oil, and $20,000 in cash. Cecil Hicks, the district attorney of Orange County, fingered Leary as "the Godfather" of the largest drug smuggling network in the world and vowed to press for his extradition from Switzerland. "Leary is responsible for destroying more lives than any other human being," Hicks declared.

Leary felt the heat from Operation BEL as he pondered his next move in Europe. Further complications arose when Joanna grew weak and yellow with hepatitis. She refused hospitalization, telling Leary that unless they kept traveling, American agents would catch up with them. The wandering fugitives were short on cash, but Joanna suggested they head east, perhaps to Ceylon, where they could rendezvous with some of her friends and charter a yacht. An idyllic life in the South Seas was envisioned. But first, at Joanna's insistence, they would stop in Afghanistan, a country that had no extradition treaty with the US. Martino was in contact with some hash smugglers there, and Joanna said she knew the royal prince. Certainly he'd help them get to Ceylon.

The decision to fly to Afghanistan proved to be a fatal mistake. Kabul, the capital city, was swarming with American narcotics police who were investigating the hashish smuggling ring associated with the Brotherhood of Eternal Love. The three were taken into custody while Terrence Burke, a former CIA agent assigned by the BNDD to work on the Brotherhood conspiracy case, convinced the Afghan authorities to deport Leary.

In an unusual display of largesse Joanna was permitted by US officials to accompany Leary on a flight to Los Angeles at a cost to taxpayers of $1,086 for her one-way first-class ticket. Why this was done, neither the State Department nor the BNDD was willing to say. Perhaps it was Joanna's reward for leading Leary into a trap. Although she had known him for only a month, it was Joanna who persuaded Leary to leave Switzerland and embark on a whirlwind tour that ended with the debacle in Kabul. Tim never suspected that she might have had anything but the purest of motives for seeking him out. A few hours before they landed in the States, he took out pen and paper and scribbled a note that would serve as Joanna's introduction to radical circles in America: "The right to speak for me I hereby lovingly give to Joanna Harcourt-Smith, who is my love, my voice, my wisdom, my words, my output to the world."

On January 17, 1973, four days after being nabbed in Afghanistan, Timothy Leary stepped off a plane in Los Angeles and looked out at fifty helmeted policemen with riot guns lining the path to the Volkswagen bus that would take him away. When BNDD agent Burke formally placed him under arrest, Leary responded by flashing his trademark ear-to-ear smile to the camera crews. But it was little more than a mask, for the High Priest was actually in quite a fix. In addition to the grand jury indictment alleging his involvement with the Brotherhood of Eternal Love, he now had to answer for his prison escape. Leary was in no position to scoff at these charges. With bail set at $5,000,000 (the highest ever for an American citizen), the Justice Department looked forward to Leary's escape trial as a means of getting at one of their prime targets: the Weathermen, whose members topped the FBI's Ten Most Wanted list.

The escape trial began in March, 1973. The jury took less than two hours to return a guilty verdict, and Leary was sentenced to five years in addition to the twenty he was serving when he escaped. This time it would be hard time at Folsom. Undaunted, Joanna predicted that Leary would be out of prison in a few weeks. "We'll simply leave our bodies.... We believe in miracles," she told a reporter. "Timothy Leary is a free man.... He's stronger than ever. He's happy."

Joanna rented an apartment on Telegraph Hill in San Francisco and proceeded to organize a Leary Defense Committee. Fund-raising benefits were held in the Bay Area and Los Angeles, but she squandered all the money on cocaine, jewelry from Cartier's, and long-distance calls to her mother in Spain. Joanna's erratic antics and high-rolling lifestyle alienated many of Leary's friends. When Allen Ginsberg, accompanied by Joanna and Lawrence Ferlinghetti, visited Tim in Folsom, he warned that she might be some kind of "double agent." Joanna looked at Tim and sloughed it off. "Oh, you know, he just hates women," she said, apparently in reference to Ginsberg's homosexuality. Leary asked Ginsberg if he would take over the defense committee, but Ginsberg was unable to assume such a heavy responsibility. In exasperation Leary threw up his hands as if to say, "Even if she is an agent, she's all I've got."

In November, 1973, Leary was transferred from Folsom to Vacaville Prison, previously the site of an extensive CIA drug testing program. While in Vacaville, he learned that Dennis Martino had been working as a government informer and that he and Joanna were having a relationship. Martino had struck a deal with the BNDD after they were busted in Kabul. As an undercover narc he was instrumental in arranging the arrests of at least two dozen people, some of whom were old associates from his dope-dealing days with the Brotherhood. His diligent service earned him some brownie points, but Martino's controllers refused to let him off the hook until he persuaded Leary to cooperate with the feds.

For Leary the confirmation that the people closest to him were working with his captors had to be a terrible blow. Joanna privately maintained that she was really a double or triple agent. According to Martino she routinely met US marshals at the door of her Telegraph Hill apartment in the nude, hoping to catch them in compromising situations; Martino hid in an adjacent room and taped the conversations. Joanna later told Ginsberg that she was monitoring the feds so she could blackmail them by threatening to make public the various "deals" they had proposed for Tim's release.

Leary, meanwhile, had begun to wither under the systematic pressure exerted by his most intimate contacts. Little by little Joanna and Martino brought him closer to the break desired by his jailers. The turning point came in April 1974. Leary indicated he was ready to talk. The FBI made it official when they pegged him with the code name of the songbird, "Charlie Thrush."

Leary defended his decision to collaborate with the feds by invoking the spectacle of Watergate. He compared his own situation with that of President Nixon, who would soon face impeachment for obstruction of justice and conduct unbefitting a chief of state. "You've got to tell the truth," said Leary.

> I can't condemn Richard Nixon for shutting his mouth because I'm shutting my mouth. I'm not getting paroled until I'm rehabilitated. I'm not getting out behind the lawyers. I've had a chance to analyze, as a psychologist, Nixon's downfall. I've had a chance to see that I'm locked up because of the way I played secrets. I know some people might get hurt. But if I can tell my story and get it all out, karmically, I think I'm free within. And if I'm free within, it will reflect without.... When I look at Socrates, I see that all they wanted him to do was just say he was sorry. He didn't have to drink the hemlock. Maybe if the offer was poison, I'd take that, I don't know. But it is prison. I'm a rat in a maze, staring at the door, looking for another door and there isn't one. Like it or not, when you're in the prison system, you come out through the system, unless you escape, and that didn't work."

Leary was grilled by the FBI and the Drug Enforcement Administration (DEA), but most of the information he gave was already common knowledge among law enforcement experts. But the feds had other uses for Leary. They wanted his assistance in setting up the arrest of George Chula, an attorney who had previously defended both Leary and the Brotherhood of Eternal Love. Leary told a grand jury that Chula had given him a small chunk of hash when they met at the Orange County courthouse the previous year. Joanna also gave damaging testimony, describing an encounter with Chula wherein he allegedly offered her marijuana and cocaine. When asked why she was testifying, Joanna told the grand jury that she found 99% of the drug culture "to be dishonest, lying people [who didn't know] where they were coming from and where they were going."

Chula was subsequently convicted of a minor marijuana violation and served forty-five days in jail.

"LEARY WILL SING," declared a *Chicago Tribune* headline. Soon there were rumors of a massive grand jury circus, with Leary fingering many of his former associates. After all, one of the main reasons the authorities went to such trouble to have Leary inform was to let everyone know about it in order to create fear and distrust among political and cultural activists. Also, it would be a way of trashing their values—the High Priest would turn out to be a fighter for his own skin just like everybody else. The media had always latched onto Leary as the one figure who personified the psychedelic movement, and by exposing him as a fink the entire subculture was implicitly discredited.

Although he insisted he was innocent on the "karmic" level, those who felt threatened by his actions took a different view. "I'm digesting news of Herr Doktor Leary, the swine," wrote Abbie Hoffman, who went underground after being busted for cocaine possession (which he claimed was a police setup). "It's obvious to me he's talked his fucking demented head off to the Gestapo. . . . God, Leary is disgusting. It's not just a question of being a squealer but a question of squealing on people who *helped* you. . . . The curses crowd my mouth. . . . Timothy Leary is a name worse than Benedict Arnold."

Out of anxiety as much as a desire to get the facts, a unique press conference was called at the Saint Francis Hotel in San Francisco on September 18, 1974. It was sponsored by a group calling itself People Investigating Leary's Lies, or PILL. A panel of counterculture heroes organized and moderated by journalist Ken Kelley addressed an audience of nearly two hundred. Jerry Rubin spoke first, reciting the facts as he knew them. It was a loose chronology and not much was certain. Rubin wondered what had really happened to Leary. Was he brainwashed in Vacaville—a prison with a reputation for behavior modification abuse of its inmates? Had only a phantom Leary survived? Or did his finking demonstrate that he never really took his politics seriously? "He may have gotten frightened—experienced an ego break," Ram Dass suggested, "or he may have lost control under the pressures of prison and developed a direct paranoid state where the ends justify the means."

When it was Allen Ginsberg's turn to speak, he began by chanting *OM* for a few minutes. He had written something for the conference called "Om Ah Hum: 44 Temporary Questions on Dr. Leary." These questions, ranging from witty to paranoid, brought out all the contradictions Leary's informing posed for the New Left. Ginsberg's open-ended tirade went in all directions, and that was its purpose— not to defend the informer, but to illustrate that the left versus right conflicts of the 1960s were no longer black and white, if they ever had been, and that the gaps in Leary's recent history made it imperative not to simply denounce him.

"Should we stop trusting our friends like in a Hotel room in Moscow?" Ginsberg asked.

> Is he a Russian-model prisoner brought into courtroom news conferences blinking in daylight after years in jails and months incommunicado in solitary cells with nobody to talk to but thought-control police interrogators?...Is he like Zabbathi Zvi, the False Messiah, accepted by millions of Jews centuries ago, who left Europe for the Holy Land, was captured by Turks on his way, told he'd have his head cut off unless he converted to Islam, and so accepted Allah? Didn't his followers split into sects, some claiming it was a wise decision?...
>
> Is Leary exaggerating and lying to build such confused cases and conspiracies that the authorities will lose all the trials he witnesses, and he'll be let go in the confusion?...Is he trying to clean the karmic blackboard by creating a hippie Watergate? . . . Is Joanna Harcourt-Smith, his one contact spokes-agent, a sex spy, agent provocateuse, double agent, CIA hysteric, jealous tigress, or what?...Will citizens be arrested, indicted, taken to jail for Leary's freedom?...Doesn't the old cry "Free Tim Leary!" apply now urgent as ever?

A can of worms had been opened. Paranoia was rampant among radicals who feared that Leary might be talking about any number of people he'd been in contact with over the years. Some blamed Leary for being a turncoat, others directed their anger at the government and the criminal justice system. The discussion grew increasingly acrimonious as the afternoon wore on. There for all to see were the signs of disintegration—fear, backstabbing, confusion, resentment, animosity. "The 1960s are finally dead," said Ken Kelley after the conference adjourned. "That was just the funeral."

The Great LSD Conspiracy

While Leary was in the slammer, his erstwhile patron Billy Hitchcock got tangled in a legal mess of his own making. It had taken almost four years for the government to gather enough evidence to indict the young Mellon heir for income tax evasion. He also faced charges stemming from stock market malpractice. A lengthy jail term seemed almost certain unless he struck a bargain with the authorities. He called Tim Scully, who had dropped out of the acid business a few years ago, and explained the situation. Would Scully also be willing to make a deal and possibly save his own skin? Certainly not. Hitchcock was on his own. In March 1973 he surrendered at a federal attorney's office in New York and offered to talk about the Brotherhood of Eternal Love in exchange for leniency.

The following month Hitchcock was in San Francisco testifying before a grand jury on the Brotherhood LSD conspiracy. He told everything he knew, naming all the key figures he had associated with in the drug trade over the years. He also identified the Swiss and Bahamian banks that had been used to launder drug profits. This information was just what the jury needed to indict Scully and his onetime partner, Nick Sand, who'd been apprehended earlier that year at an underground drug lab in Saint Louis. In the coming months both would stand trial for manufacturing and distributing LSD.

While the prosecution was preparing its case against Sand and Scully, DEA officials appeared before a Senate Judiciary Subcommittee and outlined the dimensions of the Brotherhood conspiracy. "In many ways," said DEA director John Bartels, "the evolution of the drug trafficking activities of the members of the Brotherhood of Eternal Love is a tragic illustration of the cynicism into which the youthful drug revolution of the mid-1960's has fallen."

At its peak the organization had approximately three thousand members, according to the DEA, and it operated "in a virtually untouchable manner" until 1971, when federal and state officials began their investigation. Since then, the senators were told, the Brotherhood inquiry had resulted in the arrest of over a hundred individuals, including Timothy Leary, who was inaccurately described as the group's founder. Four LSD factories had been seized, along with thirty-five hundred grams of acid in powdered form (equivalent to fourteen million dosages), a pill press, six hashish oil facilities, 546 acres of property in Southern California, and sizable quantities of marijuana, cocaine, peyote and amphetamine. In addition $1,800,000 in cash had either been seized or located in foreign banks. DEA officials concluded with a pitch for a budget increase, and Congress dutifully obliged.

The case against the Brotherhood acid chemists came to trial in

San Francisco in November 1973 and lasted thirty-nine days. The trial pitted Billy Hitchcock against his former colleagues, Sand and Scully, who were accused of being the largest suppliers of LSD in the US during the late 1960s. Since Hitchcock had already been granted immunity, the defense strategy was to pin all the blame on him, portraying him as the "Mr. Big" who single-handedly directed the entire acid operation. Hitchcock, for his part, tried to walk a fine line, giving just enough information to satisfy the prosecution, but not enough to convict the defendants. (He even put up money for Scully's legal fees.) The publicity generated by the trial crystallized in a sensational *Village Voice* article by Mary Jo Worth, "The Acid Profiteers." The article depicted Leary as a Madison Avenue huckster who was a front for Hitchcock's money. The whole psychedelic movement, according to Worth, was nothing more than a scam perpetrated by a profit-hungry clique.

But this was not the impression given by Sand and Scully during the trial. Both of them came off as remarkably idealistic fellows who got involved in the drug trade from altruistic motives. When Sand was arrested, the police discovered papers containing formulas for over a hundred psychedelic compounds unknown to the general public. He and Scully claimed the drug they produced was not LSD-25 but a related compound known as ALD-52, which was not illegal simply because the narcs had never heard of it. Ingenuity, however, was not a plausible defense, and it failed to sway the jury.

Hitchcock was not a particularly strong witness at the San Francisco trial. He acknowledged that his own drug usage had been extensive, and he listed all the substances he had experimented with over the years, including LSD and heroin. Mr. Billy had already pleaded guilty to income tax evasion and violation of SEC regulations, but he had not yet been sentenced for these charges. The defense contended that Hitchcock had been promised leniency in his other cases if he lied in this one. Although he admitted that he had perjured himself four times during Internal Revenue and SEC investigations and before a federal grand jury, his testimony was deemed reliable enough to send both of the defendants to the pen. Scully got twenty years, Sand got fifteen, while Hitchcock received a five-year suspended sentence, a $20,000 fine, and a ceremonial slap on the wrist.

Sand jumped bail and disappeared while out on appeal, leaving Scully to fend for himself. Scully's lawyers argued for a mistrial but lost. While in federal prison on McNeil Island, Washington State, he became a model inmate, designing a computer system for the staff and biofeedback equipment to help drug addicts and the handicapped. This helped him win an early parole in 1979. Shortly before his release from prison Scully was named Man of the Year by the Junior Chamber of Commerce of Washington for his scientific innovations.

As it turned out, Scully served a longer jail term than any other person associated with the Brotherhood of Eternal Love. At least twenty members of the Brotherhood chose the fugitive route while drug charges were pending against them. One of those who vanished was Ronald Stark, the mysterious entrepreneur who had assumed a commanding role in the illicit acid trade. In November 1972 a team of IRS and BNDD agents visited his drug lab in Brussels, but Stark was nowhere to be found. He was later indicted—but never prosecuted—as a co-conspirator in the Sand-Scully case.

The fact that Stark was wanted on a drug rap in the US hardly put a damper on his international escapades. He spent much of his time in Italy during the 1970s, cavorting with Sicilian Mafiosi, secret service officials, and political extremists of the far left and far right. Stark's antics took him far afield. Occasionally he traveled to the Baalbek region of Lebanon, where he negotiated with a Shiite Muslim sect for shiploads of hashish. Stark claimed to be a business representative of Imam Moussa Sadr, a powerful Shiite warlord who controlled vast hashish plantations and a private army of 6,000 men. The area under his dominion was said to include training camps used by the Palestine Liberation Organization and other terrorist groups.

Back in Italy, Stark rented a small apartment in Florence. But he rarely stayed there, preferring the posh hotels of Rome, Milan, Bologna and other cities. By day he carried on as a smooth and successful businessman. At night he donned a pair of faded blue jeans and a work shirt and mingled with student radicals and other extremists. Moving in left-wing circles was nothing new for Ronald Stark. He had a knack for popping up wherever trouble was brewing. An American expatriate bumped into him on the streets of Paris during the peak of the Sorbonne uprising in 1968. In London he frequented the clubs and bars that were hangouts for dissident elements, and he made his first appearance in Milan during the "hot autumn" of 1969, when massive student demonstrations and labor strikes nearly paralyzed Italy. Furthermore, Stark was tight with the Brotherhood leaders who contributed money to the Weather Underground for Timothy Leary's prison escape.

Whatever game Stark was playing took an abrupt turn in February 1975 when Italian police received an anonymous phone call about a man selling drugs in a hotel in Bologna. A few days later at the Grand Hotel Baglioni they arrested a suspect in possession of 4,600 kilos of marijuana, morphine, and cocaine. The suspect carried a British passport bearing the name Mr. Terrence W. Abbott. Italian investigators soon discovered that "Mr. Abbott" was actually Ronald Stark. Among his belongings was the key to a safe deposit box in Rome that contained documents on the manufacture of LSD and a synthetic version of cocaine. There was also a vial of liquid that scientists could not precisely identify (they figured it was something like LSD). Other items seized by police included letters from a certain Charles C. Adams written on stationery with the letterhead of the American embassy in London. The messages from Adams, a foreign service officer, began with a confidential "Dear Ron," and were addressed to Stark's drug laboratory in Brussels, which had been raided in the fall of 1972 by a team of American agents.

If Stark's contacts with American embassy personnel were difficult to fathom, then his association with some of Italy's most notorious terrorists was equally curious. In the spring of 1976, while he was being held in Don Bosco prison in Pisa, Stark befriended Renato Curcio, a top leader of the Red Brigades that had stalked Italy since the early 1970s. Curcio and his radical cohorts apparently had no idea that Stark was an American when they took him into their confidence. As soon as he succeeded in penetrating the underground terrorist network, Stark asked prison officials to arrange a meeting with the chief prosecutor of Pisa. He said that Curcio had told him of a plot to assassinate Judge Francesco Coco of Genoa, who was scheduled to preside over a trial of fifty Red Brigadesmen. There was also talk of abducting a prominent Italian politician who lived in Rome. In June 1976 Judge Coco was murdered, just as Stark predicted. (Aldo Moro, five times Italy's premier, may have been the other victim. Stark's name would later surface in connection with the Moro kidnapping and execution.)

Transferred to a jail in Bologna, Stark continued to expand his terrorist contacts. During this period he received a steady flow of visitors from the British and American consulates. (Curiously, the

280

US government never pressed for his extradition, even though he was wanted on drug charges related to the Brotherhood of Eternal Love.) Stark also communicated on a regular basis with representatives of the Libyan diplomatic corps and had a series of meetings with Italian secret service personnel. Documents show that he was in direct contact with General Vito Miceli, who received $800,000 from the CIA during the early 1970s while serving as chief of Italian military intelligence. Miceli was later implicated in a series of neofascist coup attempts in Italy.

It was quite a juggling act, to be sure, and a judge in Bologna eventually sentenced Stark to fourteen years' imprisonment and a $60,000 fine for drug trafficking. At his appeals trial Stark changed identities once again, this time passing himself off as "Khouri Ali," a radical Palestinian. In fluent Arabic he spelled out the details of his autobiography, explaining that he was part of an international terrorist organization headquartered in Lebanon, called "Group 14." Stark's appeal failed, and he was sent back to jail. But Italian police took a renewed interest in his case after they captured Enrique Paghera, another terrorist leader who knew Stark. At the time of his arrest Paghera was holding a hand-drawn map of a PLO camp in Lebanon. The map, Paghera confessed, had come from Stark, who also provided a coded letter of introduction. The objective, according to Paghera, was to forge a link with a terrorist organization that was planning to attack embassies.

In June 1978 Graziano Gori, a magistrate in Bologna, was assigned to investigate and clarify Stark's ties to the US, the Arabs, Italian terrorists, and other mysteries. A few weeks later Gori was killed in a car accident. The Italian government subsequently charged Stark with "armed banditry" for his role in aiding and abetting terrorist activities. But he never stood trial on these charges. True to form, Stark dropped out of sight shortly after he was released from prison in April 1979 on orders from Judge Giorgio Floridia in Bologna. The judge's decision was extraordinary: he released Stark because of "an impressive series of scrupulously enumerated proofs" that Stark was actually a CIA agent. "Many circumstances suggest that from 1960 onwards Stark belonged to the American secret services," Floridia stated.

The facts about Ronald Stark raise more questions than they answer. Was he a CIA operative throughout his drug dealing days? Or was the espionage link merely the work of a brilliant con artist who played both ends off the middle to his own advantage? An Italian parliamentary commission recently issued a lengthy report on domestic terrorism that included a section called "The Case of Ronald Stark." The commission asserted that Stark was an adventurer who was used by the CIA. But proof as to exactly when his espionage exploits began is hard to pin down. If Stark was connected to the CIA from 1960 on, as Judge Floridia suggested, then the entire Brotherhood operation, with its far-flung smuggling and financial networks, must be reinterpreted. "It could have been that he was employed by an American intelligence agency that wanted to see more psychedelic drugs on the street," Scully acknowledged. "Then again, he might have tricked the CIA, just like he fooled everyone else."

Reflecting upon the sixties, a surprising number of counterculture veterans endorsed the notion that the CIA disseminated street acid en masse so as to deflate the political potency of the youth rebellion. "LSD makes people less competent," contends William Burroughs. "You can see their motivation for turning people on. Very often it's not necessary to give it more than just a little push. Make it available and the news media takes it up, and there it is. They don't have to stick their necks out very much."

Burroughs was one of the first to suspect that the acid craze of the 1960s might have been a manipulated phenomenon—an opinion shared by John Sinclair, the former White Panther leader who once sang the praises of LSD as a revolutionary drug. "It makes perfect sense to me," Sinclair stated. "We thought at the time that as a result of our LSD-inspired activities great things would happen. And, of course, it didn't. . . . They were up there moving that shit around. Down on the street, nobody knew what was going on."

Even Ken Kesey, who still views LSD in a positive light, would not dismiss the possibility that the CIA might have meddled in the drug scene. "Could have been," Kesey admitted. "But, then again, they were giving us the cream, and once you've seen the cream, you know how good it is. And once you know how good it is, you know they can never take it away from you. They can never take that strength away."

Nearly a decade before Kesey was introduced to psychedelics as part of a government-funded drug study in Palo Alto, the CIA embarked upon a major effort to develop LSD into an effective mind control weapon. The CIA's behavior modification programs were geared toward domestic as well as foreign populations; targets included selected individuals and large groups of people. But in what way could LSD be utilized to manipulate an individual, let alone a subculture or a social movement? LSD is not a habit-forming substance like heroin, which transforms whole communities and turns urban slums into terrains of human bondage. Whereas opiates elicit a predictable response, both pharmacologically and socially, this is not necessarily the case with psychedelics. The efficacy of acid as an instrument of social control is therefore a rather tenuous proposition.

The CIA came to terms with this fundamental truth about LSD only after years of intense experimentation. At first CIA researchers viewed LSD as a substance that produced a specific reaction (anxiety), but subsequent studies revealed that "set and setting" were important factors in determining its effects. This finding made the drug less reliable as a cloak-and-dagger weapon, and the CIA utilized LSD in actual operations—as an aid to interrogation and a discrediting agent—only on a limited basis during the Cold War. By the mid-1960s the Agency had virtually phased out its in-house acid tests in favor of more powerful chemicals such as BZ and related derivatives, which were shown to be more effective as incapacitants. But that did not mean the CIA had lost all interest in LSD. Instead the emphasis shifted to broader questions related to the social and political impact of the drug. A number of CIA-connected think tanks began to examine the relationship between the grassroots psychedelic scene and the New Left.

An accurate investigation would have shown that sizable amounts of street acid first appeared around college campuses and bohemian enclaves in 1965. This was an exceptionally creative period marked by a new assertiveness among young people. LSD accentuated a spirit of rebellion and helped to catalyze the expectations of many onto greatly expanded vistas. The social environment in which drugs were taken fostered an outlaw consciousness that was intrinsic to the development of the entire youth culture, while the use of drugs encouraged a generalizing of discontent that had significant political ramifications. The very expression of youth revolt was influenced and enhanced by the chemical mind-changers. LSD and marijuana formed the armature of a many-sided rebellion whose tentacles reached to the heights of ego-dissolving delirium, a rebellion as much concerned with the sexual and spiritual as with anything traditionally political. It was a moment of great anticipation, and those who marched in that great Dionysian rap dance were confident that if they put their feet down on history, then history would surely budge.

But the mood had changed dramatically by the end of the decade, and the political fortunes of the New Left quickly plummeted. There were many reasons for this, not the least of which involved covert intervention by the CIA, FBI, and other spy agencies. The internecine conflicts that tore the Movement apart were fomented in part by government subversion. But such interference would have been far less effective if not for the innate vulnerability of the New Left, which emphasized both individual and social transformation as if they were two faces of an integral cultural transition, a rite of passage between a death and a difficult birth. "We had come to a curious place together, all of us," recalls Michael Rossman.

> As politics grew cultural, we realized that deeper forces were involved than had yet been named, or attended to deliberately. We were adrift in questions and potentials: the organizational disintegration of the Movement as a political body was an outer emblem of conceptual incoherence, the inability to synthesize an adequate frame of understanding (and program) to embody all that we had come to realize was essential for the transformation we sought.

An autopsy of the youth movement would show that death resulted from a variety of ills, some self-inflicted, others induced from without. There was the paramilitary bug that came in like the plague after Chicago, a bug transmitted by provocateurs and other government geeks who were welcomed by the Movement's own incendiaries. A vicious crackdown on all forms of dissent ensued, while domestic violence played on the TV news as a nightly counterpoint to the appalling horror of Vietnam. It was the war, more than anything else, that drove activists to the brink of desperation. If not for the war, the legions of antiauthoritarian youth would never have endured the totalitarian style of the dogmatic crazies and the militant crazies who combined to blow the whole thing apart.

"What subverted the sixties decade," according to Murray Bookchin, "was precisely the percolation of traditional radical myths, political styles, a sense of urgency, and above all, a heightened metabolism so destructive in its effects that it loosened the very roots of 'the movement' even as it fostered its rank growth." In this respect the widespread use of LSD contributed significantly to the demise of the New Left, for it heightened the metabolism of the body politic and accelerated all the changes going on—positive and negative, in all their contradictions. In its hyped-up condition the New Left managed to dethrone one president and prevent another from unleashing a nuclear attack on North Vietnam. These were mighty accomplishments, to be sure, but the Movement burnt itself out in the process. It never mastered its own intensity; nor could it stay the course and keep on a sensible political track.

During the intoxicating moments of the late 1960s, many radicals felt they were on the verge of a cataclysmic upheaval, an imminent break, a total revolution. In their dream world apocalypse was never far away. The delusions of grandeur they entertained were amplified by psychedelic drugs to the point that some felt themselves invested with magical powers. They wanted to change the world *immediately*—or at least as fast as LSD could change a person's consciousness. By magnifying the impulse toward revolutionism out of context, acid sped up the process by which the Movement became unglued. Even activists who never took an LSD trip were affected by this process.

The use of LSD among young people in the US reached a peak in the late 1960s, shortly after the CIA initiated a series of covert operations designed to disrupt, discredit, and neutralize the New Left. Was this merely a historical coincidence, or did the Agency actually take steps to promote the illicit acid trade? Not surprisingly, CIA spokesmen dismiss such a notion out of hand. "We do not target American citizens," former CIA director Richard Helms told the American Society of Newspaper Editors in 1971. "The nation must to a degree take it on faith that we who lead the CIA are honorable men, devoted to the nation's service."

Helms' reassurances are hardly comforting in light of his own role as the prime instigator of Operation MK-ULTRA, which utilized unwitting Americans as guinea pigs for testing LSD and other mind-altering substances. During Helms's tenure as CIA director, the Agency conducted a massive illegal domestic campaign against the antiwar movement and other dissident elements in the US. The New Left was in a shambles when Helms retired from the Agency in 1973. Most of the official records pertaining to the CIA's drug and mind control projects were summarily destroyed on orders from Helms shortly before his departure. The files were shredded, according to Dr. Sidney Gottlieb, chief of the CIA's Technical Services Staff, because of "a burgeoning paper problem." Lost in the process were numerous documents concerning the operational employment of hallucinogenic drugs, including all existing copies of a classified CIA manual titled "LSD: Some Un-Psychedelic Implications."

What was Helms trying to hide? The wholesale destruction of these memoranda suggests there may have been a lot more to the CIA's LSD program than the revelations that came to light during the post-Watergate housecleaning of the mid-1970s. Of course, it's highly improbable that the CIA would ever have drawn up a "smoking gun" document describing the details of a plot to dump millions of hits of acid on the black market. Nor is it likely that the Agency anticipated the catalytic impact of LSD and its disruptive effect on the youth movement. The CIA is not an omniscient, monolithic organization, and there's no hard evidence that it engineered a great LSD conspiracy. (As in most conspiracy theories, such a scenario vastly overestimates the sophistication of the alleged perpetrator.) If anything, it seems that a social phenomenon as complex and multifaceted as the psychedelic subculture was beyond the control of any single person or entity.

But there's still the puzzling saga of Ronald Stark, which begs for some kind of explanation. How does one distinguish between an international confidence trickster and a deep-cover spy when both professions are based on pretense and deception? Stark was a man who thrived in a clandestine netherworld where "facts are wiped out by artifacts," as Norman Mailer wrote of the espionage metaphysic, and "every truth is obliged to live in its denial." He appeared on the psychedelic scene like a meteor and produced more acid than any other underground source from 1969 through 1972. While pursuing his exploits as an LSD chemist, he communicated on a regular basis with American embassy personnel, and on numerous occasions he hinted of ties with the intelligence community. At one point he told an associate that he shut down his LSD laboratory in France on a tip from the CIA. He also haunted the radical fringes of Paris, London, and Milan during the heyday of the youth rebellion.

What does it all mean? Was Stark a hired provocateur or a fanatical guerrilla capable of reconciling bombs and LSD? When did the CIA learn of his role as a drug dealer, and was his activity tolerated because he passed information on the counterculture and the radical left to the Agency?* Although it is highly improbable that the CIA

---

*The CIA's continuing interest in the illicit drug trade is indicated in a once-

would have gotten involved in trafficking street acid as a matter of policy, it's not at all certain that stopping the flow of black market LSD was a particular priority either. Perhaps the best explanation is that certain CIA officials were willing to condone Stark's exploits in the drug trade as long as he functioned as an informant.

Stark's name surfaced once again in 1982 when he was arrested in Holland on charges of trafficking hashish, cocaine, and heroin. The following year he was deported without fanfare to the United States, where he was still wanted on drug charges stemming from the Brotherhood of Eternal Love conspiracy case. The entire matter was handled so discreetly that the press never learned of his return. Stark spent a few months in a San Francisco jail until charges were dropped by the US Justice Department, which claimed that too many years had passed to prosecute the case. In December 1984 he died of a heart attack, leaving others to ponder his ambiguous legacy.

Above all Ronald Stark remains an extraordinary international enigma. "A genius, but a tortured soul"—that was how an Italian magistrate described him. Even if he was never anything more than a brilliant private operator, his remarkable career illustrates the tangled web of espionage, crime, and extremist politics that is so much a part of the secret history of LSD—a story as wild and perplexing as the drug itself. Indeed, as Hunter Thompson wrote, "History is hard to know, because of all the hired bullshit, but even without being sure of 'history' it seems entirely reasonable to think that every now and then the energy of a whole generation comes to a head in a long fine flash, for reasons that nobody really understands at the time—and which never explain, in retrospect, what actually happened."

---

classified document dated March 24, 1969—a few months before Stark joined the Brotherhood. The document refers to the CIA's liaison with the Bureau of Narcotics and Dangerous Drugs: "It appears that the activities of the BNDD, ongoing and planned, could under the appropriate arrangements provide valuable information to the Agency in new drug effects, drug abuse and drug traffic areas. For this reason they will be followed very closely."

Postscript

Acid and After

Ronald Stark liked to brag to members of the Brotherhood that he had developed a new process for synthesizing LSD-25 of exceptional quality. But as was often the case with Stark, this was only a partial truth. Actually it was Stark's assistant in France, a young British chemist named Richard Kemp, who in 1970 discovered the cheap and easy method Stark took credit for. Kemp had been working for Stark in his French laboratories. Eventually they had a falling out, and Kemp left with his payoff—200 grams of pure LSD—and returned to England.

A self-described political revolutionary, Kemp viewed LSD as a tool for furthering the radical cause. While living in a cottage in Wales, he gathered around him a core of like-minded individuals and set up an elaborate network for disseminating his product. During the mid-1970s Kemp's group succeeded the Brotherhood of Eternal Love as the main psychedelic distribution operation in the world. Kemp's high-quality acid flowed from the United Kingdom to France, Israel, the Netherlands, Australia, West Germany, and the US. The British smuggling ring, however, had none of the mythos attached to the Brotherhood. Their notoriety would only come after they were busted. For even as Kemp was completing a manufacturing run of a kilo and a half of crystalline LSD, the police were watching him closely.

Scotland Yard assigned twenty-eight detectives to nail Kemp's operation. The thirteen-month investigation became known as Operation Julie, so named after the key undercover agent, Sergeant Julie Taylor, who penetrated Kemp's network. (She was immortalized in the song by the British rock group the Clash: "Julie's been working for the drug squad . . .") The police arrested a hundred and twenty people, including Kemp, in the spring of 1977. Six million doses of

LSD were seized in the raid. (Curiously, all of the acid later disappeared, prompting speculation that the police may have sold the drug.) During the trial the prosecution claimed that Kemp's group produced half the world's supply of LSD in the mid-1970s. Kemp, unrepentant to the end, was convicted and sentenced to thirteen years in prison. Sixteen others also received jail terms.

But this wasn't the end of the Julie story. By quirk of legal necessity, Kemp had to reveal the formula he used for making LSD. Once this new information entered into the public record, it quickly moved along the underground grapevine, sparking a major acid renaissance that continues to this day. A United Nations survey in the early 1980s noted that LSD was reappearing in considerable amounts in many countries. During this period tens of millions of doses were seized in a few busts in California. As any special agent for drug enforcement knows, supply like that means demand. According to the National Institute of Drug Abuse, 8% of today's high school seniors are using LSD, and 25% of people from eighteen to twenty-six years of age have experimented with hallucinogens.

Acid has indeed outlived the 1960s, but the psychedelic underground has changed in many ways. The recent recrudescence of LSD use has occurred without the press fanfare of years past. As John Lennon noted shortly before his death in 1980, "You don't hear about it any more, but people are still visiting the cosmos. We must always remember to thank the CIA and the army for LSD. That's what people forget.... They invented LSD to control people and what they did was give us freedom. Sometimes it works in mysterious ways its wonders to perform."

The most prevalent form of LSD currently available on the black market is blotter paper soaked with the drug. The "blotters" are cut into small squares and adorned with various emblems: R. Crumb's Mr. Natural, rocket ships, the atomic rings, or Walt Disney characters such as Goofy and Mickey Mouse. The dosage level of street acid usually falls between 100 and 125 micrograms, which is half the average dose found on the black market during the 1960s. As one San Francisco-based dealer put it, "It's just another high now. Doses are lower, just enough to put a smile on your face, give you a buzz, not like the heavy colors and trips of the sixties."

The return of acid in the 1980s has spawned a new wave of psychedelic rock bands. These acts frequently dress in granny glasses, sport pudding-bowl haircuts, and play hits from the 1960s. In London the psychedelic bands constitute a movement of sorts on the club circuit, where they are known as the "Paisley Underground." But the bands openly proclaiming themselves psychedelic do not represent a unique genre of music; rather, they blend in with the contemporary pop music scene, where the parameters of personal and group identity have been pushed to the outer limits.

A few of the original psychedelic bands from San Francisco still tour—most notably, Jerry Garcia and the Grateful Dead. The Dead made a mystical pact with their fans, vowing to carry the psychedelic torch as long as they can play their music. They still attract the old sixties Deadheads, as well as younger people who feel they are connecting with that era through the music. Cults have formed around legendary rock figures such as Jim Morrison and Jimi Hendrix. (Morrison's gravesite in Paris is a magnet for young people who regularly come to pay their respects to the Lizard King.) Dr. David Smith of the Haight-Ashbury Free Clinic reports that teenagers today are taking LSD and listening to Beatles records as a rite of passage. "They seek a nostalgic cultural experience, to individually experience what happened in the sixties," Smith said.

In the same spirit people still visit the Haight as a kind of pilgrimage. They come to the famous corner of Haight and Ashbury as if it were a shrine or a power place. Some take the ritual walk up the street to Golden Gate Park and sit atop "Hippie Hill" near the Polo Fields, where the first be-in was held. A few familiar places remain from the old days, such as the Free Clinic, and scattered street freaks still haunt the neighborhood. But these are ghosts from the past now that the area has been gentrified after ten years as a slum.

Many turned-on youth continue to view LSD as a sacrament and approach the drug experience with due respect and caution. But for others, acid is primarily a recreational buzz. Psychedelics are used by more people than ever before, appealing to a larger cross-section of American society—from young debutantes tripping at the disco to high school joyriders downing acid with their six-packs. LSD has made inroads among blacks, Latins, and gays in addition to middle-class whites. The drug is prevalent on the club scene in big cities, as well as on the college campus. Today's students, whether buttoned-down or punked-out, seek a strong dose of intense fun, and that's what acid gives them. LSD parties are common on weekends with psychedelic clans hitting the drugs as heavily as they hit the books. It's for getting guiltlessly—if not righteously—high. LSD is one among many popular drugs on the campus scene: alcohol, marijuana, cocaine, nitrous oxide, Quaaludes, and new compounds such as "ecstasy" (an MDA-related substance) and ketamine (a "psychedelic anesthetic").

While more people are using psychedelics than ever before, bad trips are much less frequent, largely because the psychosocial matrix surrounding LSD has evolved. When the social and political movements symbolically entangled with LSD collapsed in the early 1970s, the climate informing expectations about the drug lost much of its emotional charge. The new generation of acid trippers has not been weaned on the psychedelic controversies of yesteryear, when taking LSD was tantamount to an act of social defiance. Without the shrill warnings about psychosis or chromosome damage, or all the hubbub about the glories of expanded consciousness, there are fewer freak-outs and untoward incidents.

The recreational use of LSD as a "technology of the self" has its corollaries in the proliferating hi-tech leisure industry that includes computer video games, cable television, home video, and films whose multimillion-dollar special effects threaten to outstrip the theater of the mind. Ways of playing with reality are big business indeed. Many of today's TV commercials are more "psychedelic" than the most far-out acid poster of the 1960s. (Psychedelic poster art was recently shown in a special exhibit at the Museum of Modern Art in New York.) The corporate cooptation of psychedelia is evident in the army's television ads, which feature flashing images, strobe effects, hard rock, and the slogan "Be all that you can be ... you can *do it* in the army."

The resurgence of LSD in the 1980s is part of a boom in recreational drug usage throughout the US and Western Europe (where a highly politicized counterculture continues to thrive in various cities, most notably Amsterdam and West Berlin). Marijuana is now a $15-to-$20-billion-a-year industry (making it the third-largest American business, behind Exxon and GM), even though federal allocations for drug law enforcement have grown more than 75%, to $1.2 billion, during the last five years. Although marijuana possession is currently a parking ticket fine in some places, the laws governing LSD are as stringent as ever. LSD remains classified as a Schedule I drug, a category reserved for substances deemed to have no medical value whatsoever. Scientific investigations into LSD are at a com-

291

plete standstill, and psychiatrists who once used the drug for therapeutic purposes are pessimistic about future prospects. Despite—or
perhaps because of—these restrictions, an underground network of
LSD therapists quietly persists in the United States.

Meanwhile the CIA, which has always been at the cutting edge
of developments in psychopharmacology, continues to conduct secret research aimed at creating more sophisticated forms of chemical
control. There are new superpowerful mind drugs that affect sensory
modalities in highly specific ways. (One substance, for example, only
alters auditory perception; under its influence all sounds become
atonal, while other human faculties remain unaffected.) Scientists
have developed other compounds with recreational applications, including aphrodisiacs and a "two-martini pill" that produces a euphoric state without the subsequent hangover. Some of these drugs—
such as "designer heroin" and "designer cocaine"—have already
moved from the laboratory to the street, and the consequences have
been fatal.

The use of acid in a recreational context is a far cry from how the
LSD pioneers of the 1950s—both the spies and the doctors—originally envisioned its future. It was Timothy Leary who first spoke
of LSD in terms of "hedonic engineering." He promoted acid as a
sacrament of play, the drug of *homo ludens*. "The American people
today are quantum jumps more sophisticated," Leary said recently.
"About consciousness, about the nervous system...about self-ac-
tualization and self-indulgence, about pleasure being itself a reward.
Pleasure is now the number one industry in this country. Recreational travel, entertainment, sensory indulgence. There's no question about that being Number One. Now *that* was my goal."

Leary was granted an early parole for good behavior in 1976, shortly
after sensational reports of secret CIA acid tests began to surface in
the press. Publicity surrounding the sordid details of the CIA's drug
programs only added to the negative mystique of LSD, giving it an
even worse name. For Leary, however, these revelations were something of a pardon—the same government that had put him behind
bars for abusing drugs was guilty of far more heinous crimes.

Tim and Joanna split up as soon as he was released from jail. She
left for the island of Grenada and points beyond. Her confidant,
Dennis Martino, died of an apparent drug overdose in Spain in 1975.
It wasn't long before Leary turned up on the college lecture circuit,
hyping space migration and life extension with the same zeal he

once displayed for psychedelics. His next venue was nightclubs, where he performed as a "stand-up philosopher," a self-described "cheerleader for change." It was soft stuff by sixties standards, but Leary still managed to stir up controversy in his public and private life. When he appeared as a guest on a TV talk show, Art Linkletter called the station. Linkletter, whose twenty-year-old daughter committed suicide in the mid-1960s, blames Leary and LSD for her death.

In February 1979 Leary showed up at an "LSD Reunion" in Los Angeles, hosted by Dr. Oscar Janiger. An animated discussion ensued among the thirty psychedelic pioneers who attended this private gathering. Dr. Humphry Osmond and Laura Huxley were there, along with Sidney Cohen, John Lilly, Willis Harmon, and Nick Bercel. The legendary Captain Al Hubbard, then seventy-seven years of age, swaggered into Janiger's home wearing his security uniform, with a pistol and a bandolier around his hip. "Oh, Al! I owe everything to you," Leary greeted the Captain. "The galactic center sent you down just at the right moment." To which Hubbard responded, "You sure as heck played your part." It was the last time most of them would see the Captain, for he died a few years later, not long after receiving a card from President Reagan wishing him a happy birthday.

Leary popped up in the news again when he was busted at his home in Beverly Hills in the spring of 1979. But the only drugs found were new brain-changers that were not yet illegal and virtually unknown to the general public. A few years later he went on tour with his old nemesis, G. Gordon Liddy. Both men had come a long way since the Millbrook days, when Liddy first made a name for himself by arresting the High Priest of LSD. Liddy went on to work for CREEP (Committee to Re-Elect the President) in Washington, serving as a "plumber" and hatchet man for Nixon. In this capacity he proposed dosing columnist Jack Anderson and other "enemies" of the Nixon administration with an LSD-like substance. After doing time for his involvement in the Watergate break-in, he gladly teamed up with Leary for a tongue-in-cheek debate that caricatured their former roles.

The Liddy-Leary spectacle provided additional fodder for a flood-tide of antisixties propaganda that has reduced the memory of that era to a battered corpse. Nevertheless, the shockwaves of those tumultuous years continue to reverberate throughout society. The 1960s remain the watershed of our recent history, and the decade's warring impulses are still being played out on the cultural and political landscape. Ronald Reagan began his ascent to the White House by riding a crest of backlash sentiment against hippies, blacks, and student radicals in California. When Reagan became president, he "unleashed" the CIA, which continues to function as an international Pinkerton organization—company cops running amok in the Third World and spying on domestic dissidents. Indeed, the concerns of the 1960s have hardly withered away. Racism, sexism, militarism, and economic injustice are still the burning issues of the day. Opposition movements arising in response to Reagan will champion these same causes. And the new wave of political activists will also inherit the complex and unresolved legacy of the 1960s.

The tremendous outburst of energy in the sixties did not succeed in revamping the American power structure, but it had a profound effect in other ways. Avenues of choice were irrevocably opened, and a new set of options became available to everyone. Experimenting with psychedelic drugs was one of these options. This practice, now firmly rooted in the culture for good or ill, will endure no matter what the legal restrictions may be. People are still starving with the same hungers, and they will take LSD to satisfy a deep-rooted need for wholeness and meaning. In all likelihood acid will continue to ravage as many people as it liberates and deceive as many as it enlightens. Whether it will play a more significant role in the future remains a matter of conjecture, for the psychedelic experience carries the impress of a constellation of social forces that are always shifting and up for grabs.

It's not over yet.

Afterword

Since *Acid Dreams* was first published, six years ago, we have been treated to a series of congressional and news media revelations about CIA involvement with international drug traffickers. Massive amounts of still-unaccounted-for U.S. aid to Pakistani military officers and Afghan guerrilla leaders helped grease a major arms-for-heroin pipeline in Southwest Asia during the Reagan-Bush era. Much of the dirty cash was laundered through institutions such as the scandal-ridden Bank of Credit and Commerce International (BCCI), which functioned, not coincidentally, as a conduit for CIA operations in the region.

At the same time in Central America, Lieutenant Colonel Oliver North and high-level CIA personnel aided and abetted big-time cocaine smugglers who were ferrying weapons to the Nicaraguan contras. North and three other Iran-contra conspirators were banned for life from Costa Rica after that country's government came up with evidence of the Reagan administration's role in secretly facilitating the flow of narcotics—all this while U.S. officials were preaching about the war on drugs.

Then came the December 1989 Panama invasion, which the U.S. military undertook for the stated purpose of nabbing a drug pusher, General Manuel Noriega, who had been on the CIA's payroll for years. Noriega is now standing trial in Miami on charges of cocaine trafficking, while his U.S.-installed successors in Panama revel in narco-dollars.

If the Noriega case tells us anything, it's that U.S. intelligence officials will dutifully ignore evidence of dope smuggling when they deem it expedient to do so. That appears to be what happened with acid kingpin Ronald Stark, who, like Noriega, was adept at playing many sides off of one another.

"Drugs and covert operations go together like fleas on a dog," said former CIA analyst David MacMichael. When congressional probers scratched the surface of the drug trade, it became clear that certain cocaine and heroin dealers were okay by the CIA as long as they snorted the anticommunist line. Anything goes in the fight against communism—that could also have been the motto of MK-ULTRA and related CIA mind control projects hatched during the Cold War.

A number of victims of CIA drug tests have since come forward, seeking compensation for the injuries they sustained and the hardships their loved ones endured. In 1988 nine former psychiatric patients at Allain Memorial Hospital in Montreal reluctantly agreed to a meager out-of-court settlement after suing the CIA and the Canadian government. Adding insult to injury, during the legal proceedings a CIA attorney compared the plaintiffs to mice in a scientific laboratory, but the Agency steadfastly denied any responsibility for the cruelty they had underwritten. No apologies were forthcoming from the CIA or the Canadian government, which also sanctioned the controversial research program at Allain.

A Federal judge in Manhattan awarded $700,000 to the family of Harold Blauer, the tennis professional who died nearly four decades ago during an army chemical warfare experiment. Jim Stanley, another unwitting guinea pig in an army drug test, took his case all the way to the Supreme Court, which in 1987 ruled that enlisted personnel can't sue for injuries related to their service. After this judicial rebuff, Stanley testified before Congress that in 1958 he volunteered to test protective clothing for the army but instead was given a clear liquid to drink at Edgewood Arsenal, headquarters of the Army Chemical Corps. Stanley subsequently experienced severe behavioral changes that ruined his marriage and adversely affected his job.

As a result of congressional pressure, the Defense Department eventually consented to pay Stanley $625,000 in damages. But Congress assiduously sidestepped one of the thornier issues raised by the Stanley affair. For nearly twenty years the staff at Edgewood included Nazi scientists who were brought to the United States after World War II under the auspices of Project Paperclip, a program designed to harness the skills of German researchers and technicians. At least eight Nazi scientists were employed by the U.S. Army Chemical Corps, where they tinkered with deadly nerve gas and super-hallucinogenic drugs. Some of these men were involved in administering psychochemicals to soldiers like Stanley.

Meanwhile, CIA drug research plows ahead. Agency spokespersons are tight-lipped about this activity, but a former CIA contract employee indicates that much of the work is being conducted at universities in foreign countries.

Even as the ghosts of the Cold War continue to haunt us, the psychedelic underground marches on. According to U.S. drug authorities, a recent study showed that more high school students have tried LSD than cocaine. It's not uncommon for today's chemical astronauts to blast off by swallowing LSD-laced pictures of cartoon characters like the Simpsons. One way or another, the Promethean fire still burns in the local soul.

December 17, 1991

REFERENCES

The citations for sources from which material in the text is derived are arranged by Section and Chapter, with the beginning of a quotation or relevant phrase in italics.

CODE: **A** = Article
B = Book
CR = Congressional report
D = Declassified document (CIA, FBI, military, etc.)
I = Interview
L = Letter
O = Other (including unpublished interviews by other authors)

PROLOGUE

Description of discovery of LSD-25. **B** Albert Hofmann, *LSD: My Problem Child*, pp. 1–15.

"*Dr. Hofmann...there are thousands*" **A** quoted in Spencer Rumsey, "The Most Exquisite Rascals of the Age," *Berkeley Barb*, October 21–27, 1977.

"*Am I, Allen Ginsberg*" **B** Allen Ginsberg, "From Journals," *Poems All Over the Place*, p. 53.

"*The LSD movement was started by the CIA*" **A** quoted in Walter Barney, "Grandfather of LSD Meets the Acid Children," *San Francisco Sunday Chronicle and Examiner*, October 16, 1977.

"*As I look at my colleagues*" **A** quoted in Rumsey.

"*LSD came along before*" **A** quoted in Rumsey.

"*We must disentangle ourselves*" **A** quoted in Daniel Golden, "Allen Ginsberg: Politics of Emptiness," *City on a Hill Press*, October 20, 1977.

"*close the book on this chapter*" **CR** *Human Drug Testing by the CIA*, 1977, Hearings before the Subcommittee on Health and Scientific Research of the Committee on Human Resources, United States Senate, p. 2.

"*The knowledge that the Agency*" **D** (CIA) Inspector General's Memorandum to the Director of Central Intelligence, "Kennedy Committee Interest in IG Surveys of OTS," 31 October 1975, p. 2.

"*to investigate whether and how it was possible*" **CR** *Human Drug Testing By the CIA*, p. 169.

"*The bottom line on this whole business*" **A** Assassination Information Bureau, "Congress and the MK-ULTRA Whitewash," *Clandestine America*, November-December 1977.

witnesses conferred among themselves, agreeing to limit **B** John Marks, *The Search for the Manchurian Candidate*, p. 207.

programmed assassins who would kill on command **D** (CIA) "ARTICHOKE Report," 22 January 1954.

"hypnotically-induced anxieties" **D** (CIA) MK-ULTRA, Subproject 5, Memorandum for the Record, 11 May 1953.

"We lived in a never-never land" **A** Tad Szulc, "The CIA's Electric Kool-Aid Acid Test," *Psychology Today*, November 1977.

nearly every drug that appeared on the black market **A** Martin A. Lee, "High Spy," *Rolling Stone*, September 1, 1983.

CHAPTER ONE: IN THE BEGINNING THERE WAS MADNESS...

—The Truth Seekers—

"We were not afraid to try" **O** quoted in *Mission: Mind Control*, ABC News Close-up, January 30, 1979.

"There is no reason to believe" **D** (OSS) Memorandum for the File, 5 April 1946.

"injected into any type of food" ibid.

"TD appears to relax all inhibitions" ibid.

"to discuss psychologically charged topics" **D** (OSS) "Report on TD 'Truth Drugs,'" 2 June 1943.

"The drug defies all but" **D** (OSS) Memorandum for the File, "TD Material," 31 January 1946.

Description of Project CHATTER. **D** (CIA) Memorandum for the File, "Meeting with IAC Representatives of Project BLUEBIRD," 25 July 1951; and **CR** *Biomedical and Behavioral Research, 1975*, Joint Hearings before the Subcommittee on Health of the Committee on Labor and Public Welfare and the Subcommittee on Administrative Practice and Procedure of the Committee on the Judiciary, United States Senate, September 10, 12, and November 7, 1975, p. 989.

"impossible to impose one's will" **D** (navy) "German Aviation Medical Research at the Dachau Concentration Camp," US Naval Technical Mission (Report no. 331-N45), October 1945.

Strughold, the German scientist whose chief subordinates **A** Charles R. Allen, Jr., "Hubertus Strughold, Nazi in USA," *Jewish Currents*, December 1974.

"the amounts of scopolamine" **D** (CIA) 8 June 1954 (untitled.).

"we're now convinced that we can maintain" **D** (CIA) " 'ARTICHOKE,' Special Comments," 26 November 1952.

"to justify giving the green light" **D** (CIA) "ARTICHOKE Techniques," 21 June 1952.

"not fit for public consumption" **D** (CIA) "Subconscious Isolation," July 1951.

"broad and comprehensive, involving both domestic" **D** (CIA) Memorandum to the File, "Notes on meeting held 23 July 1951 in Room 2519 H Building and Room 2505-A H Building."

"exploitable alteration of personality" **D** (CIA) "Report of the Ad Hoc Medical Study Group," 15 January 1953.

"potential agents, defectors, refugees" **D** (CIA) "Organization of a Special Defense Interrogation Program," 11 June 1951.

fact-finding missions... to procure samples of rare herbs **D** (CIA) "Exploration of Potential Plant Resources in the Caribbean Region," 7 February 1956.

"Cocaine's general effects have been" **D** (CIA) "Cocaine" (undated).

"produced free and spontaneous speech" ibid.

heroin that ex-Nazi pilots under CIA contract smuggled **B** William R. Corson, *Armies of Ignorance: The Rise of the American Intelligence Empire*, pp. 321–22.

mobsters who moonlighted as CIA hitmen **B** Henrik Kruger, *The Great Heroin Coup: Drugs, Intelligence, and International Fascism*.

"can be useful in reverse because of the stresses" **D** (CIA) Memorandum for Assistant Director of Scientific Intelligence from R.J. Williams, Project Coordinator, "AR-TICHOKE," 26 April 1952.

—Enter LSD—

Stoll reported that LSD produced **A** Arthur W. Stoll, "LSD, a Hallucinatory Agent from the Ergot Group," *Swiss Archives of Neurology* 60 (1947): 279.

"on the conscious suppression of experimental" **D** (CIA) 21 October 1951 (untitled).

"at least twelve human subjects" **D** (CIA) "Experiments with LSD-25," 13 August 1954.

"he gave all the details of the secret" **D** (CIA) 20 July 1954 (untitled).

"for eliciting true and accurate statements" **D** (CIA) "Potential New Agent for Unconventional Warfare, LSD," 5 August 1954.

"We had thought at first that this was the secret" **B** quoted in Marks, p. 101.

"The most fascinating thing about it" **O** John Gittlinger quoted in *Mission: Mind Control*.

"serious mental confusion . . . and render the mind" **D** (CIA) "An OSI Study on the Strategic Medical Significance of Lysergic Acid Diethylamide (LSD-25)," 30 August 1955.

"Since information obtained from a person." **CR** "Truth Drugs in Interrogation," *Project MK-ULTRA, The CIA's Program of Research In Behavior Modification*, Joint Hearing before the Select Committee on Intelligence and the Subcommittee on Health and Scientific Research of the Committee on Human Resources, United States Senate, August 3, 1977, p.32

"Although no Soviet data are available" **D** (CIA) "An OSI Study on the Strategic Medical Significance of Lysergic Acid Diethylamide (LSD-25)," 30 August 1955.

"I'm sure they were" **O** quoted in *Mission: Mind Control*.

"to produce anxiety or terror" **CR** "Truth Drugs in Interrogation," *Project MK-ULTRA*, p. 32.

Security officials proposed that LSD be administered **D** (CIA) Memorandum for the Record, to Chief of Security Research Staff, from Chief, Technical Branch, "ARTICHOKE conference 22 October 1953," 16 November 1953.

"confined merely to male volunteer trainee" **D** (CIA) Memorandum for the Record, 19 November 1953.

smart shots, memory erasers, *"anti-vitamins"* **D** (CIA) Draft pertaining to MK-ULTRA, Subproject 35, 5 May 1955; "Report of Trip, 6–11 April 1955 to [deleted]"; Memorandum for Deputy Director of Plans, from Marshall S. Carter, "Report of Inspection of MK-ULTRA," 14 August 1963; Memorandum for Inspector General, "Project OFTEN," 6 May 1974; and **A** Martin A. Lee, "CIA: Carcinogen," *Nation*, June 5, 1982.

LSD was employed as an aid to interrogation **D** (CIA) "Specific Cases of Overseas Testing and Application of Behavioral Drugs" (undated); and Office Memorandum, 20 January 1959.

300

—Laboratories of the State—

CIA-linked conduits or cutouts **A** "Private Institutions Used in CIA Efforts to Control Behavior," *New York Times*, August 2, 1977.

The Boston Psychopathic Institute . . . one hundred volunteers **A** Joseph B. Treatser, "Researchers Say That Students Were among 200 Who Took LSD in Tests," *New York Times*, August 9, 1977.

"LSD and mescaline disorganize the psychic integration" **A** Paul H. Hoch, "Comments: Experimental Psychiatry," *American Journal of Psychiatry*, 111 (April 1955): 789.

"Don't worry . . . it won't work" **O** Nick Bercel, comments at LSD Reunion in Los Angeles, February 16, 1979.

"If the concept of contaminating" **D** (CIA) "Information from Europe Related to the Ego-Depressants, 6 August to 29 August 1952," 4 September 1952.

"open the mind to the power of suggestion" **D** (CIA) "An OSI Study on the Strategic Medical Significance of Lysergic Acid Diethylamide (LSD-25)," 30 August 1955.

Description of Dr. Ewen Cameron's CIA research. **B** Marks, pp. 131–42.

NIMH and NIH were fully cognizant **D** (CIA) Memorandum for Liaison & Security Officer/TSS, "An Account of the Chemical Division's Contacts in the NIH," 24 July 1953.

a new drug (usually supplied by American pharmaceutical firms) **D** (CIA) Memorandum for Director of Central Intelligence on CIA R & D Testing of Behavioral Drugs, from Inspector General Donald F. Chamberlain, 5 February 1975.

black inmates . . . given LSD for more than seventy-five consecutive days **B** Marks, p. 63.

"double, triple, quadruple doses" **D** (CIA) untitled report from Dr. Harris Isbell, 14 July 1954.

"continuous gales of laughter" **D** (CIA) H. Isbell, "Comparisons of the Reactions Induced by Psilocybin and LSD-25 in Man," 5 May 1959.

"will most probably be found in the biochemistry departments" **D** (CIA) untitled cable, 26 May 1954.

the purchase of ten kilos of LSD **D** (CIA) Memorandum to Chief of Security Research Staff, from Chief of Technical Branch, "ARTICHOKE Conference, 22 October 1953," 16 November 1953.

"This is a closely guarded secret" **D** (CIA) Memorandum to Director of Central Intelligence via Deputy Director of Plans, "Potential Large-Scale Availability of LSD through Newly-Discovered Synthesis by [deleted]," 26 October 1954.

—Midnight Climax—

"The minds of selected individuals" **D** (CIA) "Summary of Remarks by Dulles at the National Alumni Conference of the Graduate Council of Princeton University—Brain Warfare," 10 April 1953.

"Aside from the offensive potential" **D** (CIA) Memorandum from Assistant Deputy Director of Plans Helms to Director of Central Intelligence Dulles, 3 April 1953.

attempting to have a hypnotized subject kill **D** (CIA) "ARTICHOKE Report," 22 January 1954; and **A** "CIA Document Tells of 1954 Project to Create Involuntary Assassins," *New York Times*, February 9, 1978.

"to high officials would be a relatively simple matter" **D** (CIA) "Summary of Conversations with [deleted] on 11 January 1952," 5 February 1952.

"There was an extensive amount of self-experimentation" **CR** *Human Drug Testing by the CIA*, p. 185.

"produce serious insanity for periods" **D** (CIA) Memorandum to Chief of Security Research Staff, "Subject: Attached," 15 December 1954.

"I didn't want to leave it" **B** Marks, p. 69.

"He reported afterwards...that every automobbile" **B** ibid., p. 71.

"a psychotic state...with delusions of persecution" **B** ibid., p. 81.

a mildly worded reprimand **D** (CIA) Memorandum from Allen W. Dulles to Chief of Chemical Division, TSS, 10 February 1954.

White's harem of prostitutes became the focal point **B** Marks, pp. 94–97.

"So far as I'm concerned...'clear thinking' was non-existent" **L** George Hunter White to Harvey Powelson, September 30, 1970.

There he sat with gun in hand shooting wax slugs **O** *Mission: Mind Control.*

"concepts involved in manipulating human behavior" **D** (CIA) "Report of Inspection of MK-ULTRA," 14 August 1963.

"positive operational capacity to use drugs" **D** (CIA) Memorandum for Director of Central Intelligence, via Deputy Director of Central Intelligence, "Unwitting Testing," 9 November 1965.

"Soviet research in the pharmacological agents" **D** (CIA) Memorandum for Mr. J. Lee Rankin, General Counsel, President's Commission on the Assassination of President Kennedy, "Soviet Brainwashing Techniques," 26 June 1964.

"I was a very minor missionary" **B** quoted in Marks, p. 101.

Helms, who characterized the drugs as "dynamite" **CR** "Kirkpatrick Diary," 2 December 1953, *Biomedical and Behavioral Research*, p. 1090.

One scheme involved dusting Castro's shoes **CR** *Alleged Assassination Plots Involving Foreign Leaders*, Interim Report of the Select Committee to Study Govermental Operations with respect to Intelligence Activities, United States Senate, November 20, 1975, p. 72.

Gottlieb carried a stash of acid overseas **D** (CIA) "Project MK-ULTRA," 9 June 1954.

—The Hallucination Battlefield—

"I do not contend that driving people crazy" **A** "An Interview with Major General William M. Creasy," *This Week*, May 17, 1959.

"attacks the sensory, perception, and nerve centers" **CR** *Biological and Radiological Warfare Agents*, Hearings before the Committee on Science and Astronautics, United States House of Representatives, June 16 and 22, 1959, p. 3.

"How can we determine it! What is the test" ibid., pp. 24–25.

"we could possibly have you dancing on the desks" ibid.

Blauer, a tennis professional, was the subject of a drug study **D** (army) "Inspector General's Report of Inquiry into the Facts and Circumstances surrounding the Death of Mr. Harold Blauer at the New York State Psychiatric Institute (NYSPI) and Subsequent Claims and Actions, DAIG-IN 27–75, 1975.

"immediate, massive, and almost shocklike picture" ibid.

"It is possible that a certain amount of brain damage" **B** Hoch quoted in Marks, p. 123.

a hallucinogen was administered along a local **A** Martin Porter, "Crimes over the Cuckoo's Nest," *Village Voice*, September 4, 1978.

"obviously having paranoid ideas" **O** *Mission: Mind Control.*

"from total incapacity to marked decrease" **D** (army) "Use of Volunteers in Chemical

Agent Research," Report of the Inspector General, DAIG-IN 21–75, 1975, pp. 116–18.

Some staff members even tried to teach ibid., pp. 118–25.

Soldiers ... were given LSD and confined to sensory deprivation chambers **CR** *Foreign and Military Intelligence,* Final Report of the Select Committee to Study Governmental Operations with respect to Intelligence Activities, United States Senate, Vol. I, p. 412.

"interrogator of limited experience could compel" **D** (army) "Use of Volunteers in Chemical Agent Research," p. 117.

"Stressing techniques employed included silent treatment" **D** (army) "SPT Trip Report, Operation THIRD CHANCE," 6 September 1961.

"The subject often voiced an anti-communist line" **D** (army) "Report on Army Drug Testing: Material Testing Program EA 1729, Project THIRD CHANCE, and Project DERBY HAT," 23 January 1976.

"I was attempting to put on, with a good cover" **CR** *Chemical, Biological and Radiological Warfare Agents,* p. 5.

four hundred chemical "rejects" every month ibid., p. 32.

"During the period of acute effects" **CR** *Biomedical and Behavioral Research,* pp. 210–11.

Sim said he sampled LSD "on several occasions" **A** Bill Richards "Army Stockpiles BZ Drugs in Bombs," *Washington Post,* August 3, 1975.

"It's not a matter of compulsiveness" **A** "Self-Exposure to Psychochemicals," *Armed Forces Journal,* May-June 1960.

"It zonked me for three days" **A** Bill Richards, "Army Stockpiles BZ Drugs in Bombs," *Washington Post,* August 3, 1975.

"at the risk of grave personal injury" **A** "Self-Exposure to Psychochemicals, *Armed Forces Journal,* May-June 1960.

"The Army's testing of BZ was just a sideshow" **A** quoted in Bill Richards, "Army Test Subjects Got Super Hallucinogen," *Washington Post,* July 25, 1975.

"The last time I saw him" **A** quoted in Normal Kempster, "U.S. Didn't Check Gas Test Subjects," *Los Angeles Times,* July 19, 1979.

The superhallucinogen was ready for deployment **B** Seymour Hersh, *Chemical and Biological Warfare,* p. 45.

"We will use these things" **CR** *Chemical, Biological and Radiological Warfare Agents,* p. 3.

CHAPTER TWO: PSYCHEDELIC PIONEERS
—The Original Captain Trips—

Unless otherwise indicated, all quotes from Captain Al Hubbard in this section of the text are based on an interview with Hubbard by Dr. Oscar Janiger, October 13, 1978.

"Most people are walking in their sleep" **B** quoted in Gunther M. Weil, Ralph Metzner, and Timothy Leary, eds. *The Psychedelic Reader,* p. 83.

"I did not relish the possibility" **B** quoted in Aldous Huxley, *Moksha,* p. 36.

"It was ... without question the most extraordinary" ibid., p. 42.

"what Adam had seen on the morning" **B** Aldous Huxley, *The Doors of Perception,* p. 17.

"come about as the result of biochemical discoveries", **B** *Moksha,* p. 156.

"Your nice Captain tried a new" ibid., p. 69.

"What came through the closed door" ibid. p. 81.

"What Babes in the Wood" ibid., p. 70.

"a deep and genuine religious experience" **B** quoted in John W. Aiken, "The Church of the Great Awakening," in Osmond and Aaronson, eds., *Psychedelics*, p. 174.

"extensive emotional re-education" **A** J.R. MacLean, B.C. MacDonald, U.P. Byrne, and A.M. Hubbard, "The Use of LSD-25 in the Treatment of Alcoholism and Other Problems," *Quarterly Journal of Studies on Alcoholism*, 22 (1961): 43–44.

"Cost me a couple of thousand dollars" **O** Hubbard, remarks at LSD Reunion in Los Angeles, February 16, 1979.

"We humbly as Our Heavenly Mother" **O** church bulletin by Rev. J.E. Brown, "Introduction to the LSD Experience," December 8, 1957.

"We waited for him like the little old lady" **O** Dr. Oscar Janiger, remarks at LSD Reunion in Los Angeles, February 16, 1979.

"I don't know how Al's Washington affairs" **I** Dr. Humphry Osmond with M. Lee, May 13, 1978.

[Hubbard] was employed by Teledyne **L** Leon H. Steinman, Assistant to the Executive Vice-President, Teledyne, Inc., to J.L. Goddard, FDA Commissioner, May 23, 1966.

"Cappy was sort of a double agent" **I** Oscar Janiger with M. Lee, February 2, 1979.

"If you don't think it's the most amazing thing" **I** A.M. Hubbard with M. Lee, February 16, 1979.

—Healing Acid—

"perhaps by coincidence, LSD" **CR** Letter from Robert Bernstein to Lieutenant Colonel William R. Jordan, in *Biomedical and Behavioral Research*, pp. 96–97.

"To make this trivial world sublime" **B** quoted in Peter Stafford, *Psychedelics Encyclopedia*, p. 5.

"To fathom hell or soar angelic" ibid.

"include concepts of enriching the mind" **B** Humphry Osmond, "Clinical Effects of Psychotomimetic Agents," in David Solomon, ed., *LSD: The Consciousness Expanding Drug*, p. 148.

"corresponds better to the effects" **A** Michael Horowitz, "Interview with Albert Hofmann," *High Times*, July 1976.

schizophrenics did not experience the wealth **A** John M. MacDonald and James A. Galvin, "Experimental Psychotic States," *American Journal of Psychiatry* 112 (June, 1956): 972.

"The self disappears" **B** Octavio Paz, *Alternating Current*, p. 84.

"You start with yourself" **A** quoted in J.R. MacLean, et al., "The Use of LSD-25 in the Treatment of Alcoholism and Other Problems," *Quarterly Journal of Studies on Alcoholism*, 22 (1961): 43.

"All my life" **B** quoted in Allen Geller and Maxwell Boas, *The Drug Beat*, p. 220.

"[Whatever] reduces integrative capacity" **D** (CIA) "Report of the Ad Hoc Medical Study Group," 15 January 1953.

"LSD favors the prepared mind." **I** Oscar Janiger with M. Lee, May 28, 1985.

Description of Allen Ginsberg's first LSD experience. **I** Allen Ginsberg with M. Lee and B. Shlain, April 1980.

"It is a multiple million eyed monster" **B** Allen Ginsberg, "Lysergic Acid," *Kaddish*, p. 86.

"being part of a cosmic conspiracy" **B** quoted in Larry Sloman, *Reefer Madness*, p. 177.

—Psychosis or Gnosis?—

"what they felt might be an essential matrix" **A** Oscar Janiger "The Use of Hallucinogenic Agents in Psychiatry," *California Clinician*, July-August 1959.

"Under the influence of mescaline" **B** William Burroughs, "Points of Distinction Between Sedative and Consciousness-Expanding Drugs," in David Solomon, ed., *The Marijuana Papers*, p. 443.

"Our preoccupation with behavior" **B** Humphry Osmond, "Clinical Effects of Psychotomimetic Agents," in Solomon, *LSD: The Consciousness Expanding Drug*, p. 144.

"Those idiots want to be Pavlovians" **B** Huxley, *Moksha*, p. 186.

"Primitive man explored the" ibid., p. 23.

Certain scholars believe that the fabled Soma **B** R. Gordon Wasson, *Soma: Divine Mushroom of Immortality.*

strong evidence that ergot ... was the mysterious kykeon **B** R. Gordon Wasson, Carl A.P. Ruck, and Albert Hofmann, *The Road to Eleusis.*

"a Truth which the world of Europe" **B** Antonin Artaud, *The Peyote Dance*, p. 34.

"the cataclysm which was my body" ibid., p. 45.

"Once one has experienced a visionary state" ibid., p. 38.

"it transcends those fashionable ruts" **B** Humphry Osmond, "Clinical Effects of Psychotomimetic Agents," in Solomon, *LSD: The Consciousness Expanding Drug*, p. 146.

Hoch was ... "an opinion leader" **B** Sanford M. Unger, "Mescaline, LSD, Psilocybin and Personality Change," in Solomon, *LSD: The Consciousness Expanding Drug*, p. 207.

"essentially anxiety producing drugs" **A** Paul H. Hoch, "Remarks on LSD and Mescaline," *Journal of Nervous and Mental Disease*, 125 (1957): 442.

"results obtained in patients where tranquilizing drugs" **A** Paul H. Hoch, "Remarks on LSD and Mescaline," *Journal of Nervous and Mental Disease*, 125 (1957): 444.

"In my experience ... no patient asks for it" **B** "Group Interchange," in Harold Abramson, ed., *The Use of LSD in Psychotherapy: Transactions of a Conference*, p. 58.

"He had some visual hallucinations" **A** Paul H. Hoch, "Experimentally Produced Psychoses, *American Journal of Psychiatry*, 107 (February 1951): 609.

"It did not influence the symptoms" ibid.

"An interesting theory can always outrun" **A** Audrey R. Holliday, "The Hallucinogens: A Consideration of Semantics and Methodology with Particular Reference to Psychological Studies," in R. Featherstone and A. Simon, eds., *A Pharmacologic Approach to the Study of the Mind*, p. 260.

CHAPTER THREE: UNDER THE MUSHROOM, OVER THE RAINBOW

—Manna From Harvard—

[Luce] encouraged his correspondents to collaborate ... with the CIA **A** Carl Bernstein, "The CIA and the Media," *Rolling Stone*, October 20, 1977.

[Luce] turned on a half dozen times **B** W.A. Swanberg, *Luce and His Empire*, p. 463; and Wilfred Sheed, *Clare Boothe Luce*, p. 125.

"Oh sure, we all took acid" **O** Clare Boothe Luce, remarks on *The Dick Cavett Show*, April 9, 1982.

"We wouldn't want everyone doing too much" **B** quoted in Abbie Hoffman, *Soon to Be a Major Motion Picture*, p. 73.

"We were never more awake" **A** R. Gordon Wasson, "Seeking the Magic Mushroom," *Life*, May 27, 1957.

"The Leary," which was used by the CIA **A** Richard Levine, "Ram Dass' USA," *Rolling Stone*, April 22, 1976.

"It was above all and without question **A** Timothy Leary, "The Religious Experience: Its Production and Interpretation," in Weil, et. al., *The Psychedelic Reader*, p. 191.

"I discovered that beauty" **B** Timothy Leary, *High Priest*, p. 12.

"handsome, clean-cut, witty" **B** quoted in Stewart Tendler and David May, *The Brotherhood of Eternal Love*, p. 46.

"We rode out to his place" **O** Humphry Osmond, remarks at the LSD Reunion in Los Angeles, February 16, 1979.

"We would avoid the behaviorist approach" **B** Leary, *High Priest*, p. 66.

"indistinguishable from, if not identical with" **B** quoted in Huston Smith, "Do Drugs Have Religious Import?" in Solomon, *LSD: The Consciousness Expanding Drug*, p. 159.

—Chemical Crusaders—

"We're going to teach people to stop hating" **B** quoted in Leary, *High Priest*, p. 120.

"the very technology stereotyping" **B** Allen Ginsberg, Introduction to *Jail Notes* by Timothy Leary, p. 9.

"We were thinking far-out history thoughts" **B** Leary, *Neuropolitics*, p. 3.

"Politics, religion, economics" **B** Leary, *High Priest*, p. 340.

"Oh yeah...anything" **I** Allen Ginsberg (quoting Dizzy Gillespie) with M. Lee and B. Shlain, April 1980.

"perceived the interrelationship of all life" **B** quoted in J. C. Thomas, *Chasin' the Trane*, p. 215.

"It's philosophical...the Rolls-Royce of dope" **B** quoted in Leary, *Flashbacks*, p. 55.

"Mainly I felt like a floating Khan" **L** Jack Kerouac to Timothy Leary, undated.

"I was so high on bourbon" **B** Charles Olson, *Muthologos*, Vol, 1, p. 22.

"a love feast, a truth pill" ibid., p. 32

"wretched shame that we don't have it" ibid., p. 23.

"When they come after you" **I** Allen Ginsberg (quoting Charles Olson,) with M. Lee and B. Shlain, April, 1980.

"Leary used to argue" **B** Olson, p. 38.

"we were probably too proselytizing" **I** Allen Ginsberg with M. Lee and B. Shlain, April 1980.

"Love conquers all" ibid.

"This is wonderful, no doubt" **B** quoted in Leary, *Flashbacks*, p. 59.

"You don't need drugs to get high" **A** William Burroughs, "Academy 23," *Village Voice*, July 6, 1967.

"At the immediate risk of finding" **B** William Burroughs, *Nova Express*, p. 13.

"What I had experienced" **B** Michael Hollingshead, *The Man Who Turned on the World*, p. 10.

"The reality on which I had consciously" ibid., p. 12.

"It came sudden and irresistible" **B** Leary, *High Priest*, p. 246.

"LSD involved risk" **B** Hollingshead, p. 12.

"Uncontrolled experimentation has in the past" **D** (CIA) Memorandum for the Re-

cord, "International Federation for Internal Freedom (IFIF), ALPERT, Richard, LEARY, Timothy," 1 November 1963.

"I have this friend who's a very important" **B** quoted in Leary, *Flashbacks*, pp. 128–29.

"I can't give you all the details" ibid., p. 154.

she and JFK smoked pot together **A** Christopher Lehmann-Haupt, review of *The Kennedys* by Peter Collier and David Horowitz, *New York Times*, June 13, 1984.

"De Quincey's Confessions of an Opium Eater" **B** quoted in Alan Harrington, "A Visit to Inner Space," in Solomon, *LSD: The Consciousness Expanding Drug*, p. 87.

Kelman, recipient of a small grant **A** Al Larkin, "The CIA Funded Opponent of Leary," *Boston Globe*, September 1, 1977.

"I question whether this project" **A** quoted in Noah Gordon, "the Hallucinogenic Drug Cult," *New Yorker*, August 15, 1963.

"These drugs apparently cause panic" **B** quoted in Geller and Boas, p. 166.

"I liked Tim when we first met" **O** Al Hubbard, interview with Oscar Janiger, October 13, 1978.

"LSD is so powerful...a thousand rumors" **O** Leary to reporter Bob Gaines, quoted in "LSD: Hollywood's Status-Symbol Drug."

"Some day it will be quite humorous" **A** quoted in Noah Gordon, *New Yorker*, August, 15, 1963.

"the Establishment's apparatus for training" **B** quoted in Geller and Boas, p. 164.

"From this time on...dimly understand" **B** Leary, *High Priest*, p. 131.

—The Crackdown—

"with the proper precautions psychedelics are safe" **A** Sidney Cohen, "Lysergic Acid Diethylamide: Side Effects and Complications," *Journal of Nervous and Mental Disease*, 130 (1960): 30, 39.

"sensitive to their scientific integrity" **CR** Letter from Alexander Naimon to Senator Edward Kennedy, *Biomedical and Behavioral Research*, p. 1144.

"It was a very intense period" **A** "The Compass Rose of Consciousness: An Interview with Dr. Oscar Janiger," *L.A. Weekly*, November 13–19, 1981.

"may have been subject to the deleterious effects" **B** Jonathan O. Cole and Martin M. Katz, "The Psychotomimetic Drugs: An Overview," in Solomon, *LSD: The Consciousness Expanding Drug*, p. 237.

"At one time it was impossible to find" **A** Roy S. Grinkler, Sr., "Editorial: Lysergic Acid Diethylamide," in Solomon, *LSD: The Consciousness Expanding Drug*, pp. 228–29.

"latent psychotics are disintegrating under the influence" ibid.

to orient its behavioral activities exclusively toward operations **CR** "Report of Inspection of MK-ULTRA," August 13, 1963, *Biomedical and Behavorial Research*, p. 903.

"Why if they were worthwhile six months ago" **CR** *Organization and Coordination of Federal Drug Research and Regulatory Programs: LSD*, Hearings before the Subcommittee on Executive Reorganization of the Committee on Government Operations, United States Senate, May 24–26, 1966, pp. 72–75.

"We are abdicating our statutory responsibilities" **CR** Letter from William V. Vodra to Richard A Merrill, July 28, 1975, *Biomedical and Behavioral Research*, p. 513.

The FDA collaborated with the Agency **D** (CIA) "Report of Inspection of MK-ULTRA," 13 August 1963; "ARTICHOKE Conference, 16 April 1953," 11 May 1953;

Office Memorandum for Acting Deputy Assistant Director of Scientific Intelligence, from Chief of Medical Division, SI, "Secured Personnel for Special 'ARTICHOKE' Project," 7 April 1953.

"The whole thing was just moving geometrically" O Oscar Janiger, remarks at the LSD Reunion in Los Angeles, February 16, 1979.

CHAPTER FOUR: PREACHING LSD

—High Surrealism—

"It's only a matter of time" O Leary, comments to reporter Bob Gaines, quoted in "LSD: Hollywood's Status-Symbol Drug."

"Light and free you let go" B Laura Huxley, "Oh Nobly Born!" in Huxley, *Moksha*, pp. 265–66.

"We lived out a myth" B Hollingshead, p. 99.

"It hardly registered" B Arthur Kleps, *Millbrook*, p. 51.

"How can I make more money" ibid.

Dr. Max Jacobson served as JFK's personal physician B Leary, *Flashbacks*, p. 200.

"LSD was fun" B Paul Krassner, "My First LSD Trip," in Paul Krassner, ed. *The Best of the Realist*, pp. 145–46.

NASA scientist Steve Groff turned up at Millbrook B Hollingshead, p. 124.

"Objects are seen that are not objectively there" A Ralph Metzner, "Subjective Effects of Anti-Cholinergic Drugs," *Journal of Psychedelic Drugs* October-December 1977.

"All night, I alternated between eyes open terror" B Kleps, *Millbrook*, p. 12.

"I was knocked to the floor" ibid., p. 74.

"Apparently, those in control of the instrumentalities of coercive power" ibid., p. 125.

"Art, this is not a psychedelic love message" ibid., p. 208.

—The Psychedelic Manual—

"For every clarification that one arrives at" B Kleps, *Millbrook*, p. 211.

"Zen and Buddhist stock rose sharply" ibid., p. 58.

"I have never recovered from that shattering ontological confrontation" B Leary, *High Priest*, p. 256.

"recurring science fiction paranoia" ibid., p. 257.

"incredibly specific about the sequence and nature" B Leary, *Psychedelic Prayers*, p. 3.

"the comforting darkness of selfhood" B Huxley, *Doors*, p. 56.

"everything that happened would be proof of the conspiracy" ibid., p. 57.

"if there was somebody there to tell me about the Clear Light" ibid.

"Let's face it—LSD is not the key" B Hollingshead, p. 9.

"If you can't let go and instead grab the first life-saver" B Kleps, *Millbrook*, p. 242.

"Is it entirely inconceivable" A Leary, "The Religious Experience: Its Production and Interpretation," in Weil, Leary, and Metzner eds., *The Psychedelic Review*, p. 203.

"God does exist and is to me" B Timothy Leary, *The Politics of Ecstasy*, p. 223.

"Nine times out of ten" B Kleps, *Boohoo Bible*, p. 19.

"faster and sneakier" ibid.

"It is as if Leary" B Kleps, *Millbrook*, p. 29.

"what I, as a poet" **B** quoted in Leary, *High Priest*, p. 110.

"the whole fucking cosmos broke loose around me" **B** Letter from Allen Ginsberg to William Burroughs, *Yagé Letters*, p. 55.

"Your own heart is your guru" **B** quoted in Paul Portugés, *The Visionary Poetics of Allen Ginsberg*, p. 93.

"I spent about fifteen-twenty years" **B** Allen Ginsberg, *Allen Verbatim*, p. 18.

—The Hard Sell—

"Find the wisdom" **B** Leary, *Politics*, p. 288.

"would be sold like beer" **B** Kleps, *Millbrook*, p. 25.

"In a carefully prepared, loving LSD session" **B** Leary, *Politics*, p. 106.

"It's all God's flesh" **B** quoted in Kleps, *Boohoo Bible*, p. 207.

"I would say that at present our society" **B** Leary, *Politics*, p. 243.

"Tim had what we needed" **B** Kleps, *Millbrook*, p. 203.

"Of course I'm a charlatan" ibid., p. 290.

"It was easier to see him" **B** Hollingshead, p. 57.

George Blake, the convicted spy who penetrated ibid., p. 177.

"the panties were dropping as fast as the acid" **A** G. Gordon Liddy, "The Great Dutchess County Dope Raid," *True*, June 1975.

CHAPTER FIVE: THE ALL-AMERICAN TRIP

—The Great Freak Forward—

"Before I took drugs" **B** quoted in Burton Wolfe, *The Hippies*, p. 201.

"The first drug trips were" **B** Ken Kesey, *Garage Sale*, p. 175.

"tootling the multitudes" **B** Tom Wolfe, *The Electric Kool-Aid Acid Test*, p. 88.

"The purpose of psychedelics" **B** quoted in B. Wolfe, p. 203.

"Neal Cassady drove Jack Kerouac" **B** Ginsberg, Introduction to Leary, *Jail Notes*, p. 8.

"the yoga of a man driven to the cliff edge" **B** Kesey, p. 220.

"creeping religiosity" **B** T. Wolfe, p. 113.

"It was like hail and farewell" ibid., p. 90.

"they thought we were square" **I** Michael Hollingshead with M. Lee, July 21, 1981.

"When you've got something like we've got" **B** quoted in T. Wolfe, p. 172.

"We're in the same business" **A** quoted in Warren Hinckle, "A Social History of the Hippies," *Ramparts*, March 1967.

"It was a very electric atmosphere" **B** Hunter Thompson, *Hell's Angels*, p. 300.

—Acid and the New Left—

"the storms of youth" **B** Lautréamont, *Poesies*, quoted in *Point Blank* by the Situationist International, October 1972, p. 41.

"There's a time when the operation" **B** quoted in Paul Jacobs and Saul Landau, *The New Radicals*, p. 61.

"Social radicals tend to be 'arty'" **B** Hunter Thompson, "The Nonstudent Left," *The Great Shark Hunt*, p. 403.

"When a young person took his first puff" **I** Michael Rossman with M. Lee, November 11, 1978.

"a dead wet dog on a cool morning" **B** Michael McClure, *Meat Science Essays,* p. 41

"The acid experience is so concrete" **I** Carl Oglesby with M. Lee, April 24, 1979.

"Do you want to know how to stop" **B** quoted in T. Wolfe, p. 199.

"Being a musician means" **B** quoted in Miles, *Bob Dylan: In His Own Words,* p. 114.

"He was LSD on stage" **B** quoted in Anthony Scaduto, *Dylan,* p. 235.

CHAPTER SIX: FROM HIP TO HIPPIE

—Before the Deluge—

"Beauty will be CONVULSIVE" **B** quoted in Gaëton Picon, *Surrealists and Surrealism,* p. 86.

"The general tone of things" **B** quoted in Eugene Anthony, *The Summer of Love,* p. 111.

"What the Kesey thing was depended on" **B** quoted in Michael Lydon, "The Grateful Dead," in Albert J. LaValley, ed., *The New Consciousness,* pp. 555–56.

"It seemed like we were in a time machine" **B** Stephen Gaskin, *Amazing Dope Tales,* p. 2.

"Every time we'd make another batch" **I** Tim Scully with M. Lee, November 10, 1982.

"a world famous dope center" **B** quoted in Nicholas von Hoffman, *We Are the People Our Parents Warned Us Against,* p. 123.

"We were not guilty of using illegal substances" **B** quoted in Anthony, p. 126.

"We hold these truths to be self-evident" ibid., p. 130.

—Politics of the Bummer—

"the pseudo-intellectuals who advocate the use" **B** quoted in David Zane Mairowitz, *The Radical Soap Opera,* p. 181.

"the greatest threat facing the country" **A** quoted in Richard Bunce, "Social and Political Sources of Drug Effects: The Case of Bad Trips on Psychedelics," *Journal of Drug Issues,* Spring 1979, p. 227.

"We do not want amateur or blackmarket sale" **CR** *The Narcotic Rehabilitation Act of 1966,* Hearings before a Special Subcommittee of the Committee on the Judiciary, United States Senate, January 25–27, May 12, 13, 19, 23, 25, June 14–15, July 19, 1966, p. 253.

"For six years I have been in the unfortunate position" ibid., p. 257.

"for serious purposes, such as spiritual growth" ibid., p. 241.

"I should think that in the Army of the future" ibid., p. 249.

"Would you mind telling me if you are really" ibid., pp. 423–24.

"It is difficult for us to imagine" ibid., p. 415.

"If I were to give you an IQ test" ibid., p. 414.

"We are not drug addicts" ibid., pp. 417, 424.

"I have a strong feeling" **CR** *Organization and Coordination of Federal Drugs Research and Regulatory Programs: LSD,* p. 37.

"We are now in a position to understand" **B** Paz, pp. 97–98.

REFERENCES

"Although human chromosome breaks have been reported" **CR** Dr. Van Sim, "Fact Sheet on LSD Studies at Edgewood Arsenal," in *Biomedical and Behavioral Research*, p. 228.

Those who were willing to risk their own sanity **A** Bunce, *Journal of Drug Issues*, Spring 1979, p. 227.

nearly 50% of those questioned reported having ibid., p. 218.

"We can explain the substantial historical decline" ibid.

"That was a mean and dirty trick" **I** Ken Kesey with M. Lee, July 21, 1978.

"How lucky those of us are who approached LSD" **B** Laura Huxley, "Disregarded in the Darkness," in Huxley, *Moksha*, pp. 74–75.

—The First Human Be-In—

Unless otherwise indicated, all information on John Starr Cooke in this section of the text is based on an interview with Michael Bowen by M. Lee and B. Shlain, July 9–10, 1980.

John Cooke...is said to have made the acquaintance of CIA operatives **I** William Burroughs with M. Lee, March 2, 1981.

"We knew we had the tiger by the tail" **I** Allen Cohen with Mr. Lee and B. Shlain, June 10, 1980.

"For ten years...a new nation has grown" **B** quoted in Anthony, p. 155.

"that, if necessary, we have a mass emotional nervous breakdown" **B** Allen Ginsberg, "Public Solitude," in Jessie Kornbluth ed., *Notes from the New Underground*, p. 69.

"Welcome to the first manifestation" **B** John Bryan, *What Ever Happened to Timothy Leary?*, p. 4.

"The only way out is in" **B** Steve Levine, "The First American Mehla," in Jerry Hopkins ed., *The Hippie Papers*, p. 21.

"The Be-in was a blossom" **B** Michael McClure in Anthony, p. 7.

"In about seven or eight years" **B** quoted in Mairowitz, *Soap Opera*, p. 185.

"There was a fantastic universal sense" **B** Hunter Thompson, *Fear and Loathing in Las Vegas*, p. 68.

"dresses like Tarzan, has hair like Jane" **B** quoted in Don McNeil, *Moving Through Here*, p. 145.

"in their independence of material possessions" **A** "The Hippies," *Time*, July 7, 1967.

"The hip thing was fundamentally a drug-boosted look-in" **A** Carl Oglesby, "The World Before Watergate," *Inquiry*, May 29, 1978.

"the whole problem of whether to take over" **B** Allen Ginsberg, Timothy Leary, Gary Snyder, Alan Watts, "Changes," in Kornbluth, p. 139.

"the choice is between being rebellious" ibid., p. 194.

"Don't vote. Don't politic" **B** quoted in Bryan, p. 96.

"young men with menopausal minds" **B** Ginsberg, Leary, Snyder, Watts, "Changes," in Kornbluth, p. 141.

"People should not be allowed to talk politics" **B** quoted in Bryan, p. 96.

"the first thing you have to do" **B** Ginsberg, Leary, Snyder, Watts, "Changes," in Kornbluth, p. 148–49.

"a more profound vision of themselves" ibid., p. 143.

"the flavors and ingredients of whatever happens to be cooking" **I** Michael Rossman with M. Lee, November 11, 1978.

"The private is public, and the public is" **B** *Charles Olson Reading at Berkeley*, p. 5.

"turn and face man, the body of man" **A** Antonin Artaud quoted in Ira Einhorn, "The Sociology of the Now," *The Psychedelic Review*, Winter 1970–71.

CHAPTER SEVEN: THE CAPITAL OF FOREVER
—Stone Free—

Unless otherwise indicated, information on the Diggers in this chapter is based on an interview with Peter Berg and Judy Goldhaft by Eric Noble and M. Lee, April 29, 1982.

"*Street events are rituals of release*" **A** "The Digger Papers," published in *The Realist*, August 1968.

"*a poetry of festivals and crowds, with people pouring*" **B** Antonin Artaud, quoted in Hoffman, *Major Motion Picture*, p. 102.

"*encouraging the looser and disordered sort of people*" **B** B. Wolfe, p. 63.

"*No frozen moments for tomorrow's fantasy*" **B** "The Digger Papers," in *The Realist*, August 1968.

"*Western society has destroyed itself*" ibid.

"*The U.S. standard of living is a baby blanket*" ibid.

Mundane objects... warned the straight world of a threat **B** Dick Hebidge, *Subculture: The Meaning of Style*, p. 213.

"*The media casts nets, creates bags*" **B** quoted in Kornbluth, ed., *Notes From the New Underground*, p. 284.

"*Stamp out police brutality*" **B** quoted in Hopkins, ed., *The Hippie Papers*, p. 136.

"*Say if you are hungry, we will feed*" **B** B. Wolfe, p. 71.

—The Great Summer Dropout—

"*I declare that the Beatles are mutants*" **B** quoted in Philip Norman, *Shout!*, p. 365.

"*John was crying and banging his head against the wall*" ibid., p. 305.

"*We didn't know what was going on*" **B** quoted in Jann Wenner, ed., *Lennon Remembers*, p. 73.

"*an understanding of the principles of brainwashing*" **B** quoted in Norman, p. 366.

"*trip all the time*" **B** quoted in Wenner, p. 76.

"*I got a message on acid*" ibid., p. 77.

childhood's lost "tense of presence" **B** quoted in Charles Perry, *The Haight-Ashbury: A History*, p. 259.

"*It's enabled people to see a bit more*" **B** quoted in Richard Poirier, *The Performing Self*, p. 133.

"*It was an experience we went through*" ibid.

"*the haze that blurs the corner*" **B** Mairowitz, *Soap Opera*, p. 184.

"*the pious attitudes of those spiritual bigots*" **B** John Ashbery, *Three Poems*, p. 75.

"*the ego-death of easy-prey LSD takers*" **B** Mairowitz, *Soap Opera*, p. 190.

"*The whole catalogue of craziness*" **B** Gaskin, p. 51.

"*Rape is as common as bullshit*" **B** quoted in Perry, p. 181.

"*Acid is like being let out of a cage*" **B** McNeill, p. 74.

Scientists at Edgewood tested STP **B** B. Wolfe, p. 149.

The drug was actually phencyclidine **B** David E. Smith and John Luce, *Love Needs Care*, p. 265.

the CIA employed Dr. Ewen Cameron to administer PCP **A** Nicholas M. Horrock, "Drugs Tested by CIA on Mental Patients," *New York Times*, August 3, 1977.

high dosages...can "lead to convulsions and death" **CR** *Unauthorized Storage of Toxic Agents*, Hearings before the Select Committee to Study Governmental Operations with respect to Intelligence Activities of the United States Senate, Vol. 1, September 16–18, 1975, p. 197.

"Hard-core Cosa Nostra-type criminal figures" **A** "Cosa Nostra Tied to Traffic in LSD," *New York Times*, June 28, 1967.

"Syndicate acid stinks" **B** von Hoffman, p. 35.

West...rented a pad in the heart of the Haight ibid., pp. 213–14. See also **A** Louis Joylon West and James R. Allen, "Flight From Violence: The Hippies and the Green Rebellion," *American Journal of Psychiatry*, September 3, 1968.

"The CIA is poisoning the acid these days" **B** quoted in Perry, p. 269.

"The Haight-Ashbury was our town" **B** quoted in Myra Friedman, *Buried Alive*, p. 102.

"We're trying to sabotage the word" **B** quoted in McNeill, p. 135.

"We're not going to listen to any crybabies" **B** quoted in Smith and Luce, pp. 277, 279.

"LSD hand-holding is not the end" **B** Peter Berg quoted in Leonard Wolf, *Voices from the Love Generation*, p. 263.

CHAPTER EIGHT: PEAKING IN BABYLON

—A Gathering Storm—

"a process whereby an individual casts off" **O** Frank Zappa, album liner notes of *Freak Out!*, 1966.

"No corporate leader can afford to ignore" **A** "David Rockefeller Bids Business Heed Disaffection Among Youth," *New York Times*, March 14, 1968.

Four million North Americans are said to have tried acid **B** Richard Alpert and Dr. Sidney Cohen, *LSD*.

"If some of the subjects are drawn" **A** William H. McGlothlin, "Long-lasting Effects of LSD on Certain Attitudes in Normals: An Experimental Proposal," RAND Corporation Study, May 1962.

Stanford Research Institute received a number of grants from the U.S. Army to conduct classified research **B** John Cookson and Judith Nottingham, *A Survey of Chemical and Biological Warfare*, p. 95.

"There's a war going on" **I** Michael Rossman (quoting Willis Harman) with M. Lee, November 11, 1978.

"Our investigations of some of the current social movements" **L** Willis W. Harman, Director, Educational Policy Research Center, SRI, to Dr. A. M. Hubbard, October 2, 1968.

"His services to us consisted in gathering" **L** Willis Harmon, Director, Center for the Study of Social Policy, SRI, "To Whom It May Concern," January 14, 1974.

"Impure drugs are very dangerous" **O** Al Hubbard interviewed by Oscar Janiger, October 13, 1978.

"Don't give LSD to Che Guevara" **B** quoted in "Digger Papers," *The Realist*, August 1968.

"a condition, a kind of internal 'landscape'" **A** Peter Marin, "The Open Truth and Fiery Vehemence of Youth," *Center Magazine*, January 1969.

"its first-ever dose of real fun" **B** Mairowitz, *Soap Opera*, p. 186.

—Magical Politics—

"*I wear this uniform*" **B** quoted in J. Anthony Lukas, *Don't Shoot—We are Your Children!*, p. 385.

"*A modern revolutionary headed for the television station*" **B** Hoffman, *Major Motion Picture*, p. 86.

"*If everyone did it*" **B** quoted in Lukas, p. 389.

"*makes you want to take off your clothes*" **B** quoted in Norman Mailer, *Armies of the Night*, p. 272.

"*Now, here, after several years of the blandest reports*" ibid., p. 143.

"*What possibly they shared*" ibid., p. 103.

the plan never got off the ground because of a dirty trick by the FBI **CR** *Supplementary Detailed Staff Reports on Intelligence Activities and the Rights of Americans*, Final Report of the Select Committee to Study Governmental Operation with respect to Intelligence Activities, Book III, p. 32.

"*We had symbolically destroyed the Pentagon*" **B** quoted in Lukas, pp. 389–90.

"*Once the media announces it*" **B** Jerry Rubin, *Growing (Up)* at 37, p. 97.

so they "*could look at the problem*" **B** Jerry Rubin, *Do It!*, p. 81.

a recipe for social change **B** Keith Melville, *Communes in the Counter Culture*, p. 67.

"*We figured we could create a new myth*" **B** Milton Viorst, *Fire in the Streets*, p. 431.

"*Some day, we dreamed, the myth will grow*" **B** Jerry Rubin, *We Are Everywhere*, p. 230.

"*No need to build a stage*" **B** Hoffman, *Major Motion Picture*, p. 102.

"*Our lifestyle—acid, long hair*" **B** quoted in Gene Marine "Chicago and the Trial of the New Culture," in Editors of *Rolling Stone*, eds., *Age of Paranoia*, p. 232.

"*Once one has experienced LSD*" **B** Abbie Hoffman, *Revolution for the Hell of It*, p. 13.

"*Mostly it's a catch-as-catch-can affair*" **B** Hoffman, *Major Motion Picture*, p. 244.

"*At community meetings all over the land*" **B** Rubin, *Do It!*, p. 256.

"*We had many analytical discussions*" **B** Leary, *Flashbacks*, p. 269.

"*I studied his technique of karmic salesmanship*" **B** Hoffman, *Major Motion Picture*, p. 90.

"*When movements become too 'mediated'*" **B** quoted in David Armstrong, *Trumpet to Arms*, p. 133.

"*I don't know if I was headed*" **B** Rubin, *Growing (Up)*, p. 90.

"*I purposefully manipulated the media*" ibid., p. 98.

"*seemed like Central Casting's gift*" **I** Todd Gitlin with M. Lee, August 13, 1980.

"*These brothers would get halfway high*" **A** Bobby Seale, "The Biography of Huey P. Newton," *Ramparts*, November 17, 1968.

"*Eldridge wanted a coalition*" **B** Rubin, *Do It!*, p. 196.

"*Let us join together*" ibid., p. 199.

"*the fateful merging of anti-war and racial dissension*" **B** quoted in Todd Gitlin, *The Whole World is Watching*, p. 55.

—Gotta Revolution—

"*This is a ferocious but effective way to be*" **B** Carl Oglesby, "The Idea of the New Left," in Oglesby, ed., *New Left Reader*, p. 15.

"We were willing to experiment with anything" **I** Julian Beck with M. Lee, April 19, 1984.

"LSD carried with it a certain messianic" ibid.

"We pushed reefers on them all the time" ibid.

"We competed for attention like media junkies" **B** Rubin, *Growing (Up)*, p. 191.

"Television [kept] us escalating" **B** Rubin, *Do It!*, p. 107.

"We will burn Chicago to the ground" **B** Hoffman, *Revolution for the Hell of It*, p. 106.

"It's not the Republicans and Democrats" **B** Rubin quoted in Armstrong, p. 122.

"The effect of LSD was really heavy" **I** John Sinclair with M. Lee, February 3, 1981.

"Anything to the right of Malcolm X" ibid.

"In my case it was the idealistic poetry stuff" ibid.

"When the beatniks started taking acid" **O** John Sinclair interview with Bret Eynon, February 1977.

"They're the ones who had it" **I** John Sinclair with M. Lee, February 3, 1981.

"School sucks. The white honkie culture" **B** John Sinclair, "White Panther State/ Meant," *Guitar Army*, p. 104.

"I could never see what was more important" **O** John Sinclair, interview with Bret Eynon, February 1977.

"We believe that people should fuck all the time" **B** quoted in Viorst, p. 448.

"but young, you know, and nice" **B** quoted in Gene Marine, "Chicago and the Trial of the New Culture," in *Age of Paranoia*, p. 237.

"We were dirty, smelly, grimy, foul" **B** Rubin, *Do It!*, p. 169.

"For me that week in Chicago" **B** Hunter S. Thompson, "Freak Power in the Rockies," in *Age of Paranoia*, p. 186.

"Chicago, I think, was the place where all America" **B** quoted in Nancy Zaroulis and Gerald Sullivan, *Who Spoke Up*, p. 200.

CHAPTER NINE: SEASON OF THE WITCH

—Armed Love—

the school they attended was known as "Hoover University" **A** Jeff Cohen, "Cril Payne: Undercover for the FBI," *L.A. Weekly*, December 28, 1979–January 3, 1980.

Between lectures on the New Left, drug abuse, and FBI procedure ibid.

the Yippies were infiltrated by an FBI agent named George Demmerle **B** Rubin, *We Are Everywhere*, pp. 142–43, 216–18.

one out of six demonstrators at the Chicago Convention was an undercover operative **A** Todd Gitlin, "Seizing History," *Mother Jones*, November 1983.

Bob Pierson, a Chicago cop disguised as a…biker **B** Viorst, pp. 453, 455, 461.

a quarter-million Americans were under "active surveillance" **B** Robert Justin Goldstein, *Political Repression in Modern America*, p. 463.

Nixon pressed CIA director Richard Helms to expand the parameters of Operation CHAOS ibid., pp. 477–479.

the CIA provided training, technical assistance, exotic equipment **A** Philip H. Melanson, "The CIA's Secret Ties to Local Police," *Nation*, March 26, 1983.

The Agency [sprinkled] itching powder…on toilets near leftist meetings **O** Tuli Kupferberg, "News Poem"; and **A** *Toronto Star*, July 7, 1975.

"depraved nature and moral looseness" **D** (FBI) Memorandum from Director, FBI, to SAC, Albany, 9 October 1968.

"Since the use of marijuana and other narcotics" **D** (FBI) Memorandum from Di-

rector, FBI; to SAC, Albany, "Counter Intelligence Program—Internal Security, Disruption of the New Left," 5 July 1968.

targets of the anti-drug campaign were often involved in radical politics **B** Goldstein, p. 514.

Jack Martin... testified that he was asked to [frame] Allen Ginsberg **A** Peter Stafford, "Law and the Future of Psychedelics," *L.A. Free Press*, September 30, 1966.

the narcs maintained a file... which included a photograph of the well-known poet "in an indecent pose" **D** (Narcotics Bureau) "Photograph of Allen Ginsberg," 28 September 1967.

Hoover's men shadowed John Lennon... **B** John Wiener, *Come Together*, pp. 225– 55.

the FBI kept tabs on Jimi Hendrix, Janis Joplin, Jim Morrison, the Fugs **D** (FBI) Letter from FBI Director J. Edgar Hoover to Hon. Charles Crutchfield, 26 March 1969; memorandum from SAC, Buffalo to Director, FBI, 16 June 1968, "James Marshall Hendrix"; memorandum from SAC, Miami, to Director, FBI, "Possible Racial Violence," 4 March 1969.

"All of these and many more items of popular culture" **B** Gitlin, *The Whole World is Watching*, p. 202.

"armchair bookquoting live-ass honky leftists..." **B** Peter Stensill and David Zane Mairowitz, eds., *BAMN (By Any Means Necessary): Outlaw Manifestos and Ephemera 1965–1970*, p. 155.

"A permanent fermenting agent, encouraging action" ibid. p. 158.

they denounced Timothy Leary... for "limiting the revolution" **B** Mairowitz, *Soap Opera*, pp. 186–187.

"We are the freaks of an unknown space/time..." **B** Stensill and Mairowitz, p. 161.

PL castigated SDS regulars for being "escapist" **B** Kirkpatrick Sale, *SDS*, pp. 485, 537.

PL also criticized propaganda tactics like guerrilla theater ibid., p. 540.

they even claimed that Timothy Leary was a CIA agent **A** Stew Alpert, "Free Timothy Leary," *Georgia Straight*, April 1–9, 1970.

"The SDS prize continues to be fair game" **D** (CIA) "Situation Information Report," April 1969.

"I remember when it hit the Weathermen" **O** Ken Kelley, interview with Bret Eynon, September 1978.

"We have one task" **B** Billy Ayers quoted in Sale, p. 583.

"You're right, I am a pig" **B** Sale, p. 625; and Goldstein; p. 476.

"We all live in a Weather machine" **B** Jonah Raskin, *Out of the Whale*, p. 127.

"Inside the movement... without time to learn from the experience." **B** Gitlin, *Whole World*, p. 234.

"It was like a cheap form of shrinkdom" **O** Ken Kelley, interview with Bret Eynon, September 1978.

"a sequence of tenuously linked exclamation points" **B** Gitlin, *Whole World*, p. 234.

"Organizing is just another way of going slow." **B** quoted in Gitlin, *Whole World*, p. 204.

—The Acid Brotherhood—

"Operation White Wing" **B** Wil D. Wervey, *Riot Control Agents and Herbicides in War*, p. 181.

the super-hallucinogen was used on at least five other occasions, ibid.

"have dosage ranges into lethality" **B** S. Hersh, p. 49.

One scheme involved the use of tiny remote-controlled model airplanes **A** Zodiac News Service, "Civil War Plans," *Colorado Daily*, December 15, 1976; and "Army Stockpiles BZ Drug in Bombs," *Washington Post*, August 3, 1975.

"Trends in modern police action" **D** (CIA) "Proposal to Study the Toxic Properties of Highly Poisonous Natural Products," 4 September 1970.

80% of American servicemen got stoned **B** Editors of *Ramparts* and Frank Browning, *Smack!*, p. 29.

15% of those who saw action...returned home as heroin addicts ibid.

Federal investigators described them as a "hippie Mafia" **B** Tendler and May, p. 13.

"Although unschooled and unlettered" ibid., pp. 90–91.

"to bring to the world a greater awareness" **B** Joe Eszterhas, *Narc!*, p. 103.

"Big deal" **B** quoted in Tendler and May, p. 158.

"It was like the Dead End Kids who took acid" ibid., p. 96.

[Hitchcock] helped Scully move to the premises, hauling large **A** Mary Jo Worth, "The Acid Profiteers," *Village Voice*, August 22, 1974.

"to pay tribute to this most honorable profession" **A** Timothy Leary, "Deal for Real," *East Village Other*, September 3, 1969.

"They were very good dealers on a spiritual trip" **A** quoted in Terry McDonnell, *LA*, August 19, 1972.

IOS, a fast-money laundry for organized crime **B** Jim Hougan, *Spooks*, pp. 161–74.

At Clapp's urging he poured over $5,000,000 ibid., pp. 390–91.

Hitchcock maintained a private account at Castle Bank **B** Hougan, pp. 390–91; and **B** Penny Lernoux, *In Banks We Trust*, p. 86.

Castle Bank...set up by the CIA **A** Jim Drinkhall, "IRS Versus CIA: Big Tax Investigation..." *Wall Street Journal*, April 18, 1980.

A number of Mellons served in the OSS **B** R. Harris Smith, *OSS*, pp. 15–16, 163–64, 223.

Mellon family foundations...conduits for Agency funds **A** John S. Freeman, "Culture War II," *Nation*, April 18, 1981.

Helms was a frequent weekend guest of the Mellon patriarchs **B** Thomas Powers, *The Man Who Kept the Secrets*, p. 40.

$67,000,000 illegally sloshed through Paravacini Bank **B** Burton Hersh, *The Mellon Family*, p. 487.

"It's just between me and God" **B** quoted in Tendler and May, p. 160.

"We were definitely very gullible in believing the stuff" **I** Tim Scully with M. Lee, November 10, 1982.

Stark claimed a relationship to the Whitneys **B** Tendler and May, p. 174.

The Brothers...had no idea he was running a separate cocaine ring **I** Tim Scully with M. Lee, November 10, 1982.

It was a tip from the Agency...that prompted him to shut down his French operation **B** Tendler and May, p. 202.

Stark communicated on a regular basis with officials at the American embassy in London **A** Maurizio de Luca and Pino Buongiorno, "Giallo Amerikano," *Panorama*, October 31, 1978.

Stark had made twenty kilos of LSD **I** Tim Scully with M. Lee, November 10, 1982.

"He must have pegged us as real softies" ibid.

—Bad Moon Rising—

Woodstock "was less a festival than a religious convocation" **B** Friedman, p. 206.

"Fuck hippie capitalism. . . . Events like the Woodstock gentleness freakout" **B** Zaroulis and Sullivan, p. 261.

"The revolution is more than digging rock" **B** Abbie Hoffman, *Woodstock Nation*, p. 77.

"a completely frustrating and pointless exercise" **B** Jann Wenner, "Everybody's Chicago Blues," in *Age of Paranoia*, p. 199.

"It's like television, loud, large television" **B** quoted in Michael Lydon, "The Grateful Dead," in LaValley, p. 559.

"We are a people . . . a nation." **B** Sinclair, pp. 207–27.

"which mistook its demographic proliferation" **B** Stanley Aronowitz, "When the New Left was New," in Sayres, et al., eds., *60s Without Apology*, p. 25.

"Woodstock was political because everybody was tripping" **I** Carl Crazy with M. Lee, April 11, 1982.

"I didn't have a sense of how unique I was" **I** John Sinclair with M. Lee, February 3, 1981.

"Drugs had a lot to do with placing people" **B** quoted in John Burks, "The Underground Press," in *Age of Paranoia*, p. 10.

"The pill was no longer a sacrament" **I** Michael Rossman with M. Lee, June 3, 1985.

Manson's "cherub face and sparkling eyes" **B** Viorst, p. 523.

"First they killed those pigs, then they ate dinner" **B** quoted in Sale, p. 628.

"Any kind of action that fucks up the pig's war" ibid., p. 629.

CHAPTER TEN: WHAT A FIELD DAY FOR THE HEAT

—Prisoner of LSD—

"Drug Crazed Hippies Slay Mother and Children" **B** Leary, *Flashbacks*, p. 288.

"using violent tactics which were light-years removed" **B** quoted in Mairowitz, *Soap Opera*, p. 236.

"As the beast falls, a new culture of life arises" ibid., p. 268.

"Somewhere in the nightmare of failure" **B** Hunter Thompson, "Freak Power in the Rockies," in *Age of Paranoia*, p. 171.

"the new depression" **B** quoted in Robert Sam Anson, *Gone Crazy and Back Again*, p. 160.

Subsequent revelations, however, topped any conspiracy theory **B** Alfred W. McCoy, *The Politics of Heroin in Southeast Asia*; Henrik Kruger, *The Great Heroin Coup*; and the editors of *Ramparts* and Frank Browning, *Smack!*.

"Better to be good than to do good" **A** Martin A. Lee, "Disarmament on the Material Plane," *Win*, July 15, 1982.

"You may remember me as Mr. LSD, Jr." **A** Richard Levine, "Ram Dass' USA," *Rolling Stone*, April 22, 1976.

"If he's there, that's where he should be" **B** quoted in Rubin, *We Are Everywhere*, p. 165.

"We are at war" **B** quoted in Tendler and May, p. 192.

"To Shoot a genocidal robot policeman" **A** Timothy Leary, "Shoot to Live," *Berkeley Barb*, January 13–20, 1971.

—A Bitter Pill—

"Panthers are the hope" **L** Leary to Ginsberg, October 10, 1970.

"Dr. Leary is part of our movement" **A** "Leary, If It Was Leary, Appears Briefly in Beirut," *New York Times*, October 27, 1970.

"you've got to free yourself" **A** quoted in Michael Zwerin, "Revolutionary Bust," *Village Voice*, February 11, 1971.

"the split with Panther leader Huey Newton, fomented...by FBI subterfuge" **A** Lowell Bergmann and David Weir, "Revolution on Ice," *Rolling Stone*, September 9, 1976.

Tim and Rosemary were busted at gunpoint...while black CIA agents who had penetrated Cleaver's entourage monitored the situation **D** (CIA) "Situation Information Report," 12 February 1971; and **A** Seymour Hersh, "CIA Reportedly Recruited Blacks for Surveillance of Panther Party," *New York Times*, March 17, 1978.

"Something's wrong with Leary's brain" **A** quoted in Michael Zwerin, "Acid, Guns, and Love," *Vancouver Free Press*, February 24, 1971.

"We want people to gather their wits" **A** Michael Zwerin, "Acid, Guns, and Love," *Vancouver Free Press*, February 24, 1971.

"To all those of you who look to Dr. Leary" **A** "Panthers Bust Learys," *Vancouver Free Press*, February 3, 1971.

"He's liberal CIA" **B** Leary, *Flashbacks*, p. 308.

a mysterious benefactor named Michel-Gustave Hauchard ibid., p. 313.

"aid to meditation aimed at the mystical experience" **B** Albert Hofmann, *LSD: My Problem Child*, p. 209.

Joanna met Michel Hauchard for drinks **A** Craig Vetter, "Bring Me the Head of Timothy Leary," *Playboy*, September 1975.

"Whoever eats this" ibid.

"The pre-dawn raids were ordered on the basis of twenty-nine secret indictments" **B** Eszterhas, p. 99.

"Leary is responsible for destroying" ibid., p. 99.

Joanna was permitted to accompany Leary to Los Angeles at a cost to taxpayers of $1,086 **B** Bryan, p. 228.

"the right to speak for me" **A** Vetter.

"We'll simply leave our bodies" **B** Bryan, p. 231.

"Oh, you know, he just hates women" **I** Allen Ginsberg with M. Lee and B. Shlain, July 23, 1978.

Vacaville prison, previously the site of an extensive CIA drug testing program **B** Marks, p. 201.

Martino had struck a deal with the BNDD **A** David Weir, "Timothy Leary: Soul in Hock," *Rolling Stone*, August 28, 1975.

Joanna met U.S. marshalls at the door in the nude **A** Vetter.

Joanna later told Ginsberg she was trying to blackmail the feds **I** Allen Ginsberg with M. Lee and B. Shlain, July 23, 1978.

The FBI...pegged him with the code name of the songbird **A** Weir.

"You've got to tell the truth" **A** quoted in Tom Thompson, "The Drug Puzzle," *Los Angeles Free Press*, April 4, 1975.

Leary told a grand jury that Chula had given him a small chunk of hash **A** Vetter.

Joanna also gave damaging testimony **A** Thompson, "The Drug Puzzle."

"to be dishonest, lying people" **A** quoted in Weir.

"It's obvious to me he's talked" **B** Abbie Hoffman and Anita Hoffman, *To America with Love: Letters from the Underground*, p. 108.

"He may have gotten frightened—experienced an ego break" **A** David Johnston, "The Bitter Pill," *Berkeley Barb*, September 20–26, 1974.

"Om Ah Hum: 44 Temporary Questions on Dr. Leary" **B** Ginsberg quoted in Bryan, p. 271.

"The 1960s are finally dead" **B** quoted in Bryan, p. 273.

—The Great LSD Conspiracy—

"In many ways," explained DEA Director John Bartels **CR** Hashish Smuggling and Passport Fraud: The Brotherhood of Eternal Love, Hearings Before the Subcommittee to Investigate the Administration of the Internal Security Act and other Internal Security Laws of the Senate Judiciary Committee, 1973, p. 3.

it operated "in a virtually untouchable manner" ibid., p. 30.

Four LSD factories have been seized ibid., pp. 23–24.

He acknowledged his own drug use had been extensive **B** David E. Koskoff, *The Mellons*, pp. 549–50.

a team of IRS and BNDD agents visited his drug lab in Brussels **CR** Hashish Smuggling and Passport Fraud, p. 22.

Stark claimed to be a business representative of Imam Moussa Sadr **A** Jonathan Marshall, "The Strange Career of Ronald Stark," *Parapolitics*, November 1984 (Paris); and **A** Maurizio de Luca and Pino Buongiorno, "Giallo Amerikano," *Panorama*, October 31, 1978.

An American expatriate bumped into him in the streets of Paris **I** David Solomon with M. Lee, June 28, 1982.

Italian investigators soon discovered that "Mr. Abbott" was actually Ronald Stark **B** Tendler and May, pp. 269–70.

a safe deposit box in Rome that contained **A** de Luca and Buongiorno, *Panorama*, October 31, 1978.

Stark befriended Renato Curcio ibid.; and **B** Tendler and May, p. 271.

Stark asked prison officials to arrange a meeting **B** Tendler and May, p. 271.

he received a steady flow of visitors from the American and British consulates **A** Marshall, "The Strange Career of Ronald Stark," *Parapolitics*, November 1984.

Stark also communicated . . . with members of the Libyan diplomatic corps ibid.; and **A** "Ronald Stark, agente triplo fra Gheddafai, i fedain e la cia," *Giorno*, November 6, 1981.

he was in direct contact with General Vito Micelli **A** Marshall, *Parapolitics*, November 1984.

Stark changed identities once again **A** "Stark e americano o un palestinese?" *Giorno*, November 8, 1978; and **B** Tendler and May, p. 272.

he was part of an international terrorist organization . . . called "Group 14" **A** Marshall, *Parapolitics*, November 1984.

The objective, according to Paghera **A** de Luca and Buongiorno, *Panorama*, October 31, 1978.

he was released from prison . . . on orders from Judge Giorgio Floridia **A** Marshall, *Parapolitics*, November 1984; and **B** Tendler and May, p. 272.

"an impressive series of scrupulously enumerated proofs" **A** quoted in Marshall, *Parapolitics*, November 1984.

"Many circumstances indicate that . . . Stark belonged to the American secret services" ibid.; and **B** Tendler and May, pp. 272–73.

an adventurer who was used by the CIA **B** *Relazione della Commissione Parlamentare d' Inchiesta sulla strage di via fani sul sequestro e l'assassinio di Aldo Moro e sul terrorismo in Italia*, Roma, 1983, pp. 144–46.

"It could have been that he was employed by an American intelligence agency" **I** Tim Scully with M. Lee, November 10, 1982.

"LSD makes people less competent" **I** William Burroughs with B. Shlain, February 6, 1978.

"It makes perfect sense to me" **I** John Sinclair with M. Lee, February 3, 1981.

"Could have been" **I** Ken Kesey with M. Lee, July 21, 1978.

"We had come to a curious place together" **B** Michael Rossman, *New Age Blues*, p. 101.

"What subverted the sixties decade" **B** Murray Bookchin, "Between the 30s and the 60s," in Sayres, et al., eds., *60s Without Apology*, p. 250.

"We do not target American citizens" **B** quoted in Thomas Powers, *The Man Who Kept the Secrets*, pp. 350, 479.

"a burgeoning paper problem" **A** quoted in Assassination Information Bureau, "Congress and the MK-ULTRA Whitewash," *Clandestine America*, November-December 1977.

"LSD: Some Un-Psychedelic Implications" **CR** *Biomedical and Behavioral Research*, p. 935.

"facts are wiped out by artifacts" **B** Norman Mailer, "A Harlot High and Low," *Pieces and Pontifications*, p. 160.

Stark's name surfaced once again in 1982 **B** Tendler and May, p. 274.

"A genius, but a tortured soul" **I** Claudio Nunziato with M. Lee and Dorianna Fallo, October 29, 1983.

"History is hard to know" **B** Hunter Thompson, *Fear and Loathing in Los Vegas*, p. 67.

POSTSCRIPT: ACID AND AFTER

Kemp's group succeeded the Brotherhood of Eternal Love as the main psychedelic distribution operation **A** Heathcote Williams, "The Great LSD Bust," *Village Voice*, April 17, 1978.

all of the acid later disappeared, prompting speculation ibid.

Kemp's group produced half the world's supply of LSD in the mid-1970's ibid.

A United Nations survey in the early 1980s **B** Tendler and May, p. 218.

According to the National Institute of Drug Abuse **A** Lloyd Johnson, Patrick M. O'Malley, and Gerald G. Bachman, "Use of Licit and Illicit Drugs by America's High School Students, 1975–1984," Department of Health and Human Services, 1985.

"You don't hear about it anymore" **A** John Lennon and Yoko Ono Interview, *Playboy*, January 1981.

"It's just another high now" **A** Katy Butler, "LSD Is Back, After a Long Trip," *San Francisco Chronicle*, October 27, 1979.

"They seek a nostalgic cultural experience" **A** David Smith, *Zodiac News Service*, January 1980.

bad trips are much less frequent **A** Bunce, "Social and Political Sources of Drug

Effects: The Case of Bad Trips on Psychedelics," *Journal of Drug Issues*, Spring 1979, pp. 218, 230.

"The American people today are quantum jumps more" O Timothy Leary, remarks at the LSD Reunion in Los Angeles, February 16, 1979.

"Oh Al, I owe everything to you," ibid.

"You sure played your part" O Al Hubbard, remarks at the LSD Reunion in Los Angeles, February 16, 1979.

BIBLIOGRAPHY

Nearly 20,000 pages of once-classified government documents secured through the Freedom of Information Act provided the basic source material for the chapter on CIA and military drug experiments. Some of this information is discussed in *The Search for the "Manchurian Candidate"* by John Marks. His book offers a detailed analysis of the CIA's secret control projects.

Two anthologies were particularly helpful in examining the scientific debate over LSD and the definition of its effects: *Psychedelics: The Uses and Implications of Hallucinogenic Drugs*, edited by Bernard Aaronson and Humphry Osmond, and *LSD: The Consciousness Expanding Drug*, edited by David Solomon. Several lengthy conversations with Dr. Oscar Janiger provided valuable insight into the above-ground LSD research scene during the 1950s. Janiger also made available his voluminous files, which included interviews with Captain Al Hubbard and other LSD pioneers.

A number of books on the psychedelic subculture of the 1960s warrant special mention. The story of Ken Kesey and the Merry Pranksters has been described in great detail by Tom Wolfe in *The Electric Kool-Aid Acid Test*. *Millbrook* by Arthur Kleps offers an anecdotal and philosophical chronicle of Leary's psychedelic fraternity in the mid-1960s. *High Priest* and *Flashbacks* by Timothy Leary are also useful for acid historians.

Emmett Grogan's autobiographical novel *Ringolevio* captures the unique spirit of the Haight-Ashbury community. Charles Perry gives a detailed appraisal of the rise and fall of the acid ghetto in *Haight-Ashbury: A History*. These written accounts were supplemented by interviews with Peter Berg and Judy Goldhaft, who shared their perspective on the Diggers.

The Brotherhood of Eternal Love by two British authors, Stewart

Tendler and David May, is the most comprehensive and well-researched book on the principal figures involved in the manufacture and distribution of the blackmarket LSD in the 1960s and 1970s.

Other works on the sixties counterculture worthy of note are *Moving Through Here* by Don McNeill, *A Generation in Motion* by David Pichaske, and *Bomb Culture* by Jeff Nuttall. Dick Hebidge provides a sociological analysis of rebellious trends in *Subculture: The Meaning of Style*.

Our discussion of the New Left relied heavily on three sources: *The Radical Soap Opera* by David Mairowitz, a well-written and insightful book; *The Whole World is Watching: Mass Media in the Making and Unmaking of the New Left* by Todd Gitlin; and the extensive oral history archives compiled by Bret Eynon, who guided our thinking in this area.

Books —

Aaronson, Bernard and Osmond, Humphrey, eds. *Psychedelics: The Uses and Implications of Hallucinogenic Drugs.* New York: Doubleday, 1970.

Abramson, Harold, ed. *The Use of LSD in Psychotherapy.* New York: The Josiah Macy, Jr. Foundation, 1960.

Abramson, Harold, ed. *The Use of LSD in Psychotherapy and Alcoholism.* Indianapolis: Bobbs-Merrill, 1967.

Agee, Philip. *Inside the Company: CIA Diary.* New York: Stonehill, 1975.

Aldiss, Brian. *Barefoot in the Head.* New York: Avon, 1981.

Allegro, John. *The Sacred Mushroom and the Cross.* London: Hodner and Stoughton, 1970.

Alpert, Richard. *Be Here Now.* San Cristobal, New Mexico: Lama Foundation, 1971.

Alpert, Richard, Cohen, Sidney, and Schiller, Lawrence. *LSD.* New York: New American Library, 1966.

Anderson, Chester. *The Butterfly Kid.* New York: Pocket Books, 1980.

Andrews, George and Vinkenoog, Simon., eds. *The Book of Grass.* New York: Grove Press, 1967.

Anson, Robert Sam. *Gone Crazy and Back Again.* New York: Doubleday, 1981.

Anthony, Gene. *The Summer of Love.* Millbrae, California: Celestial Arts, 1980.

Armstrong, David. *A Trumpet to Arms: Alternative Media in America.* Los Angeles: J.P. Tarcher, 1981.

Artaud, Antonin. *The Peyote Dance.* New York: Farrar, Straus and Giroux, 1976.

Ashbery, John. *Three Poems.* New York: Viking, 1975.

Baudelaire, Charles. *Artificial Paradise.* New York: Herder and Herder, 1971.

Beck, Julian. *The Life of the Theatre.* San Francisco: City Lights, 1972.

Bedford, Sybille. *Aldous Huxley, A Biography.* New York: Alfred A. Knopf, 1975.

Blum, Ralph. *The Simultaneous Man.* New York: Bantam, 1971.

Blum, Richard, and associates. *Utopiates: The Use and Users of LSD-25.* New York: Atherton Press, 1965.

Booth, Stanley. *Dance with the Devil.* New York: Random House, 1984.

BIBLIOGRAPHY

Bowart, Walter H. *Operation Mind Control*. New York: Dell, 1978.

Braden, William. *The Age of Aquarius*. New York: Pocket Books, 1971.

Braden, William. *The Private Sea: LSD and the Search for God*. New York: Bantam, 1968.

Breines, Wini. *Community & Organization in the New Left, 1962–1968: The Great Refusal*. South Hadley, Massachusetts: J.F. Bergin Publishers, 1982.

Breton, André. *What is Surrealism? Selected Writings*. Franklin Rosemont, ed. New York: Monad Press, 1978.

Brown, Anthony Cave. *Wild Bill Donovan: The Last Hero*. New York: Times Books, 1982.

Brown, Peter, and Gaines, Steven. *The Love You Make: An Insider's Story of the Beatles*. New York: Signet, 1983.

Browning, Frank, and the editors of *Ramparts*. *Smack!* New York: Harper & Row, 1972.

Bryan, John. *What Ever Happened to Timothy Leary?* San Francisco: Renaissance Press, 1980.

Burroughs, William S. *The Job*. New York: Grove Press, 1974.

Burroughs, William S. *Naked Lunch*. New York: Grove Press, 1966.

Burroughs, William S. *Nova Express*. New York: Grove Press, 1965.

Burroughs, William S., and Ginsberg, Allen. *The Yagé Letters*. San Francisco: City Lights, 1963.

Bylinsky, Gene. *Mood Control*. New York: Charles Scribner's Sons, 1978.

Caldwell, W. V. *LSD Psychotherapy*. New York: Grove Press, 1969.

Carey, James T. *The College Drug Scene*. Englewood Cliffs, New Jersey: Prentice-Hall, 1968.

Case, John, and Taylor, Rosemary C.R., eds. *Co-ops, Communes & Collectives: Experiments in Social Change in the 1960s and 1970s*. New York: Pantheon,1979.

Cashman, John. *The LSD Story*. Greenwich, Connecticut: Fawcett Publishers,1966.

Castenada, Carlos. *The Teachings of Don Juan—A Yaqui Way of Knowledge*. Berkeley: University of California Press, 1968.

Charbonneau, Louis. *Psychedelic-40*. New York: Bantam, 1965.

Charters, Ann, ed. *The Beats: Literary Bohemians in Postwar America* (Vols. I and II). Detroit: Gale Research Company, 1973.

Chavkin, Samuel. *The Mind Stealers*. Boston: Houghton Mifflin, 1978.

Cholden, Louis, ed. *Lysergic Acid Diethylamide and Mescaline in Experimental Psychiatry*. New York: Grune & Stratton, 1956.

Clark, Walter Houston. *Chemical Ecstasy*. New York: Sheed and Ward, 1969.

Cleaver, Eldridge. *Soul on Ice*. New York: Dell, 1968.

Cohen, Sidney. *The Drug Dilemma*. New York: McGraw-Hill, 1969.

Cohen, Sidney. *Drugs of Hallucination*. London: Paladin, 1973.

Cook, Bruce. *The Beat Generation*. New York: Scribners, 1971.

Cookson, John, and Nottingham, Judith. *A Survey of Chemical and Biological Warfare*. New York: Monthly Review Press, 1969.

Corson, William R. *Armies of Ignorance: The Rise of the American Intelligence Empire*. New York: Dial Press, 1977.

DeRopp, Robert S. *Drugs and the Mind*. New York: Grove Press, 1961.

Dick, Philip. *The Three Stigmata of Palmer Eldritch*. New York: New American Library, 1964.

Dick, Philip. *A Scanner Darkly*. New York: New American Library, 1977.

Dickstein, Morris. *Gates of Eden: American Culture in the Sixties*. New York: Basic Books, 1977.

Didion, Joan. *Slouching Towards Bethlehem*. New York: Simon and Schuster, 1979.

Donner, Frank J. *The Age of Surveillance: The Aims and Methods of America's Political Intelligence System*. New York: Vintage, 1981.

Durr, R. A. *Poetic Vision and the Psychedelic Experience*. Syracuse, New York: Syracuse University Press, 1970.

Ebin, David, ed. *The Drug Experience*. New York: Grove Press, 1965.

Eisen, Jonathan, ed. *The Age of Rock*. New York: Random House, 1969.

Epstein, Edward J. *Agency of Fear*. New York: Putnam, 1977.

Eszterhas, Joe. *Nark!* San Francisco: Straight Arrow Books, 1974.

Evans, Arthur. *Witchcraft and the Gay Counter-culture*. Boston: Fag Rag Books, 1978.

Farina, Richard. *Been Down So Long It Looks Like Up to Me*. New York: Dell, 1971.

Felton, David, ed. *Mindfuckers: A Source Book on the Rise of Acid Fascism in America*. San Francisco: Straight Arrow Books, 1972.

Fort, Joel. *The Pleasure Seekers: The Drug Crisis, Youth and Society*. Indianapolis: Bobbs-Merrill, 1969.

Friedman, Myra. *Buried Alive: The Biography of Janis Joplin*. New York: Bantam, 1974.

Frith, Simon. *Sound Effects*. New York: Pantheon, 1981.

Fuller, John C. *The Day of St. Anthony's Fire*. New York: Macmillan, 1968.

Furst, Peter T. *Hallucinogens and Culture*. San Francisco: Chandler & Sharp, 1976.

Gaskin, Stephen. *Amazing Dope Tales and Haight Street Flashbacks*. Summerton, Tennessee: The Book Publishing Company, 1980.

Geller, Allen, and Boas, Maxwell. *The Drug Beat*. New York: McGraw-Hill, 1969.

Gerzon, Mark. *The Whole World is Watching*. New York: Paperback Library, 1970.

Ginsberg, Allen. *Allen Verbatim*. New York: McGraw-Hill, 1975.

Ginsberg, Allen. *Composed on the Tongue*. Bolinas, California: Grey Fox Press, 1980.

Ginsberg, Allen. *Howl and Other Poems*. San Francisco: City Lights, 1956.

Ginsberg, Allen. *Kaddish and Other Poems 1958–60*. San Francisco: City Lights, 1961.

Ginsberg, Allen. *Planet News 1961–1967*. San Francisco: City Lights, 1968.

Ginsberg, Allen. *Poems All Over the Place, Mostly 'Seventies*. Cherry Valley Editions, 1978.

Gitlin, Todd. *The Whole World is Watching: Mass Media in the Making and Unmaking of the New Left*. Berkeley: University of California Press, 1980.

Gleason, Ralph. *The Jefferson Airplane and the San Francisco Sound*. New York: Ballantine, 1969.

Goldstein, Richard. *1 in 7: Drugs on Campus*. New York: Walker and Company, 1966.

Goldstein, Robert Justin. *Political Repression in Modern America: 1870 to the Present*. Cambridge, Massachusetts: Schenkman Publishing Co., 1978.

Goodman, Mitchell, ed. *The Movement Toward a New America*. New York: Pilgrim Press, 1970.

Greenfield, Robert. *The Spiritual Supermarket: An Account of Gurus Gone Public*. New York: Saturday Review Press, 1975.

Grinspoon, Lester, and Bakalar, James B. *Psychedelic Drugs Reconsidered*. New York: Basic Books, 1979.

Grof, Stanislov. *Realms of the Human Unconscious*. New York: Viking, 1975.

Grof, Stanislov, and Halifax, Joan. *The Human Encounter With Death*. New York: Dutton, 1978.

Grogan, Emmett. *Ringolevio, A Life Played for Keeps*. London: Heinemann, 1972.

Halperin, Morton H., et al. *The Lawless State: The Crimes of the U.S. Intelligence Agencies*. New York: Penguin, 1976.

Hamalian, Leo, and Karl, Frederick R., eds. *The Radical Vision*. New York: Thomas Y. Crowell Co., 1970.

Harner, Michael J., ed. *Hallucinogens and Shamanism*. London: Oxford University Press, 1973.

Hayes, Harold, ed. *Smiling Through the Apocalypse*. New York: Delta, 1971.

Hebidge, Dick. *Subculture: The Meaning of Style*. London: Methuen, 1979.

Henderson, David. *'Scuse Me While I Kiss the Sky: The Life of Jimi Hendrix*. New York: Bantam, 1983.

Hersh, Burton. *The Mellon Family: A Fortune in History*. New York: William Morrow, 1978.

Hersh, Seymour M. *Chemical and Biological Warfare: America's Hidden Arsenal*. New York: Doubleday, 1969.

Hinckle, Warren. *If You Have a Lemon, Make Lemonade*. New York: Bantam, 1976.

Hoffman, Abbie. *Revolution for the Hell of It*. New York: Pocket Books, 1970.

Hoffman, Abbie. *Soon To Be a Major Motion Picture*. New York: Perigee, 1980.

Hoffman, Abbie. *Woodstock Nation*. New York: Vintage, 1969.

Hoffman, Abbie, and Hoffman, Anita. *To America with Love*. New York: Stonehill, 1976.

Hofmann, Albert. *LSD: My Problem Child*. New York: McGraw-Hill, 1980.

Hollander, Charles, ed. *Student Drug Involvement*. Washington, DC: The National Student Association, 1967.

Hollingshead, Michael. *The Man Who Turned on the World*. London: Blond & Briggs, 1973.

Hopkins, Jerry, ed. *The Hippie Papers*, New York: Signet, 1968.

Horman, Richard E., and Fox, Allen M. *Drug Awareness: Key Documents on LSD, Marijuana, and the Drug Culture*. New York: Avon, 1970.

Hougan, Jim. *Decadence*. New York: William Morrow, 1975.

Hougan, Jim. *Spooks: The Haunting of America—The Private Use of Secret Agents*. New York: William Morrow, 1978.

Howe, Irving. *Beyond the New Left*. New York: Horizon Press, 1965.

Huxley, Aldous. *Brave New World*. New York: The Modern Library, 1952.

Huxley, Aldous. *Brave New World Revisited*. New York: Bantam, 1960.

Huxley, Aldous. *Doors of Perception*. New York: Perennial Library, 1970.

Huxley, Aldous. *Heaven and Hell*. New York: Harper, 1956.

Huxley, Aldous. *Island*. New York: Bantam, 1971.

Huxley, Aldous. *Moksha: Writings on Psychedelics and the Visionary Experience (1931–1963)*. Michael Horowitz and Cynthia Palmer, eds. New York: Stonehill, 1977.

Huxley, Aldous. *The Perennial Philosophy*. New York: Meridian Books, 1967.

Huxley, Laura Archera. *The Timeless Moment*. New York: Farrar, Straus and Giroux, 1968.

Hyde, Margaret O. *Mind Drugs*. New York: McGraw-Hill, 1973.

Inglis, Brian. *The Forbidden Game: A Social History of Drugs*. London: Hodder & Stoughton, 1975.

Jacobs, Harold, ed. *Weatherman*. Palo Alto: Ramparts Press, 1970.

Jacobs, Paul, and Landau, Saul. *The New Radicals: A Report with Documents*. New York: Vintage, 1966.

James, William. *The Varieties of Religious Experience*. New York: Modern Library, 1929.

Kerouac, Jack. *Dharma Bums*. New York: Viking, 1958.

Kerouac, Jack. *On the Road*. New York: Viking, 1957.

Kesey, Ken. *One Flew Over the Cuckoo's Nest*. New York: Viking, 1962.

Kesey, Ken. *Ken Kesey's Garage Sale*. New York: Viking, 1973.

Kleps, Art. *The Boohoo Bible*. San Cristobal: The Toad Press, 1971.

Kleps, Art. *Millbrook*. Oakland: The Bench Press, 1975.

Kornbluth, Jesse, ed. *Notes From the New Underground*. New York: Ace Publishing Corporation, 1968.

Koskoff, David E. *The Mellons: The Chronicle of America's Richest Family*. New York: Crowell, 1978.

Krassner, Paul, ed. *Best of the Realist*. Philadelphia: Running Press, 1984.

Krim, Seymour. *Shake It For the World, Smartass*, New York: Delta, 1971.

Kruger, Henrik. *The Great Heroin Coup: Drugs, Intelligence, & International Fascism*. Boston: South End Press, 1980.

Kuhn, Thomas. *The Structure of Scientific Revolutions*. Chicago: University of Chicago Press, 1970.

Laing, R.D. *The Politics of Experience and the Bird of Paradise*. London: Penguin, 1967.

Lamb, F. Bruce. *Wizard of the Upper Amazon*. Boston: Houghton Mifflin, 1974.

Lasby, Charles G. *Project Paperclip: German Scientists and the Cold War*. New York: Atheneum, 1971.

LaValley, Albert J., ed. *The New Consciousness*. Cambridge, Massachusetts: Winthrop Publishers, 1972.

Leary, Timothy. *Confessions of a Hope Fiend*. New York: Bantam, 1973.

Leary, Timothy. *Flashbacks: An Autobiography*. Los Angeles: J.P. Tarcher, 1983.

Leary, Timothy. *High Priest*. Cleveland: World Publishing Company, 1968.

Leary, Timothy. *Jail Notes*. New York: Douglas Book Corporation, 1970.

Leary, Timothy. *The Politics of Ecstasy*. London: Paladin, 1970.

Leary, Timothy. *Psychedelic Prayers*. Kerhonkson, New York: Poets Press, 1966.

Leary, Timothy. *What Does Woman Want?* Beverly Hills: 88 Books, 1976.

Leary, Timothy, Metzner, Ralph, and Alpert, Richard. *The Psychedelic Experience*. Secaucus: The Citadel Press, 1970.

Leary Timothy, with Wilson, Robert Anton, and Koopman, George A. *Neuropolitics*. Los Angeles: Starseed/Peace Press, 1977.

Lee, Dick, and Pratt, Colin. *Operation Julie*. London: W. H. Allen, 1978.

Legman, G. *The Fake Revolt*. New York: Breaking Point, 1967.

Lem, Stanislas. *The Futurological Congress*. New York: Seabury Press, 1974.

Lennard, Henry L. and associates. *Mystification and Drug Abuse*. New York: Harper & Row, 1971.

Lerner, Michael P. *The New Socialist Revolution*. New York: Delacorte Press, 1973.

Lernoux, Penny. *In Banks We Trust*. New York: Anchor Press, 1984.

Lewis, Roger, *Outlaws of America*. London: Penguin, 1972.

Lilly, John. *The Scientist: A Novel Autobiography*. Philadelphia: Lippincott, 1978.

Lingeman, Richard R. *Drugs From A to Z: A Dictionary*. New York: McGraw-Hill, 1974.

London, Perry. *Behavior Control*. New York: New American Library, 1977.

Lothstein, Arthur, ed. *"All We Are Saying..." The Philosophy of the New Left*. New York: Capricorn Books, 1970.

Louria, Donald. *Nightmare Drugs*. New York: Pocket Books, 1966.

Lukas, J. Anthony. *Don't Shoot—We Are Your Children!* New York: Random House, 1971.

Mailer, Norman. *The Armies of the Night*. New York: Signet, 1968.

Mailer, Norman. *Miami and the Siege of Chicago*. New York: Signet, 1968.

Mailer, Norman. *Pieces and Pontifications*. Boston: Little, Brown, 1982.

Mairowitz, David Zane. *The Radical Soap Opera: Roots of Failure in the American Left*. New York: Avon, 1976.

Marchetti, Victor, and Marks, John D. *The CIA and the Cult of Intelligence.* New York: Dell, 1974.

Marks, John. *The Search for the "Manchurian Candidate."* New York: Times Books, 1979.

Marsh, Dave, and Stein, Kevin. *The Book of Rock Lists.* New York: Dell, 1981.

Masters, R.E.L. and Houston, Jean. *The Varieties of Psychedelic Experience.* New York: Holt, Rinehart & Winston, 1966.

McClure, Michael. *Meat Science Essays.* San Francisco: City Lights, 1970.

McCoy, Alfred W. *The Politics of Heroin in Southeast Asia.* New York: Harper Colophon Books, 1973.

McNeill, Don. *Moving Through Here.* New York: Lancer Books, 1970.

Meerloo, Joost A.M. *The Rape of the Mind.* New York: Grosset and Dunlap, 1961.

Melville, Keith. *Communes in the Counter Culture: Origins, Theories, Styles of Life.* New York: William Morrow, 1972.

Metzner, Ralph. *The Ecstatic Adventure.* New York: Macmillan, 1968.

Michaux, Henri. *The Major Ordeals of the Mind and the Countless Minor Ones.* New York: Harcourt Brace Jovanovich, 1974.

Michaux, Henri, *Miserable Miracle.* San Francisco: City Lights, 1963.

Miles. *Bob Dylan In His Own Words.* New York: Quick Fox, 1978.

Miller, Richard. *Bohemia: The Protoculture Then and Now.* Chicago: Nelson-Hall, 1977.

Mungo, Raymond. *Famous Long Ago: My Life and Hard Times with the Liberation News Service.* New York: Pocket Books, 1971.

Nahal, Chaman, ed. *Drugs and the Other Self: An Anthology of Spiritual Transformations.* New York: Harper & Row, 1971.

Naranjo, Claudio. *The Healing Journey.* New York: Ballantine, 1975.

Newfield, Jack. *A Prophetic Minority.* New York: Signet Books, 1967.

Newland, Constance A. *My Self and I.* New York: Coward-McCann, 1962.

Norman, Philip. *Shout!* New York: Warner Books, 1981.

Nowlis, Helen H. *Drugs on the College Campus.* New York: Anchor Books, 1969.

Nuttall, Jeff. *Bomb Culture.* London: Paladin, 1970.

Oglesby, Carl, and Shaull, Richard. *Containment and Change.* New York: Macmillan, 1967.

Oglesby, Carl, ed. *The New Left Reader.* New York: Grove Press, 1969.

Olson, Charles. *Muthologos* (Volume I). Bolinas, California: Four Seasons Foundation, 1977.

O'Neill, William L. *Coming Apart.* Chicago: Quadrangle, 1971.

Papworth, M.H. *Human Guinea Pigs.* Boston: Beacon Press, 1967.

Paz, Octavio. *Alternating Current.* New York: Viking, 1973.

Perkus, Cathy. *COINTELPRO: The FBI's Secret War on Political Freedom.* New York: Monad Press, 1975.

Perry, Charles. *The Haight-Ashbury: A History.* New York: Random House, 1984.

Pichaske, David. *A Generation in Motion: Popular Music and Culture in the Sixties.* New York: Schirmer Books, 1979.

Picon, Gaëton. *Surrealists and Surrealism.* New York: Rizzoli, 1983.

Poirier, Richard. *The Performing Self: Compositions and Decompositions in the Languages of Contemporary Life.* New York: Oxford University Press, 1971.

Pope, Harrison, Jr. *Voices from the Drug Culture.* Boston: Beacon Press, 1974.

Portugés, Paul. *The Visionary Poetics of Allen Ginsberg.* Santa Barbara: Ross-Erikson, 1978.

Powers, Thomas. *The Man Who Kept the Secrets.* New York: Pocket Books, 1981.

Pynchon, Thomas. *Gravity's Rainbow.* New York: Viking, 1973.

Raskin, Jonah. *Out of the Whale: Growing Up in the American Left*. New York: Links Books, 1974.

Reich, Charles. *The Greening of America*. New York: Random House, 1970.

Rips, Geoffrey. *Unamerican Activities: The Campaign Against the Underground Press*. San Francisco: City Lights, 1981.

The editors of *Rolling Stone*. *The Age of Paranoia*. New York: Pocket Books, 1972.

Roseman, Bernard. *LSD: The Age of the Mind*. Hollywood: Wilshire Book Company, 1963.

Rossman, Michael. *New Age Blues: On the Politics of Consciousness*. New York: E.P. Dutton, 1979.

Rossman, Michael. *On Learning and Social Change*. New York: Vintage, 1972.

Rossman, Michael. *Wedding Within the War*. New York: Doubleday, 1971.

Roszak, Theodore. *The Making of a Counter Culture*. New York: Anchor Books, 1969.

Rubin, Jerry. *Do It!* New York: Simon and Schuster, 1970.

Rubin, Jerry. *Growing (Up) at 37*. New York: Warner Books, 1976.

Rubin, Jerry. *We Are Everywhere*. New York: Harper Colophon Books, 1971.

Ruether, Rosemary. *The Radical Kingdom*. New York: Paulist Press, 1970.

Sale, Kirkpatrick. *SDS*. New York: Vintage, 1974.

Sanders, Ed. *The Family*. New York: Dutton, 1972.

Sanders, Ed. *Shards of God*. New York: Grove Press, 1970.

Sayres, Sohnya, Stephanson, Anders, Aronowitz, Stanley, and Jameson, Fredric, eds. *The 60s Without Apology*. Minneapolis: University of Minnesota Press, 1984.

Scaduto, Anthony. *Dylan*. New York: Grosset and Dunlap, 1971.

Scheflin, Alan W., and Opton, Edward M., Jr. *The Mind Manipulators*. New York: Paddington Press, 1978.

Schein, Edgar. *Coercive Persuasion*. New York: W. W. Norton, 1971.

Schrag, Peter. *Mind Control*. New York: Pantheon, 1978.

Sheed, Wilfred. *Clare Boothe Luce*. New York: Dutton, 1982.

Siegel, Ronald K., and West, L. J., eds. *Hallucinations: Behavior, Experience, and Theory*. New York: John Wiley, 1975.

Sinclair, John. *Guitar Army*. New York: Douglas Book Corporation, 1972.

Situationist International. *Point Blank!* Berkeley, 1972.

Slack, Charles W. *Timothy Leary, the Madness of the Sixties, and Me*. New York: Peter H. Wyden, 1974.

Sloman, Larry. *Reefer Madness*. New York: Bobbs-Merrill, 1979.

Smith, David, ed. *The New Social Drug*. Englewood Cliffs, New Jersey: Prentice-Hall, 1970.

Smith, David E., and Luce, John. *Love Needs Care*. Boston: Little Brown, 1971.

Smith, Huston. *Forgotten Truth: The Primordial Tradition*. New York: Harper & Row, 1976.

Smith, R. Harris. *OSS: The Secret History of America's First Central Intelligence Agency*. New York: Delta, 1973.

Solomon, David, ed. *LSD: The Consciousness-Expanding Drug*. New York: Berkeley-Medallion, 1966.

Solomon, David, ed. *The Marijuana Papers*. New York: Mentor, 1968.

Spellman, A.B. *Four Lives in the Be-Bop Business*. New York: Pantheon, 1966.

Spitz, Robert Stephen. *Barefoot in Babylon*. New York: Viking, 1979.

Stafford, P.G. and Golightly, B.H. *LSD: The Problem-Solving Psychedelic*. New York: Award Books, 1967.

Stafford, Peter. *Psychedelic Baby Reaches Puberty*. New York: Delta, 1971.

Stafford, Peter. *Psychedelics Encyclopedia*. Los Angeles: J.P. Tarcher, 1983.

Stensill, Peter, and Mairowitz, David Zane, eds. *BAMN (By Any Means Necessary): Outlaw Manifestos and Ephemera 1965–70*. London: Penguin, 1971.

Stone, Robert. *Dog Soldiers*. Boston: Houghton Mifflin, 1973.

Swanberg, W.A. *Luce and His Empire*. New York: Charles Scribner's Sons, 1975.

Szasz, Thomas. *Ceremonial Chemistry*. New York: Anchor Press, 1975.

Tart, Charles T. *On Being Stoned*. Palo Alto: Science and Behavior Books, 1971.

Taussig, Michael. *The Devil and Commodity Fetishism in South America*. Chapel Hill: University of North Carolina Press, 1983.

Taylor, Norman. *Flight From Reality*. New York: Duell, Sloane and Pearce, 1949.

Tendler, Stewart, and May, David. *The Brotherhood of Eternal Love*. London: Panther Books, 1984.

Teodori, Massimo, ed. *The New Left: A Documentary History*. Indianapolis: Bobbs-Merrill, 1969.

Thomas, J.C. *Chasin' the Trane*. New York: Doubleday, 1975.

Thompson, Hunter S. *Fear and Loathing in Las Vegas*. New York: Popular Library, 1971.

Thompson, Hunter S. *The Great Shark Hunt*. New York: Summit Books, 1979.

Thompson, Hunter S. *Hell's Angels*. New York: Ballantine, 1966.

Viorst, Milton. *Fire in the Streets: America in the 1960s*. New York: Simon and Schuster, 1979.

von Hoffman, Nicholas. *We Are the People Our Parents Warned Us Against*. Greenwich, Connecticut: Fawcett Publications, 1973.

Wakefield, Dan. *The Addict*. Greenwich, Connecticut: Fawcett Publications, 1963.

Wasson, R. Gordon, Ruck, Carl A.P., and Hofmann, Albert. *The Road to Eleusis: Unveiling the Secrets of the Mysteries*. New York: Harcourt Brace Jovanovich, 1978.

Wasson, R. Gordon. *Soma: Divine Mushroom of Immortality*. New York: Harcourt, Brace & World, 1968.

Watts, Alan W. *The Joyous Cosmology*. New York: Pantheon, 1962.

Weil, Andrew. *The Natural Mind*. Boston: Houghton Mifflin, 1972.

Weil, Gunther M., Metzner, Ralph, and Leary, Timothy, eds. *The Psychedelic Reader*. Secaucus, New Jersey: The Citadel Press, 1973.

Weiner, Rex, and Stillman, Deanne. *Woodstock Census*. New York: Viking, 1979.

Wells, Brian. *Psychedelic Drugs*. Baltimore: Penguin, 1973.

Wiener, John. *Come Together: John Lennon in His Time*. New York: Random House, 1984.

Wilkinson, Paul. *The New Fascists*. London: Pan Books, 1983.

Wolf, Leonard. *Voices from the Love Generation*. Boston: Little, Brown, 1968.

Wolfe, Burton H. *The Hippies*. New York: New American Library, 1968.

Wolfe, Tom. *The Electric Kool-Aid Acid Test*. New York: Bantam, 1969.

Yablonsky, Lewis. *The Hippie Trip*. Baltimore: Penguin, 1973.

Young, Warren, and Hixson, Joseph. *LSD on Campus*. New York: Dell, 1966.

Zaroulis, Nancy, and Sullivan, Gerald. *Who Spoke Up!* New York: Doubleday, 1984.

U.S. Government Reports—

Alleged Assassination Plots Involving Foreign Leaders. An Interim Report of the Select Committee to Study Governmental Operations with respect to Intelligence Activities, United States Senate, November 20, 1975.

Biomedical and Behavioral Research, 1975. Joint Hearings before the Subcommittee on Health of the Committee on Labor and Public Welfare and the Subcommittee on Administrative Practice and Procedure of the Committee on the Judiciary, United States Senate, September 10, 12; and November 7, 1975.

Chemical, Biological and Radiological Warfare Agents. Hearings before the Committee on Science and Astronautics. United States House of Representatives, June 16 and 22, 1959.

CIA: The Pike Report. Nottingham: Spokesman Books, 1977.

The CIA and the Media. Hearings before the Subcommittee on Oversight of the Permanent Select Committee on Intelligence, House of Representatives, December 27, 28, and 29, 1977; January 4, 5; and April 20, 1978.

Drug Safety. Hearings before a Subcommittee of the Committee on Government Operations, House of Representatives, March 9, 10; May 25, 26; June 7, 8 and 9, 1966.

Final Report of the Select Committee to Study Governmental Operations with Respect to Intelligence Activities. United States Senate, Books I-VI.

Hashish Smuggling and Passport Fraud: The Brotherhood of Eternal Love. Hearings before the Subcommittee to Investigate the Administration of the Internal Security Act and other Internal Security Laws of the Senate Judiciary Committee, 1973.

Human Drug Testing by the CIA, 1977. Hearings before the Subcommittee on Health and Scientific Research of the Committee on Human Resources, United States Senate.

Individual Rights and the Federal Role in Behavior Modification. A Study Prepared by the Staff of the Subcommittee on Constitutional Rights by the Committee on the Judiciary, United States Senate, 1974.

The Narcotic Rehabilitation Act of 1966. Hearings before a Special Subcommittee of the Committee on the Judiciary, United States Senate, January 25–27; May 12, 13, 19, 23 and 25; June 14–15; July 19, 1966.

The Nelson Rockefeller Report to the President. Commission on CIA Activities. New York: Manor Books, 1975.

Organization and Coordination of Federal Drug Research and Regulatory Programs: LSD. Hearings before the Subcommittee on Executive Reorganization of the Committee on Government Operations, United States Senate, May 24–26, 1966.

Project MK-ULTRA, The CIA's Program of Research in Behavior Modification. Joint Hearing before the Select Committee on Intelligence and the Subcommittee on Health and Scientific Research of the Committee on Human Resources, United States Senate, August 3, 1977.

Unauthorized Storage of Toxic Agents. Hearings before the Select Committee to Study Governmental Operations with respect to Intelligence Activities of the United States Senate, Volume 1, September 16–18, 1975.

INDEX